Globalizing L.A.

Strictly by itself, and on its own terms, metropolitan Los Angeles is a city-state, a world force, the de facto capital of the Asia/Pacific community. In this compelling, exhaustively researched study, Steven P. Erie offers a preeminent example of how global and local energies are converging to create a new kind of global city and a new kind of global economy.

—Kevin Starr, *State Librarian of California*

Steven Erie provides a distinctive and persuasive analysis of political strategies that have been central to shaping the growth of the complex Los Angeles region. The book should be of much interest to scholars who are concerned with the development of the L.A. region and the role of semi-autonomous governments in the United States and beyond.

—Jameson Doig, *professor of politics and public affairs, Princeton University*

Although there have been several books about the area [L.A.], largely by geographers of the L.A. School, none has captured the interaction of politics and economic interest in the context of key infrastructure investments as Steve Erie is able to do. His combination of mastery of political, financial, and technical elements of development is outstanding. It will be an important contribution to our understanding of regional development.

—Michael B. Teitz, *program director, economy, and senior fellow, Public Policy Institute of California and emeritus professor, University of California, Berkeley*

A significant new contribution to the study of urban development. . . . This book will change the way we think about Los Angeles and Southern California. . . . It is the next great book on the region.

—David Perry, *director, Great Cities Institute, University of Illinois at Chicago*

This is the first major study of L.A.'s trade infrastructure and goes far beyond earlier books on L.A. It will add significantly to the existing literature on urbanization, the impact of globalization on local communities, the emergence of economic regions or city-states, and the history of the Los Angeles region itself.

—Earl Fry, *professor of political science, Brigham Young University*

Globalizing L.A. is a major achievement. I know of nothing in the existing literature on urban politics, regional policy studies, regime theory, or developmental policy that is of comparable quality. This book makes major contributions to the existing literature in political science, and equally to new schools of thought surfacing in economic geography, sociology, and urban planning.

—David J. Olson, *professor of political science, Harry Bridges Chair Emeritus, University of Washington*

Globalizing L.A.

Trade, Infrastructure, and Regional Development

Steven P. Erie

STANFORD UNIVERSITY PRESS
STANFORD, CALIFORNIA
2004

Stanford University Press
Stanford, California

Printed in the United States of America on acid-free, archival-quality paper

Library of Congress Cataloging-in-Publication Data
Erie, Steven P.
  Globalizing L.A. : Trade, infrastructure, and regional development / Steven P. Erie.
    p.   cm.
  Includes bibliographical references and index.
  ISBN 0-8047-4680-X (alk. paper)—ISBN 0-8047-4681-8 (pbk. : alk. paper)
    1. Los Angeles (Calif.)—Commerce—History. 2. Los Angeles (Calif.)—Economic
policy. 3. Regional planning—California—Los Angeles. I. Title.
HF3163.L7 E75 2004
382'.09794'94—dc22

                                                                2003022782

Typeset by G & S Typesetters in Sabon 9.7/11.5

Original Printing 2004

Last figure below indicates year of this printing:
13   12   11   10   09   08   07   06   05   04

Contents

Tables, Figures, and Photos

Figures

Photos (*following page 42*)

To Kathleen, for love and support

Preface

San Diego, California, offers a unique vantage point for studying Los Angeles trade, infrastructure, and regional development. San Diegans daily experience (and frequently resent) L.A.'s regional reach and global grasp, which have been created by its infrastructure dominion. Early on, these two urban rivals (located 125 miles apart) battled fiercely for harbor, railroad, airport, and regional supremacy. San Diego held the early advantage. It had a natural harbor, thought to be a prime lure for a transcontinental rail line. Not so Los Angeles, which had only shallow sloughs and unprotected open-sea anchorages. When L.A. finally built a breakwater and began dredging a deep-water port, San Diego's newspapers derided L.A.'s effort as a mere "harborette."[1] Later, San Diego would dedicate Lindbergh Field, its municipal airport, before L.A. created Mines Field, predecessor to Los Angeles International Airport (LAX). Attending Lindbergh Field's 1928 inaugural ceremony, Hollywood actor Wallace Beery wisecracked: "If Los Angeles doesn't hurry and fix up its own airport it will soon be one of San Diego's suburbs."[2]

Yet San Diego, not L.A., would prove to be the suburb. "America's Finest City" (as local boosters call it) lost the key infrastructure battles. Displaying "Bismarckian municipal will" (in historian Kevin Starr's inimitable phrase), Los Angeles secured the transcontinental rail line and built what are now the world's third busiest port and airport facilities. L.A. and its suburbs also created the regional water system that serves San Diego. Los Angeles became the regional hegemon and one of the world's great cities, regional economies, and trade centers because it was willing to make the huge public infrastructure investments needed for growth.

San Diego did not. The city may be "Futureville," as *The Economist* dubbed it, because of its high-tech promise and North American Free Trade

Agreement (NAFTA) trade with Mexico, but its port, rail, airport, and water facilities remain inadequate.[3] As a result, L.A.'s ports and airports, not diminutive Lindbergh Field and the Port of San Diego, serve as San Diego's chief gateways to the Pacific Rim region. San Diego also depends on an L.A.-based agency for water. The result of this regional infrastructure imbalance is a little-understood colonial relationship between the nation's second and seventh largest cities. Arguably, San Diego's recent efforts at securing independent water supplies from the Imperial Valley, reforming airport governance, and developing its port and cargo rail service can be viewed as a belated revolt against L.A.'s infrastructure dominion.

This project has enjoyed an unusually long gestation period. In graduate school at UCLA, my interest in the role played by public bureaucracies and infrastructure in L.A.'s development was kindled in coursework with Professors Francine Rabinovitz, John C. Bollens, Chuck Ries, and Stephan Thernstrom. But this interest remained dormant until the early 1990s, when I embarked on a study of L.A.'s "crown jewels"—mega-projects such as the L.A. Aqueduct, San Pedro Bay ports, Colorado River Aqueduct, LAX, and the public agencies that built and managed them—and their catalytic roles in L.A.'s improbable twentieth-century development. *Globalizing L.A.* is the first of the "crown jewels" projects; it will be followed by studies of the Metropolitan Water District of Southern California, the gigantic regional water agency serving seventeen million customers from Ventura to San Diego, and L.A.'s storied but still controversial Department of Water and Power.

I want to thank a corps of able UC San Diego graduate researchers: Jessica Hills, Jim Ingram, Henry Kim, Tommy Kim, Mike Malloy, and David Shirk. I also wish to acknowledge the help of Claremont Graduate University students in a policy clinic class I taught on the region's trade mega-projects. Both scholars and practitioners kindly read—and improved—earlier drafts of the manuscript. I wish to thank Mike Armstrong, Jim Doig, Jack Driscoll, Richard Feinberg, Earl Fry, Dan Garcia, Mark Griffin, Gill Hicks, Sam Kernell, Geraldine Knatz, Abe Lowenthal, Julia Nagano, Ethel Pattison, Julie Puentes, Ken Sulzer, and Art Wong for their valuable comments and suggestions. Elmar Baxter provided invaluable help in locating photographs. David Abel, Wally Baker, Chris Becker, Norm Emerson, and Lee Harrington offered needed encouragement. Harold Brackman provided first-rate research help. My most profound debt is owed to Greg Freeman for indispensable assistance in turning an ungainly manuscript into a book.

I would like to express my deep appreciation to the following public agencies for their generous cooperation: the Los Angeles Harbor Department, Long Beach Harbor Department, Los Angeles World Airports, Alameda Corridor Transportation Authority, On-Trac Joint Powers Authority, Southern California Association of Governments, and the San Diego Association of Governments. I also am grateful to the many individuals interviewed for this project who so generously gave their time and effort. Further, I wish to express my gratitude for the able assistance provided by the L.A. City Archives, the UCLA and USC libraries, and the Huntington Library.

I owe a special thanks to the John Randolph Haynes and Dora Haynes Foundation for underwriting much of the research for this book. Project support was also furnished by the California Policy Research Center, USC's Southern California Studies Center, the James Irvine Foundation, the Pacific Council on International Policy, the Los Angeles County Economic Development Corporation, and UC San Diego.

Steven P. Erie
La Jolla, California
January 2004

Part One Overview

1

"Gateway for the Pacific Rim"

The development of this city as a gateway for the Pacific Rim in particular, but really the whole world, . . . was something so clear to me that I never questioned it. International trade and the Southern California jobs created directly or indirectly by the Harbor Department prompted me to improve the Port of Los Angeles. . . . And the international terminal at the airport was something which I recognized was important. . . . I either called or visited the airport every day just to see how the construction was going. . . . [The port and the airport] have become a truly major force in the economy of Southern California, . . . tied in with international trade, . . . and I'm proud of that achievement.

—*former Los Angeles Mayor Tom Bradley, 1995*[1]

Central to our region's economic vitality is international trade. To be the Los Angeles of the 21st century, we must invest [in infrastructure] today to increase our capacity for international trade tomorrow.

—*former Los Angeles Mayor Richard Riordan, 1996*[2]

Globalizing L.A. is a study of trade, infrastructure, and regional development in Greater Los Angeles: from the fierce railroad and harbor battles of the late nineteenth century, to the twentieth-century building of one of the world's greatest trade-transportation complexes, to L.A.'s emergence as a leading trade center, and, finally, to new uncertainties regarding its twenty-first-century global future.

A major focus of this book is the epic battles fought since the early 1990s over the nation's most ambitious trade-infrastructure development plan: the development of the Los Angeles and Long Beach ports; the Alameda Corridor rail project; the Los Angeles International Airport (LAX) Master Plan; the plans for a new international airport at the former El Toro military air base in Orange County; and the North American Free Trade Agreement (NAFTA) border-infrastructure improvements. I consider the myriad of challenges to these mega-projects, pitting the forces of globalization and the economy against community and environmental resistance, and analyze the strategies devised by project supporters and opponents to shape Southern California's community, regional, and global future.

Los Angeles has become one of the world's great regional economies and global laboratories. In 2001, the five-county Los Angeles metropolitan area (consisting of Los Angeles, Orange, Ventura, San Bernardino, and Riverside counties) had a gross regional product of $651 billion, making it one of the

Table 1.1   Placing the Los Angeles Economy in Global Perspective:
Countries Ranked by Year 2001 Gross Domestic Product
(in billions of dollars)

Rank	Country	Gross Product
1	United States	10,208
2	Japan	4,145
3	Germany	1,849
4	United Kingdom	1,431
5	France	1,307
6	China	1,160
7	Italy	1,089
8	Canada	700
	Los Angeles Metropolitan Area[a]	**651**
9	Mexico	594
10	Spain	585
11	India	507
12	Brazil	505
13	South Korea	423
	Los Angeles County	**390**
14	Netherlands	380
15	Australia	355
16	Russia	310
17	Taiwan	282
18	Argentina	260
19	Switzerland	247
20	Belgium	228
21	Sweden	210
22	Austria	188
23	Poland	177
24	Saudi Arabia	170
25	Norway	164

SOURCE: Data from United States Conference of Mayors, *U.S. Metro Economies: The Engines of America's Growth* (Lexington, Mass.: DRI/WEFA, 2001), Table 5, p. 9.
[a] Los Angeles, Orange, Ventura, San Bernardino, and Riverside counties.

world's largest economies. Table 1.1 compares the Los Angeles regional product for 2001 with the gross domestic product of the top twenty-five national economies. If Greater Los Angeles were a nation, its economy would rank ninth in the world, below those of Italy and Canada and above those of Mexico, Spain, and India. Were L.A. County a separate country, its $390 billion economy would rank fourteenth in the world, below those of Brazil and South Korea but above those of the Netherlands, Australia, Russia, and Taiwan.

Greater L.A.'s global significance extends well beyond its world-scale economy. The region has become a premier crossroads for migration from the Pacific Rim, Mexico, and Latin America. The region is now home to one-fifth of the country's new immigrants. With Hollywood and major industries in multimedia, fashion, and design, L.A. is a capital of the global entertainment industry and a leading incubator of global culture and design innovation. Yet, Southern California also aspires to be the nation's leading Pacific Rim gateway and a major center for trade with Mexico under NAFTA. L.A.'s trade ambitions and the catalytic role of its trade infrastructure supply the main focus here.[3]

Building L.A.'s Gateways and Trade

This study weaves together history and policy analysis to trace the arc of the region's trade, infrastructure, and economic development. I explore Southern California's meteoric rise historically as well as its still uncertain future as a leading center for global trade and transshipment. A primary concern involves the strategies devised to plan, finance, and build one of the world's great trade-transportation complexes—the ports of Los Angeles and Long Beach and LAX. These are the world's third busiest port and airport facilities. I also examine the development of major trade corridors, such as the landmark Alameda Corridor rail project, which connects the ports with the downtown rail yards, as well as the extensive network of rail, highway, and land port-of-entry links to Mexico and the rest of North America.

More so than most regions, L.A. trades on its superior infrastructure; its other trade-development efforts pale in comparison. Yet, as these pages reveal, the building of L.A.'s global gateways was an improbable and remarkable achievement. In 1900, Los Angeles lay a distant twenty miles from the ocean. The region had no natural harbor. San Pedro, then a separate city, had a small, inadequate port with shallow sloughs and unprotected open-sea anchorages. Neighboring Long Beach also had no natural harbor. The present site of LAX was a bean field. The region's seaport and airport sites originally lay in private, not public, hands. How the municipalities of Los Angeles and Long Beach improbably came to own these facilities and, despite daunting challenges, to publicly develop them (albeit with federal, state, and private assistance) into the mighty trade portals now globalizing the Southern California economy is a major focus of inquiry.

Of paramount importance was the fashioning of appropriate local institutional arrangements for infrastructure provision. Progressive-era Southern California rejected the eastern model of regional public authorities. Instead, L.A. and Long Beach created powerful municipal proprietary departments (semi-autonomous agencies armed with formidable city-charter protections and powers) to develop and manage the region's early "crown jewels": its public water, power, harbor, and airport facilities, which were crucial to the region's improbable yet dramatic twentieth-century economic development. A key question addressed here is whether early reliance on city agencies to provide regional infrastructure vitiated the later growth of regional institutions and cooperation, which are now being called for to address pressing areawide problems such as airport development.[4]

Powerful, semi-autonomous public enterprises created strong incentives for public entrepreneurs to engage in long-range strategic planning and innovative development policies. My concern with the dynamic interplay between structure and agency borrows from Jameson W. Doig's study of the semi-autonomous Port Authority of New York/New Jersey and its troika of leaders—General Counsel Julius Henry Cohen, Chief Engineer Othmar Ammann, and Executive Director Austin Tobin. Because multiple agencies and actors complicate the Southern California story, I examine how organizational structures and roles have shaped strategic behavior and policy. With institutional structure thus playing a conditioning role, strategies for public-agency trade and infrastructure development ranged from early trade programs and missions, to competitive pricing and agile market responses, to building electoral and interest-group coalitions for infrastructure financing and development, to lobbying City Hall and the state and federal governments, and, more recently, to managing and mitigating community and environmental concerns regarding today's mega-projects.[5]

While acknowledging the catalytic roles of high-profile elected officials such as Mayor Tom Bradley as well as local business organizations and leaders, I also highlight the unsung public actors who profoundly shaped the region's trade and infrastructure development: public servants and citizen commissioners. For example, Clarence Matson was an early visionary manager of L.A.'s Harbor Department, mapping out L.A.'s Pacific Rim trade strategy as early as the 1920s. In the post–World War Two era, Frances Fox and Clifton Moore served as innovative managers of L.A.'s Department of Airports. Both were effective proponents of airport expansion and international passenger and air-cargo service. L.A. airport commissioners such as Donald Belding masterminded successful bond campaigns for facility expansion. In Long Beach, early Mayor and later City Manager Charles Windham, considered the port's founding father, led the city's harbor and trade-development efforts in the pre–New Deal era. Later, Eloi Amar, a long-serving Port of Long Beach general manager, and David Hauser, a Long Beach harbor commissioner, facilitated harbor and rail projects. These and other unheralded public servants were master politicians whose influence rivaled that of elected officials and business leaders.

Policy Debates

Today, the nation's metropolitan areas, from New York to San Diego, are examining their global engagements. Local officials, businesses, and civic and community organizations are concerned with developing regional strategies to increase globalization's local benefits while reducing its costs. This study contributes to the growing dialogue concerning globalization's local impacts and appraisals of various ameliorative strategies.[6]

There also is a current scholarly rethinking of the role of global cities and regions not merely as corporate and financial command centers but as vibrant places for international trade and commerce. The L.A. case illuminates new theories of trade regionalization and particularly the advantages of superior trade infrastructure. Compared with earlier trade theories, the so-called New Economic Geography, exemplified in Paul Krugman's *Geography and Trade* (1990), shifts the focus from nations to regions and firms. As national tariffs are reduced or eliminated, transportation costs become a major trade determinant. World-class port and airport facilities can confer substantial regional advantage by lowering such costs, which, in a just-in-time economy, now include shipping time and reliability.[7]

This study seeks to bring physical capital investments and transportation infrastructure back into contemporary policy debates concerning regional and trade development. Today, there is a preoccupation with the role of social capital in regional growth. Thus, sociologist Richard Florida offers a creative-capital theory of regional prosperity, in which a bohemian "artistic class" is seen as the new catalyst of development. Political scientist Robert Putnam and others see economic growth as tied to a community's level of civic participation and social cohesion. Economists stress the role of "human capital"; according to this theory, growth is driven by workforce educational levels. Yet successful regions also require enormous physical capital investments in infrastructure—ranging from water and power systems to ports, airports, highways, and rail lines—to attract and retain businesses and remain competitive.[8]

A related aim is to restore infrastructure's pride of place in trade-development debates, where its importance is frequently downplayed. The development of ports and airports is, after all, a lengthy, expensive, and contentious process. As a result, such mega-projects have become anathema to many local public officials, who, in an era of term limits and poll-driven policymaking, have short-term policy horizons and seek to avoid angering voters. Local politicians tend to prefer trade initiatives with immediate benefits and few costs: sister-cities programs, local and overseas trade offices, and high-visibility trade missions.[9]

Despite growing political impediments, infrastructure retains extraordinary value as regional trading strategy. For places such as Los Angeles, infrastructure remains the sturdy bedrock of trade and regional development. L.A.'s innovative port, rail, and airport governance, financing, and developmental policies merit serious study by policymakers concerned with infrastructure and trade across the nation and around the world. In the 1990s, with the telecommunications and dot.com speculative bubbles, it became fashionable to dismiss transportation systems as somehow antiquated and primitive and to focus instead on telecommunications as the new conduit of global trade for the then high-flying, high-tech economy. In the so-called new economy, trade was about intellectual property rights, not the movement of people and goods. Yet, as argued here, the now-struggling new economy also depends fundamentally on the global connectivity supplied by gateway airports such as LAX.

Closer to home, I endeavor to bring issues of trade, infrastructure, and local government's catalytic role to the forefront of debate concerning L.A.'s globalization and regional development. I critically evaluate the leading perspectives on global restructuring in Southern California—the so-called L.A. School and what might be termed the New Boosterism—pointing out their failure to take seriously the region's trade infrastructure and local government's role. I also assess the benefits and costs to a region such as Greater Los Angeles of becoming a major trade center and transportation complex, a topic of interest to regional policymakers everywhere.

Although L.A. has a reputation as a trade underachiever, these pages reveal a different story. Its goods exports may lag, but its strong service exports and enormous imports warrant its status as one of the nation's and world's leading trade centers. The crucial question concerns the overall trade/infrastructure balance sheet for local communities, Southern California, and the nation as a whole. Premier gateway regions such as L.A. facilitate both regional and national trade. However, trade can create regional losers as well as winners. Further, infrastructure investments in ports and airports generate sizeable dispersed economic benefits (jobs), but in dense, urban environments they also can produce significant, concentrated environmental costs (noise, traffic, and air pollution).

Also explored here is why mega-projects in Los Angeles, as elsewhere, are so much harder to build today than in the past. Projects now face fierce community and environmental opposition and constrained funding. I thus examine how the strategic environment for infrastructure development has changed dramatically since the 1970s because of the breakdown in the consensus on growth, the rise of NIMBY ("not in my backyard") community resistance, and the creation of supralocal regulatory-policy regimes. New environmental policies have included the National Environmental Policy Act (NEPA) and the California Environmental Quality Act (CEQA), which mandated project environmental-impact reviews and mitigation. In California, the passage of Proposition 13 (1978) and later tax-reform measures dramatically altered local-government finance and thus further threatened L.A.'s mega-projects.

I analyze these stringent environmental and fiscal rules and assess their potentially inhibiting effects on the region's ambitious port, rail, and airport plans under L.A. Mayors Richard Riordan (1993–2001) and James Hahn (elected in 2001). Significantly, these are the first two L.A. mayors under term limits (two four-year terms both for the mayor and for the city council). As argued here, term limits can adversely affect long-term capital planning and investments. Port and airport projects have twenty-year to as much as fifty-year planning and investment cycles, a span that closely matches the career horizons of bureaucrats. Yet, term-limited politicians receive little short-term benefit from such long-term investments. In the case of infrastructure projects, they can be exposed to significant short-term political costs because of NIMBY voter anger. Under term limits, politicians have little incentive to champion expensive, controversial, and lengthy projects that promise long-term regional economic benefits but impose short-term political costs.

Los Angeles's recent troubled history with its trade mega-projects is a cautionary tale concerning the potentially adverse effects of these new regulatory and electoral rules. Faced with state property-tax raids, Mayor Riordan saw the ports and airports as convenient "cash cows" to be milked to balance the city's budget and to pay for additional police. I chronicle the epic battles in the 1990s over the Riordan administration's revenue-diversion efforts, which pitted City Hall against the shippers, airlines, and even state and federal governments. In the Hahn administration, the threat of municipal secession (by the San Fernando Valley and Hollywood) became another incentive to placate short-term community and environmental concerns at the expense of long-term infrastructure development. Further, the September 11, 2001, terrorist attacks made security, not expansion, the watchword at the region's ports and airports.

The Riordan and Hahn policies reveal the growing tensions between political and bureaucratic leadership and priorities and between democratic accountability and market efficiency. Public enterprises such as the L.A.–area ports and airports are hybrid institutions that function in the dual and conflicting arenas of democracy and the market. I analyze the resulting conflict between voter-sensitive elected officials, who seek increased control in order to use agency revenues to balance budgets and pay for popular services without raising taxes, and market-sensitive bureaucrats, who seek increased autonomy.

L.A. as Trade Entrepôt

Once a trade backwater, Southern California has emerged as one of the world's leading centers for trade and transshipment. From the early 1970s to the late 1990s, global trade in the Southland (as Southern California is also known) experienced remarkable growth, increasing at an average rate of 16 percent annually. As a result, Los Angeles in 1994 surpassed New York as the nation's busiest customs district. In less than thirty years, the trade fortunes of the nation's two leading metropolises were dramatically reversed. Between 1972 and 2000, Los Angeles's share of the nation's global merchandise trade climbed from 6 to 14 percent, while New York's share dropped from 21 to 12 percent. However, for 2001, with a looming recession and the immedi-

Table 1.2   Year 2001 Merchandise Trade: Imports and Exports, Major
U.S. Customs Districts (in millions of dollars)

District	Imports[a]	Exports[b]	Total
Los Angeles	200,670	69,111	269,781
New York	139,110	76,239	215,349
San Francisco	50,041	45,803	95,844
Seattle	56,404	41,372	97,776
San Diego	20,706	12,342	33,048
U.S. total	1,141,959	731,026	1,872,985

SOURCE: Data from U.S. Bureau of the Census, *U.S. Merchandise Trade: Selected Highlights*,
FT 920 Series (Washington, D.C., 2002).
[a]Import values for district of unlading.
[b]Export values exclude shipping charges.

ate trade-dampening effects of terrorist attacks, L.A.'s trade growth, like that
of other areas in the nation, was (at least temporarily) reversed.[10]

Table 1.2 displays the value of merchandise trade in the year 2001—imports, exports, and total trade—as measured by district of unlading (where
goods actually are unloaded) for the four West Coast customs districts (Los
Angeles, San Francisco, Seattle, and San Diego) and for New York. With
$270 billion in trade, Los Angeles had become the "gateway for the Pacific
Rim," for both the West Coast and the nation as a whole. The Los Angeles
Customs District (LACD) had a 54 percent share of the total West Coast merchandise trade, mostly from Pacific Rim countries. Overall, one-seventh of total U.S. global trade (and roughly one-twentieth of the world's commerce)
coursed through Los Angeles's gateways.[11]

Most striking was Los Angeles's heavy import activity. Three-quarters
of L.A.'s merchandise trade consisted of imports, a significantly larger share
than nationwide (60 percent). Overall, the LACD handled 18 percent of the
nation's total imports but only 9 percent of goods exports. While half of
LACD imports served the massive Southern California market of twenty million customers, the other half was transshipped to other places in the state
and nation. Facilitating L.A.'s entrepôt role were excellent rail and highway
connections to the rest of North America. As Abraham Lowenthal and colleagues observe, "Southern California . . . serves as the single largest transshipment point 'between' the most active exporting region, East Asia, and the
world's number one source of demand, the United States." [12]

L.A. serves as the chief hub for U.S. waterborne commerce, which accounts for much of its import and transshipment activity. Table 1.3 shows
year 2001 merchandise trade by shipping mode for the five major U.S. customs districts. Twenty-eight percent of the nation's total waterborne commerce passed through the ports of San Pedro Bay (the LACD), nearly two-
and-one-half times more than went through the once-mighty New York–area

Table 1.3   Year 2001 Merchandise Trade by Shipping Mode, Major
U.S. Customs Districts (in millions of dollars)

District	Water	Air	Total[a]
Los Angeles	203,700	64,119	269,781
New York	86,026	126,509	215,349
San Francisco	29,006	66,367	95,844
Seattle	48,168	10,610	97,776
San Diego	4,283	153	33,048
U.S. total	718,448	518,602	1,872,985

SOURCE: Data from U.S. Bureau of the Census, *Merchandise Trade: Selected Highlights*, FT 920 Series (Washington, D.C., 2002).
Note: Import values by district of unlading; export values exclude shipping charges.
[a] Total includes trade shipped by truck through land ports.

ports. Trade through the L.A.–area ports also dwarfed that of their West Coast rivals. San Pedro Bay (consisting of the ports of Los Angeles and Long Beach) handled over 70 percent of all Pacific Coast waterborne trade. However, L.A.'s trade preeminence did not extend to airborne commerce. LACD airports (primarily LAX) handled only 12 percent of the nation's airborne commerce compared with 24 percent for New York–area airports. On the West Coast, LAX battled for air-freight supremacy with the Bay Area's three gateway airports: San Francisco International, Oakland International, and San Jose International. In 2001, with a slumping high-tech economy, the Bay Area airports (at $66 billion) barely edged out LAX (at $64 billion) in global air-cargo value.

Los Angeles has become the nation's leading Pacific Rim gateway. As measured by port-of-entry merchandise trade, three-quarters of the region's two-way trade is with Pacific Rim countries. In 2001, L.A.'s chief trading partners were Japan ($45.6 billion), China ($44.9 billion), South Korea ($15.7 billion), Taiwan ($14.9 billion), Malaysia ($10.1 billion), Singapore ($7.7 billion), and Thailand ($6.7 billion). Leading Pacific Rim imports were electronic machinery, automobiles and trucks, consumer electronics, apparel, footwear, and toys. Top regional exports worldwide were high-tech equipment, industrial machinery, aircraft, plastics and polymers, engines and pumps, and chemicals.[13]

However, port-of-entry data (reflecting where customs papers are filed rather than the actual site of production or final destination) seriously underreport L.A.'s NAFTA trade. Most of L.A.'s trade with Mexico and Canada is transported by truck or train (not by ship or airplane) and thus is recorded in border-area customs districts such as San Diego, Laredo, and Seattle. In contrast, Exporter Location data (which tally the location of the exporter of record) reveal L.A.'s growing NAFTA trade. From 1993 (the year before NAFTA's implementation) to 1999, the Mexico/Canada share of

L.A.–area exports rose from 17 percent to 27 percent, while shares for other world regions, including the Pacific Rim, declined. In all, NAFTA trade generated nearly 60 percent of the region's export growth from 1993 to 1999. This figure underscores the growing importance of L.A.'s trade corridors— highways and rail lines—to Mexico and Canada.[14]

Notwithstanding the threat of terrorism, global trade promises to play an important role in Southern California's long-term future, and thus it will place unprecedented demands on the region's already congested transportation system. Despite the East Asian currency devaluation, financial turmoil, and sluggish recovery, up to half the world's economic growth in the early twenty-first century is projected to occur in East Asian countries, L.A.'s chief trading partners. As a result, Southern California's ports, rail lines, airports, and highways could face a doubling, even tripling, of demand by the mid-2020s. NAFTA trade with Mexico also is projected to double and further congeal the region's north/south arteries.

Sinews of Trade

The Importance of Infrastructure

Although conventional wisdom holds that international trade flows are driven by global trade agreements, international currency markets, national trade and fiscal policies, and corporate sourcing decisions, new understandings are emerging of the potent stimulus provided by a superior import/export infrastructure. In an era of growing free trade, just-in-time manufacturing and delivery, and supply-chain logistics, regions are fast becoming multimodal transportation centers; they speed the flow of people, goods, information, and finance throughout the world economy. Metropolitan areas that build world-class transportation infrastructures lower transportation costs (including time and reliability) for businesses, thus strengthening their competitive advantage in the global economy while building cost barriers to the entry of competing regions.[15]

Although the received account holds that globalization can "hollow out" the national state, it actually may strengthen urban governance arrangements. Growing evidence indicates that what local governments do to provide trade infrastructure fundamentally matters to their global competitiveness. In the movement of international trade, the orientation of private-sector actors such as shippers and carriers is primarily global and national. Yet, in the United States, the public-sector responsibility for transporting trade is primarily subnational. Unlike many other countries, which have nationally run port and airport systems, the United States has a decentralized system; nearly all such U.S. facilities are managed by regional or municipal governmental entities. International ports, airports, and rail and highway trade corridors give grassroots governments considerable leverage over regional trade flows and economic competitiveness.[16]

A growing body of research attests to the trade-inducing role of regional ports, airports, and trade corridors. In regard to Seattle, arguably the most trade-oriented region in the country, Frederic Morris notes, "One reason Seattle is home to so many larger multinationals, particularly global technology companies, is its success in creating its own competitive advantage. This edge starts with physical infrastructure [the Seattle-Tacoma International Airport, the ports of Seattle and Tacoma], which continues to be an important determinant of success in the global economic system."[17] Similarly, Tony Robinson argues that the Denver International Airport is a lynchpin of Denver's global aspirations. In contrast, as Sara Bachman shows for the San Francisco Bay Area and Richard Feinberg demonstrates for San Diego, their regional infrastructure deficiencies have led to business and trade losses to Los Angeles, which is advantaged by superior infrastructure. In the world economy, a superior import/export infrastructure strengthens regional advantage by reducing transportation costs. This logic extends to new-economy industries engaged in time-based competition. To minimize transport time, delays, and uncertainties, high-tech firms have a real incentive to locate near hub airports.[18]

L.A.'s Global Gateways

The catalytic role of infrastructure is particularly evident in Southern California, where a world-class transportation system has been constructed to handle huge volumes of global trade, primarily with Pacific Rim countries and Mexico. These are among the nation's—and the world's—busiest global gateways and trade corridors. Because of San Diego's limited port, rail, and airport facilities, Los Angeles's gateways serve California's trade needs from San Luis Obispo to the Mexican border. In 2001, over 70 percent of the Golden State's total international trade (by value) passed through the L.A.–area ports and airports.[19]

As Table 1.4 shows, for 2001 the ports of San Pedro Bay together ranked third, behind Hong Kong and Singapore, among the world's top container ports; San Pedro Bay handled 9.6 million twenty-foot equivalent units (TEUs). Separately, the Los Angeles and Long Beach ports ranked seventh and tenth worldwide. New York/New Jersey, the next largest U.S. container port, ranked fourteenth internationally. L.A.'s nearest competitors for Pacific Rim container trade, the ports of Oakland, Seattle, and Tacoma, ranked twenty-eighth, thirty-third, and thirty-seventh, respectively. Connecting the San Pedro Bay ports to the North American market, L.A.'s two transcontinental rail systems—the best systems on the West Coast—handled nearly 70 percent of total West Coast trade shipped by rail.

Table 1.4   World's Top Fifteen Container Ports Ranked by Year 2001 Traffic (in millions of TEUs[a])

Rank	Port	Country	TEUs
1	Hong Kong	China	17.80
2	Singapore	Singapore	15.57
	Ports of San Pedro Bay	*United States*	**9.64**
3	Pusan	South Korea	7.91
4	Kaohsiung	Taiwan	7.54
5	Shanghai	China	6.33
6	Rotterdam	Netherlands	6.10
7	*Los Angeles*	*United States*	5.18
8	Shenzhen	China	5.07
9	Hamburg	Germany	4.69
10	*Long Beach*	*United States*	**4.46**
11	Antwerp	Belgium	4.22
12	Port Kelang	Malaysia	3.76
13	Dubai	United Arab Emirates	3.50
14	New York/New Jersey	United States	3.32
15	Bremen/Bremerhaven	Germany	2.92

SOURCE: Data from "Special Report: World's Top 50 Container Ports," *Journal of Commerce Week*, July 8-14, 2002, pp. 22-27.
[a]Twenty-foot equivalent units

Tables 1.5 and 1.6 display the world's leading passenger and cargo airports in 2001. LAX was the world's third busiest passenger and fourth busiest air-cargo facility. In passenger traffic, LAX ranked behind Atlanta and Chicago, but ahead of London, Tokyo, Dallas/Fort Worth, and Frankfurt. As for air cargo, LAX ranked behind Memphis (the FedEx hub), Hong Kong, and Anchorage (a Pacific Rim transit-freight hub) but ahead of Tokyo's Narita, Miami, Frankfurt, and Paris airports. LAX handled nearly half of California's global air cargo and one-eighth of the U.S. total (see Table 1.3).

With looming capacity constraints threatening to act as bottlenecks to trade growth and regional job creation, public officials in the 1990s feverishly worked on ambitious port, rail, airport, and highway projects to dramatically increase system capacity well into the early twenty-first century. These mega-projects (whose planning, financing, and development are analyzed in this book) included

- The $4 billion program of Los Angeles and Long Beach port development, 1995–2020.
- The $2.4 billion Alameda Corridor separated-grade rail project, 1995–2002, designed to facilitate the movement of goods from the San Pedro Bay ports to the downtown L.A. intermodal rail yards; and the planned $3 billion Alameda Corridor East and Orange County On-Trac separated-grade rail projects from the downtown railheads to San Bernardino/Colton.

Table 1.5 World's Ten Busiest Passenger Airports Ranked by Year 2001 Passenger Volumes (in millions)

Rank	Airport	Country	Passengers
1	Atlanta (ATL)	United States	75.85
2	Chicago (ORD)	United States	66.81
3	Los Angeles (LAX)	United States	61.02
4	London (LHR)	Great Britain	60.74
5	Tokyo (HND)	Japan	58.69
6	Dallas/Fort Worth (DFW)	United States	55.15
7	Frankfurt (FRA)	Germany	48.56
8	Paris (CDG)	France	48.00
9	Amsterdam (AMS)	Netherlands	39.53
10	Denver (DEN)	United States	36.09

SOURCE: Data from Airports Council International, *Traffic Data: World Airports Ranking by Total Passengers—2001.* www.airports.org.

Table 1.6 World's Ten Busiest Cargo Airports Ranked by Year 2001 Freight Volumes (in millions of metric tons)

Rank	Airport	Country	Metric Tons
1	Memphis (MEM)	United States	2.63
2	Hong Kong (HKG)	China	2.10
3	Anchorage (ANC)	United States	1.87[a]
4	Los Angeles (LAX)	United States	1.77
5	Tokyo (NRT)	Japan	1.68
6	Miami (MIA)	United States	1.64
7	Frankfurt (FRA)	Germany	1.61
8	Paris (CDG)	France	1.59
9	Singapore (SIN)	Singapore	1.53
10	Louisville (SDF)	United States	1.47

SOURCE: Data from Airports Council International, *Traffic Data: World Airports Ranking by Total Cargo—2001.* www.airports.org.
[a] Includes transit freight.

- The $2.3 billion in "NAFTA-network" border-infrastructure improvements, such as State Routes 905 and 125 in San Diego; plans for truck-only lanes on selected L.A. freeways; and the ambitious "Southwest Compact" strategy for improving highway and rail connections between the metropolitan regions of the Southwest and the northern states of Mexico.
- The $8–12 billion LAX Master Plan, 1999–2015; Ontario International Airport expansion; and plans to convert El Toro and other former military air bases in the region into international and air-cargo commercial airports.

For 1996–2000, spending for the region's port, rail, and airport megaprojects was $4.3 billion, which was the nation's largest five-year capital spending program for trade infrastructure. Los Angeles's chief trade rivals—the Bay Area, Seattle/Tacoma, and New York—unveiled less ambitious capital programs. During this period, the Bay Area invested $3.2 billion in projects at San Francisco International Airport and at the Port of Oakland's maritime and airport facilities. The ports of Seattle and Tacoma earmarked $1.5 billion for port and airport development. The Port Authority of New York/New Jersey's capital expenditure for airport and seaport development was $2.1 billion.[20]

Yet, these mega-projects, designed to enhance regional competitiveness in the global economy, became objects of intense local debate in regard to their regional benefits and costs. They were ground zero for escalating conflicts that pitted the forces of globalization and the economy against community and the environment. While lacking the violence of the antiglobalization protests at the World Trade Organization meetings in Seattle and the G-8 Summit in Genoa, Italy, community and environmental opposition was strong in regard to Port of Los Angeles and Port of Long Beach terminal projects, the Alameda Corridor rail project, NAFTA border projects, the LAX Master Plan, and a proposed commercial airport at El Toro.

Balanced against their promised economic benefits, the mega-projects threatened to impose substantial environmental costs—traffic congestion, air pollution, and noise—on neighboring communities. As a result, affected local communities such as San Pedro/Wilmington, Compton, South Gate, Lynwood, Tecate, Westchester, El Segundo, Irvine, and Lake Forest organized in NIMBY fashion to oppose or at least to mitigate the worst effects of port, rail, highway, and airport expansion. Environmental groups also entered the fray as project opponents. These challenges are explored in this book. They had major implications for L.A.'s trade aspirations. As the Southern California Association of Governments (SCAG), the area's multicounty council of governments, warned, "Failure to adequately address and plan for . . . significant growth in airport demand will not only result in major air and ground congestion, it will also seriously jeopardize Southern California's position as a national and international trade center."[21]

Overview of the Study

The eight chapters that follow explore trade, infrastructure, and regional development in Greater Los Angeles—from the early railroad and harbor fights, to the building of one of the world's greatest trade-transportation complexes, to L.A.'s emergence as a leading trade center, to recent challenges to its mega-projects, and to its uncertain infrastructure and trade future.

Part One (Chapters One and Two) provides an introduction and relevant context. Chapter Two explores the local pillars of trading regions such as Greater Los Angeles. Although tariff-lowering international and binational trade agreements (such as the General Agreement on Tariffs and Trade and NAFTA) and new globe-spanning transportation technologies such as containerization and air-cargo express have been potent trade catalysts, I focus on the catalytic roles of local markets and governments. What is there about regional economies such as L.A.'s that is making them key trading units in the global economy? What role in trade is played by local government? Here I focus on public ports, airports, and trade corridors, analyzing how institutional arrangements shape capital-development policies, regional trade competitiveness, and growth. Particularly examined are the innovative municipal-governance arrangements for Southern California's major ports and airports.

The remainder of the book consists of three parts. Part Two (Chapters Three and Four) examines the historical evolution of the region's port and airport systems. I analyze early public port and airport creation and the subsequent development of their governance systems, strategic planning, infrastructure financing and development, and trade-promotion policies. I also consider how these agency policies affected trade development and the regional economy. Except for fierce railroad and harbor battles between rival economic elites, this is a story largely of unchallenged development. There was little organized community and environmental opposition until the region's growth consensus began to fray, a process that started with community resistance to LAX expansion in the 1960s. By the 1990s, community and environmental opposition was unrelenting.

Chapter Three examines L.A.'s great regime transformation from 1880 to 1932; during this time a classic laissez-faire growth regime and caretaker local state controlled by the Southern Pacific Railroad were replaced by a powerful local developmental state apparatus that provided critically needed infrastructure. The chapter traces the epic battle between the railroad and the local business community over the location and ownership (private versus public) of the region's harbor; the rise of a powerful local reform movement that invoked the formidable powers of the local state to promote regional development; the creation of the ports of Los Angeles and Long Beach and their subsequent development as semi-autonomous proprietary departments; and the creation in 1928 of Mines Field, L.A.'s municipal airport and predecessor to LAX. I also explore the catalytic role of the twin ports in Los Angeles's "branch-plant" industrialization and the ports' early quests for trade, both domestic and foreign.

Chapter Four traces the development of the region's global gateways, trade, and economy from 1933 to 1992; this development took place under the transformative conditions of depression, war, and new postwar transportation technologies. The chapter explores the role of New Deal financing in early port and airport projects; L.A.'s wartime transformation into a major arsenal of democracy; the maturation of L.A.'s municipal-airport system, which culminated in 1947 in proprietary-department status, and its evolution in the 1960s into a regional airport system with the acquisition of Ontario and Palmdale airports; the Port of Long Beach's rise as a major competitor to L.A.; and agile local agency responses to new technologies such as containerization and the jet airplane.

With roots in their semi-autonomous governance arrangements and entrepreneurial leadership, the Los Angeles and Long Beach port and airport systems throughout the postwar era demonstrated the capacity for long-range strategic planning and innovation. Yet development would no longer be unchallenged. The 1960s saw the rise of strong community opposition to jet noise and LAX growth. And, beginning in the 1970s, new federal and state environmental and fiscal regulatory regimes were installed that later would challenge L.A.'s mega-projects.

Part Three (Chapters Five through Seven) examines the substantial threats —fiscal, environmental, community-based, and governance—to trade-infrastructure development during the administration of Mayor Riordan, the city's first term-limited chief executive. Chapter Five considers challenges to expansion of the San Pedro Bay port system. It examines the differing visions and plans of the competing ports; analyzes City Hall revenue raids; highlights environmental challenges to port development; and examines community and governance disputes involving the L.A. port, ranging from charter reform to secession threats from San Pedro/Wilmington.

Chapter Six explores planning and development strategies in the 1990s for the region's chief trade corridors: the rail and highway projects linking the ports, airports, and borders to the North American market. I explore the landmark Alameda Corridor intermodal freight-rail project; planned rail extensions through Orange County, the San Gabriel Valley, and the Inland Empire (San Bernardino and Riverside counties); and NAFTA port-of-entry and highway projects linking Mexico to Greater Los Angeles. I examine how Alameda Corridor decision makers devised innovative institutional mechanisms (such as the joint-powers authority) to overcome financing, governance, and community challenges.

Chapter Seven dissects the Achilles' heel of L.A.'s global engagement: the uncertain future of its international airports, a crisis that started in the Riordan years. I examine the pivotal battle among the mayor, airlines, and federal government over LAX revenue diversion. Also examined are the fierce struggles over the LAX Master Plan and the intense conflict over a proposed new international commercial airport at El Toro in south Orange County. I trace the rise of well-organized community opposition to both projects and analyze the political strategies used by airport supporters and opponents. I also consider other regional airports, such as Ontario and Palmdale (part of the L.A. municipal airport system), and facilities at former military bases in the Inland Empire. Unlike trade-corridor projects, airports represented a major failure of regional cooperation and problem solving.

In Part Four (Chapter Eight), I consider Los Angeles's current status and uncertain future as a trade and transportation center. I explore the contemporary debates over L.A. globalization and consider the overall benefits and costs of Southern California's global engagement. I also look closely at new challenges and new leadership. The September 2001 terrorist attacks in New York and Washington adversely affected trade and infrastructure, both nationally and regionally. As a result, new and expensive security measures have been installed at U.S. ports, airports, and land ports of entry. I consider the short- and long-term effects of this new security regime on Southern California trade and infrastructure.

Also considered are the trade and infrastructure plans since 2001 of L.A. Mayor Hahn; these plans include a $10 billion LAX Master Plan proposal stressing security and modernization at the expense of large-scale expansion. Although Hahn had been given additional powers under a new city charter, he faced resurgent localism in the form of neighborhood councils and secession threats from the San Fernando Valley, Hollywood, and the harbor district of San Pedro/Wilmington. Localistic forces and short-term expediency appeared to shape the new mayor's port and airport plans. Finally, I consider the region's search for alternative global-trade formulas, ranging from increased private-sector involvement, to capitalizing on the area's renowned ethnic diversity, to building greater equity into regional policies, to championing telecommunications rather than transportation investments. I conclude by reexamining the role of infrastructure in regional trade and economic development. Thus, how Southern California's looming airport crisis is handled will profoundly shape the region's global future.

Perhaps owing to the sheer difficulty of the task, too many who tell the story of the development of sprawling, complex Los Angeles rely on secondary source materials and thus can only repackage the conventional wisdom. In contrast, this study utilizes a treasure trove of unexplored primary source materials to offer a fresh perspective on L.A.'s trade "crown jewels" and their largely unsung roles in the political economy of the city and region. For a public historian, Los Angeles is a first-rate archeological dig. This study relies heavily on a rich vein of untapped archives (such as annual departmental reports, budgets, and planning studies) from L.A.'s harbor and airports departments, the Long Beach Harbor Department, and regional agencies such as the Alameda Corridor Transportation Authority and SCAG. These archival materials, as well as the official letters, memos, and consulting reports herein cited, can be difficult to locate. They can be accessed from departmental archives and websites, from public officials' offices, or from the author.

I also have canvassed the extensive holdings of the Los Angeles municipal archives and, at UCLA's Department of Special Collections, the extraordinary John Randolph Haynes Collection (on early L.A. politics and governance) as well as oral histories of former L.A. Mayors Norris Poulson, Sam

Yorty, and Tom Bradley, and of early airport officials. I interviewed more than seventy-five former and current public officials (mayors, city councilpersons, departmental managers, and their staffs) as well as knowledgeable business and community leaders. Newspapers, particularly the *Los Angeles Times*, were heavily utilized. Finally, I have tapped an invaluable regional resource: interviews with infrastructure policymakers published in the *Metro Investment Report*, a monthly newsletter devoted to public investment in Southern California.

As these pages reveal, the story told by the archives, oral histories, newspapers, and interviews departs in major respects from the conventional view of Los Angeles as a West Coast Dallas or Houston—another Sunbelt city tightly run by a conservative, business-controlled oligarchy with a fragmented, limited governmental system serving as a formula for policy weakness and incoherence. Until the multiple crises of the early 1990s (recession, riots, and earthquake) shook civic confidence, the City of the Angels never behaved as a city with limits. Instead, Los Angeles acted as a sovereign city-state, using the extensive powers of local government (particularly development bureaucracies and massive infrastructure investments) to create, in an unlikely setting, one of the world's great cities, regions, and hubs of global commerce. However, whether Los Angeles can continue to marshal sufficient civic leadership and public support for its ambitious infrastructure projects and global future remains to be seen.

2 Regional Trade Catalysts

Local Markets and Governments

Cities . . . are being reshaped as national economies open up to virtually unmediated global market forces. . . . The economic future of the city, the employment and incomes of its citizens, comes to be much more closely related to the ease, cheapness and reliability of flows of goods and services to and from the rest of the world. Cities with the capacity to invest in the infrastructure of movement, sea, air and road, thus enormously strengthen their competitive capacity and build barriers to the entry of competing cities.

—*Nigel Harris, "The Emerging Global City: Transport" (1994)* [1]

Conventional wisdom maintains that ports are driven by the combined forces of geographic location, technology, and economics, and that port governing structures lack influence on the behavior and performance of ports. . . . This argument ignores, of course, the reasons why ports were converted from private to public ownership in the first place. It is also incorrect, or at least incomplete, because it leaves out the role of government, whose activities can serve to retard or enhance the success of ports in attaining their goals. . . .

—*David Olson,* Governance of U.S. Public Ports *(1992)* [2]

This chapter seeks to account for the rise of trading regions such as Los Angeles. I focus on two grassroots catalysts: (1) local economies and the growing regionalization of trade and (2) local governments. Although local governments have launched a variety of trade-development initiatives, I focus here on the local public infrastructure of trade: international ports, airports, and trade corridors. Particularly examined are the institutional arrangements governing Southern California's global gateways. Yet, the explosive postwar growth in trade has also been the result of global forces such as international trade agreements and innovations in transportation and information technologies. As tariff and transportation costs have fallen, global trade has grown dramatically. While recognizing that trade patterns also are profoundly shaped by such factors as international currency markets and corporate sourcing decisions, I start by considering global policy and technological catalysts. [3]

Global Catalysts

The major postwar policy impetus involved tariff-reducing international trade agreements such as the 1947 General Agreement on Tariffs and Trade (GATT) and preferential agreements such as the 1993 North American Free Trade Agreement (NAFTA). Under GATT's successive trade liberalizations, world trade (in year 2000 dollars) grew from $365 billion in 1950 to $6.4 trillion in 2000. Los Angeles was a primary beneficiary of this flood tide of trade. Roughly one-twentieth of the world's trade now comes through Los Angeles. Facilitating the region's trade growth have been international and bilateral agreements with its major trading partners: Japan, the East Asian newly industrialized countries, Mexico, and China.[4]

Despite supposed favored treatment of "least developed countries," GATT's center of gravity long remained its North American and European founders. Newly industrializing countries such as Taiwan and South Korea, which had emerged as leading exporters of inexpensive manufactured goods, were disadvantaged by the imposition of "voluntary" export restrictions, such as formal caps on Japanese automobiles. Despite such restrictions, Asian exports rose (in real terms) from $741 billion in 1980 to $1.8 trillion in 2000. During this twenty-year period, they accounted for 35 percent of the growth in overall world trade. Los Angeles particularly has benefited from trade liberalization with East Asia, which accelerated L.A.'s aspirations as a Pacific Rim trading entrepôt. L.A. was also helped by progress toward a "North American Common Market," embodied in the NAFTA preferential trading agreement with Mexico and Canada, implemented in 1994. Since 1993, U.S. trade with Mexico (in real terms) more than doubled, from $97 billion to $248 billion in 2000.[5]

Even without the benefit of preferential status, the People's Republic of China now rivals Mexico as a U.S. trading partner and exceeds its importance for Los Angeles. Southern California–based multinationals, such as Mattel Toys, depend on Chinese trade, which has seen remarkable growth despite the political turmoil long marking Sino-American trade relations. A stabilizing force was the passage in 2000 of the Permanent Normal Trading Relations with China Act. With the accession of both the People's Republic of China and Taiwan into the World Trade Organization in late 2001, the complicated trade relationship between China and the United States entered a new era. Los Angeles was well positioned to be a prime beneficiary.[6]

A second global catalyst involves the intertwined revolutions in transportation and information technologies, which dramatically reduced transport costs (which are increasingly measured by time and reliability). Given pressures to cut sourcing, production, and delivery cycle times (and thus inventory), logistical innovations such as synchronized supply-chain management and just-in-time techniques have been widely implemented worldwide.

With lowered transportation costs has come substantial growth in international sourcing. Component-production and final-assembly sites now are globally dispersed on the basis of raw-material availability, labor costs, and markets.[7]

Since the 1960s, containerization and air-cargo express shipping have revolutionized the global transportation of goods and placed a premium on the capacity, efficiency, and ground accessibility of local port and airport facilities. Containerization radically transformed the shipping, port, trucking, and railroad industries. An oblong box (twenty, forty, or even fifty-four feet in length) could be stacked in ships, then directly transferred to a truck chassis or rail flatcar for land transportation. This innovation changed the appearance and equipment of ports everywhere, rendered entire fleets of cargo ships useless, cut labor costs drastically, and reduced ship turnaround time from a week or more to two or three days. Starting in 1960, West Coast ports such as Los Angeles and Long Beach feverishly made massive investments in container facilities in order to capture larger market shares of the burgeoning trans-Pacific containerized-cargo trade. Between 1970 and 1994, the amount of containerized cargo passing through West Coast ports grew from 8.8 million tons to 122.1 million tons. While in 1975 only one-quarter of all cargo passing through West Coast ports was containerized, by 1994 that share had climbed to over 60 percent.[8]

Another global transportation revolution has taken place in air cargo and air express. Heralding the coming age of air cargo, John Kasarda argues

> With international transactions, production flexibility, and speed characterizing the new economy, it is absolutely certain that air cargo and air express will play increasingly important roles. . . . No other means of transit is better equipped to meet the economic realities of the emerging era where global sourcing and selling and just-in-time logistics require that producers receive and ship smaller quantities more frequently and quickly over long distances. Already air freight accounts for more than one-third of the value of U.S. products exported, a percentage that is continuously rising.[9]

As a result, Los Angeles and other regions with trade aspirations have added new international-airport capacity to handle growing trade volumes. Air cargo, increasingly shipped in all-cargo freighters rather than in the belly of passenger planes, is fast becoming the primary conduit for exports. For 2001, half of Southern California's exports (by value) were shipped by air; these exports added more value to the local economy than did waterborne exports. High-technology, high value-added manufactured products are especially conducive to air shipment.[10]

Trading regions like Southern California also recognize the need to reduce trade-related highway and rail congestion. The watchword of the global logistics revolution is intermodalism: efficient connections between different modes of transportation. For the San Pedro Bay ports, where roughly half of imports are transshipped to inland markets such as Chicago, the promotion of intermodalism has meant expediting rail projects like the Alameda Corridor. For gateway airports like Los Angeles International Airport (LAX), ground transportation is critical because trucks transport both air-cargo exports and imports. Regional competitiveness for places such as Southern California increasingly depends on providing a seamless intermodal transportation network that efficiently links shippers, carriers, ports and airports, highway and rail systems, and ultimately customers.

Some futurists, though, claim that information technologies soon will supplant physical transportation systems such as port and airport facilities as the primary platform for global trade, particularly in knowledge-based, high-tech economies. While telecommunications and information technologies such as the Internet, e-commerce, and teleconferencing have indeed become important trade conduits, it is far too early to write an obituary for the nation's ports, airports, and railways.

Indeed, the relationship between information technology and transportation systems appears to be more one of synergy than of substitution. Thus, while e-mail is reducing overnight air-express deliveries, e-commerce is generating unprecedented demand for air-cargo deliveries. Just as the invention of the telephone did not reduce the need for business meetings (but rather increased them because of greater business contacts), so has information technology increased the demand for moving people and goods. Despite the temporary surge in teleconferencing after the September 2001 terrorist attacks, a substantial need for face-to-face meetings and for the physical movement of goods and services remains, even in knowledge-based economies.

Airports are a critical underpinning of the new economy. In Southern California, high-tech industries have among the highest air-passenger and air-cargo rates. Examining 312 U.S. metropolitan areas, Kenneth Button and Roger Stough found that a hub airport increased a region's high-technology employment on average by more than twelve thousand jobs. In the metro areas surveyed, hub airports accounted for nearly two-thirds of the variation in high-tech employment.[11]

From Global Cities to Trading Regions

Although tariff-reducing trade pacts and cost-reducing transportation technologies, among other factors, have facilitated overall global trade, they do not fully explain the rise of trading regions such as Los Angeles. An additional explanation is supplied by such factors as local markets and local government's provision of trade infrastructure. Cities and regions have been the primary loci of trade for centuries, but the rise of the nation-state and the erection of national trade barriers drew attention away from their historical role. Today, however, there are new theoretical understandings of the rise of subnational regions in the global economy. In sociology and urban planning, these new understandings have brought about a rethinking of global cities, not only as corporate and financial headquarters but as vital centers for exchange and trade. In economics, theories of trade have shifted their focus from nations to regions and firms, with transport costs now seen as critical determinants.

Global Cities

Despite grandiose claims by some futurists that modern information-based economies render place irrelevant, growing evidence indicates that cities and regions, especially "world cities," may matter more than ever in the world economy. John Friedman describes the "world-city hypothesis" as follows:

1. The form and extent of a city's integration with the world economy and the functions assigned to the city in the new spatial division of labor will be decisive for any structural changes occurring within it.
2. Key cities throughout the world are used by global capital as "basing points" in the spatial organization and articulation of production and markets. The resulting links make it possible to arrange world cities into a complex spatial hierarchy.
3. Global control functions of world cities are directly reflected in the structure and dynamics of their production sectors and employment.
4. World cities are major sites for the concentration and accumulation of global capital.
5. World cities are points of destination for large numbers of both domestic and international migrants.
6. World-city formation brings into focus the major contradictions of industrial capitalism—among them spatial and class polarization.
7. World-city growth generates social costs at rates that tend to exceed the fiscal capacity of the state.[12]

In this essentially functionalist account, cities are cast in "roles" assigned by international capital. World cities are command centers for managing globally dispersed economic activities such as manufacturing. Thus, Saskia Sassen details the seemingly inexorable triumph of late-twentieth-century finance and business capital located in a handful of global metropolises—New York, London, and Tokyo, but not, pointedly, Los Angeles. For Sassen, the "postindustrial" thesis of a shift to a service economy and the "multinational" thesis of the triumph of transnational corporations fail to capture the more recent global concentration of economic power in these few world cities, which function as highly specialized international corporate and financial markets built around the provision of "producer services"—for example, speculative investment markets, real estate, insurance, legal services, accounting, advertising, and management consulting. Located at the apex of a hierarchy of world cities, these metropoles supposedly function as corporate and financial command-and-control centers directing worldwide investment flows and production processes.[13]

Yet, Carl Abbott, among others, suggests that a focus on only a handful of world cities and their corporate and financial command functions misses key dimensions of global restructuring. In Abbott's countering "international-city hypothesis," cities are not merely loci of control activities but are also vital centers for exchange activities across political borders. As Abbot argues, "Connected outward to world markets and constituencies," international cities, which well outnumber world cities, occupy "specialized roles and niches in the international economy . . . , [serving] as nodes, junctions, outposts, and relays." They include "production cities" (export centers for finished goods), "transaction cities" (suppliers of professional expertise), and "gateway cities" (entry points to resource regions and markets). Although not a center of finance or of corporate headquarters, Los Angeles is one of the world's leading gateway and transaction cities. Finally, nearly alone among the world-systems theorists, David Keeling argues that efficient goods-transportation networks, such as L.A.'s ports and airports, remain key to a region's global integration.[14]

The New Economic Geography

Economics is witnessing the emergence of regionally based theories of trade; these theories emphasize competitive advantage, early entry, and the role of trade and transport costs in shaping regional production decisions. Such concepts of place and distance are relative newcomers to the world of economic theories of international trade. Mainstream theory has focused on countries, not regions or firms. Emphasizing comparative national advantages, this approach depicted international trade as taking place between nations with different fixed endowments of capital and labor. Abundant labor in one country made labor-intensive goods cheaper to produce, while abundant capital in another made capital-intensive goods cheaper. Thus, a country's factor abundance determined its exports. Despite mounting criticism for its lack of real-world applicability, this approach remained the dominant paradigm until rigorous methods for modeling imperfect competition and increasing returns were developed.[15]

The New International Trade Theory, pioneered by J. A. Brander and B. J. Spencer and by Paul Krugman, deemphasizes the old concern with comparative factor advantages of nations and instead stresses the importance of early start and competitive advantage. A key element here is increasing returns from scale. This cost structure suggests that once a business is set up and operating, it is difficult for newcomers to compete. Thus, nations that can quickly enter new markets such as high technology, where there are few established participants, can capture and dominate those markets. Although the new thinking sparked a hot debate over strategic trade policy and national industrial policy, it too viewed nations as the units of analysis. Yet, as Michael Porter pointed out, the reality is that nations rarely engage in production or trade with one another, although they may regulate such activities. Firms are the real trade participants; they, not nations, are either competitive or noncompetitive. Both national and regional characteristics affect the competitive advantages of firms.[16]

With the advent of the New Economic Geography, as propounded in, for example, Krugman's *Geography and Trade*, the focus in debates about trade shifted from nations to regions. A central question was how a particular region or city became a center of economic activity. The new approach took seriously the location decisions of firms and workers and the costs of engaging in trade. Increasing returns from scale offered a useful vehicle for shifting the focus of trade from nations to regions. Industries, obviously, cannot be spread out evenly across entire countries. The logic of increasing returns implied that they be concentrated where they are most efficient. Indeed, real-life observations of industries, ranging from those in Silicon Valley to the ceramics industry's center in Northern Italy, seemed to confirm the theory.[17]

On the basis of the work of Alfred Marshall, Krugman develops a model of core and periphery. The relationship between the two is determined by trade costs. If moving goods from core to periphery is too expensive, the periphery may retain its industries; in such cases it can do well enough serving local demand despite its smaller scale. As transport costs fall, industry in the periphery is threatened because it becomes cheaper to import goods from the core. Krugman offers the example of pre–Gold Rush California, where demand was so small that it was more profitable to import goods from outside rather than engage in local production. As in Walter Christaller's central-place theory in geography, for Krugman core concentrations of economic activity service a "hinterland" whose size is determined by the transport technology available or by applicable trade costs.[18]

The New Economic Geography has generated studies of regional trade, transportation costs, and the "hub effect." For example, Hideo Konishi has developed an intriguing model of transport costs and the development of hub cities. Rather than assuming transport costs are dissipated, he suggests that they are expended on transport workers and others along the route. This model offers an understanding of how industry agglomeration processes might start at centers of transportation such as Los Angeles. Similarly, Masahisa Fujita, Krugman, and Anthony Venables demonstrate that a port or other form of transportation hub presents the most obvious location for economic activity for it allows firms to minimize transport costs while serving a larger market—all the regions connected through the region's transportation infra-structure. Fujita and Tomoya Mori also use a Krugmanesque approach to an-swer the question of how port cities become and remain great. Port cities like Los Angeles/Long Beach enjoy the advantage of being early starters and benefit from increasing returns from scale, and they can prevent latecomers such as nearby San Diego from rising as rivals. Industries and related eco-nomic activities that emerge in such transportation hubs likely will persist be-cause of increased returns.[19]

The New Regionalism

Grounded in these fresh approaches, a "new-regionalism" movement has arisen to highlight the growing importance of regions in the global economy. According to Kenichi Ohmae, "As investment, industry, technology and con-sumption have become global in orientation," "region states," which form natural "business units," have arisen throughout the world to become the new engines of global prosperity and trade in a borderless economy. Ohmae identifies a series of emerging regional states, each inhabited by five million to twenty million people; they include the San Francisco Bay Area/Silicon Valley, San Diego/Tijuana, Singapore, and Hong Kong/Guangdong Prov-ince. In similar fashion, Neal Peirce and Rosabeth Moss Kanter trace the rise of regionally articulated and globally integrated "citistates" such as Seattle, Boston, and Miami, which use their comparative advantages—for example, location, infrastructure, human capital, regulatory and tax policies—to lure foreign trade and investment.[20]

There also are different types of trading regions. Those areas with a dom-inant export industry, such as Seattle and the Bay Area, have become "export monocultures," while places such as Buffalo and New Orleans have become near-pure trade entrepôts, where only a small proportion of exports and im-ports are locally produced or consumed. As Abraham Lowenthal and col-leagues observe, infrastructure needs and attendant financing strategies may well be different depending on regional trade roles and beneficiaries.[21]

New regionalists such as Peirce and Kanter claim that the governance arrangements of metropolitan areas, particularly their central cities, are key institutional factors affecting global competitiveness. Yet, their concept of governance remains incomplete. Although the notion of "citistates" brings to mind once-powerful Renaissance centers of global commerce and finance such as Venice and Amsterdam, today the concept prosaically refers to infor-mal public/private partnerships that foster regional cooperation and policy-making in the general absence of metropolitanwide government. The new approach depicts businesses, not local governments, as the chief architects of and actors in global trade and regional competitiveness.[22]

Thus, scant attention is paid to local-government structure and capacity

—that is, to formal governmental institutions, resources, and powers. When the value of local government is recognized, the concern is primarily with telecommunications infrastructure, not transportation policies, which are viewed as somehow antiquated and primitive. Hence, Thomas Bonnett argues, "Telecommunications infrastructure investment . . . may be the most significant investment decision that public sector leaders can influence."[23] Many new regionalists thereby sharply limit the role of local development bureaucracies and physical infrastructure in shaping a region's global competitiveness. They see grassroots government's proper roles as investing in nontargeted infrastructure, primarily to expedite communications and transportation, and as fostering industrial districts or clusters where positive spillovers will occur without the benefit of additional government intervention.[24]

The Local Governmental Apparatus

Nevertheless, governmental structure can profoundly shape a region's global competitiveness. Here I consider the local governmental apparatus as a critical (and underrecognized) regional trade regime.

Developmental State Structures

As work on the role of government in less-developed countries attests, state structure—particularly powerful development bureaucracies—can decisively shape patterns of growth and global competitiveness. Peter Evans, for example, contrasts two types of states—predatory and developmental—to explain the different growth trajectories of African and East Asian countries. In predatory African states, such as the former Zaire, rent-seeking politicians and bureaucrats have siphoned off private capital for personal use, thereby substantially reducing incentives for business investment. In contrast, East Asian nations such as Taiwan and South Korea feature a different kind of state apparatus—the developmental state—which, though severely criticized since the economic crises of the 1990s, apparently promoted, not hindered, growth.[25]

According to Evans, developmental states share three essential features. First, strong meritocratic state bureaucracies under civil service rules direct the development process. Second, state bureaucracies possess the resources—legal, financial, and political—needed to play a transformative role in the economy. Third, effective state bureaucracies have "embedded autonomy" vis-à-vis economic actors. Public servants are more than mere instruments of the business community. Instead, they possess the political capacity to mobilize private-sector actors and resources behind state development projects.

This concept fruitfully might be applied to subnational governments in the United States. As Peter Eisinger argues, state and local governments have

greater capacity than the national government to fashion coherent development policies because of their smaller size and greater homogeneity of economic interests. For Eisinger, subnational governments function as entrepreneurial states when they creatively mobilize and deploy the public and private
resources needed for economic development.[26]

Metropolitan areas, with coherent economies built around industry clusters, would appear to have particularly strong incentives to create developmental state structures, such as ports and airports, for regional infrastructure
provision. Not surprisingly, the nation's strongest development bureaucracies
have formed at the grassroots. These normally take the form of regional public authorities (in the East) or special districts (in the West) that address regionwide problems. New York City, for example, is famed for its Triborough
Authority and Port of New York Authority, which operated under the stew-
ardship of public entrepreneurs such as Robert Moses and Austin Tobin.[27]

Yet even more than New York, Chicago, or other leading cities and metropolitan areas, Los Angeles offers perhaps the most fruitful application of
the concept of the local developmental state. In seemingly fragmented L.A.
and neighboring Long Beach, port, airport, and other key development
bureaucracies are proprietary departments—semi-autonomous municipal
agencies. Functioning as part of general-purpose governments (in contrast to
limited-purpose regional authorities) and under the nominal control of mayors and city councils, these agencies serve as potent local instruments of
trade, urban/regional development, and global competitiveness.[28]

As Chapter Three argues, like postwar East Asian countries, the City of
Los Angeles early in the twentieth century transformed itself into a prodigious public growth machine in order to jump-start a backward regional
economy. In light of Southern California's subsequent transformation into
one of the world's great trade and transshipment centers, Los Angeles represents a Weberian ideal-typical case of local state-directed development. Its
municipal government features strong meritocratic bureaucracies with ample
resources for economic transformation and substantial capacity for "embedded autonomy" relative to private-sector actors.

Although L.A.'s government has developed a reputation for being expensive and inefficient, it performs valuable stimulus roles, such as business promotion. Yet its core development function is as a provider of collective goods.
At the heart of municipal Los Angeles lie the three powerful proprietary, or
semi-autonomous, departments: water and power, harbor, and airports. For
fiscal year 2000–2001, these mammoth public enterprises accounted for over
60 percent of the city's $11.3 billion budget and nearly 60 percent of its
$9.5 billion gross direct debt. Although other cities have resorted to regional
public authorities for infrastructure provision, Los Angeles has made infrastructure the centerpiece of municipal governance. No other major U.S. city
has all four of these functions under the aegis of city government. In similar

fashion, neighboring Long Beach created independent proprietary departments modeled on Los Angeles's semi-autonomous agencies in order to manage critical facilities such as the Port of Long Beach.[29]

While crown jewels normally serve as ceremonial objects of sovereignty, Los Angeles's and Long Beach's port and airport facilities are industrial-grade gems that drive the engines of Southern California trade and development. They are operated by powerful local development bureaucracies. In Southern California, their political influence and regional impact are rivaled only by the City of Los Angeles's storied and still-controversial Department of Water and Power; the mammoth Metropolitan Water District of Southern California; the Community Redevelopment Agency, responsible for the postwar rebuilding of downtown L.A.; and the conflict-plagued Metropolitan Transportation Authority. In contrast, Los Angeles's City Planning Department has neither the political influence nor the transformative capacity of the proprietary departments.

Does Governance Matter?

A key question is why some of the nation's global gateways—such as the San Pedro Bay ports and, until recently, LAX—and not others have responded agilely to global forces through long-range strategic planning, market-sensitive pricing, and ambitious capital-improvement programs. Are such policy responses attributable in some fashion to their governance systems?

Outside of California, the nation's ports are managed primarily by regional, not municipal, authorities. Of the eighty-six members of the American Association of Port Authorities, 55 percent are governed by regional special districts; 19 percent by state and bistate authorities; 9 percent by county agencies; and only 17 percent by city agencies. Nearly half the municipal ports are in California—Los Angeles, Long Beach, Oakland, San Francisco, Redwood City, and Richmond. This pattern of port governance by regional districts is particularly evident in the nation's largest cities and metropolitan areas. Eight of the fifteen biggest cities have seaports; seven are governed by special districts. The lone exception is the municipal Port of Los Angeles.[30]

In contrast with port governance, airport governance is as much a municipal as a regional affair. Of the nation's ten largest airports, half are city-run, and the other half are governed by special districts, joint-powers authorities, counties, or multijurisdictional agencies. Of the nation's fifteen largest cities, eight are served by municipal airports while seven have airports managed by regional public authorities/special districts or joint-powers authorities.[31]

There is growing debate concerning the impact of governance systems on the policies and performance of ports and airports. Does it matter that Los Angeles's and Long Beach's ports and airports are municipally run affairs endowed with substantial policy and fiscal autonomy while in New York and other metropolitan areas such facilities are managed by regional authorities? One leading school of thought, represented by Michael Denning, argues that local infrastructure policies and outcomes are driven primarily by market and technological forces, not governance systems. According to Denning, external market forces such as the containerization revolution, not internal governance arrangements, transformed these ports from conservative public monopolists (like public utilities) to public entrepreneurs and shifted their pricing policies from a public- to a more private-good orientation as market-sensitive terminal leases replaced administered harbor tariffs.[32]

A competing school of thought argues that governance structures do in fact matter. In his study of U.S. port governance, David Olson contends that port governance systems can and do make a difference in seven areas: strategic planning, finance, pricing, investment, regulatory requirements, commercialization, and stability. For Olson, formally autonomous structures such as regional authorities and public corporations appear to be organizationally superior to more politicized local structures such as the Los Angeles and Long Beach municipal port and airport systems. Regional authorities such as the Port Authority of New York/New Jersey seem better able than Southern California's city departments to engage in long-term strategic planning while they face fewer local short-term pressures to be revenue generators for supervisory jurisdictions. Similarly, Alan Tucker in his study of airport expansion in Denver and St. Louis argues that metropolitan integration (as with regional authorities) facilitates airport development by reducing the number of actors and veto points and by allowing for a more equitable distribution of project costs and benefits across jurisdictions.[33]

Governance and organizational structure also may matter in other ways. According to John Gulick in a study of the Port of Oakland, what is important about governance structures is whether they facilitate or retard the building of "regional development alliances" with adjacent communities and environmentalists to mitigate the negative externalities of harbor development. Further, as Herman Boschken argues in his study of Pacific Rim seaports, the most critical factor for strategic planning may not be the macrostructure of port organization but the microstructure of planning, engineering, and environmental design and management. At the more microlevel, he concludes that "organizational structure proved to be [a] subtle but powerful influence" in determining which West Coast ports adopted strategic plans and behavior and which did not in the face of rapid technological and market changes.[34]

Governing Southern California's Global Gateways

Historical Foundations

Local governmental power in early twentieth-century Southern California was erected on the sturdy pillars of federalism, home-rule charter powers, and direct democracy. To this day, these institutional factors undergird the region's port and airport systems and shape their governance, policies, and performance.

The system of federalism vitally affects municipal autonomy and the capacity for effective local policymaking. California cities early on enjoyed unusual legal and financial latitude in shaping their economic destinies. Here, as in much of the West, urbanization had preceded state building. San Francisco representatives controlled the 1879 state constitutional convention and wrote provisions favoring urban interests.[35]

Southern California's powerful local developmental state apparatuses could not have been constructed early on without the extensive municipal powers permitted under the California constitution. In 1879, California was the second state in the nation to institute local home rule; in 1888 Los Angeles was the state's first city (and the nation's second, after St. Louis) to adopt a voter-approved freeholders' charter. Long Beach would soon follow. California also gave its cities the fiscal capacity needed to finance large-scale public infrastructure projects. The state's debt ceiling for municipal borrowing was 15 percent of assessed valuation, double the national average. These extensive powers were invoked to create Los Angeles's and Long Beach's development bureaucracies and to finance their ambitious harbor, water, and power projects. However, since the passage of Proposition 13 (1978), a much more restrictive state/local fiscal regime has been put into place.[36]

The region's version of "frontier statism" also required other forms of federal and state government assistance.[37] Federal legislation and subsidies helped underwrite the region's ambitious harbor, water, power, and airport projects. State legislation allowed Los Angeles to annex the harbor cities of San Pedro and Wilmington and to capture the tidelands from railroad control. More recently, though, state and federal environmental laws have created a new, more restrictive regulatory regime and oversight process governing port and airport development.

Since the early advent of home rule in California, the municipal governance structures of Los Angeles and Long Beach have undergone major transformations that affect port and airport governance and development. Los Angeles's 1889 charter established the institutional precedent for independent departments with special fiscal and property powers, which were applied to the Port of Los Angeles by ordinance in 1909 and by charter in 1911. This institutional foundation was strengthened by the passage of the 1925 charter and its enshrinement of a citizen commission to protect the port from the short-term pressures that elected officials might otherwise place on it. Later, the airport would be given similar powers and protections. L.A.'s 2000 charter provided increased representation for local residents on the port and airports commissions and gave the mayor a greater voice. The charter also left largely intact the powers of the harbor and airports departments and even the managing role of their commissions.[38]

Long Beach's first home-rule charter also addressed the needs of its port. The 1907 charter provided that the city would control its waterfront, and harbor development proceeded under the supervision of the mayor and council. When Long Beach moved to a commission charter in 1915, the city further enhanced its harbor powers and established the precedent for an ordinance-created harbor commission. In 1921, the city adopted a council-manager charter, but borrowed L.A.'s provision of an independent citizen commission to manage the Port of Long Beach. Later charter amendments made its port panel more independent than Los Angeles's Board of Harbor Commissioners.[39]

Although much attention has been devoted to the urban political roles of interest groups and the business community, less work has been done on citizen/state relations.[40] *Ballot-box growth*—municipal bond referenda and charter, referendary-ordinance, and annexation elections—was an essential underpinning to early local statist growth regimes. The ballot also helped build the region's powerful bureaucratic machines. For example, the L.A. Harbor Department and Long Beach Harbor Department managers skillfully orchestrated a series of charter amendments to gain public blessing for enhancing their agencies' legal autonomy and fiscal powers. The West's early embrace of political reform, particularly direct democracy, made voters key actors in urban development policy. The local initiative is still being used today to decide the fate of mega-projects, such as the proposed El Toro commercial airport in Orange County.

Compulsory referenda on local bond issues accompanied the Progressive-era direct-democracy movement. By 1914, thirteen states (eight of them west of the Mississippi) had mandatory voting on local bond propositions. California required two-thirds voter approval on all municipal general-obligation bonds backed by the "full faith and credit of the city."[41] In the mid-twentieth century, however, California's governments would begin switching to revenue-bond financing (not requiring voter approval) for revenue-producing projects such as ports and airports. New forms of citizen participation were mandated by the federal and state environmental regulatory regime created in the early 1970s. In project environmental-impact reports/environmental-impact statements, public participation and input were mandated.

Contemporary Governance

Table 2.1 summarizes the current organization, powers, and authority of Los Angeles's and Long Beach's proprietary port and airport departments. As this study argues, local constitutions—the Los Angeles and Long Beach city charters—provide a key explanation for these bureaucratic agencies' political autonomy and transformative capacity. Though city agencies, the proprietary departments historically have approached the independence and influence of regional authorities such as New York's port and Triborough authorities. In L.A.'s and Long Beach's decentralized systems of government, commission-run bureaucracies share power with the mayor, city manager, and city council.

The proprietary departments are first among bureaucratic equals. Under their respective city charters, they are semi-autonomous departments with broad formal powers, particularly with respect to their budgets. They are not subject to the kinds of controls that Congress and the president can exercise over federal agencies. While federal agencies are creatures of Congressional statute and delegated authority, L.A.'s and Long Beach's city charters, not the local legislature, are the primary source of authority for the proprietary departments. Voter-approved local constitutional protections limit the ability of the mayor, city council, or, as was the case in Long Beach, the city manager to micromanage the departments' affairs.[42]

The harbor and airports departments, though, are not rogue bureaucracies unanswerable to voters and elected officials. By simple majority vote, the electorate can approve charter amendments that rewrite the rules of the bureaucratic game. In the history of charter reform in L.A. and Long Beach, the bureaucrats first mastered the game; they persuaded voters from the 1920s to the early 1980s to insulate their agencies from extensive political oversight. Since the Proposition 13 tax revolt (1978), however, local politicians have had strong incentives to rewrite the rules of the bureaucratic game in an effort to funnel agency revenues into the city's general fund, and they have been successful in securing voter passage of charter amendments enhancing their control over the bureaucracy.[43]

Mayors and city councils do possess some means of political oversight. Departments are managed by five- or seven-member boards of commissioners appointed by the mayor subject to council confirmation. Since the 1980s, mayors in the two cities have actively used their appointments to impose their own policy agendas. In Los Angeles, but not in Long Beach, the council can veto (with a two-thirds vote) board decisions. The council also must approve major contracts. Both city councils have broad investigatory powers over the bureaucracy. However, the mayor and council (and, in the case of Long Beach, the city manager) still have little direct authority over the proprietary departments' budgets and capital-spending programs. In this fashion, the two charters maintain a delicate (albeit somewhat different) balance between political oversight and agency financial independence and ability to initiate policy.

This constitutional balance reflects the fact that these are public bureaucracies responsible for revenue generation and economic development. Public enterprises are hybrid institutions. Operating as governmental enterprises that provide collective goods and charge user fees, they function in the dual— and conflicting—arenas of market and democracy. As such, they face the inevitable trade-off between market efficiency and democratic accountability. To achieve market efficiency, public enterprises must be free of interference

Table 2.1 Governance Systems: Los Angeles World Airports, Port of Los Angeles, and Port of Long Beach

Governance Structure	Los Angeles World Airports	Port of Los Angeles	Port of Long Beach
Governing board	Seven members; five-year, staggered terms with no term limits. One member must live near LAX, and another must live near Van Nuys Airport. Mayor appoints members; council confirmation. Mayor removes without council action.	Five members; five-year, staggered terms with no term limits. One member must live in the harbor district. Mayor appoints members; council confirmation. Mayor removes without council action.	Five members; six-year, staggered terms with a limit of two full terms plus portion of initial term if first appointed mid-term. No residency requirements. Mayor appoints members; council confirmation. Council may remove, with appeal to council. Removal for cause only.
Board authority	Possesses, manages, and controls all airport assets, but council approval is required or veto provided for virtually every decision that the board makes, under Section 245 of the charter—formerly Prop. 5. Hires executive director (ED) with confirmation by mayor and council. Fires ED with mayor's confirmation, unless two-thirds of council reinstates ED within twenty days.	Possesses, manages, and controls all harbor assets, but council approval is required or veto provided for virtually every decision that the board makes, under Section 245 of the charter—formerly Prop. 5. Hires executive director (ED) with confirmation by mayor and council. Fires ED with mayor's confirmation, unless two-thirds of council reinstates ED within twenty days.	Holds "exclusive control and management authority of the Harbor Department." Has extensive authority over franchises, streets, property, etc., within the harbor district. Employs and appoints executive director (ED) and assistant, both of whom serve at pleasure. Council may not impose other tasks on the Harbor Department without board approval. Manages all affairs and activities under board jurisdiction.
Authority delegated to executive director	Administers affairs of the department; supervises its employees, subject to civil service; recommends and implements budget; exercises other powers conferred by	Administers affairs of the department; supervises its employees, subject to civil service; recommends and implements budget; exercises other powers conferred by	

Authority retained by city council	board, which may also authorize ED to enter contracts within council-set limits. Council approval required for contracts beyond five years or above certain monetary amounts. Council can veto almost any board decision, as long as it acts within time deadlines by two-thirds majorities.	board, which may also authorize ED to enter contracts within council-set limits. Council approval required for contracts beyond five years or above certain monetary amounts. Council can veto almost any board decision, as long as it acts within time deadlines by two-thirds majorities.	Council may change boundaries of Harbor District upon board request.
Legal restraints on boards	Must hold open meetings at which anyone may observe most proceedings, except those regarding personnel and litigation (Brown Act). City Administrative Officer (CAO) must approve agenda items of board (Executive Directive #39). Must submit biennial debt accountability and major capital-improvement plan.	Must hold open meetings at which anyone may observe most proceedings, except those regarding personnel and litigation (Brown Act). City Administrative Officer (CAO) must approve agenda items of board (Executive Directive #39). Must submit biennial debt accountability and major capital-improvement plan. May not sell or dispose of rights; may make federal or state grants only with voter majority.	Must hold open meetings at which anyone may observe most proceedings, except those regarding personnel and litigation (Brown Act). Cannot grant franchises that exceed sixty-six years; grants over five years must be made by board ordinance, so they may be subjected to voter referendum. May not sell or dispose of rights; may make federal or state grants only with voter majority.
Staffing authority	Civil service for most employees, and collective bargaining rules for others. Four civil service–exempt employees, plus up to ten more with mayor and council approval by one process,	Civil service for most employees, and collective bargaining rules for others. Four civil service–exempt employees, plus up to ten more with mayor and council approval by one process,	Board may employ needed staff by resolution. Exempt from civil service are most management staff, with one clerical person for each; a chief wharfinger and those in other expert positions; *(continued)*

Table 2.1 (*continued*)

Governance Structure	Los Angeles World Airports	Port of Los Angeles	Port of Long Beach
Staffing authority (*continued*)	and up to 150 persons with special skills under another mayor-council approval process.[a]	and up to 150 persons with special skills under another mayor-council approval process.	sales, traffic and promotion personnel; and personnel intermittently employed in handling cargo and freight. Coverage of bargaining units under state collective bargaining rules.
Litigation authority	Legal staffing provided by city attorney; outside legal counsel approved by city attorney. Board makes client decisions in litigation and settlement.	Legal staffing provided by city attorney; outside legal counsel approved by city attorney. Board makes client decisions in litigation and settlement.	Legal staffing provided by city attorney. Council may employ outside legal counsel at the request of city attorney. Board has some client authority, but council controls litigation.
Financial obligations to city	Board may transfer revenues to city's general fund only under strictly specified conditions such as those specified in state and federal law. City may also charge for services to airports, such as fire, sewage, etc.	Charter does not list transfers to city's general fund as a permitted use of the Harbor revenue fund. City may also charge for services to ports, such as fire, sewage, etc.	Up to 10 percent of net income may be transferred from the harbor revenue fund to tideland operating fund upon approval by board majority, followed by a two-thirds council vote.

SOURCES: Data from Los Angeles and Long Beach city charters.
[a]The Los Angeles World Airports and Harbor Departments both draw from the same pool of ten exempt positions and compete with all city departments for a share of the 150 exempt employees with special skills.

from rent-seeking politicians. Such political autonomy can yield enormous economic benefit. In the short run, it allows agencies to respond quickly to changing market conditions to ensure cost recovery and profitability. In the long run, it encourages them to undertake major capital investments that promise long-term yield. Long-term project horizons closely match the lengthy thirty-to-forty-year career perspectives of professional civil servants. In contrast, local elected officials in Los Angeles face short career horizons under voter-approved term limits of two four-year terms. As a result, local office seekers increasingly favor current expenditures popular with voters (such as more police) over long-term capital investments with little immediate political payoff (such as port and airport expansion). Los Angeles's and Long Beach's charters recognize these different budgetary priorities. The proprietary departments have their own special revenue funds, which still remain largely shielded from raids by politicians.

The charters also strive for democratic accountability, through which elected officials and voters can influence bureaucratic decision making. From 1925 through the 1980s, the Los Angeles charter enshrined efficiency. More recently, however, a series of voter-approved charter amendments made the city's bureaucracies more responsive to the mayor and council. As noted, the mayor and council choose the proprietary department's policymaking boards. In Los Angeles, the board-appointed general manager requires further confirmation by the mayor and city council. Since the early 1990s L.A.'s city council has veto power (by extraordinary-majority vote) over major agency decisions. These changes appeared to disadvantage the Port of Los Angeles relative to the Port of Long Beach. As a result, there was pressure to reduce the competitive handicap during the L.A. charter-reform process of the late 1990s, which culminated in a new charter. As Chapter Five argues, the new L.A. charter, by measures such as weakening the council veto, shifted the balance back by granting greater autonomy to the city's proprietary departments.[44]

Table 2.1 highlights the different political environments in Los Angeles and in Long Beach for the ports and other proprietary departments. It is more difficult for elected officials to remove commissioners in Long Beach than in L.A. Long Beach has established a "for-cause" standard for removal of commissioners prior to the end of their terms. It is easier for the Los Angeles city council to micromanage departments because it has a veto over all commission decisions—a power that Long Beach's legislative body does not enjoy. Los Angeles's elected officials have some authority over department CEOs; in Long Beach, this power belongs to the port commission. In Long Beach, commissioners largely control contracts for franchises, leases, and purchases, while in Los Angeles nearly all contracts involving large amounts of money or for lengthy periods require council approval. The Long Beach Board of Harbor Commissioners also has greater power over staff than do Los Angeles commissioners.[45]

Bureaucratic Development, Policymaking, and Leadership

In addition to investigating the local-government apparatus, this study also analyzes bureaucratic/institutional development, policymaking, and leadership. How were the Southern California port and airport agencies created? What were their strategies for amassing power? What were their major planning, financing, and development strategies? How have governance systems shaped the policies and performance of these public enterprises? As Matthew Crenson has argued, there is no theory of urban bureaucracy comparable to existing theories of the urban party machine. Here, three strategies of bureaucratic empowerment are explored. The first approach was electoral mobilization. To secure needed project financing, sympathetic city officials, and charter protections, the managers of the global gateways early on transformed their agencies into potent ballot-box organizations. The second formula for bureaucratic independence and effectiveness involved clientelism. The crown jewels mobilized their customer base—shippers, carriers, and the airlines—as political allies in battles with City Hall. The third approach was lobbying city, state, and federal officials.[46]

In regard to policymaking, Los Angeles and Long Beach became national innovators in public finance in order to build their ambitious infrastructure projects. The City of the Angels emerged as an exemplar in targeting municipal debt for revenue- and growth-generating projects. Early on, the city charter earmarked 75 percent of L.A.'s total bonded indebtedness for the revenue-producing proprietary departments. In contrast, no other city in the nation targeted as much as 50 percent of its general-obligation debt for such projects.[47] Starting in the 1930s, as the politics of hard times made voter approval of general-obligation bonds difficult, Los Angeles led the nation's cities in shifting local infrastructure financing to revenue bonds, which did not require voter approval. L.A. also pioneered developmental pricing strategies. In the pre–World War Two era, L.A. offered the nation's lowest water, power, harbor, and airport charges. Although low prices increased business volume (sufficient to cover operating expenses and retire debt), they left little cash available for new projects. As a result, the proprietary departments were continually conducting bond campaigns to raise new project capital.

In the postwar era, as the city's public enterprises shifted to revenue-bond financing, a new higher rate structure was installed. To receive favorable bond ratings (thus lowering borrowing costs), L.A.'s crown jewels raised their user fees to create self-sustaining project revenue yields. More recently, the Port of Los Angeles has chosen a higher pricing strategy—monopoly rent seeking. Rent seeking builds ample cash reserves, which can be funneled into facility modernization and expansion. However, monopoly pricing has downside risks. The port risked losing market share to lower-priced competitors such as the Port of Long Beach. Monopoly pricing also encouraged the city's elected officials to divert cash reserves targeted for port improvements into the city's general fund to pay for items such as police, which were popular with voters.[48]

Yet, the management of L.A.'s and Long Beach's global gateways has involved more than governance arrangements and policymaking. It has also involved human agency. The region's public enterprises have attracted a visionary breed of public entrepreneurs with the political and technical talents needed to realize the region's great infrastructure projects. This study considers some of the master public builders of modern Southern California; it recognizes unheralded public servants as major actors who shape the development of the bureaucracy and the city and regional economy. These enterprising bureaucrats have not always served as handmaidens of the business community, as conventional wisdom suggests, or as faithful servants of mayors, city managers, and city councils. Public entrepreneurs helped create powerful and autonomous professional bureaucracies, engineered the elite and mass consent necessary for an enormous expansion of urban debt, and planned, financed, constructed, and operated massive municipal infrastructure projects.

Los Angeles's emergence as one of the world's great trade and transshipment centers owes much to these global and local regimes of trade. International and binational trade agreements coupled with new transportation and information technologies have dramatically reduced trade and transportation costs. In this facilitating context, regions such as Southern California blossomed as trade centers in the world economy. Yet, Los Angeles would not be so globally positioned today without timely development of its trade infrastructure. The semi-autonomous public port and airport system that evolved was capable of long-term strategic planning, competitive pricing, and major capital improvements. How these public enterprises historically developed and how they were entrepreneurially operated are subjects to which I now turn.

1. *(above)* San Pedro Harbor, 1906. Photo courtesy of the Port of Los Angeles.

2. *(below)* Los Angeles Harbor, 1925. Photo courtesy of the Port of Los Angeles.

3. *(opposite, above)* Los Angeles Harbor, 1975. Photo courtesy of the Port of Los Angeles.

4. *(opposite, below)* Los Angeles Harbor, looking toward Santa Monica Bay, 2003. Photo courtesy of the Port of Los Angeles.

5. *(above)* Long Beach Inner Harbor, looking toward downtown Long Beach, 1929. Photo courtesy of the Port of Long Beach.

6. *(below)* Long Beach Harbor, 2000. Photo courtesy of the Port of Long Beach.

7. *(opposite, above)* Alameda Corridor Rail Project. Photo courtesy of the Alameda Corridor Transportation Authority.

8. *(opposite, below)* U.S. and Mexico Customs Cargo Inspection Facilities at Otay Mesa, 2002. Photo courtesy of Caltrans District Eleven.

9. *(above)* Mines Field Air Races, 1930. Photo courtesy of Los Angeles World Airports.

10. *(below)* LAX and Century Boulevard, 1997. Photo courtesy of Los Angeles World Airports.

11. *(above)* LAX Air Cargo Loading. Photo courtesy of Los Angeles World Airports.

12. *(below)* El Toro Marine Corps Air Station, 1993. Photo courtesy of Air Photo Services.

Part Two Historical Development

Entrepreneurial Visions and Deeds, 1880–1992

3 Local Foundations

Creating the Global Gateways, 1880–1932

The Board of Harbor Commissioners believes that Los Angeles is destined to be one of the really great ports of the world. . . . It is the purpose of this Board to . . . plan . . . improvements and administer the affairs of the harbor as will build up great commerce for this city and the territory tributary to it.

—*Los Angeles Board of Harbor Commissioners, 1913*[1]

We are just awakening to the fact that two-thirds of the world's population lies across the Pacific, of which we are the gateway. . . . The Pacific Ocean and not the Atlantic is going to have the world's shipping. . . . Shall Long Beach stand still, or forge ahead? . . . If Long Beach sits back and insists on letting her neighbor to the north do it, detrimental reaction resulting in stagnation and deferred hopes will come to our city as sure as death itself.

—*Harry Krotz, Long Beach Harbor Bonds Committee, 1922*[2]

Mines Field [now LAX] is far and above all others [rival local sites] in desirability as a municipal airport.

—*Charles Lindbergh, 1928*[3]

This chapter explores the genesis and early development of Southern California's global gateways—the ports of Los Angeles and Long Beach, and Mines Field, predecessor to Los Angeles International Airport (LAX)—in the period from 1880 to 1932. This was an epochal half century for regional infrastructure development. In 1880, the area's waterfront was privately owned and controlled, particularly by the powerful Southern Pacific Railroad. The landlocked City of Los Angeles lay a distant twenty miles from the ocean. Long Beach, although situated seaside, would not be incorporated until 1888. Initially, both cities lacked the home-rule charter powers needed to develop their waterfronts. In the 1890s, the Southern Pacific, which monopolized the region's transportation system and controlled local politics, unveiled its own port-development plans at Santa Monica rather than Los Angeles or Long Beach. Given this trajectory, private, not public, hands should have guided Southern California harbor development.

But by 1930 the region was vigorously pursuing a strategy of public port development. By then, both Los Angeles and Long Beach were armed with new charters and powers under California's liberal home-rule laws. The federal government, by choosing San Pedro rather than Santa Monica for federally assisted harbor development, thwarted the railroad's plans. Next, Los Angeles, over local opposition, consolidated the small port cities of San Pedro and Wilmington within its boundaries and launched an ambitious program of port development. The State of California wrested ownership of tidelands from private hands and designated L.A. and Long Beach as trustees responsible for local tidelands development.

To promote public development of their waterfronts, both Los Angeles and Long Beach, under their home-rule charter authority, created powerful, semi-autonomous proprietary harbor departments, which were armed with significant charter powers and autonomy. Created in 1907, the Los Angeles Harbor Department, headed by a citizen commission, became a proprietary department (like the storied Department of Water and Power) in 1913; and, in 1925, it was given additional authority and independence under a new city charter. Created by ordinance in 1917, the Long Beach Harbor Department in 1921 became a citizen commission–managed and charter-sanctioned department. Under Long Beach's 1925 charter, the Harbor Department also became a proprietary department, and it secured enlarged authority by charter amendment in 1931. In regard to airports, in 1928 the City of Los Angeles leased Mines Field, now the site of LAX. In 1930, the L.A. Airports Department was created by ordinance as a council-controlled agency. Only in 1947 would the Airports Department become, like the city's harbor and water and power departments, a proprietary agency.

Local public projects such as the ports (the largest artificial harbor in the world) became essential pillars of Southern California's precocious population growth and early industrialization. Such public investments were an essential precondition to private development, particularly the burgeoning real estate market. In no small part because of the catalytic role of its harbor, water, and power agencies, the City of Los Angeles in fifty-plus years became the Colossus of the West, growing from an 1880 population of 10,000 to over 1.2 million in 1930. By 1930, Los Angeles ranked fifth in population, second in territory (442 square miles, through annexation and consolidation), and ninth in manufacturing among the nation's cities. Federal military spending during World War Two (a prime catalyst for Sunbelt urban growth elsewhere) merely solidified Los Angeles's position as the premier Western city and regional hegemon.[4]

Using its superior infrastructure (such as its monopoly water supply), L.A. pursued an aggressive annexation policy, capturing half of the five-county region's early population growth. In 1880, the city was home to only one-quarter of the region's population; by 1930, its share had risen to nearly 50 percent. Neighboring Long Beach, which also annexed surrounding territory, quickly grew to nearly 150,000 residents by 1930, becoming the area's second largest city.

In the Progressive era, Los Angeles experienced a dramatic regime transformation as a classic laissez-faire growth regime (with a caretaker local government) was replaced by an activist, state-centered regime that provided the necessary infrastructure (harbor, water, power) for rapid urban and regional development. Although the conventional wisdom holds that economic elites and private development strategies were the central forces shaping Los Angeles's growth throughout the pre-1930s era, this received account underestimates the budding role of local public enterprises and civil servants in shaping regional development.[5] I turn now to L.A.'s great regime transformation and the early development of its public port and airport systems.

From a Laissez-Faire to a Statist Growth Regime

One must be careful when "bringing the local state back in." Although it has become fashionable to call for more state-centered interpretations of urban political economy, few have attempted to define the term precisely. The crucial distinction between laissez-faire and statist growth regimes is a relative, not an absolute, one. The essential difference refers to the relative influence and autonomy of private-sector actors versus public-sector actors in shaping urban growth and to the relative importance of private versus public development strategies.[6]

Los Angeles's pre-1900 laissez-faire regime featured business hegemony and primary reliance on real estate speculation and booster advertising to produce growth. But a business-led regime was not devoid of state action. Thus, in the 1860s, Yankees used the legal system to wrest control of the Mexican land grants from the ranchero class. In the 1870s, the business community skillfully orchestrated voter approval for the large subsidy needed to bring the Southern Pacific Railroad to L.A. Yet these early political interventions by business interests were ad hoc and episodic. The caretaker state was not systematically organized to direct the process of growth.

L.A.'s post-1900 state-centered growth regime, however, was organized for growth. It featured semi-autonomous public bureaucracies and large-scale infrastructure projects as the centerpiece of a more public growth strategy. With the construction of the municipal harbor, water, and power systems, public bureaucrats began challenging the long-standing hegemony of the business community. But this more state-centered regime was not without entrepreneurial force. The Los Angeles Chamber of Commerce, in particular, wielded significant power in the post-1906 era, more so with the Harbor Department than with the Department of Water and Power (DWP). Under the new statist growth regime, the city's power structure shifted from business-led elitism to increased pluralism, while public development strategies complemented private ones.[7]

The Caretaker State

The closest approximation to Stephen Elkin's entrepreneurial regime (in a study of Dallas) and to Todd Swanstrom's conservative growth coalition (in a study of Cleveland) occurred in Los Angeles between 1880 and 1906. The business community, particularly the Southern Pacific Railroad, firmly controlled a small, essentially caretaker, local-state apparatus. Private development strategies, particularly an aggressive national promotional campaign and a speculative local real estate market, completely overshadowed public efforts.[8]

In late-nineteenth-century Los Angeles, the local state exercised limited functional responsibilities. The 1889 freeholders' charter created only six departments: police, fire, education, libraries, health, and parks. Authority over city departments was divided between the mayor and the nine-member city council. Although the charter authorized municipal regulation and ownership of public utilities, little was done along these lines until after the turn of the century. Operating under liberal, long-term, public franchises, private utilities supplied the region's water, electricity, gas, telephone, and transportation needs. These firms tightly controlled the local state's limited regulatory apparatus. Not until 1904 did the city council finally pass an ordinance to regulate private utility rates; it did not exercise that power until 1907.[9]

The result was Los Angeles's version of the night-watchman (or minimalist) state. Municipal taxes and spending were kept low. In 1905, the city's debt was $5.5 million, small for a rapidly growing city of two hundred thousand. In 1903, city employment stood at only 1,123. Under the entrepreneurial regime, Los Angeles's voters played a limited growth-promoting role. Between 1889 and 1898, voters were asked to approve only seven small-scale water and sewer bond issues; they passed six. The city's territorial ambitions also remained parochial. Between 1880 and 1905 the city's boundaries increased only from twenty-nine to forty-three square miles.[10]

The Southern Pacific Machine

Before the turn of the century, business elites thoroughly controlled the caretaker state and the region's economic development. Yet, unlike early Dallas, with its pure entrepreneurial regime and homogeneous and consensual business community, Los Angeles early on developed a more complex regime featuring business heterogeneity and conflict. By the mid-1880s, a railroad/utility combination shaped the local political economy. However, by the early 1890s, fault lines were growing within the business community. A local commercial, financial, and real estate elite rose to challenge absentee corporate control of the region's infrastructure, economy, and politics.

The major actor in late-nineteenth-century Los Angeles's economy and polity was the Southern Pacific Railroad, the first long-distance rail line in the West, which quickly demonstrated the power of monopoly. Popularly known as the SP or the "Octopus," the railroad was founded by "the Big Four" (Collis Huntington, Leland Stanford, Charles Crocker, and Mark Hopkins), who had grown wealthy as merchants for the forty-niners. Huntington emerged as the Big Four's spokesperson and was the driving force behind the railroad's dictatorial policies in Southern California.[11]

Extending its tracks (or tentacles) south from the Bay Area, the Octopus ruthlessly bypassed towns that refused to accede to its demands. As it neared Los Angeles, the railroad made known its plans to circumvent the city entirely and to head instead southeast to Yuma and Texas unless its exorbitant terms were accepted. The SP's demands included a $602,000 bond subsidy (equaling 5 percent of L.A. County's assessed valuation at that time and equivalent to over $30 billion in year 2000 dollars), choice publicly owned property, and the recently completed Los Angeles & San Pedro Railroad, which linked the city to the harbor. San Diego, which also wanted the transcontinental rail link, then hired some of L.A.'s ablest lawyers to convince local voters that they would be foolish to bond themselves so lavishly to the SP. Notwithstanding San Diego's meddling and believing that "Los Angeles must place herself on the world's highway," the county's voters in 1872 approved the deal. In 1876, L.A.'s vital railroad connection with San Francisco and the East was completed.[12]

This proved to be a Faustian bargain. The economic benefits were immediate. The SP connection ensured Los Angeles's dominance over regional competitors such as San Diego, San Bernardino, and Ventura. Owning vast tracts of Southern California land, the railroad, at least initially, was a willing promotional partner of local boosters. But the Southern Pacific was a true economic behemoth; by 1885 it controlled fully 85 percent of California's railroad lines. Its economic stranglehold over Los Angeles was even greater. Representing the interests of San Francisco and eastern capital, the SP treated Southern California as a colony. The railroad's major concerns were its massive federal debt load (which financed construction of the transcontinental line) and its substantial waterfront, terminal, and land investments in the Bay Area. To service its debt and protect these core investments, the railroad saddled Southern California with high shipping rates and poor schedules.[13]

Not content to exercise economic power alone, the Southern Pacific created a powerful bipartisan machine to control Los Angeles's political destiny. The railroad particularly valued control of the local police and judiciary (useful in labor disputes) and, as a large property owner, the tax assessor's office. Walter Parker, the railroad's local agent, ran the dominant Republican Party, and Tom "Espee" McGaffrey, his loyal lieutenant, oversaw the Democrats. The SP's chief allies included the city's private utilities, street railways, public-works contractors, liquor dealers, vice and gambling interests, and small-scale real estate interests.[14]

Local Business as a Counter Elite

A junior partner at best to machine power, the city's downtown business establishment increasingly did not share the vision of a railroad-controlled Los Angeles. The land boom of the 1880s, which triggered a fivefold increase in population, had produced a new local elite of merchants, bankers, publishers, and large-scale real estate developers and investors. This group (the so-called boomers of the 1880s) viewed the railroad's regional transportation monopoly, exorbitant rates, and political power as potent brakes on Los Angeles's future development and on their own business and real estate investments. Harrison Gray Otis, owner and publisher of the *Los Angeles Times*, served as their self-appointed dean. Arriving in Los Angeles in 1882, Otis quickly became the city's ultimate booster. In the wake of the land boom's collapse in 1888, Otis and his business partners helped organize the Los Angeles Chamber of Commerce as a vehicle for their personal and regional economic ambitions. Surveying the boom's wreckage, Otis and the Chamber solemnly pledged a new beginning for Los Angeles: the creation of a commercial/industrial "Empire in the Sun." [15]

Essential to the region's new beginning, Otis and his colleagues believed, was an end to the Southern Pacific's economic and political stranglehold on Los Angeles. The land boom's collapse had fractured the city's growth coalition, revealing the weaknesses of too great a reliance on the dynamics of the real estate market to produce economic development. The SP had been a willing partner to the land boom, inaugurating a special low-fare "immigrant train" from the East. But the railroad had little interest in developing the region's economy. Having built its Southern California business around passenger service and imports from Northern California and the East, the Southern Pacific would do little to build up Los Angeles's commerce and industry. Whereas the railroad saw Los Angeles's future as the Riviera of the West, a tourist resort and retirement community for the affluent, Otis and the Chamber saw the city as a future West Coast Chicago. These sharply contrasting visions of the region's future sparked a colonial revolt to liberate Los Angeles from the SP's grasp.

The conflict between the two private-sector elites and their competing visions would be played out starting in the mid-1890s over the construction and ownership of an artificial deep-water harbor for Los Angeles. Here, Otis and his downtown allies would invoke the substantial powers of the local state to counter absentee corporate control and to help realize their vision of L.A. as a commercial and industrial empire.

Building a Statist Growth Regime

The years from 1895 to 1909 constituted a transformative era in Los Angeles's political economy. After the harbor, water would prove to be the next battleground between the contending business elites, their conflicting economic visions, and private-versus-public development strategies. Water, not the harbor, was the fundamental barrier to the region's growth. The Los Angeles River and nearby artesian wells could support a population no larger than three hundred thousand. After the harbor battle, the *Times* and its business allies launched a relentless campaign to bring more and cheaper water to the city to attract people and industry.

Their first target was the privately owned Los Angeles City Water Company, a political ally of the Southern Pacific. The company's high prices and poor service led to an attempted municipal buyout of the waterworks in 1897. Even though the local business community, public officials, and voters strongly backed a city-owned water system, it took a bruising five-year battle, featuring two bond elections and court litigation, before Los Angeles gained control of its water system in 1902. The water battle served as the crucible for a new strategy of public development: the organized bond campaign. In an 1899 special election, voters were asked to approve the city's largest bond issue to date —$2 million—to purchase the private waterworks; they did so overwhelmingly. In later years, municipal agencies such as the Harbor Department and the DWP would raise bond financing and campaigning to a high art.[16]

By the turn of the century, the Southern Pacific machine also faced challenges from a burgeoning political-reform movement. Reform originated in the 1890s among a cadre of young professionals, including lawyers, journalists, physicians, and clergymen. Yet, support from the city's small professional classes was not sufficient to tip the balance of power. Reformers realized that the battle would be won or lost in the downtown business community. Arguing that reform was good for business, progressives successfully proselytized the local economic establishment. Soon, the business community embraced reform as a potent antidote to railroad/utility power.[17]

In 1906 reformers launched a successful frontal assault on the SP machine, electing seventeen of twenty-three candidates to local office. In 1909, as reformers swept city offices and instituted a program of nonpartisanship, direct primaries, and at-large elections, the railroad juggernaut was effectively eliminated as a force in local politics. After reformer Hiram Johnson's election as governor on an antirailroad platform in 1910, the Southern Pacific would be mustered out of state politics. In the process, the activist state replaced the caretaker state as a reformed Los Angeles turned to the mammoth task of building the public infrastructure necessary for the region's commercial and industrial development. Two harbingers of a strengthened, growth-oriented local state were territorial expansion to the harbor (in 1906) and passage of the massive $23 million Los Angeles Aqueduct bond issue (in 1907). The aqueduct, in turn, paved the way for public power.[18]

The "Great Free-Harbor Fight"

The free-harbor battle of the 1890s served as the real catalyst for regime transformation. It was the first major challenge to railroad power and, along with the water battle, the first systematic invocation of the countervailing powers of the state. In the 1870s, Los Angeles's poor harbor had paradoxically provided an enticement for regional development. When choosing between Los Angeles and San Diego as the location for its southern trunk line, the SP had viewed San Diego's chief natural asset—its magnificent harbor—as a serious competitive liability. With commercial development, San Diego could challenge San Francisco as the West Coast's principal port and in the process endanger the railroad's substantial Oakland waterfront investments and its coastal shipping trade. Not so Los Angeles. The region had only shallow sloughs and unprotected open-sea anchorages. The railroad picked the weaker rival. By the late 1880s, however, as the land boom and demand for building materials overwhelmed the region's primitive infrastructure, the lack of a decent harbor proved a bottleneck to growth.[19]

The Octopus quickly tightened its hold over Southern California. It imposed suffocating conditions, warning all shippers through San Pedro that they had better use the Southern Pacific or else. Freight rates were raised to exorbitant levels—just below what the SP's agents decided a company could pay without going bankrupt. Perceived troublemakers were driven out of business. Furious demands for legislation to curtail the rail monopoly's runaway power were futile, thanks to the SP's well-paid political cronies in Sacramento and Washington.[20]

Bristling at any hint of competition, Huntington and his partners then quietly began acquiring all available waterfront property in the new resort town of Santa Monica, where an SP-controlled commercial harbor and a mile-long wharf to the sea were constructed; they opened in 1893. The Southern Pacific fiercely promoted its deep-water harbor. A railroad-controlled port would further monopolize the region's transportation network and would give the SP a decided advantage in its battle with the Santa Fe Railroad (which completed its own cross-country line into L.A. in 1885) for the transcontinental market. The Southern Pacific used its considerable influence in Washington to lobby for funds to build a breakwater in Santa Monica Bay. But the railroad baron's bulldozing tactics ignored two stubborn facts: first, no length of breakwater could protect their port from the open sea; and second, porous soil in Santa Monica made waterfront development difficult.[21]

As the railroad's designs on the Southland became clearer, publisher Otis and his Chamber allies in 1895 created the Free Harbor League as a potent anti-SP lobbying organization. Los Angeles's business community then countered with a proposal for a municipally owned harbor at San Pedro. Not only would their port attract commerce, it would anchor a rival railroad network —the Santa Fe—and a proposed Salt Lake City rail line that would import cheap Utah coal into Southern California. As Huntington tried to force Los Angeles to abandon San Pedro altogether and to adopt Santa Monica as its official port, the so-called Great Free-Harbor Fight commenced. One of the bitterest conflicts in L.A. history, it lasted nearly a decade.[22]

Both sets of contestants knew that federal assistance was crucial. Each site required at least $3 million for dredging and a breakwater. Several federal boards of engineers decided in favor of San Pedro over Santa Monica, but each time Huntington's congressional allies killed the proposed appropriation. In 1896, the railroad even succeeded in turning a bill for San Pedro improvements into a $3 million appropriation for Santa Monica. Los Angeles's lobbyists could scarcely match the Southern Pacific's power in Congress, particularly in the Rivers and Harbors Committee and the Commerce Committee.

Heavily lobbied by Otis and the L.A. Chamber of Commerce, California Senator Stephen White, Otis's personal attorney and a Los Angeles resident, took the fight to the floor of the Senate. White presented a devastating picture of a how an SP-controlled harbor would permanently stifle development in the Los Angeles area. He then proposed yet another board of experts and introduced a provision stating that if Santa Monica were chosen as the site for improvements, the Southern Pacific would have to allow other railroads to use the harbor at reasonable rates. White's plan became law, and in March 1897 a new board of army engineers favored San Pedro 4-to-1. Even so, Huntington loyalists managed to delay work on a new breakwater section until 1899.

The harbor fight signaled the beginning of a shift in the balance of power between the SP and Los Angeles's commercial and *rentier* interests. At the time, the railroad and its allies still controlled the Republican machine and the local caretaker state. But the free-harbor campaign strengthened the local business community's resolve to use public power to limit corporate influence over the region's political economy.

Building the Port of Los Angeles

Controlling the Harbor and Tidelands

The harbor contest of the 1890s had begun, but did not complete, L.A.'s shift to public strategies of economic development in the service of an enlarged vision of the city's and region's future. The principle of municipal ownership was embraced as a counter to external corporate control of the region's infrastructure. Yet building a federally subsidized breakwater at San Pedro was one thing; control by Los Angeles and necessary (but expensive) harbor improvements were another.

As federal dredging at San Pedro brought the harbor's depth to eighteen feet for most of the present main channel (giving ships greatly increased access to the inner harbor), Los Angeles launched the second phase of its aggressive campaign to control the harbor. In 1900, the independent port cities of San Pedro and Wilmington lay a distant sixteen miles from Los Angeles. The SP still controlled the inner harbor. Upward of $40 million dollars—well over ten times the initial federal investment—would be needed by 1930 for harbor dredging, sea walls, wharves, docks, and other improvements. Los Angeles would invoke the powers of the state to overcome these formidable barriers.

Spurred by the prospect of the Panama Canal, L.A.'s political and economic leaders began campaigning for municipal ownership of the harbor. In 1906, voters approved the so-called Shoestring Addition, a narrow, sixteen-mile-long strip of annexed land linking Los Angeles with San Pedro and Wilmington. The nineteen-square-mile annexation increased the city's size by nearly 50 percent. This became the prototype for a new municipal policy of infrastructure-based territorial expansion.[23]

Creating a three-member harbor commission (without a port) by ordinance in December 1907, Los Angeles turned to the state legislature for the requisite authority to consolidate the two port cities into Greater Los Angeles. In Sacramento, L.A. needed all the help it could get—the influence of Assembly Speaker Phillip Stanton of Los Angeles, a united city legislative delegation, and lobbying by L.A. Mayor Arthur Harper and the city's leading commercial and civic organizations—to pass the consolidation bill over spirited opposition from some political and business leaders in San Pedro and Wilmington. In 1909, with a well-financed campaign organization and promises of $10 million in harbor and highway improvements as well as borough-style government as inducements to port-city voters, Los Angeles secured the needed voter approval for consolidation in San Pedro, Wilmington, and Los Angeles. The merger became official in August 1909, and a new, official harbor commission was then established.[24]

Two urgent matters of unfinished business remained. The first concerned official harbor boundary lines, which had never been settled. Until a federal board fixed the lines (which remain in place today), port development was delayed because few would invest in property whose status was uncertain. The second, more contentious, issue involved ownership of waterfront property, much of which had been claimed by various entities but never legally approved. The city itself owned only the ends of two San Pedro streets, and their access to the main channel was blocked by a Southern Pacific right-of-way.

The federal Harbor Line Board, which was established to set the port boundaries, uncovered the old State Admission Act, dating back to 1848. The law made "all navigable waters" within California "forever free." This meant that there could be no leasing, that all private claims to tidelands and other property along the channel were illegal, and that waterfront land belonged to the state and not to private parties. The City of Los Angeles then initiated a series of tidelands lawsuits (including several involving its old adversary, the Southern Pacific), particularly over valuable port properties that the railroad had long considered its own. Finally, in 1911, the California state legislature passed the Tidelands Trust Act, which made port cities such as Los Angeles and Long Beach trustees of the state tidelands and gave enforcement responsibility to the State Lands Commission.[25]

Ballot-Box Prowess

Los Angeles's Board of Harbor Commissioners then turned to the task of building an adequate infrastructure for the port. Because the board defined its mission primarily as attracting industry rather than as producing profits, it deliberately set low rates that left little room for financing needed capital improvements. This developmental pricing system had undeniable benefits in generating port business and regional growth. Yet it had costs as well because it necessitated public subsidies for new infrastructure. Lacking a surplus to pay for needed capital projects, such as the reclamation of additional water frontage and the building of wharves, piers, docks, bridges, and highways, the Harbor Department turned to general-obligation bonds, which required two-thirds voter approval. Working in close collaboration with the L.A. Chamber of Commerce, the department formed election-campaign committees, the Greater Harbor Committee of Two Hundred and the Harbor Bond Campaign Committee, to secure the necessary voter approval. Formed in 1924, the Greater Harbor Committee of Two Hundred included representatives from major wholesale and retail businesses, oil companies, shipping concerns, railroads, banks, and law firms but not, significantly, labor unions.[26]

Unlike L.A.'s DWP, which used its employees as a formidable precinct organization, the Harbor Department chose to contract out to private companies for laborers. Lacking in-house precinct workers, the port relied instead on interest-group supporters and their well-financed campaign advertising to win elections. Save for the SP, which the port began to court assiduously, the department, in stark contrast to the DWP, had few potential adversaries. (The embattled public power system was fiercely opposed by private utilities and the *Los Angeles Times*.) To reduce conflict, harbor manager Clarence Mat-

Table 3.1   The Port of Los Angeles and the Ballot Box: Bond Votes, 1906–1932

Date (month/year)	Election Type[a]	Amount ($)	Outcome	Yes Vote (%)	Total Vote	Turnout (%)	Registered Voters
04/1910	Special	3,000,000	Passed	90.2	14,041	14.8	94,680
04/1913	Special	2,500,000	Passed	88.5	53,505	31.4	170,220
05/1919	Primary	4,500,000	Passed	71.1	51,974	26.6	195,142
06/1921	General	4,800,000	Passed	68.1	82,470	33.8	244,348
06/1923	General	15,000,000	Passed	80.5	76,743	28.1	272,848
05/1924	State primary	400,000	Passed	80.1	151,563	52.1	291,009

SOURCES: Data from Los Angeles City Clerk, *Records of Election Returns*, vol. 1, Dec. 5, 1904-Dec. 9, 1920; *Records of Election Returns*, vol. 2, Apr. 5, 1921-Nov. 2, 1926; *Elections 1902-1930*, Haynes Papers, box 108, UCLA; *Los Angeles Times*, election-day published registration statistics, post-election published turnout statistics; *Los Angeles City Charter*, 1889, 1925.
[a] Municipal election unless otherwise specified.

son worked closely with local SP official Paul Shoup to find common ground on issues of railroad switching, terminals, rights of way, and a municipal belt line. The city's leading newspapers and commercial organizations enthusiastically backed the department's electoral campaigns.[27]

Tables 3.1 and 3.2 demonstrate the prowess of the port/business coalition from 1906 to 1932 in getting department-sponsored bond referenda, charter amendments, and referendary ordinances passed by the voters. The Harbor Department won all six bond elections, totaling over $30 million, by an average 80 percent of the vote. Yet the Board of Harbor Commissioners frequently found itself in competition for electoral support with the powerful Board of Public Service Commissioners (predecessor to the Board of Water and Power Commissioners). In five of the six harbor-bond elections from 1910 to 1924, the Harbor Department competed for electoral favor with water and power bonds as the city's bonding capacity was approached. The capital-intensive campaigning of the Harbor Department (featuring newspaper advertising and mailed brochures) was consistently more successful than the DWP's labor-intensive politics (featuring precinct-based get-out-the-vote efforts by departmental employees). In part this success was due to the fact that harbor bonds had few opponents while public power bonds faced strong opposition from powerful private utilities. While the Harbor Department overwhelmingly won all six bond elections, the DWP won approval of only three of nine bonds appearing on the same ballots.[28]

The port also turned to the federal government for financial assistance in its campaign for harbor improvements. Establishing a close working relationship with the Army Corps of Engineers, it secured further congressional appropriations of $9.5 million to dredge the outer harbor, widen the main channel, and double the length of the breakwater. But federal harbor improvements represented only part of a broader federal subsidization campaign that included U.S. Shipping Board support for creating the Los Angeles Steamship Company in competition with San Francisco–based Matson lines.[29]

Until November 1932, when three charter amendments failed in a high-turnout presidential election, the department also enjoyed remarkable success in securing voter approval for greater legal authority and autonomy. Overall, it secured passage of 72 percent of the thirty-two charter amendments and referendary ordinances from 1906 to 1932 and thereby strengthened its administrative, land-use, contracting, and leasing powers. Thus, in 1911 the Board of Harbor Commissioners was created as a charter body and was later given authority to oversee harbor development and rate setting. In 1924, at part of a new city charter, the port commission was expanded to five members, the new position of general manager was created, and the Harbor Department was given near total control over port development, financing, and personnel. The port's strongest supporters at the ballot box were Republican, middle- and upper-class, native-white of native-parentage voters.[30]

One controversy, though, concerned leasing and franchises. As discussed, the port charged low rates to attract business and then asked taxpayers to pay for capital improvements. The Municipal League, an influential good-government organization, complained loudly about taxpayers' subsidizing large companies such as Pan American Petroleum. In response, the harbor worked hard for financial self-sufficiency, which was finally achieved in 1926. With the advent of self-financing, bond elections were no longer needed. Thus, the port had less incentive to seek local business support. Instead, it could focus attention on its customer base of shippers and carriers. This switch in business loyalties did not go unnoticed. The Chamber of Commerce, perhaps wishing to keep the port on a tight leash, successfully opposed the department's 1932 attempts to broaden its rate and leasing authority, which would have increased the port's bargaining position with shippers.[31]

A key feature of Los Angeles's Progressive-era bureaucracies such as the Harbor Department was their reliance on low-turnout special municipal elections. The city council frequently colluded with departments to call special elections in which the electoral leverage of municipal employees could be maximized. Of the harbor-bond, charter, and ordinance referenda (Tables 3.1 and 3.2), over 75 percent were in municipal elections; over half of these involved special elections. Turnout in municipal elections was low; generally, fewer than one-third of Los Angeles's registered voters bothered to go to the polls. Turnout was even lower in special elections. City employees (numbering 13,000 on average between 1912 and 1932) could be a powerful force both in municipal-bond (72,000 average turnout) and in nonbond elections (107,000 average turnout) from 1906 to 1932.[32]

The 1925 charter furthered the process of bureaucratic empowerment.

Table 3.2 The Port of Los Angeles and the Ballot Box: Charter-Amendment and Ordinance Votes, 1906-1932

Date (month/year)	Election Type[a]	Purpose (Type)	Outcome	Yes Vote (%)	Total Vote	Turnout (%)	Registered Voters
11/1906	Special	Shoestring annexation-vote within city (Ordinance)	Passed	87.9	7,523	N/A	N/A
11/1906	Special	Shoestring annexation-vote outside city (Ordinance)	Passed	51.2	416	N/A	N/A
02/1909	Special	Leasing/improving (Amendment)	Passed	65.0	15,404	16.3	94,680
08/1909	Special	Wilmington consolidation-vote within city (Ordinance)	Passed	98.4	13,960	14.7	94,680
08/1909	Special	Wilmington consolidation-vote outside city (Ordinance)	Passed	63.7	168	N/A	N/A
08/1909	Special	San Pedro consolidation-vote within city (Ordinance)	Passed	99.1	11,696	12.4	94,680
08/1909	Special	San Pedro consolidation-vote outside city (Ordinance)	Passed	76.2	953	N/A	N/A
03/1911	Special	Established department (Amendment)	Passed	76.5	14,259	15.1	94,680
03/1911	Special	Franchise authority (Amendment)	Passed	81.1	14,225	15.0	94,680
05/1912	Special	Land exchange (Ordinance)	Passed	87.1	30,816	21.3	144,742
05/1912	Special	Pacific Ave. improvements (Ordinance)	Not Passed	35.9	31,827	22.0	144,742
06/1912	General	Franchise authority (Amendment)	Passed	79.4	50,320	34.8	144,742
03/1913	Special	Created Harbor District with appointed commission (Amendment)	Passed	51.9	34,256	20.6	166,626
03/1913	Special	Created Harbor District with elected commission (Amendment)	Not Passed	40.0	38,462	23.1	166,626
06/1913	General	Franchise authority (Ordinance)	Passed	80.7	52,737	29.3	180,206

Date	Election	Description	Result	%	Votes	Turnout %	Registration
06/1913	General	Franchise authority-alternate (Ordinance)	Not Passed	78.5	50,920	28.3	180,206
10/1916	Special	Contract authority (Amendment)	Not Passed	40.4	46,793	24.2	193,640
06/1917	General	Federal land grant (Ordinance)	Passed	85.1	73,895	32.5	227,452
06/1920	State primary	Strengthened department management (Amendment)	Passed	50.8	95,705	40.8	234,600
05/1923	Primary	Franchise authority (Ordinance)	Passed	55.4	78,151	29.4	265,910
05/1924	State primary	New charter strengthens department (Amendment)	Passed	86.7	145,345	49.9	291,009
05/1925	Primary	Public-land authority (Ordinance)	Passed	87.6	145,353	38.3	379,553
04/1926	Special	Federal land grant (Ordinance)	Passed	82.7	164,901	48.9	337,448
04/1926	Special	Unified port district (Advisory)	Passed	58.6	175,667	52.1	337,448
06/1927	General	Steam/electric plant (Ordinance)	Not Passed	41.9	116,186	29.9	388,098
06/1927	General	Franchise authority (Ordinance)	Passed	60.8	93,018	24.0	388,098
11/1928	State general	Tidelands leases (Amendment)	Not Passed	38.4	226,815	43.4	522,667
11/1928	State general	Interest from harbor bond funds transferred to DWP (Amendment)	Passed	70.9	241,446	46.2	522,667
11/1930	State general	Contract authority (Amendment)	Passed	68.6	173,156	37.7	459,679
11/1932	State general	Rate authority (Amendment)	Not Passed	30.5	322,335	46.1	699,664
11/1932	State general	Lease authority (Amendment)	Not Passed	17.9	322,686	46.1	699,664
11/1932	State general	Contract authority (Amendment)	Not Passed	45.4	320,303	45.8	699,664

SOURCES: Data from Los Angeles City Clerk, *Records of Election Returns*, vol. 1, Dec. 5, 1904–Dec. 9, 1920; *Records of Election Returns*, vol. 2, Apr. 5, 1921–Nov. 2, 1926; *Records of Election Returns*, vol. 3, Jan. 19, 1927–June 2, 1931; *Records of Election Returns*, vol. 4, Sept. 29, 1931–Nov. 26, 1935; *Elections 1902–1930*, Haynes Papers, box 108, UCLA; *Los Angeles Times*, election-day published registration statistics, post-election published turnout statistics.

^aMunicipal election unless otherwise specified.

Approved overwhelmingly by 87 percent of the voters, the new charter gave the proprietary departments personnel and budget-making powers independent of the mayor and city council. Their governing boards also were given the power to appoint department heads, to set overall policy, and to supervise operations. By expanding board memberships and staggering the terms of appointment, the new charter reduced the leverage of newly elected mayors over city commissioners. The advent of district elections in 1925 reduced the city council's interest in the proprietary departments, except for the San Pedro/Wilmington council member. The Board of Public Works became the center of attention for the rest of the council as members became preoccupied with delivering divisible benefits to their districts.

Under managers such as Matson (1912–20) the Harbor Department deliberately pursued a collaborationist strategy with the business community. This was a prototype for later public/private partnerships in port and rail development. In its ballot-box pursuit of harbor improvements and agency autonomy, the department enjoyed the near-continuous blessing of the business community and the city's leading newspapers. The high point of collaboration was achieved during the 1920s with the creation of the Harbor Trunk Line Railroad, jointly owned by the Harbor Department and its old railroad antagonists, including the Southern Pacific; the partnership was a prototype for later public/private collaborative port/rail ventures such as the Alameda Corridor project.

Trade and Development

Under Matson's leadership, the fledgling Harbor Department quickly sought foreign trade opportunities. In 1915, the port wrote American consuls throughout the world for reports on what products of the Southwest might find a market in their respective districts, what foreign products of their districts might be shipped to Los Angeles, what transportation facilities existed in their districts, and for the names of local importers and exporters with whom business relations might be -created. Matson disseminated these reports widely "to make Los Angeles business men foreign trade minded." By 1917, the Harbor Department had issued its first foreign trade report, and it soon was complaining of substantial trading opportunities lost to San Francisco because of the L.A. port's limited trade with Latin America. Although Matson would leave the port in 1920, he continued to extol the virtues of the port and regional trade in his new position as head of the Chamber of Commerce's trade-extension department. Matson then joined banker George Carpenter to form the World Traders of Los Angeles, later reorganized as the Foreign Trade Association of Southern California.[33]

The major catalyst for early L.A. port and trade development, as well as for the established rival port of San Francisco, was the construction of the

Panama Canal. Here, geography favored Los Angeles. Compared with San Francisco, L.A. was 413 miles (or thirty-six hours sailing time) closer to the Panama Canal. Not only the port of entry for the fastest-growing city in the West, San Pedro was positioned on the earth's curvature just seventy miles off the great-circle route between the canal and Asia. This location made it the most convenient port of call for trans-Pacific trade with Southern California, the Southwest, and even the Middle West.[34]

The canal's trade possibilities were immediately placed on hold, however, when England declared war on Germany in August 1914, just eleven days before the canal was scheduled to open. With sections of the canal soon blocked by rock and dirt slides, it was forced to close for repairs for the war's duration and for several years thereafter. During World War One, Pacific Coast trade languished. Most of the facilities in L.A. harbor were turned over to the Navy for use as a training center, as a submarine base, and for ship repair. The only local war-related commercial jobs were in shipbuilding. By 1918, four San Pedro shipyards, employing twenty thousand workers, had contracts for $115 million to build steel and wooden ships.[35]

Benefiting from prewar dredging of the channel to thirty feet and completion of thousands of feet of municipal and commercial wharves, postwar L.A. port traffic soared. However, the port's early business was chiefly domestic, not foreign. With Southern California's 1920s' building boom, imported lumber from the Pacific Northwest accounted for most port traffic. Although L.A. soon reigned as the world's busiest lumber port, its shortcomings were becoming apparent. Lumber carriers from the Northwest left empty and stopped on the return trip in San Francisco to pick up supplies and merchandise. Latin American merchants bypassed Los Angeles and shipped to San Francisco markets. Ship captains were reluctant to stop in Los Angeles unless they could leave with outgoing cargo.

L.A., however, would soon discover a potent local export—oil. The timing of the Panama Canal's reopening in 1921 was fortuitous for Southern California. Oil had just been discovered throughout the Los Angeles area, and the harbor made possible the development of this industry. The volume of production was so great that there were few places to store it locally. Absent nearby refineries to process it, crude oil was shipped aboard every available vessel through the canal to East Coast refineries. Between 1922 and 1924, the number of barrels shipped out of the port increased over sixfold, from 21 million to 138 million barrels. The endless parade of oil tankers alone made the Panama Canal (and the L.A. port) profitable. In this way, the port helped develop (and then benefited from) the Southern California oil industry. Soon, L.A.-based technology and innovation helped spark a worldwide oil boom.[36]

With lumber and oil monopolizing nearly all the port's facilities, voters in 1923 overwhelmingly passed a $15 million general-obligation bond for extensive wharf construction to serve other industries. Los Angeles also launched an aggressive campaign to market its port services; the campaign highlighted the fact that it was four times cheaper to ship goods by vessel than by rail or truck. As the region's economy began diversifying in the 1920s, local exports increased significantly. Dozens of shipping lines that formerly had paused only to refuel began making regularly scheduled stops.

In the campaigns to market the port, the Harbor Department worked closely with the Chamber of Commerce to attract new industries. These campaigns yielded dividends when the Goodyear Tire & Rubber Company became the first large-scale manufacturer to build a branch plant in Los Angeles. One critical selling point was the low shipping cost of Indonesian rubber through the Port of Los Angeles.

Other public entrepreneurs also assisted the industrialization campaign. Ezra Scattergood, the DWP's chief electrical engineer, joined Matson and other port officials in successfully lobbying Akron tire firms and, later, Detroit automobile companies to set up branch plants in the Southland. The port's chief drawing cards were low shipping costs both for raw materials and for component parts for automobile assembly. The DWP's drawing cards were abundant and inexpensive public water and power. Los Angeles's electrical power rates (the lowest of any major city in the nation) served as a potent magnet for eastern industry.[37]

As a result of these marketing campaigns, port traffic soared over sixfold between 1920 and 1930, from 3.5 million to 23 million net tons. Los Angeles quickly overtook San Francisco as the leading West Coast port. Whereas in 1920 Los Angeles shipped slightly more than half the tonnage of San Francisco, by 1930 it was shipping more than twice as much. With the lowest tariffs on the West Coast, the best rail connections, deep-draft dredging, and wharfage improvements, the Port of Los Angeles also captured much of the Port of San Diego's business.[38] As Matson archly observed of the two local ports' contest for the coveted Hawaiian sugar trade:

> San Diegans had poked a great amount of fun at the harbor aspirations of
> Los Angeles. The San Diego newspapers referred to Los Angeles Harbor as a
> "harborette," and if the truth must be told, this practice rather irritated those
> of us in Los Angeles whose duty it was to make the world understand that
> Los Angeles was a real seaport. So when the American-Hawaiian Company
> announced its intention of passing up San Diego it was a staggering blow to
> that delightful community. Plans were rushed for harbor improvements [at
> San Diego], but it was too late to catch up with Los Angeles.[39]

With the industrialization and diversification of the Southern California economy in the 1920s, the region's export trade grew dramatically. In 1930, the L.A. port shipped $161 million in exports to other countries, up from only $748,000 in 1915. Thus, the city's hard-won investment in a municipally owned harbor had realized the dream of the 1919 Harbor Bond Campaign Committee to make L.A. a "seat of world commerce." Los Angeles quickly became a world-class port. By 1932 the Port of Los Angeles was first on the Pacific Coast and third nationwide (behind New York and Philadelphia) in total tonnage. In a few short years, Los Angeles had become the shipping and wholesale center for the Southwest.[40]

The local state—the Los Angeles Harbor Department and DWP—played a central role in both shaping and accelerating this pre–New Deal economic development. As then–L.A. Mayor George Cryer observed, these "magic agencies" were chiefly responsible for the city's phenomenal early growth. To empower themselves, however, public bureaucracies in the reformed West were forced to adopt political-machine methods. Unlike insulated and autocratic eastern bureaucratic power brokers such as New York's Robert Moses, West Coast bureaucratic boosters such as the L.A. Harbor Department's Matson and the DWP's William Mulholland and Ezra Scattergood were forced to compete in the democratic arena of electoral politics. Borrowing the campaign tactics of their enemies—the railroads and private utilities—Los Angeles's bureaucratic entrepreneurs skillfully orchestrated voter legitimization for ambitious strategies of public infrastructure development and regional growth.[41]

Building the Port of Long Beach

A dazzling oil windfall also transformed the perennially cash-short town of Long Beach on the other side of San Pedro Bay. Founded in the 1880s as a failed model city and fractured by a rancorous, long-running conflict over liquor, the City of Long Beach early on struggled financially. Its hopes of raising the large sums needed to build a world-class harbor seemed a distant dream until the night of June 23, 1921, when the first oil strikes came in on nearby Signal Hill. A tidal wave of sudden wealth—in the form of oil royalties—soon financed an ambitious plan of port development. Within a half-century the international Port of Long Beach would be competing neck and neck with the Port of Los Angeles for the title of the nation's busiest and most profitable harbor.[42]

Competition between Los Angeles and Long Beach would shape the development of both ports, as the two keenly vied for access to rail lines, the tidelands, surrounding territory, harbor improvements, maritime trade, and economic growth. However, the early development of the Port of Long Beach would differ from L.A.'s because of a much lengthier transition from private-sector to public-sector ownership and control. Yet, as with Los Angeles, in order to understand the early history of the Port of Long Beach, one must begin by examining the critical role played by railroads.

Railroad/Port Battles

Long Beach first gained rail access via the efforts of Los Angeles. L.A.'s construction of the Los Angeles & San Pedro line (1869) and the county voters' subsidy to the SP (1872) meant that a mere three miles separated Long Beach from a transcontinental rail system. In 1882, Long Beach's founders contracted for construction of a railway linking the city to the downtown L.A. rail heads. However, the railroad was undercapitalized and poorly constructed and operated. Soon, the Long Beach Development Company (LBDC), the town's leading real estate and promotion firm, purchased the line and deeded it over to the SP. Long Beach became a city on February 10, 1888; a mere ten days later, the SP began operating its trains into Long Beach. The SP dominated Long Beach even more than it did Los Angeles, especially when Big Four member Crocker in 1888 bought a controlling interest in the LBDC.[43]

Thus, the free-harbor battle meant as much to Long Beach as it did to Los Angeles. In fact, Long Beach fought the Southern Pacific's attempt to monopolize access to its water frontage by making an alliance with the L.A. Terminal Railroad (LATR). LATR's near monopoly over rail access to both San Pedro Bay ports hardened Huntington's resolve to build a rival harbor at Santa Monica. Santa Monica thus presented as great a threat to Long Beach as to San Pedro.[44]

Although Long Beach celebrated along with Los Angeles when the federal government chose San Pedro for harbor funding, intercity harmony would not last long. In 1903, Long Beach successful lobbied the federal government for a $300,000 appropriation to dredge the Cerritos Slough. The slough was all that separated Long Beach from reaping as much benefit from the free-harbor victory as San Pedro had. Further, Long Beach moved to annex Terminal Island, which set off a series of bitter annexation wars. Long Beach, Los Angeles, San Pedro, and Wilmington fiercely contested control of the island, which later would host two of the world's great ports.

Controlling the Harbor and Tidelands

Long Beach expansionists urged their city to annex Terminal Island, "which would give Long Beach a ready-made port of its own and immediate access to harbor commerce." In August 1905, Long Beach citizens voted nearly unanimously to annex all of Terminal Island. Yet the margin of victory among voters in the accompanying election on Terminal Island was only a single questionable vote. As a result, a local judge ruled the election invalid. San Pedro retaliated "by trying to annex the western end of Long Beach." Later, the cities of Long Beach and San Pedro both tried to annex Wilmington (which included the inner-harbor channel to the ocean), but that area incorporated and became the third city in San Pedro Bay.[45]

Long Beach was not about to give up its fight for control of the water-front. In 1905, the city annexed further water frontage on its southeast border. Two months later, the city annexed a piece of land that brought its bound-aries all the way to Wilmington's east border. Long Beach was not alone in seeking control of this valuable waterfront territory. Los Angeles could not afford to let the three small cities reap the benefits accrued from its hard-won free-harbor fight. One way that L.A. attempted to control port development throughout all of San Pedro Bay was by pressing for a city-county consolida-tion bill, but the statute failed in the 1905 state legislature. Annexation and consolidation then became the only alternatives available to Los Angeles. In 1906, Los Angeles annexed the Shoestring Addition and thereby brought its southern border to the city limits of San Pedro and Wilmington. Long Beach then retaliated by annexing more southeast water frontage.[46]

In 1909, Long Beach again moved to annex Terminal Island and suc-ceeded in taking the 620 acres that constituted its eastern portion. Within a matter of days, Los Angeles brought San Pedro and Wilmington into its boundaries. But the annexation wars did not end with Los Angeles's hasty ac-quisition of the two tiny port cities. L.A. next pressured Long Beach to fol-low suit and seek consolidation with its larger neighbor. In response, Long Beach seriously explored becoming part of Orange County to escape L.A.'s imperial grasp. In early 1910, Long Beach permanently blocked Los Angeles's access to any further water frontage south and east of Long Beach. Long Beach administered this *coup de grâce* by annexing a 100-foot-wide strip of land all the way to the Orange County line.[47]

By 1910, Long Beach had quadrupled its original land area; its popula-tion grew even faster—by nearly 700 percent from 1900 to 1910, the great-est percentage increase in the nation. Although Long Beach's acquisitions would also protect the city's water rights and coincidentally secure future benefits in oil revenues, the primary goals of annexation were increasing wa-ter frontage (essential to port development) and preventing encirclement by Los Angeles. In 1923, Long Beach completed its annexation plan by bringing in Alamitos Bay and Naples. As a result, Los Angeles dropped its plans to consolidate with Long Beach.[48]

In the years before 1909, when voters approved the first large-scale mu-nicipal investment in the harbor, Long Beach port development was largely a private concern. In 1887, the LBDC had bought 802 acres of "salt marsh." The property was not choice and later was purchased by a private syndicate known as the Long Beach Land and Navigation Company. This firm desired to bring industries to the west side of Long Beach and even gave a smelting company free land as an inducement. Its founders soon realized the salt-marsh property's potential for harbor development and devised a plan to give Long Beach "more dockage area than San Pedro, second only to that of San Francisco on the West Coast."[49]

In late 1905, two of Long Beach Land and Navigation Company's owners formed the Los Angeles Dock and Terminal Company (LADT). This company was "no kin to the city of the same name" and put lengthy, Herculean efforts into making Long Beach Harbor possible. From 1905 until it went out of business in 1923, LADT privately "expended about $2,000,000 in the harbor area, including $800,000 for dredging and $225,000 for building and maintaining rock jetties to protect the ocean entrance." Yet it was never a profitable undertaking. Only the constant sale of property enabled the firm to defray the immense costs of maintenance and regular dredging required to offset the flooding and tons of silt swept into the bay from the Los Angeles River. As LADT's president later lamented, "Our company had never paid a dividend." [50]

Between 1905 and 1923, LADT worked closely with the City of Long Beach to develop the harbor. In 1906, both the city and the company faced the problem that the harbor could not be improved because two trestle bridges owned by the Salt Lake Railroad (formerly LATR) made it impossible to develop both the inner and outer harbors. LADT sought relief in the courts. The Long Beach city council and the Chamber of Commerce Harbor Committee supported LADT's position, and the courts forced the railroad to remove both trestles. The Salt Lake line had to construct expensive drawbridges in order to resume operations. Like the free-harbor fight, this contest involved active cooperation between local businesses and political leaders against the railroads and ultimately required federal intervention. The U.S. Department of War forced the removal of the trestle blocking the channel to the outer harbor, and the U.S. district engineer enforced the court's orders. Yet, despite local, state, and federal assistance, the Long Beach port remained a privately held asset. [51]

The close relationship between the private and public sectors was strengthened by the fact that one of LADT's directors, Charles Windham, served as Long Beach's mayor from 1908 to 1912. In his private capacity, Windham helped attract businesses to the harbor. He negotiated the deal with the first major manufacturer to choose Long Beach as its new home—Craig Shipbuilding. Long Beach, San Diego, and San Pedro competed for Craig's patronage, but Long Beach submitted the winning bid. Craig Shipbuilding then assisted LADT in improving the harbor, dredging an ocean entrance, building a "powerful electric dredger" as its first West Coast contract, and even performing emergency dredging. In this way, John Craig developed both the harbor and his own business. Craig's shipyards served (in conjunction with Western Boat Works) to make Long Beach Harbor an important site for the construction of seagoing vessels—one of the port's first key industries. Craig's construction of vessels for the U.S. Navy prefigured Long Beach's and the port's future role as centerpieces of Southern California's once-mighty military-industrial complex. [52]

Thus, the early history of the Port of Long Beach differs from that of Los Angeles in its lengthier transition from private-sector to public-sector owner-

Table 3.3   The Port of Long Beach and the Ballot Box: Bond Votes, 1892–1932

Date (month/ year)	Election Type[a]	Amount ($)	Outcome	Yes Vote (%)	Total Vote	Turnout (%)	Registered Voters
07/1892	Special	15,000	Passed	84.5	142	N/A	N/A
03/1901	Special	6,600	Passed	90.9	287	N/A	N/A
11/1903	Special	100,000	Passed	97.0	466	N/A	N/A
12/1905	Special	16,000	Passed	77.6	143	N/A	N/A
09/1909	Special	245,000	Passed	80.8	1,515	N/A	N/A
04/1910	Special	75,000	Passed	90.5	1,167	N/A	N/A
04/1910	Special	50,000	Passed	67.1	1,140	N/A	N/A
04/1912	Special	162,500	Not Passed	55.0	3,408	N/A	N/A
09/1912	Special	100,000	Not Passed	57.5	1,974	N/A	N/A
09/1913	Special	50,000	Not Passed	61.9	3,253	N/A	N/A
09/1913	Special	400,000	Not Passed	58.3	4,827	N/A	N/A
01/1914	Special	50,000	Passed	76.2	3,755	N/A	N/A
01/1914	Special	650,000	Passed	84.8	4,730	N/A	N/A
02/1916	Special	4,450,000	Passed[b]	93.5	7,920	N/A	N/A
10/1916	Special	500,000	Not Passed	62.7	7,921	N/A	N/A
10/1916	Special	300,000	Passed	78.5	7,812	N/A	N/A
01/1920	Special	25,000	Not Passed	66.2	3,724	N/A	N/A
04/1922	Special	500,000	Not Passed	56.8	15,281	62.9	24,300
04/1922	Special	2,000,000	Not Passed	52.5	15,398	63.4	24,300
05/1924	Special	5,000,000	Passed	94.9	25,112	58.1	43,233
05/1928	Special	2,700,000	Passed	91.0	38,743	N/A	N/A
05/1928	Special	2,800,000	Passed	87.4	38,521	N/A	N/A
05/1930	Special	300,000	Not Passed	58.1	28,655	N/A	N/A
01/1932	Special	225,000	Not Passed	40.8	25,357	N/A	N/A
01/1932	Special	300,000	Not Passed	46.5	25,496	N/A	N/A
11/1932	State general	3,450,000	Not Passed	58.0	62,112	69.0	90,045

SOURCES: Data from Long Beach City Clerk, *Long Beach City Council Minutes*, 1892, 1899; *Long Beach City Ordinances and Resolutions*, microfiche, date n.a.; *Elections History File*, 1888-Present; "All the Proposals Get a Majority of Total Vote Cast," *Daily Telegram*, April 19, 1922, p. 1; "Birth of World Metropolis," *Long Beach Press*, May 9, 1924, p. 1.

[a] Municipal election unless otherwise specified.

[b] This was actually a vote on an L.A. County bond issue providing flood-control protection for Long Beach Harbor from San Gabriel River silting.

ship and control. From 1905 to 1909, LADT controlled the harbor. The period 1909–1914 featured growing public involvement in port development. From 1914 to 1923, LADT slowly disengaged from harbor development, offering in 1922 to sell its property to the city. When the bonds needed for the purchase failed, the company sold off its holdings to other private companies. Only later would these lands become public property.

Ballot-Box Prowess

Like Los Angeles, Long Beach created a powerful port/business political coalition that operated as a potent force at the ballot box. Tables 3.3 and 3.4 demonstrate the alliance's prowess at getting harbor bond referenda, charter

Table 3.4 The Port of Long Beach and the Ballot Box: Charter-Amendment and Ordinance Votes, 1892–1932

Date (month/ year)	Election Type[a]	Purpose (Type) Amendment or Ordinance	Outcome	Yes Vote (%)	Total Vote	Turnout (%)	Registered Voters
08/1905	Special	Terminal Island/East San Pedro annexation-vote within city (Ordinance)	Passed	97.7	265	N/A	N/A
08/1905	Special	Terminal Island/East San Pedro annexation-vote outside city (Ordinance)	Passed	50.3	145	N/A	N/A
02/1907	Special	New charter (city claims management and control of waterfront) (Amendment)	Passed	88.5	1,398	N/A	N/A
07/1909	Special	Terminal Island annexation-vote within city (Ordinance)	Passed	100	135	N/A	N/A
07/1909	Special	Terminal Island annexation-vote outside city (Ordinance)	Passed	100	5	N/A	N/A
01/1913	Special	City may "own" the waterfront (Amendment)	Passed	81.8	5,012	N/A	N/A
01/1913	Special	Harbor franchises (Amendment)	Passed	51.3	5,054	N/A	N/A
01/1913	Special	Harbor franchises-alternate (Amendment)	Not Passed[b]	53.9	4,516	N/A	N/A
10/1914	Special	Increase in 1914-15 tax levy for harbor ($0.10/$100) (Ordinance)	Passed[c]	65.3	4,245	N/A	N/A
10/1914	Special	New charter authorizes commissioners of public works and property to handle harbor matters (Amendment)	Passed	50.7	3,256	N/A	N/A
04/1921	Special	Harbor franchises (Amendment)	Not Passed[d]	57.3	3,151	N/A	N/A
04/1921	Special	New council/manager charter creates three-member Harbor Commission with powers; stipulates that harbor assets may be transferred only with two-thirds voter majority approval (Amendment)	Passed	56.2	5,419	N/A	N/A
04/1923	Special	City Manager given authority to select Harbor Department employees	Passed	N/A	N/A	N/A	30,890
04/1925	Special	Exclusive franchises-wharves and piers (Amendment)	Passed	56.0	10,169	N/A	N/A

Date	Election	Description	Result	%	Votes		
04/1925	Special	Cooperation with other government bodies (Amendment)	Passed	65.4	9,963	N/A	N/A
04/1925	Special	Beach franchises (Amendment)	Not Passed	34.7	10,746	N/A	N/A
04/1925	Special	Puts Harbor Department under control of five-member Harbor Commission with separate harbor revenue fund expended with council permission; creates port superintendent appointed by Commission with council confirmation (Amendment)	Passed	60.5	10,093	N/A	N/A
07/1926	Special	Unified port district (Advisory)	Passed	50.2	15,782	33.6	47,000
03/1927	Special	New oil wells prohibited in specified places (Ordinance)	Passed	59.0	23,612	N/A	N/A
08/1928	Special	Exchange of lands (Amendment)	Passed	70.7	11,744	N/A	N/A
02/1929	Special	Harbor District boundaries defined by charter; commissioner terms staggered rather than ending with council terms; leasing altered (Amendment)	Passed	62.3	9,549	N/A	N/A
06/1930	General	Neptune Pier franchise (thirty-five years) (Ordinance)	Passed	57.4	22,793	N/A	N/A
02/1931	Special	Port manager made a commission appointee serving at pleasure; harbor commissioners removed only by council for cause or by recall; Commission given discretion over harbor revenue fund (Amendment)	Passed	73.3	9,736	N/A	N/A

SOURCES: Data from Long Beach City Clerk, *Long Beach City Ordinances and Resolutions*, microfiche, date n.a.; *Elections History File*, 1888–Present; *Long Beach City Charter*, 1907, 1914, 1915, 1921, 1929.

[a]Municipal election.

[b]This alternate amendment did not pass because of a smaller number of affirmative votes. The winning amendment allowed for thirty-five-year franchises and protected harbor interests by explicitly vesting municipal "plenary control" over use of public places.

[c]Section 3 (Fourteenth) of the 1907 Long Beach charter required a three-fifths majority for tax increases.

[d]This secured the needed majority but lost because it amended the old commission-plan charter, which was replaced by a new council/manager charter.

amendments, and referendary ordinances passed. From 1892 to 1932, Long Beach voters went to the polls on twenty-six separate occasions for port-related bond measures. Yet they were not nearly as willing as their Los Angeles counterparts to assume bonded debt on behalf of their harbor. Long Beach's electorate approved slightly over half (fourteen) of the bond propositions. The requested bond issues totaled nearly $25 million for harbor development, of which nearly $17 million was ultimately approved. The try–try again method of persuading voters to go into debt for port construction was as important to Long Beach's efforts as it was for L.A.'s DWP. Low-turnout elections also appear to have been as utilized by bond supporters in Long Beach as they were in Los Angeles. Special municipal elections were the venue for twenty-five of the city's twenty-six port bond measures.[53]

Port development in Long Beach depended as well on voter approval of charter amendments and ordinances. From 1892 to 1932, the city's voters considered twenty-three port-related charter amendments and ordinances. Here the record of popular approval was much stronger than with bonds. Of these, only a single measure failed for lack of a simple majority. Low-turnout special municipal elections were utilized as heavily for port-related charter changes and ordinances as for bond measures.

Given that Long Beach's port initially lay in private hands, public-harbor proponents soon developed a tandem strategy of seeking both charter changes and bond measures to develop the port as a public enterprise. As a result, from 1907 onward Long Beach harbor development entered a more statist phase. The new 1907 charter changed Long Beach from a general-law municipality run by a board of trustees to a home-rule, charter city with a mayor/council system of governance. In ratifying their new charter, voters simultaneously made decisions concerning their harbor because the charter, which was drawn largely word for word from the 1905 Los Angeles city charter, addressed the issue of control of public utilities and infrastructure. It provided explicitly for city "control" and improvement of Long Beach's waterfront, wharves, and other harbor assets. From this modest beginning, the city began to assert control over its harbor.[54]

In 1913, the city took the next step toward public ownership of the harbor. Voters overwhelmingly approved new charter language providing that the city would "own" the waterfront. (The previous language only allowed the city to "control" the harbor.) The amendment also permitted the city "to incur a bonded indebtedness" so as to pay for municipal ownership, control, improvement, and maintenance of the harbor.

In 1914, pro-harbor forces sought the passage of a $650,000 bond issue for improving Long Beach's inner harbor. This was the largest port-related bond issue in the city's history, and it followed a series of bond defeats. Bond proponents took no chances this time. Campaign leaders passed out one-dollar bills to everyone who showed up to listen to arguments in favor of the harbor-improvement bonds. However, the bonds were made contingent on federal-government assistance and supervision. When the ranking federal district engineer refused to play any such role because "there was 'no need' for a second deep-water harbor so close to San Pedro," the pro-harbor forces, although victorious as the polls, were stymied once again.[55] The 1914 bond misadventure did have one positive long-term institutional consequence. On June 29, 1917, the city government created a new board of harbor commissioners.

Later, Long Beach's voters supported harbor dredging through a temporary tax levy. Heavy floods had made it impossible for LADT to meet the costs of dredging, and severe winter storms brought tons of silt into Long Beach's harbor. In response, Los Angeles County created a flood-control district, which diverted the Los Angeles and San Gabriel rivers upstream and separated them into two concrete-lined channels. L.A. and Long Beach cooperated on the project, which protected both ports from further silting.[56]

In 1921, Long Beach adopted a new city charter—featuring the council/manager system—with important effects on the harbor. First, the charter protected the city's harbor assets from being sold or given away by requiring two-thirds voter approval for such an action. Second, harbor assets were explicitly defined as involving "commerce, navigation and fisheries." Third, the charter established a harbor department, run by a three-member commission (appointed by the city manager, subject to council confirmation, and serving at the manager's pleasure) that would manage the new agency, subject to council oversight. This was the foundation for the modern Long Beach Harbor Department.[57]

LADT's mounting financial problems finally furnished Long Beach the opportunity to completely municipalize port property. In 1924, Charles Henderson—who had chaired the unsuccessful 1922 Harbor Bond Campaign and served as president of the Chamber of Commerce—worked with City Manager Windham to secure the passage of $5 million in harbor bonds to publicly purchase LADT's property and improve the port. The victory was overwhelming. Ninety-five percent of the voters supported the measure, the largest bond issue in the city's history. The special election also featured unusually high turnout—58 percent of registered voters. In 1928, harbor-bond proponents enjoyed their final victories at the polls. The ballot included two bond propositions, totaling $5.5 million, to be used to fund improvements in both the inner and outer harbors. This would be the last successful campaign for port bonds, as economic hard times led voters to reject the next four measures. After 1933, however, with oil royalties financing port development, there would be no need for another voter-approved harbor bond in Long Beach.[58]

Public-port supporters also were successful with charter amendments that created a semi-autonomous public agency. In 1925, voters approved charter changes increasing the Harbor Department's authority, particularly over a separate harbor revenue fund. Harbor property was further protected in that it could be granted in the future only to state or federal authorities and even then only with majority voter approval. Finally, in 1929 and 1931, voters enacted charter amendments that gave the Long Beach Board of Harbor Commissioners and the Harbor Department powers comparable to those granted by Los Angeles's 1925 charter to its proprietary departments and citizen commissions. Thus, Long Beach harbor board members were appointed to fixed and staggered terms. This arrangement freed them from the short-term political forces to which elected officials were subject. The 1931 charter change completed the transformation of the Harbor Department into a semi-autonomous proprietary department. John Craig, who had brought Craig Shipbuilding to Long Beach a quarter-century earlier, served as the first president of the newly constituted board.[59]

As early as the mid-1920s Long Beach was making such progress with its ambitious harbor-development projects that an earlier proposal resurfaced that the two side-by-side ports function as a single entity administered by a central authority. The plan gained so much support that the California state legislature in 1925 passed the Port District Enabling Act, providing for the appointment of a central administration to operate the two ports if both cities agreed to such an arrangement. Long Beach, however, would have none of it. Flush with new oil millions and an unaccustomed sense of independence, Long Beach was not about to share its modern, state-of-the-art port with anyone, especially its powerful next-door neighbor. It considered the proposal yet another stratagem by which imperial Los Angeles, thwarted in its recent consolidation drive, might gain control over Long Beach's harbor development.

Trade and Development

Developing later than Los Angeles's harbor, Long Beach's port would need time to generate the commerce its northern neighbor enjoyed. By 1930, L.A.'s harbor handled nearly six times as much tonnage as Long Beach's port did—twenty-three million tons compared with four million tons. Yet Long Beach worked hard to catch up, relying on the ceaseless efforts of Windham, who was called the "the Father of the Port of Long Beach." For nearly three decades, Windham pursued Long Beach harbor and trade development in both private and public capacities. As an LADT director, he brought Craig Shipbuilding to Long Beach. As mayor, he oversaw city approval for and expenditure of the first harbor bonds, which allowed construction of a municipal dock.[60]

Later, Windham served as Long Beach city manager from 1922 to 1926.

In that capacity, he oversaw "beach acquisition, re-routing the railroad thru [sic] the city[,] . . . developing the harbor[,] . . . building of highways to facilitate oil drilling and refining. . . . His services, advice, and engineering experience were invaluable during the period of harbor building and general expansion." He also helped negotiate deals to bring both Ford Motor Company and Procter & Gamble to Long Beach.[61]

By 1932, Long Beach had developed a port system comparable to Los Angeles's, although it operated on a smaller scale. Its waterfront and tidelands were finally under public ownership and control. In organization and function, its semi-autonomous Harbor Department closely resembled L.A.'s proprietary departments, complete with substantial charter protections and powers. Its port was beginning to function as a potent economic catalyst. Using the ample municipal powers granted under the California constitution, Long Beach created its own powerful local developmental state apparatus, which also shaped patterns of trade and regional development.

Yet it was oil revenue that ultimately made Long Beach a true competitor for San Pedro Bay trade. As its capital projects became self-financed, it could lower prices and thereby lure port business away from its larger neighbor. Despite the failure of port unification, L.A. and Long Beach early on learned to cooperate when they had to. Thus, in 1929 they collaborated on the creation of the Harbor Belt Line Railroad. By merging the harbor operations of the private railroads, both ports were provided with improved rail access. This cooperative enterprise, which reduced the chances of domination by any single rail line, temporarily brought Long Beach and Los Angeles back to the mutually beneficial outcome of the free-harbor fight three decades before.[62]

LAX's Beginnings: Mines Field

The pre–New Deal era also would witness the controversy-plagued beginnings of Greater Los Angeles's third global gateway: Los Angeles International Airport. By the 1920s, as with ports in an earlier era, there was keen competition between private and public proposals for airport development. In Los Angeles, as elsewhere, the initial impetus was private. By 1927, there were fifty-two landing fields in L.A. County; forty-seven were privately owned and leased. Despite the fact that Los Angeles was one of the places where the aviation industry had its origins, the region seriously lagged behind other big cities in not having a major airport. Mindful that the Bay Area was building two municipal airports (San Francisco and Oakland) and that a public airport could serve as a catalyst for the city's economic and financial well-being, the Los Angeles Chamber of Commerce in 1926 began lobbying the L.A. city council for a municipal airport.[63]

Recognizing a burgeoning market in the aircraft-manufacturing industry (such as the local firms headed by Glenn Martin and Donald Douglas), the L.A. Chamber hired leading meteorologist Dr. Ford Ashman Carpenter to evaluate thirteen potential sites for a future municipal airport. One of those sites was a relatively small three thousand–acre swath of land then known as Mines Field on the Andrew Bennett Ranch. This would be the future site of LAX. Referring to Mines Field (then a bean and barley field) as the "Inglewood Site," Carpenter called it "an ideal location as far as level unobstructed space is concerned. Ideal weather conditions were another comparative advantage." [64]

Realizing aviation's economic value, several groups of local businesspersons and realtors began promoting various sites for a future main airport. One group included George Cleaver, Harry Culver, and Frank Parent. The three would play a critical role in the eventual selection of Mines Field as Los Angeles's municipal airport. In 1927, they formed a partnership to acquire options to purchase Mines Field. William Mines, who had leased the acreage for use as a landing strip, was brought into the partnership to promote the airport site and to arrange options for the partnership to buy the property. [65]

The partners then searched for a buyer with the capital to undertake airport development. They initially showed little interest in Mines Field as a municipal airfield. On two occasions the partners nearly arranged the site's sale to private buyers. Negotiations first were begun with Jack Maddux, who was seeking an airport for his newly founded Maddux Airlines (which eventually became Trans World Airlines). In late 1927, famed aviator Charles Lindbergh came to Los Angeles. Lindbergh flew into Mines Field on a surprise visit— the brainchild of Maddux. The resulting publicity showcased the site's aviation potential. Maddux, however, was unable to secure the necessary financing for an airport. [66]

The Ford Motor Company, which was deciding whether to become a major aircraft manufacturer, was a second potential buyer. However, the company declined, claiming that it was not ready to engage in the risky business of operating airports. The promoters then solicited the U.S. government to purchase the site as a military air base; this scheme also proved to no avail. Finally, in desperation, they offered to sell the land to the City of Los Angeles at $3,250 per acre. As other potential buyers fell by the wayside, the city loomed ever larger as a promising suitor. [67]

In July 1927, the City of Los Angeles solicited offers for future municipal airport sites. Twenty-seven bids were reduced to eight, including Mines Field. Local real estate interests spearheaded the support for each site. In March 1928, the L.A. city council narrowed the field to three sites—all to be bought by the city. They included Mines Field (the southwest site), Vale Field (the eastside site, championed by the publishers of the *Los Angeles Times*), and the Sesnon Tract in the San Fernando Valley (championed by the area's city councilperson). As for Mines Field, the city council's Finance Committee recommended that it be purchased for $3,000 per acre, noting portentously that "it is the only field outside of those in San Fernando Valley lying within the territorial limits of the City of Los Angeles, and therefore is the only one which would be subject to the legislative control of the city, and around which the city would control the development which is a very important feature."[68]

L.A. City Councilperson Peirson "Pete" Hall, a member of the body's Airport Committee, was the chief champion at City Hall for a municipal airport system and for Mines Field. Hall's visionary proposal (later to come to fruition) was to have three such airports. In April 1928, at Hall's insistence, the council called for a special municipal election to purchase three possible sites. But in a serious setback to L.A.'s airport aspirations, the $6 million bond measure failed at the polls. Temperance had triumphed over the tarmac. The "wet" Hall was called a "drunkard" and accused of secretly getting rich on the sale of airports by the Reverend Robert Schuler; a conservative "dry" force in local prohibition-era politics, Schuler led churchgoers in the anti-bond campaign.[69]

As a result, the city council was forced to choose the no-frills option of leasing a single site. Mines Field's chances were substantially improved by the National Air Races, awarded that year to Los Angeles. Supporters of Mines Field lobbied hard for the races, even offering the site for the air show's duration for one dollar. With such inducements and with endorsements by prominent aviators such as Lindbergh, the show's promoters selected Mines Field. Provided with free publicity and structural improvements, Mines Field was handed a decided advantage. Yet, the eastside Vale site continued to have strong support, particularly from the *Los Angeles Times* and the L.A. Chamber of Commerce. Led by Hall, the city council in 1928 finally selected Mines Field as Los Angeles's future airport. In 1930, Mines Field was officially dedicated as Los Angeles Municipal Airport. Soon, the lease for the 480-acre site was renegotiated for fifty years, with the city having the right to own and expand the facility in the future.[70]

In retrospect, city officials may have appeared shortsighted in not making a greater initial effort to purchase Mines Field. Yet, Mines Field was heavily criticized as a "white elephant," particularly by promoters and operators of rival airports, because it did not quickly attract the support of the airline industry. The industry did not immediately need spacious Mines Field because planes were small enough to fly in and out of the area's many smaller and better-maintained private airports. With the coming of the Depression, the city also lacked the funds to upgrade the facility; the airlines demanded an upgrade as a condition of relocation. Thus, leasing may have been the only politically palatable alternative given the spate of criticism in the airport's early years.[71]

For airport governance, Councilman Hall supported the system used by the DWP and the Harbor Department. Through his efforts, the city council seriously considered officially designating the airport as "Los Angeles Air Harbor." Yet the local legislature hesitated to give the airport the independent charter status and powers the two other proprietary departments had. Instead, the airport was kept on a short leash. By ordinance, the council created the Department of Airports, run by a council-appointed director; the agency was overseen not by a citizen commission but by the city council's Finance Committee. Thus, the council was the early airport manager, with the power to pass all rules and regulations regarding operations and rates and to approve all leases. The airport's revenues were included in the city's general fund and thus were susceptible to later raids as the Depression deepened. Only in the postwar era, with the blossoming of commercial aviation, would L.A.'s "Air Harbor" become a charter-designated proprietary department with control of a special revenue fund.[72]

Thus, by 1932 the local foundations of L.A.'s future global gateways had been laid. The ports of San Pedro Bay and L.A. Municipal Airport had been created as municipal entities. The ports, but not yet the airport, had been given governance arrangements that limited political oversight and allowed them to function as market-driven public businesses. The ports were no longer taxpayer-subsidized and were becoming financially self-sufficient. As such, they raised their initially low prices, which had been needed to attract business; the new rates allowed financing of capital improvements. By the late 1920s the ports functioned as developmental state apparatuses and were potent catalysts for trade and regional development. Later, L.A.'s municipal airport system would follow a similar trajectory.

4
Building for Regional and Global Markets

Leadership and Innovation, 1933–1992

There is no such thing as short-range in port planning. In addition to retaining our share of the maritime commerce of Southern California we are determined to . . . generate new trade in areas which have not been fully explored in the past.

—*Los Angeles Board of Harbor Commissioners, 1982*[1]

Long Beach today is the principal cargo gateway to the Pacific . . . and continues to lead all West Coast ports . . . in innovation. Port staff are constantly renovating and improving terminals, docks and roadways, striving to incorporate the latest technological advances and respond to customer needs.

—*Port of Long Beach, 1991*[2]

One thing that I kept convincing the council members that would listen, the mayor, and the [airport] commissioners [of] was that the future of Los Angeles depended on the trade that was generated, primarily on the nonstop hauls out of Europe and on the Pacific Rim.

—*Clifton Moore, former executive director,*
Los Angeles Department of Airports, 1995[3]

This chapter explores strategies of trade, infrastructure, and regional development from 1933 to 1992, under the transformative conditions of depression, war, and postwar global trade agreements and transportation innovations. In the sixty-year period from the New Deal through the administration of L.A. Mayor Tom Bradley (1973–93), the region's port and airport systems were fundamentally transformed from small-scale, local-market-oriented facilities to major wartime arsenals of democracy and, finally, to world-class trade portals serving huge regional, national, and global markets. By 1992, the L.A. Customs District, once a trade backwater, was handling $122 billion in global trade, dramatically up from $6.2 billion in 1972. By then, the San Pedro Bay ports had become the world's fourth largest container facility, handling 4.4 million twenty-foot equivalent units (TEUs) annually. Los Angeles International Airport (LAX) had become the world's fourth busiest, handling forty-seven million passengers annually and nearly 1.4 million tons of air cargo. The two ports and LAX in 1990 served 14.5 million customers in the L.A. metropolitan area—then the world's fourteenth largest economy.[4]

Public Entrepreneurship

The hallmark of the Los Angeles and Long Beach port and airport systems during these years was their public entrepreneurship, which featured long-term strategic planning, agile market responses, and innovative capital programs. With burgeoning regional and global markets to serve, L.A.'s global gateways needed both to expand massively and to restructure in order to accommodate new technologies such as the intermodal container and jet airplane. In the early 1960s, the San Pedro Bay ports entered the container age by building state-of-the-art facilities. Once a laggard, LAX by the 1960s also positioned itself on the cutting edge, becoming the nation's first airport designed for the jet age.

Innovative development continued when, in 1985, the San Pedro Bay ports launched an ambitious planning effort—the 2020 Plan—to create the world's largest marine-highway-rail trade-transportation hub. This plan also included the country's biggest intermodal project—the Alameda Corridor separated-grade rail facility, which linked the ports with the downtown rail yards. In the early 1980s LAX successfully undertook large-scale international-terminal and air-cargo expansion projects. By the late 1980s, airport planners were launching the $8–12 billion LAX Master Plan, the nation's most ambitious airport expansion project. Actively seeking new global markets, port and airport officials in the postwar era also launched new trade initiatives.

Both institutional structure and political agency contributed to long-range strategic planning and innovative infrastructure development. Proprietary-department governance (which came to L.A.'s airport system in 1947) largely shielded the ports and airports from excessive political oversight and micro-management by elected officials. Financial independence (finally achieved by the L.A. airport system in the 1960s) further aided project planning and development. (However, since the passage of Proposition 13 in 1978, local elected officials have had strong incentive to rein in the proprietary departments and raid their revenue funds.) Elected officials, professional managers, and citizen commissioners provided valuable leadership for the region's postwar mega-projects and trade-development initiatives. For example, Mayor Bradley was a fervent supporter of infrastructure and trade growth; port and airport managers and commissioners also played major leadership roles.[5]

Since the 1970s, however, the task of infrastructure development and financing has been complicated by new federal and state environmental and fiscal regulations and bureaucracies. This chapter surveys the region's entrepreneurial public leaders (ranging from mayors to port and airport officials), examines their innovative strategies of infrastructure and trade development from 1933 to 1992, and traces the rise of the new supra-local regulatory regimes that later would bedevil Southern California's mega-projects.

The Ports of San Pedro Bay

Federal Catalyst

The federal government played a major role in San Pedro Bay port development from 1930 to 1945. The ever-tightening grip of the Great Depression on world commerce had a domino effect on shipping. More fortunate than most, the Port of Los Angeles, despite experiencing a sharp slump in lumber imports because of a near-moratorium on local construction, continued to handle a large volume of oil exports. This advantage, however, proved to be short-lived. In 1930, the Hawley-Smoot Tariff Act, a misguided attempt to protect the shattered U.S. economy, imposed the highest import duties in U.S. history. Foreign retaliation decimated oil exports even though Congress in 1934 passed reciprocal trade agreements and lowered tariffs.

As a result, the L.A. port faced a fiscal crisis in the early 1930s. Throughout its early existence, the port ran a deficit (requiring taxpayer subsidies) as it pursued a developmental pricing strategy of low tariffs to attract commerce. It thus had little money left for pay-as-you-go capital financing and, as a result, incurred $30 million in bonded debt for necessary improvements. From 1930 to 1934, as port traffic plummeted, port revenues fell 28 percent, but operating expenses barely declined because of large debt payments. As the harbor's annual deficit mushroomed from $150,000 to $750,000, the city council responded in 1934 by resolving to stop port subsidies. It demanded that the port adopt a remunerative pricing scheme designed to achieve self-sufficiency and fully pay for capital improvements. Port officials complied and, after a failed 1935 bond vote, turned to lobbying for federal assistance. An obliging federal government eventually paid for new dredging and widening of the main channel, a breakwater extension, new wharves, and a concrete and steel terminal.[6]

As the national economy slowly recovered so did port activity. In 1938, L.A. harbor traffic topped twenty million tons for the first time in seven years; cargo value approached the $1 billion level first reached in 1929. The L.A. port ended the fiscal year with a first-ever net profit. On the Long Beach side, most of the new traffic (and revenue) involved oil. In 1936, tests confirmed a significant deposit of oil under Long Beach's harbor; within two years, the first harbor well began producing. Oil would both provide a valuable export and, until 1965, cover the entire costs of harbor development.[7]

In December 1941, both ports enlisted full-time in the war effort. The Navy installed a port director with absolute control over all ship movements. A total blackout went into effect, a submarine net was installed, and the approaches to the ports and Navy installations were heavily guarded. Only authorized Navy ships were allowed to pass through. Terminal Island became the center of military activity. After two years of unsuccessful negotiations with L.A., the Navy in 1937 condemned land for an air station there. Long Beach willingly donated one hundred acres of land in 1940 for a new Terminal Island naval base after being chosen as the home anchorage for the Pacific Fleet.[8]

Shipbuilding, airplane manufacturing, oil drilling, and military transport transformed the entire port area during the war. Big shipyards such as California Shipbuilding, Bethlehem Shipbuilding, and Consolidated Steel constructed more than 110 vessels while nearby Todd Shipyards built 26 warships. Smaller yards built thousands of patrol boats and landing craft. All told, wartime ship production employed ninety thousand workers. Thousands more worked at the nearby Long Beach Naval Shipyard, building and repairing combat craft. A short distance away, the enormous, camouflaged Douglas Aircraft Company plant had produced over ninety-five hundred military aircraft by 1945. Here, a key locational determinant was infrastructure: "Douglas had chosen the Long Beach site because it was close to rail lines and a harbor and had an existing airport to deliver the planes built at the factory."[9] The war also created enormous demand for petroleum; Long Beach made a singular contribution. By 1943, its oil-drilling program encompassed 126 harbor wells producing seventeen thousand barrels a day. Annual oil revenues were $10 million. A half million service personnel and fifteen million tons of equipment passed through San Pedro Bay, one of the closest major transit points to the Pacific theater. Few other areas of the country contributed more to the war effort than the Los Angeles/Long Beach port complex.[10]

Planning and Governance Innovations

In December 1945, the Navy relinquished control of the San Pedro Bay ports. On the L.A. side, the Harbor Department's most urgent tasks were to convert military installations to civilian use, resume delayed repairs, build new terminals, and extend the breakwater. In all, the L.A. port spent $25 million on a major postwar construction program from 1945 to 1954. As a result, the Port of Los Angeles positioned itself to become the West Coast's maritime leader, supplanting San Francisco. Its twenty-eight miles of waterfront included over seventy-five thousand linear feet of wharfage (with berthing space for eighty ocean-going vessels) and sufficient transit sheds for thirty-five ships simultaneously to load and unload cargo. One hundred fifteen shipping lines, two hundred commercial trucking companies, and three transcontinental railroads handled the now-diversified traffic flowing through the port. Further boosting the Port of L.A.'s trade aspirations was its designation in 1949 as the nation's fourth foreign trade zone, making it possible for ships to unload, inspect, and process goods pending reshipment without duty payments.[11]

Long Beach's postwar prospects seemed more uncertain. After ordering four thousand layoffs at his aircraft plant, Donald Douglas observed that "the future is as dark as the inside of a boot." One bright spot was oil revenue. But Long Beach's oil rights were cast in doubt by the U.S. Supreme Court, which ruled in 1947 that the oil-rich tidelands were under the federal government's jurisdiction. Further complicating matters, oil drilling caused Long Beach's harbor to subside.[12]

Through both the war and the peacetime transition, the San Pedro Bay ports benefited from skilled managers. Long-serving managers replaced elected officials and citizen commissioners as crucial agents guiding harbor development. In Los Angeles, Arthur Eldridge was the prototype of the new port professional; he served as general manager from 1934 to 1954 and was succeeded by Bernard Caughlin (1954–74). Such longevity contrasted sharply with the growing turnaround of port commissioners. During Eldridge's twenty-one-year tenure, four different L.A. mayors appointed twenty-one different harbor commissioners. On taking office in 1938, Mayor Fletcher Bowron set a precedent by calling for the resignation of all city commissioners, whether or not their five-year terms had expired. Although this move produced a clean slate and enhanced mayoral authority, it reduced commission longevity, expertise, and influence.[13]

At war's end, farsighted L.A. port officials like Eldridge made a priority of quickly resuming full-scale trade with Japan and of expanding trade elsewhere. Within one year of the signing of the Japanese Peace Pact in 1951, the number of Japanese ships stopping at the Port of Los Angeles had increased 140 percent, while seaborne trade tonnage between the United States and Japan had soared 163 percent. The port soon opened a trade-development office in Tokyo. By the late 1950s, with the introduction of Japanese automobiles to the U.S. market, most of L.A.'s port tonnage involved trade with Japan. Hoping to increase commerce between the port and Europe, L.A. port officials opened a similar office in Oslo. An international public relations firm was hired to market the port to foreign countries and shippers.[14]

L.A.'s harbor managers campaigned hard for greater port governance and financial autonomy. Table 4.1 summarizes Port of L.A. bond and charter-amendment votes from 1933 to 1992. Unlike its earlier display of ballot-box prowess, the Harbor Department's electoral fortunes waned during the Depression. In 1934, it failed to secure majority voter approval for increased leasing authority. A year later, it failed to garner the necessary two-thirds vote for a $7.7 million bond issue. From 1945 through the mid-1960s, the port regained its once-sure electoral footing, winning approval of six of seven charter amendments. Voters strongly supported loosening prior restrictions in order to give the department greater leasing and contracting authority.

L.A. port staff also fought to make the harbor financially self-sufficient. At their urging, city voters in 1959 overwhelmingly approved a charter

Table 4.1 The Port of Los Angeles and the Ballot Box: Bond and Charter-Amendment Votes, 1933–1992

Date (month/year)	Election Type[a]	Purpose or Amount (Type)	Outcome	Yes Vote (%)	Total Vote	Turnout (%)	Registered Voters
09/1934	Special	Leasing authority (Amendment)	Not Passed	49.6	166,093	22.5	739,637
11/1935	Special	$7,700,000 (Bond)	Not Passed	64.6	90,104	14.3	631,513
05/1941	General	Commission fees (Amendment)	Not Passed	36.6	201,539	N/A	N/A
04/1945	Primary	Leasing authority (Amendment)	Passed	79.9	152,900	N/A	N/A
04/1947	Primary	Leasing authority (Amendment)	Passed	68.9	228,369	32.0	714,715
05/1949	General	Contract authority (Amendment)	Passed	58.5	307,148	N/A	N/A
04/1953	Primary	Harbor Department given authority to use harbor revenue fund to construct facilities for managing, improving, or promoting harbor (Amendment)	Not Passed	40.1	370,913	N/A	N/A
04/1959	Primary	Revenue bond authority (Amendment)	Passed	78.4	340,812	34.5	986,799
05/1961	General	Temporary rules and charges (Amendment)	Passed	65.4	457,712	40.6	1,128,070
04/1963	Primary	Franchise and permit authority (Amendment)	Passed	63.0	316,479	N/A	N/A
04/1969	Primary	Council oversight strengthened (Amendment)	Passed	50.9	509,012	46.1	1,104,787
05/1973	General	Limits on contracts over certain amounts of time and money (Amendment)	Passed	58.4	589,520	48.5	1,216,173
05/1973	General	Proprietary-department management (Amendment)	Passed	77.6	606,983	49.9	1,216,173
11/1976	State general	Council two-thirds vote required for approval of specified leases (Amendment)	Passed	63.2	745,969	N/A	N/A

Date	Election	Measure	Result	%	Votes	Turnout %	Registration
04/1977	Primary	General manager made exempt from civil service (Amendment)	Passed	60.7	380,668	32.4	1,174,439
05/1977	General	Contract-approval authority for general manager (Amendment)	Passed	57.1	281,104	23.9	1,174,985
05/1977	General	Council control of salaries (Amendment)	Passed	65.1	284,146	24.2	1,174,985
05/1979	General	Tidelands transfer authority (Amendment)	Not Passed	43.6	235,463	19.4	1,214,707
06/1981	General	Investment of funds (Amendment)	Passed	74.0	321,743	25.3	1,271,612
06/1981	General	Short-term borrowing authority (Amendment)	Passed	64.3	313,226	24.6	1,271,612
04/1991	Primary	Council approval of leases of specified times and amounts (Amendment)	Passed	72.2	192,166	15.1	1,270,050
06/1991	General	City anti-apartheid policy applies to contracts (Amendment)	Passed	59.8	204,444	16.6	1,233,919
06/1991	General	Prop. 5: council veto of any and all board decisions (Amendment)	Passed	59.3	211,009	17.1	1,233,919
06/1992	State primary	Local and domestic contract bidding preferences (Amendment)	Passed	55.1	513,466	40.9	1,255,774

SOURCES: Data from Los Angeles City Clerk, *Records of Election Returns*, vol. 4, Sept. 29, 1931–Nov. 26, 1935; *Records of Election Returns*, vol. 5, Dec. 8, 1936–Nov. 5, 1940; *Records of Election Returns*, vol. 6, Apr. 1, 1941–May 10, 1943; *Charter Amendments 1961–1997*; *City of Los Angeles Voter Registration and Turnout for Mayor, City Attorney, and Controller for 1961 through 1997*; *City of Los Angeles Voter Registration and Turnout All Regularly Scheduled Elections, 1977–1997*; *Los Angeles Times*, election-day published registration statistics, post-election published turnout statistics; *Los Angeles City Charter*, 1925.

[a] Municipal election unless otherwise specified.

amendment authorizing the Harbor Department to issue revenue bonds to finance harbor expansion. Repayment would come entirely from harbor revenues at no cost to taxpayers. Revenue bonds—which did not require voter approval—enabled the port to immediately raise $50 million for new container facilities. As a result, L.A. agilely positioned itself to take advantage of one of the great technological advances in maritime commerce.[15]

From the late 1960s into the 1990s, the charter pendulum swung in the other direction, enhancing the authority of elected officials over professional managers and citizen commissioners. As a 1998 RAND charter study noted, "In the past 25 years, elected officials have consistently sought to increase their powers at the expense of departments."[16] Voters approved a series of charter amendments weakening the independence of the proprietary departments, such as the Harbor Department. These departments were stripped of their independent salary-setting authority, oversight of leases by the city council was strengthened, and general managers were made exempt from civil service protections. Finally, with the passage of Proposition 5 in 1991, the city council was given veto authority (with a two-thirds vote) over board decisions.

Other governance changes strengthened mayoral oversight. In 1972, Mayor Samuel Yorty (1961–73) issued an executive directive giving the mayor indirect power to control the agendas of proprietary-department boards; his successors would issue similar orders. Later, Mayor Bradley reputedly asked for signed, undated resignation letters from his commissioners, a move that increased his authority over port policymaking. Bradley also broke the pattern of in-house top-management appointments. In 1984, the mayor secured the appointment of Ezunial Burts, one of his key assistants, as port executive director. In this way, by either charter change or practice, the mayor and city council both increased their oversight over the port bureaucracy and policymaking.[17]

Across the bay in Long Beach, Eloi Amar ably served as port general manager from 1940 to 1958. A San Pedro native, Amar previously managed Santa Catalina Island's Avalon harbor and served as president of the Los Angeles Board of Harbor Commissioners from 1933 to 1939. He understood well Long Beach's complex challenge of providing commercial facilities, serving the Navy, and recovering harbor oil deposits. Long Beach, in turn, appreciated the value of an experienced port manager. By 1948, the port manager earned more than Long Beach's city manager.[18]

One major postwar challenge facing Amar involved keeping the naval shipyard on Terminal Island, a mainstay of the local economy. In 1950, the federal government moved to close the shipyard, in part because of subsidence caused by oil drilling. Work at the yard ceased until early 1951; however, the Korean War then gave the shipyard a new lease on life. The Navy budgeted $4.5 million to stop subsidence and keep the yard operating. By 1952, the shipyard was a $200 million annual operation, employing sixty-five hundred people with a payroll of over $30 million. The Navy also stationed in Long Beach forty thousand sailors, who contributed $127 million to the local economy.[19]

A second major challenge involved oil subsidence. Ironically, the resource that served as the key catalyst for Long Beach harbor development was also its biggest headache. So much oil had been pumped out that the harbor floor gradually began to sink. Ignored during the war years, subsidence steadily worsened and caused tremendous damage, threatening to destroy the entire harbor and even parts of the city. Finally, in the early 1960s, a massive injection of a million barrels of water per day under the harbor halted subsidence. With its remaining oil money, Long Beach set about rebuilding its ruined harbor to accommodate container facilities.

The Port of Long Beach ultimately would fight a losing twenty-year battle to keep its oil revenues. Federal legislation returned the tidelands to state control. In 1956, the California Supreme Court upheld a 50/50 split of oil revenues between the state and the Harbor Department. In 1965, the City of Long Beach and the state rewrote the Tidelands Trust Act so that 85 percent of oil royalties went to the state and 15 percent to the city's general fund. However, the port could be reimbursed by the state to mitigate subsidence. The federal government then sued for subsidence-caused damages to Navy facilities; in 1963, Long Beach and the state paid a substantial damage claim. For the port and city, then, oil proved a mixed blessing. Oil royalties that might have gone for harbor improvements instead were used to pay for damages and mitigation. As a Long Beach city manager lamented, subsidence "cost the city $90 million to stop (not cure!) and 25 years of industrial and commercial growth."[20]

Long Beach harbor officials also campaigned hard to maintain autonomous control over port governance and finances. Table 4.2 displays Port of Long Beach bond and major charter-amendment votes from 1933 to 1992. Over the years, the city manager, council, and mayor proposed charter reforms to increase their authority over port matters. Early on, the port and its community and business allies successfully resisted; later, voters approved increased oversight. In 1935, the port coalition defeated a proposal to transfer control of the Harbor Department to the city manager. In 1948, it defeated plans for greater city-manager and council authority over harbor funds and harbor oil development. Yet the port also began experiencing erosion of its authority. In 1946 and 1952, voters approved measures allowing harbor oil revenues to be used for non-port-related public improvements, although in 1956 the electorate revoked this power. Over time, however, the city council did convince a majority of voters that it should oversee port budgets and salary setting.

In 1980, voters approved several major port governance changes. First, members of the Board of Harbor Commissioners (BOHC) now were limited

Table 4.2 The Port of Long Beach and the Ballot Box: Bond, Charter-Amendment, and Ordinance Votes, 1933–1992

Date (month/year)	Election Type[a]	Purpose or Amount (Type)	Outcome	Yes Vote (%)	Total Vote	Turnout (%)	Registered Voters
11/1933	Special	$35,000 (Bond)	Not Passed	59.9	32,170	38.0	84,705
04/1935	Special	City manager-controlled Harbor Department (Amendment)	Not Passed	22.8	25,208	N/A	N/A
05/1937	Special	Harbor Board control of oil revenues (Amendment)	Passed	54.5	17,965	N/A	N/A
06/1937	Special	Harbor Department authority to drill one well per acre within Harbor District (Ordinance)	Passed	53.5	13,724	N/A	N/A
07/1946	Special	Harbor operating fund created from operating revenues (Amendment)	Passed	72.1	16,479	13.7	119,901
07/1946	Special	Authority to use specified tidelands oil funds for public improvements (Amendment)	Passed	78.1	17,488	14.6	119,901
02/1948	Special	City manager and council control of harbor funds (Amendment)	Not Passed	25.2	45,001	N/A	N/A
02/1948	Special	Council control of harbor oil development (Amendment)	Not Passed	24.0	44,489	N/A	N/A
05/1951	Primary	Authority to award emergency contracts without bidding (Amendment)	Passed	56.5	30,449	26.6	114,535
06/1951	General	Harbor Department chargebacks for use of city services (Amendment)	Passed	72.5	38,630	32.8	117,651
11/1952	State general	Authority to expend 50 percent of tidelands oil funds on nonharbor items (Amendment)	Passed	82.8	104,940	N/A	N/A
04/1953	Special	Harbor Commission authority re: employees; civil-service-exempt positions (Amendment)	Passed	60.3	40,573	29.2	138,956
05/1954	Primary	Council approval of Harbor Department budgets (Amendment)	Passed	67.2	46,306	30.4	152,381
05/1954	Primary	Harbor purchases by city purchasing agent, except for emergencies (Amendment)	Passed	79.7	39,345	25.8	152,381
05/1954	Primary	Council control over Harbor Department salaries (Amendment)	Passed	79.3	40,525	26.6	152,381
02/1956	Special	Replacement of funds used for subsidence or impounded by litigation (Amendment)	Passed	81.8	74,495	53.5	139,364

Date	Election	Description	Result	%	Votes	%	Votes
11/1956	State general	Voter approval required to alter Harbor District boundaries (Amendment)	Passed	78.2	106,116	N/A	N/A
11/1956	State general	Suspension of use of tidelands oil funds on nonharbor items (Amendment)	Passed	66.8	110,981	N/A	N/A
03/1958	Special	Authority for unit development agreements to remedy subsidence (Amendment)	Passed	93.8	40,580	25.9	156,942
11/1958	State general	Long-term leasing authority (Amendment)	Passed	66.9	106,332	60.4	176,060
05/1960	Primary	Unitization to remedy subsidence financed by tidelands oil funds (Amendment)	Passed	75.3	50,048	33.3	150,190
06/1963	General	Leasing authority enhanced (Amendment)	Passed	68.6	46,008	31.7	145,105
11/1964	State general	Long Beach payments to California for tidelands oil settlement (Amendment)	Passed	68.2	122,466	66.7	183,681
11/1968	State general	Revenue bonding authority (Amendment)	Passed	57.4	122,494	N/A	N/A
06/1976	State primary	Four-year terms for all elected officials; council terms staggered (Amendment)	Passed	53.0	86,488	N/A	N/A
11/1976	State general	City council elected by districts (Amendment)	Passed	51.4	119,435	67.2	177,725
03/1978	Special	Two-year term for mayor (Amendment)	Passed	81.1	36,459	N/A	N/A
11/1978	State general	Harbor District expansion (Amendment)	Passed	60.4	95,233	61.1	155,772
11/1980	State general	Charter streamlining: harbor commissioners appointed by mayor and subject to term limits; 10 percent annual revenue transfers permitted to city's tidelands operating fund (Amendment)	Passed	67.3	101,599	N/A	N/A
06/1984	State primary	Short-term revenue bonding authority (Amendment)	Passed	65.0	66,753	39.2	170,132
11/1984	State general	Renegotiation of all leases by harbor commissioners every five years (Amendment)	Passed	71.5	106,532	56.3	189,195
11/1986	State general	Mayor elected citywide (Amendment)	Passed	67.2	94,243	51.6	182,555
11/1986	State general	Council extension of tidelands contracts without competitive bidding (Amendment)	Not Passed	48.1	89,451	49.0	182,555
11/1992	State general	Term limits for elected officials (Amendment)	Passed	65.8	119,933	N/A	N/A

SOURCES: Data from Long Beach City Clerk, *Long Beach City Ordinances and Resolutions*, microfiche, date n.a.; *Elections History File, 1888–Present*; *Long Beach City Charter, 1931.*

[a] Municipal election unless otherwise specified.

to two six-year terms. Previously, harbor commissioners had been routinely reappointed; some had served over twenty years. Second, the mayor, not the city manager, was given the power to appoint BOHC members. Greater mayoral influence was felt immediately. Mayor Ernie Kell appointed David Hauser, a Long Beach realtor and mortgage broker, as harbor commissioner. Hauser, who questioned many port policies, sought to improve the port's management capacity and trade potential. By 1987, the mayor had appointed a majority of the board. Under Hauser's leadership, the port panel created a new international trade and marketing position and hired a new port executive director. Third, the port commission took over salary-setting authority from the city council. Fourth, by a two-thirds council vote, up to 10 percent of the port's net annual income could be transferred into the city's tidelands operating fund (used for beach and marina projects); however, a majority of the harbor board had to agree that the money was not needed by the port. In 1986, voters approved a charter amendment making the mayoralty an independently elected office with a four-year term and increased authority.[21]

The 1960s and 1970s: Containerization and Port Competition

By the early 1960s, containerization had revolutionized the global shipping and port industries; this development sharply intensified competition between the L.A. and Long Beach ports. Both targeted large-scale capital investments at state-of-the-art container facilities. In 1960, the Port of Los Angeles launched a five-year, $37 million development program (with a second $14 million revenue bond issued in 1962) to build needed facilities for full-scale container operations. In the same year, Matson Navigation Company began full container service. L.A. officials also focused on attracting Pacific Rim trade. In 1962, Mayor Yorty headed a trade mission (including port and airport commissioners and the port's public relations director) to Taipei, Hong Kong, and Manila. The next year, nearly three hundred foreign VIPs visited the port to learn about its market potential. In the late 1960s, L.A. signed trade agreements with eight Japanese prefectures. Soon, a host of Japanese container lines had inaugurated service at the L.A. port.[22]

The Port of Long Beach aggressively competed with Los Angeles for container traffic. Although he was ever mindful of the Navy's value, port manager Amar's chief priority was "an aggressive campaign to win business" for the port. The Harbor Department invested much of its available oil revenues into building state-of-the-art commercial facilities. As one close observer noted: "The emphasis on modern construction was a key factor in the rapid growth of Long Beach in the 1960s, when the facilities were in place to handle soaring traffic and total cargo tonnage quadrupled in a single decade."[23]

In 1962, Long Beach began construction on the world's then-largest landfill expansion—the 310-acre Piers J and F container facilities. In the same year, SeaLand Services began container operations in Long Beach, opening its own terminal three years later. In the 1970s, firms such as International Transportation Services and the Maersk Line inaugurated Long Beach container service. Later, South Korea's Hanjin Container Lines initiated service between Long Beach and Asia. In an ironic twist, Hanjin's fifty-seven-acre container terminal would be built on the Pier C site of the defunct Procter & Gamble plant. Thus, the port's earlier industrialization strategy was supplanted by a commercial strategy focusing on Pacific Rim trade. The two ports also aggressively competed for noncontainer trade, such as automobile imports.[24]

Debt free until 1970, Long Beach also sought to lure L.A. business away with lower prices. As Michael Denning and David Olson argue in their comparative study of West Coast ports, the smaller port pursued a "developmental operating strategy." "As long as Long Beach remained inferior to Los Angeles [in container units and tonnage], it actively sought to capture cargo away from its rival as well as increase its share of new cargo by steeply underpricing its terminals under long-term leases. Its pricing behavior in turn fueled the rivalry." [25] Long Beach's low-bid strategy paid off handsomely. In 1965, L.A. handled nearly twice the revenue tonnage of Long Beach—25.1 versus 13.6 million tons. By 1971, however, Long Beach had achieved near parity, handling 26.1 million tons compared with L.A.'s incremental growth to 27.2 million tons. Later, Long Beach surpassed its rival in cargo tonnage and container shipments.

Competition between the two ports was fierce. If one discovered that the other's tenants were the least bit dissatisfied with services, facilities, or fees, it would assiduously woo them. The battle went public when a Long Beach newspaper accused the Port of Los Angeles of gross mismanagement by supposedly hiding revenue losses and showing favoritism in awarding contracts. Los Angeles sarcastically replied that Long Beach's phenomenal progress was due mainly to the steady infusion of oil money rather than honest effort. L.A. also sharply condemned its rival's allegedly cutthroat pricing practices.[26]

The L.A. Harbor Department also was forced to keep a wary eye on the machinations of City Hall. As the West Coast leader in postwar maritime traffic and profitability, the port had soaring revenues and was thus an attractive target. City officials had long been interested in port profitability, especially at budget time. When they sought to siphon off port revenue to bolster the city's general fund, port officials protested vehemently, insisting on the need to finance massive container-age improvements. Under pressure from city officials, however, the port was forced to make concessions. It agreed to repay the city for fire protection and law enforcement on harbor property.[27] In the mid-1990s, the L.A. port's financial tug-of-war with City Hall would dramatically escalate.

L.A. saw profit in port cooperation. In 1964, Mayor Yorty revived the long-dormant port-consolidation proposal. He argued that "they should be made one harbor; it's ridiculous to compete with each other when they're right next door, but of course Long Beach had that oil revenue and we didn't have that, so they were really unfair competition."[28] Although Long Beach's mayor also supported the plan, consolidation was vetoed by the BOHC and the city council. As Long Beach councilman Raymond Keeler sarcastically observed: "This is just another effort by Los Angeles to get oil money to develop THAT PORT."[29]

By the 1970s, however, the financial positions of the two ports had equalized. After 1965, the Long Beach port no longer had oil revenues and had to rely on tariff, wharfage, and terminal fees. In 1968, Long Beach secured revenue-bonding authority (which Los Angeles had enjoyed for nearly a decade). The ports now competed in different ways. As Long Beach port manager Thomas Thorley observed: "The two ports utilize the same breakwater, the same railway systems, the same highway system, the same labor pool, and their tariffs are identical. The only thing either port has to offer over the other port is service. The result of this competition is a port system that some shippers rate as the most efficient in the nation."[30]

Yet the Port of Los Angeles found itself at growing competitive disadvantage. In the 1970s, it was forced to address a chronic problem: a shallow harbor that cost the port millions of dollars in lost shipping. Nearly fifty years had passed since the harbor had been dredged to thirty-five feet. Now, container vessels and other ships required much deeper drafts. More than one-third of the world's new container fleet was unable to enter the main channel; an even greater percentage of petroleum and chemical carriers was turned away. It made little sense for the L.A. port to construct container cranes and terminals if ships could not reach them. Working closely with port and city officials, San Pedro Congressman Glenn Anderson led a prolonged campaign for federal funding, eventually securing $36 million to dredge the harbor to forty-five feet. In 1981, after ten years of funding, permit, and approval delays, dredging finally began. In 1983, a deepened L.A. harbor was opened to hundreds of huge new container ships.[31]

Long Beach had no such problem. Subsidence unexpectedly had created a deep-water harbor, made to order for the newer, bigger ships. Further dredging deepened the Long Beach port to sixty feet and thereby made it one of the country's deepest harbors, a ready alternative for the ship traffic that Los Angeles could not take. In the 1970s, Long Beach port officials pressed their advantage. For example, Long Beach secured $30 million in new revenue-bond financing to build three new container terminals and a new container freight station and to expand operations. Completed in 1975, this new container complex had ten berths and twelve cranes. Long Beach then added a hundred-acre site for SeaLand and a fifty-one-acre site for K-Line, its two largest container shippers.[32]

For both ports, an unexpected trade bonanza resulted from diversion of Pacific Rim cargo from the Panama Canal. Cargo could be offloaded at West Coast ports and shipped by rail to U.S. destinations. This "land-bridge" system also connected the San Pedro ports to East Coast ports, where cargoes could be reloaded on vessels for European destinations. Far East shippers favored this route because of the Panama Canal's rising rates, growing political unrest, delays in passage, and, importantly, limited width. An estimated 90 percent of Pacific Rim cargo traveling to East and Gulf Coast ports and beyond eventually would be shipped via land bridges through West Coast ports. By 1980, Los Angeles harbor was processing more than 150,000 containers per year in diverted Panama Canal traffic, a significant share of its then-annual traffic of 657,000-TEU containers.[33]

Into the late 1970s, the Los Angeles/Long Beach rivalry for the nearly 50 percent of West Coast maritime traffic coming through San Pedro Bay continued unabated. Yet port financial strategies were changing. In the mid-1970s, in response to both City Hall pressures for larger payments and new market opportunities, L.A. shifted from a remunerative scheme to a monopolistic pricing system to maximize port revenues. L.A. immediately lost business to lower-priced Long Beach. As a result, by 1980 Los Angeles moved less cargo than Long Beach but led all U.S. ports in profits because of higher freight charges, terminal rents, docking fees, and charges for harbor pilots. Long Beach led in total tonnage on the West Cost with its large, low-value bulk shipments and lower-cost long-term agreements with shippers moving high-value cargo.[34]

As a result of its great trade spurt in the late 1960s and the 1970s, Long Beach finally overcame its historic also-ran status vis-à-vis Los Angeles. Yet, with terminal space at a premium and inflation rising, Long Beach's low-cost, fixed leasing and pricing agreements became counterproductive. Thus, in the late 1980s, Long Beach overhauled its leasing policy. Under the leadership of Harbor Commissioner Hauser, the port adopted a more market-sensitive revenue-sharing pricing system, which allowed the port to finance nearly three-quarters of a billion dollars of capital projects. The phenomenal postwar development of the Port of Long Beach was not a matter of happenstance. It had been carefully orchestrated by innovative, long-serving port managers Amar (1940–58), Charles Vickers (1958–64), Thomas Thorley (1964–77), James McJunkin (1977–88), and Steven Dillenbeck (1991–97). By modernizing port planning, development, and finance, they made Long Beach competitive with L.A.[35]

The two ports also actively searched for new trading partners and markets. In 1972, Los Angeles launched a series of trade-development missions all over the world. The next year, L.A.'s trade efforts were given a significant boost with the election of Mayor Bradley, who claimed that he intuitively foresaw L.A.'s global future: "It was something that was just so clear to me that I never questioned it, the development of this city as a gateway city for the Pacific Rim. It's obvious you have to do everything you can to try to build our trade between this community, Southern California, and the United States—flowing through the city of Los Angeles to the rest of the world." [36]

In 1974–75, with the new mayor's blessing, the L.A. port signed trade agreements and conducted trade missions to Japan, Hong Kong, and Taiwan. The next year, the Taiwan-based Evergreen Line established container operations at the port. In 1976, L.A. port officials embarked on a seven-country trade mission, including Australia and Europe. Three years later, the port conducted the first-ever trade mission to Mainland China as relations normalized. In 1982–83, trade missions were sent to Australia, New Zealand, the nations of the Association of Southeast Asian Nations (ASEAN), Europe, Israel, Yugoslavia, and Greece. Not to be outdone, the Port of Long Beach in 1980 sent its own trade mission to China. These efforts quickly paid off. In 1981, when China Ocean Shipping Co. inaugurated international shipping, Long Beach was its first U.S. port of call. In 1982, Long Beach opened its own foreign trade zone, allowing "duty-free manufacturing, storage, repair, testing, exhibition, assembly and labeling of products for U.S. consumption or re-export." [37]

The 1980s: Port Cooperation

Although historically the Los Angeles and Long Beach ports had been fierce rivals, cooperation began replacing competition by the early 1980s as the two ports achieved near parity in container units and tonnage. Booming Pacific Rim container trade left them facing similar developmental constraints, including little available land for port expansion; growing rail bottlenecks between the ports and the downtown railheads; and severe truck congestion in the harbor area. Shared problems encouraged joint solutions. [38]

The centerpiece of joint port action was the ambitious 2020 Plan, designed to solve land, terminal, and transportation problems well into the twenty-first century. In 1985 the Army Corps of Engineers launched a long-term planning effort with the two ports to create the largest integrated marine-highway-rail transportation hub in the world. The 2020 program was designed to develop new facilities that would meet a projected 250 percent cargo tonnage increase from 1990 to 2020. At an estimated cost of $4.8 billion, the plan was the nation's most ambitious port-development program. The fate of this mega-project is examined in detail in Chapter Five.

In the 1980s, the two ports also cooperated on major rail-access initiatives. With the container revolution, railroads became critical linchpins in the global transportation system. Panamax and post-Panamax cargo ships—those too large to pass through the Panama Canal—called on fewer ports and relied on rail transport to distribute cargo to inland and transcontinental destinations. By the 1990s, railroads handled one-quarter of total U.S. trade. Nowhere was this truer than for the San Pedro Bay ports—the leading U.S. transshipment center for Pacific Rim imports. By the early 1990s, railroads shipped more than 40 percent of San Pedro Bay imports to eastern and Gulf Coast destinations such as Chicago, Houston, and New York. A growing rail bottleneck loomed as the major challenge to L.A./Long Beach port development.[39]

Opened in 1987, a $70 million intermodal container transfer facility (ICTF), a joint venture of the two ports and the then-Southern Pacific railroad, was designed to reduce container-truck traffic between the ports and the downtown rail yards. At the 150-acre ICTF facility, cargo containers were transferred from trucks to trains, eliminating more than eight hundred thousand annual truck trips on the crowded L.A. freeway system. Starting in the mid-1980s, the two ports also developed on-dock rail facilities within their shipping terminals to further ease highway congestion.[40]

The other major cooperative rail initiative was the $2.4 billion Alameda Corridor project, the nation's largest intermodal project. The project's origins could be traced back to 1981, when the Southern California Association of Governments (SCAG) created a Port Advisory Committee and commissioned a series of port/rail–access studies. In 1989, the cities of Los Angeles and Long Beach agreed to set up a consolidated rail-corridor authority—now called the Alameda Corridor Transportation Authority—for project financing and construction. With port train traffic projected to more than triple between 1991 and 2020, the mega-project would consolidate over ninety miles of rail lines intersected by two hundred at-grade road crossings into a single, uninterrupted, twenty-mile, high-speed, grade-separated rail system linking the ports with the transcontinental rail yards located near downtown Los Angeles. Chapter Six examines the Alameda Corridor project's bumpy ride in the 1990s, when it was confronted with such challenges as lack of funding and port/community conflicts.[41]

While cooperating on port-development and rail-access projects, the San Pedro Bay ports in the 1980s continued to compete aggressively for cargo. In the 1970s, a still-shallow harbor and high prices had hurt L.A. and allowed its rival to soar ahead. By the mid-1980s, however, as crowded Long Beach was forced to raise its prices to pay for needed space, Los Angeles began closing the gap; it was aided by a massive, ten-year, $405 million capital-improvement plan. Between 1983 and 1993, a no-longer handicapped L.A. port increased its share of total tonnage through San Pedro Bay from 38 percent to 45 percent; L.A.'s share of cargo dollar value rose even higher, from 44 percent to 53 percent. Los Angeles also maintained its lead in the all-important container market. By 1993, L.A. was handling 2.3 million TEUs compared with Long Beach's 2.1 million.[42]

Relative to their West Coast rivals, the San Pedro Bay ports increasingly behaved as a duopoly seeking to capture the lion's share of Pacific Rim trade, particularly for containers. The duo enjoyed decided market advantages over competitors such as the ports of Oakland, Portland, and Seattle. First, their huge economic hinterland provided an enormous captive market. Second, with the best transcontinental rail connections on the West Coast, the two ports captured discretionary traffic being shipped eastward. By 1993, the San Pedro Bay ports had a 56 percent share of the West Coast Asian-import and container markets. This traffic, in turn, generated the enormous port revenue streams that would underwrite the 2020 Plan, which was designed to expand the ports' market share even further.[43]

Burgeoning Pacific Rim trade through San Pedro Bay had a strong stimulative effect on the region's economy. In the early 1970s, 220,000 area jobs were directly or indirectly dependent on trade through the two ports, which pumped $6.5 billion annually into the regional economy. By 1987, the number of port-dependent jobs had grown to 363,000; the ports now contributed $39 billion (a 10 percent overall share) to the region's economy. The ports, along with LAX, had become leading drivers of the region's economy and its transformation into a major trade center. These calculations of economic impacts, required since the early 1970s by federal and state environmental reviews, would be skillfully used by port officials in the 1990s to build public support as they encountered community and environmental opposition to the nation's most ambitious port-development plan.[44]

From Mines Field to LAX

Federal Catalyst

L.A.'s municipal-airport aspirations languished during the Depression years as Mines Field failed to develop into a major commercial facility. Ultimately, federal assistance would be needed here too. Early on, its facilities were cramped and inadequate, and airlines refused to relocate from private airports such as Burbank and Glendale until improvements were made. By the mid-1930s, however, the carriers started recognizing Mines Field's long-term value and began pressuring city officials for an upgrade.[45] Airport officials used the airlines' new-found support to pressure City Hall for expansion. In 1937, Ray Jones, then director of public relations for the newly constituted Los Angeles Department of Airports (LADOA), told city officials and the public that the airport had not solicited the airlines but rather that the "airlines themselves have urged the City to develop the field so that it would be available for transport operations."[46] Thereafter, airport officials would highlight airline demand and market forces in campaigns to improve and expand their facilities.

Expansion, though, faced major stumbling blocks. The Great Depression had sent city finances plummeting. Although L.A. Mayor Frank Shaw was a strong airport supporter, he had little authority over the facility. A tight-fisted city council, which oversaw the airport and its finances, refused to commit moneys from the general fund for a money-losing "white elephant." Hard times, an apathetic electorate, and fierce opposition from competing private airport operators made it difficult to construct the voter supermajorities needed to approve general-obligation bonds. As a result, Mines Field remained largely unimproved and relegated to use by private aircraft, flying schools, and repair services. Yet, foreshadowing its future role as economic catalyst, the struggling airport helped attract aircraft-manufacturing firms such as Northrop, Douglas, and North American Aviation. With a skilled, nonunion labor force and inexpensive land also available, all three firms located nearby, from Santa Monica to Long Beach. By 1940, Southern California was home to nearly half of the nation's airframe-manufacturing facilities.[47]

Given the unavailability of local funding, Los Angeles turned to the federal government. In an early victory for private interests over supporters of municipal ownership, the 1926 Air Commerce Act had forbidden the use of federal funds for local airport development. But the Depression and a new Democratic administration caused a policy change: federal airport assistance would be offered as work-relief. In 1935, L.A. received $558,000 from the federal Emergency Relief Administration to hire unemployed workers to begin the upgrade of Mines Field. Congress then transferred control of all airport funding to the Works Progress Administration (WPA), headed by Harry Hopkins. When Los Angeles asked the WPA for $1.2 million in airport-development funds, Hopkins denied the request, notwithstanding the lobbying efforts of Mayor Shaw. As one close observer noted: "The City's original bid for Works Progress Administration funds received the O.K. from everybody in Washington except one individual, and that person happened to be the Hon. Harry Hopkins, in whose hands repose[d] the strings that either loosen or tighten the aperture to the sock in which the Works Progress Administration funds are on deposit. Mr. Hopkins said 'no dice' because at that time the City did not own title to the land on which its airport is located."[48]

City officials decided to buy the site after Hopkins assured them that federal funds would be forthcoming on purchase. In 1937, Los Angeles bought 623 acres for $2.7 million, saving $3 million over the life of the lease. WPA funds were used to build three-hundred-foot-wide east-west runways, sewers, and waterlines, and to provide grading and drainage. As a result, TWA and American Airlines agreed to leases covering much of the city's annual purchase payments. By 1938, TWA, United Airlines, American Airlines, and Western Air Express had signed long-term leases for permanent relocation pending completion of improvements, much to the dismay of Burbank and Glendale airport officials.[49]

Because of ever-tightening WPA budgets, L.A. received only limited federal assistance and thus was forced to place general-obligation bonds before

Depression-weary voters to cover the remaining costs. When a $3 million bond issue failed to capture the necessary two-thirds vote in 1939, a broad-based pro-airport coalition composed of civic, business, and labor organizations redoubled its efforts. In May 1941, voters approved a $3.5 million airport-improvement bond. Yet plans for a new terminal building soon were placed on hold as the United States went to war. With expansion delayed and the major air carriers still operating out of other airports, Los Angeles entered the 1940s seriously lagging behind other major cities in municipal-airport development.[50]

In early 1942, the federal government took over wartime control of Los Angeles Municipal Airport, assuming responsibility for tower operations, installing an instrument landing system, and making needed structural improvements. In all, Washington heavily subsidized the early development of LAX. Between 1935 and 1950, the federal government paid half of the airport's total construction costs. During the war, thousands of military aircraft were built at plants at or near the airfield. For example, the North American P-51 Mustang was assembled here. These wartime facilities formed the template for a massive postwar aerospace military/industrial complex that by 1960 accounted directly or indirectly for one-third of the region's employment. It also spawned a host of nearby "model communities" for factory workers. One such planned residential community was Westchester, built adjacent to L.A.'s airport. Although it may have been desirable wartime policy (with gas rationing) to locate workers' homes within walking distance of factories, the practice would later produce fierce community conflicts at LAX over jet noise and airport expansion.[51]

Planning and Governance Innovations

At war's end, control over the airfield passed back to L.A.'s Department of Airports. LADOA's first "postwar" Master Plan (actually released in 1944) was geared toward convincing the major airlines to relocate to L.A. Municipal. The plan provided for intermediate facilities while promising long-term improvements. Finally, in 1946, the four major airlines that had signed leases in 1938 relocated from Burbank Airport. Newcomer Pacific Southwest Airlines also began service, and Pan American followed shortly thereafter. Of the region's airports, L.A. Municipal had the space to accommodate larger planes, more cargo, and future expansion.[52]

During the war, the use of large, multi-engine aircraft exposed the inadequacy of LADOA's prewar planning, which had been based on then-smaller airplanes. Because development was delayed, L.A. Municipal Airport inadvertently avoided a problem that affected most other cities' airports—facilities made obsolete by technological advances. Instead, when permanent improvements were finally completed in the 1950s, they made the airport far more modern, comprehensive, and future-oriented than other airports. These changes would give Los Angeles International Airport (renamed in 1949) a major competitive advantage.[53]

The 1953 LAX Master Plan (and 1956 jet-oriented redesign) offered a highly innovative approach. LADOA officials hired the architectural/engineering firm of Pereira/Luckman to prepare a master plan and schematics for a new terminal building. Going against the conventional wisdom, Pereira/Luckman proposed a terminal featuring "a decentralized design with individual ticketing and satellite units, constructed on two levels." When larger planes and jets arrived in the early 1960s, LAX's futuristic design allowed the airport to integrate them without the major alterations other airports were forced to undergo. In 1959, LAX inaugurated the jet age with the nation's first jet passenger flight. Two-and-a-half years later, and over twenty years after initial long-term plans had been drawn up by LADOA, then-Vice-President Lyndon Johnson dedicated the new $70 million jet-age terminal.[54]

A postwar change in airport governance facilitated LAX's capacity for long-range planning and development. Initially, the city council had overseen airport matters. The airport manager reported to the council's Finance Committee, which controlled the airport fund as part of the general-fund budget. Yet there were strong incentives for delegation. The growing complexity of airport operations and financing made council oversight cumbersome and time consuming. Early on, the struggling facility represented a drain on the city's general fund; it did not turn a profit until 1952. Further, L.A.'s district election system (1925) encouraged localistic concerns; only councilpersons representing Westchester (LAX) and Van Nuys (after L.A. acquired the San Fernando Valley airport) focused on airport matters.

As a result, the city council began delegating responsibility. In 1940, it created the Board of Municipal Airport Commissioners (BMAC) to oversee the city's airport. Although the BMAC was still nominally under council control as an ordinance-created (rather than charter) department, the three members (expanded to five in 1943) were mayoral appointees, subject to council confirmation. The BMAC ran political interference for both the mayor and the city council, where airport oversight had been shifted to the Industry and Transportation Committee.[55]

Airport officials spearheaded a drive for greater political autonomy. In 1941, they proposed turning LADOA into a semi-autonomous proprietary department similar to the Department of Water and Power and the Harbor Department. As one close observer noted, in the system created in 1940, "although relations b/w [between] the Board . . . , the Mayor, and the City Council were most cooperative, it was still a cumbersome organization. . . . It became more and more evident to all parties concerned that a so called self controlling department should be established by amending the City Charter."[56] In May 1945, momentum for semi-independent status grew when voters overwhelmingly passed a $12.5 million bond issue to extend existing runways, build new facilities, and purchase additional land. Given the challenges of planning a postwar major expansion program, public officials saw the benefit of conferring proprietary status on the LADOA. Public support for the other two proprietary departments strengthened the airport's case for equivalent status.

Critical to the independence drive was the mayor's blessing. Mayor Fletcher Bowron (1938–53) initially was opposed to municipal ownership of utilities and was disinclined to support airport development. Yet airport officials converted him into a strong supporter. In the 1945 airport-bond campaign, Bowron made airport expansion central to warding off San Francisco and San Diego competition. In early 1947, the mayor recommended to the city council that LADOA be given proprietary status; later that year, voters approved a charter amendment to that effect. The proposal was supported by the business community as an efficiency measure and by the airlines as a way to keep airport revenue separate from the city's budget. As a result, LADOA was given greater governance and financial independence.[57]

Although LADOA now had significant control over its day-to-day operations, airport officials still had to go to voters to pass general-obligation bond issues requiring two-thirds approval. The supermajority requirement delayed airport expansion. Table 4.3 displays L.A. airport bond and charter-amendment votes from 1933 to 1992. All twenty airport-related charter amendments passed; for these only a simple majority vote was needed. In contrast, airport supporters were successful in only three of six bond elections. Major airport bond issues lost in 1939, 1951, and 1953, despite the support of civic, business, and labor leaders. Thus, the 1939 $3 million bond proposal was defeated notwithstanding the support of city officials, the federal government, the *Los Angeles Times*, the airlines, and real estate groups. The 1951 and 1953 bonds lost in part because of San Fernando Valley opposition and because of growing concerns over regional burden sharing. Why should city taxpayers build and pay for a facility that benefited the entire metropolitan area? Although the losing bonds garnered voter majorities, they failed to attract the necessary two-thirds vote.

In 1956, civic and business leaders mounted a major campaign to pass a $59.7 million bond issue to build the Master Plan's proposed jet-age airport. Airport commissioner Don Belding, a public relations executive appointed by Mayor Norris Poulson (1953–61), masterminded the effort. Belding tapped realtor Charles Detoy, former president of the L.A. Chamber of Commerce, to head the bond drive. Detoy and his business associates raised several hundred thousand dollars for the effort.[58]

Belding's well-financed campaign skillfully played on local fears of national and international competition from San Francisco's new terminal and held out the added inducement of $20 million in federal matching funds (only

$12 million of which would materialize). To persuade skeptical Valley voters, an upgrade of Van Nuys airport, acquired by LADOA in 1949, was promised. Belding's efforts were aided by a companion ballot proposition that dedicated all future airport revenue surpluses to paying off the new bonds. Labor unions, taxpayers' groups, and numerous business organizations endorsed both ballot propositions. Three hundred fifty civic leaders formed the Global Air Harbor Committee to support the measures. Supporters pointed to LADOA's healthy bottom line. (The airport had shown a profit since 1952 and contributed nearly $1 million to the city's general fund from 1951 to 1957.) As Table 4.3 shows, in the May 1956 election both measures passed overwhelmingly.[59]

Airport management provided critical leadership on issues of financial independence, LAX expansion, regionalization, and global air service under visionary and entrepreneurial General Managers Francis Fox (1959–68) and Clifton Moore (1968–93), Fox's handpicked successor. In the early 1960s, Fox led the successful battle for airport financial self-sufficiency, much like that enjoyed by the Harbor Department and the Department of Water and Power. In 1963, voters approved a city-charter amendment allowing LADOA to issue revenue bonds to fund major improvements. Fox favored revenue bonds because they allowed profits to be plowed directly back into capital programs, and they were more equitable than taxation. In 1967, Fox reached a historic agreement with the airlines serving LAX to raise landing fees to pay future revenue bonds. He also developed a close working relationship with the Federal Aviation Administration (FAA) and played a key role in Najeeb Halaby's appointment as FAA head during the Kennedy years. As Fox later wryly noted, his friend Halaby "gave us his blessing with a lot of federal aid in those years." [60] Yet, from the late 1960s to the early 1990s, a series of voter-approved charter amendments subjected LADOA and its able managers, much like the Harbor Department and its managers, to increased oversight by the mayor and city council.

LAX Expansion Battles

Airport financial independence would have an unforeseen impact on the relationship between LAX and surrounding communities. Because the airport no longer needed voter approval for major capital programs, officials felt less need to educate citizens about the benefits of airport expansion. The resulting atrophy of community outreach would come back to haunt airport officials.[61]

The turbulent 1960s severely tested the relationship between LAX and its neighbors. Accelerating air traffic growth at LAX set the stage for a new master-planning effort for airport development that would produce fierce community opposition. Between 1950 and 1960, LAX passenger traffic increased nearly 400 percent, from 1.4 million annual passengers (MAP) to

Table 4.3 The Los Angeles Airports and the Ballot Box: Bond and Charter-Amendment Votes, 1933–1992

Date (month/year)	Election Type[a]	Purpose or Amount (Type)	Outcome	Yes Vote (%)	Total Vote	Turnout (%)	Registered Voters
05/1939	General	$3,000,000 (Bond)	Not Passed	59.9	261,671	38.0	689,326
12/1939	Special	Revenue bonds (Amendment)	Passed	59.8	272,539	32.7	832,257
05/1941	General	$3,500,000 (Bond)	Passed	71.6	274,813	N/A	N/A
05/1941	General	Airport revenues (Amendment)	Passed	67.2	235,507	N/A	N/A
05/1945	General	$12,500,0000 (Bond)	Passed	82.9	353,749	41.5	852,255
04/1947	Primary	Department established in charter (Amendment)	Passed	63.8	241,422	33.8	714,715
05/1951	General	$14,500,000 (Bond)	Not Passed	62.1	252,320	32.0	N/A
05/1951	General	Department authority (Amendment)	Passed	51.6	232,741	32.0	N/A
05/1953	General	$33,255,000 (Bond)	Not Passed	59.5	474,524	N/A	N/A
06/1956	State primary	$59,700,000 (Bond)	Passed	85.6	540,868	N/A	N/A
06/1956	State primary	General-obligation bonds to be paid from airport revenues (Amendment)	Passed	87.8	540,107	N/A	N/A
04/1963	Primary	Revenue bonds and efficiency survey (Amendment)	Passed	71.2	337,580	N/A	N/A
04/1969	Primary	Council oversight strengthened (Amendment)	Passed	50.9	509,012	46.1	1,104,787
06/1970	State primary	Airport revenue bonds conform to harbor and DWP model (Amendment)	Passed	62.0	577,810	N/A	N/A
05/1973	General	Limits on contracts over specified amounts of time and money (Amendment)	Passed	58.4	589,520	48.5	1,216,173
05/1973	General	Proprietary-department management (Amendment)	Passed	77.6	606,983	49.9	1,216,173

11/1976	State general	Council two-thirds vote required for approval of specified leases (Amendment)	Passed	63.2	745,969	N/A	N/A
05/1977	General	Contract approval authority for general manager (Amendment)	Passed	57.1	281,104	23.9	1,174,985
05/1977	General	Council control of salaries (Amendment)	Passed	65.1	284,146	24.2	1,174,985
04/1983	Primary	Airport property-leasing authority (Amendment)	Passed	76.0	253,977	20.3	1,253,403
11/1984	State general	Airport funds investment (Amendment)	Passed	79.2	825,589	57.9	1,426,826
04/1991	Primary	Council approval of leases of specified times and amounts (Amendment)	Passed	72.2	192,166	15.1	1,270,050
06/1991	General	City anti-apartheid policy applies to contracts (Amendment)	Passed	59.8	204,444	16.6	1,233,919
06/1991	General	Prop. 5: Council review and veto power over all board decisions (Amendment)	Passed	59.3	211,009	17.1	1,233,919
06/1992	State primary	Local and domestic contract bidding preferences (Amendment)	Passed	55.1	513,466	40.9	1,255,774
11/1992	State general	Authority for transfer from airport revenue fund to general fund (Amendment)	Passed	50.4	886,022	63.6	1,393,951

SOURCES: Data from Los Angeles City Clerk, Records of Election Returns, vol. 5, Dec. 8, 1936–Nov. 5, 1940; Records of Election Returns, vol. 6, Apr. 1, 1941–May 10, 1943; Charter Amendments 1961–1997, LACA, 1997; City of Los Angeles Voter Registration and Turnout for Mayor, City Attorney, and Controller for 1961 through 1997; City of Los Angeles Voter Registration and Turnout All Regularly Scheduled Elections, 1977–1997; Los Angeles Times, election-day published registration statistics, post-election published turnout statistics; Los Angeles City Charter, 1925.
ᵃMunicipal Election unless otherwise specified.

6.6 MAP, while air cargo grew 240 percent, from 21.7 million tons to 73.8 million tons. During the 1960s, the number of LAX passengers grew over 200 percent, to 20.8 MAP, while air cargo ballooned 461 percent, to 414 million tons.[62]

LAX also was being reconfigured as an international airport. The first regular trans-Pacific service (Pan Am) was inaugurated in 1946. Soon thereafter, Mexicana became the airport's second international airline. In 1956, polar service to Europe was inaugurated. Three years later, commercial jet service began. In the early 1960s, runway 25L was extended to twelve thousand feet, and the first jet-age terminal was dedicated. By 1970 twenty-two international airlines were serving LAX.

In 1965, William Pereira & Associates was retained to develop a new master plan, which was approved in 1967. LADOA General Manager Fox outlined the plan's key elements: "To realize the recommended airport potential and the clearly indicated future operational requirements, the two north runways must be developed. These runways are an essential part of our original master plan programmed in 1944. Current voluntary restrictions against jet landings and takeoffs must eventually be removed to permit full and effective implementation of our approved master plan. . . . Runway expansion will require additional clear zone acquisition."[63]

Mayor Yorty threw his full support behind the plan, claiming "funds for the half billion dollar expansion program will come from airport revenues and the sale of airport revenue bonds." As LADOA began adding new runways and more terminals, it sought to reestablish a buffer zone around the airport and began acquiring residential housing bordering on the west and north. Although LAX viewed this expansion as a needed noise-reduction program that required condemnation and purchase of 2,834 parcels of adjoining land totaling 579 acres for $142 million, local residents saw it as the wholesale and forcible destruction of their communities. In what became a defining moment, residents were angered when they lost three schools in addition to block after block of neighborhoods bordering the ocean. Thousands of residents were displaced by the airport's massive land-acquisition program. Airport official Fox later recalled these disruptions as "the most painful thing I felt in my years at LAX."[64]

Jet noise was a potent contributing factor to deteriorating airport/community relations. For Fox, the problem was "the most vexing in my ten years at LADOA—at times it seemed unsolvable." In neighboring communities such as Westchester, Playa Del Rey, and Inglewood, protests over jet noise levels resulted in the creation of a host of grassroots anti-airport organizations: the Greater Westchester Homeowners Association, the Airport Area Action Committee, and Inglewood's Stop the Overhead Planes. It also led to the airport-sponsored formation of the Los Angeles Sound Abatement Coordination Committee, a technically oriented task force comprised mostly of air-industry representatives. Significantly, the committee made no provision for public participation or membership. (In the mid-1990s, this pattern of community mobilization and ineffective airport response would be replayed over the LAX Master Plan.)[65]

Because airport opponents could no longer halt expansion through the ballot box by denying funding for capital improvements, affected residents turned to the legal system, relying on recently passed state and federal environmental legislation. Lawsuits stemming from runway expansion cost the airport nearly $150 million and gave LAX the dubious distinction of being the nation's most litigated airport. In 1971, the courts overturned the 1967 Master Plan, ruling that it could not be implemented until deficiencies had been corrected in its Environmental Impact Statement (EIS).

As a result, a new LAX master plan was developed in 1971–72 under the leadership of Clifton Moore. It recommended a limit of forty million annual passengers by 1990. (This limit was exceeded in 1986, as passenger traffic grew from thirty-three MAP in 1980 to forty-six MAP in 1990). In 1978, the Board of Airport Commissioners approved a $500 million expansion program that included double-decking the central-terminal roadway system. Two years later, an interim plan (with an additional $250 million outlay) designed to meet Olympic hosting needs was approved. Although this interim plan was considered part of the existing master plan, it called for yet another long-term master plan to address issues of capacity, ground access, noise, and environmental factors.[66]

In the late 1980s, a new long-range planning effort began but soon was delayed by political infighting between the mayor and the councilperson representing LAX and surrounding communities. Only in 1993, with the election of new Mayor Richard Riordan (who had campaigned on the promise of privatizing LAX but dropped the idea after assuming office), was the master-plan process finally restarted. The new LAX Master Plan raised significant issues concerning regional development and equity, environmental justice and degradation, and L.A.'s global future. The fierce battles over LAX during the administrations of Mayors Riordan (1993–2001) and James Hahn (elected in 2001) are detailed in Chapters Seven and Eight.

Going Regional/Going Global

Airport managers Fox and Moore also led efforts to create a regional airport system and (with strong support from Mayor Bradley) to transform LAX into one of the world's great international airports. As early as 1940, the Los Angeles County Regional Planning Commission had recommended a regional approach.[67] In the postwar era, though, LADOA appeared to preempt the regionalization impulse by acquiring new airports at Van Nuys, Ontario, and Palmdale. Long derided for its "water imperialism," Los Angeles, critics charged, practiced "airport imperialism" as well.

In 1949, LADOA purchased Van Nuys Airport from the U.S. War Assets Board for one dollar. In 1960, LADOA tried to encourage regional airport planning by endorsing the Regional Airport Study Commission, which included representatives from nine Southern California counties. In 1964, the group published a report recommending the creation of a single regionwide agency or, alternatively, a county-based system to achieve economies of scale and effective regional planning. When that proposal failed, airport officials decided to transform LADOA into a de facto regional airport authority. Their blueprint, codified in the defunct 1967 Master Plan, had LAX serving as the hub airport and other L.A. municipal airports serving as satellite facilities.[68]

During the 1960s LAX passenger traffic grew geometrically—16 percent per year—while air-cargo growth was even greater. Airport officials feared that LAX, even with expansion, might not be able to handle the load. Thus, they sought reliever airports. In addition, LAX's growing mix of commercial and general aviation created safety problems. As a result, Van Nuys was developed as a general-aviation airport. As Fox argued, "We had to get the little birds out of the way of the big ones."[69] A major incentive for private pilots to relocate was that Van Nuys, unlike LAX, had no landing fees. LAX traffic pressure also led to a lengthy search for new commercial airport facilities. In 1967, Los Angeles signed a joint-powers agreement with the City of Ontario for LADOA to operate Ontario Airport. (In 1985, L.A. acquired full title.) Mayor Yorty and the city council then approved issuance of $410 million in airport revenue bonds for additional development of L.A.'s regional system. As a result, the city acquired 17,500 acres in Palmdale for a future international airport to ultimately relieve LAX.[70]

The acquisition and planned development of Palmdale appears to have been the apex of the movement toward a regional airport system. Since then, efforts to foster greater regionalism have floundered. New federal and state environmental laws have been an important limiting factor. Anti-airport groups successfully used the National Environmental Policy Act, the Airport and Airways Development Act, and the California Environmental Quality Act to halt or delay expansion or at least substantially to raise the timelines and financial costs of airport expansion. Thus, a 1971 environmental lawsuit eventually halted federal assistance in Los Angeles's purchase of the Palmdale property.[71]

Since 1970 there have been two modest regionalization efforts. First, SCAG became the lead agency for regional airport planning (but not operation) in the metropolitan area. Although lacking taxation and land-use authority, SCAG provided a useful voluntary forum for elected officials in six Southland counties to debate regional airport issues. SCAG also excelled in technical studies, such as of regional air-cargo needs and the feasibility of military air-base conversion to commercial use. Second, at the urging of Executive Director Moore, LADOA in 1976 proposed the creation of a regional airport authority. Participation would be voluntary for existing airports; each facility could determine its own level of participation. In 1983 the Southern California Regional Airport Authority (SCRAA) was created with representatives from Los Angeles, Orange, San Bernardino, and Riverside counties. However, the initiative stalled when no other airport operator expressed interest. (SCRAA remained moribund until 1999, when L.A. County supervisors seeking leverage over the LAX Master Plan cynically resurrected it.)[72] The proposal also encountered opposition from local real estate and commercial interests. As airport designer William Pereira complained to Executive Director Moore:

ALL OF THE DISPUTES ARISE OVER LAND VALUES AND WHO GETS THE GRAVY, WHO LOSES OUT ON THE GRAVY. The "GRAVY" is found in those advantages inherent in the monopolizing of economic rent to land, capitalizing into values, and where tax is very light, into higher and higher prices. . . . I fear we will be spinning wheels within wheels, circumvented on all sides by interests so firmly vested that we cannot displace them.[73]

Thus, in large part, L.A.'s regional "pax aeronautica" was achieved by default.

Visionary manager Moore was much more successful in his efforts to transform LAX into one of the world's great international and air-cargo airports. For Moore, "cargo was kind of a main thing I hung my hat on, 'cause of the economic value added. . . . And it seems pretty clear that you . . . want to be identified as the principal fulcrum point of the Pacific Rim." Moore also devised ways to sell city officials on his vision: "So we started making cargo-promotion visits, where we would take the mayor and a couple of the commissioners and airline people and go to London and talk to the air-freight people. . . . In addition to having these cargo seminars, we would do sister airport relationships, like sister cities. We did one with Frankfurt because that was the big one for cargo. We did one with Korea."[74]

The airport director found a soul mate in the mayor: "Well, I'll say this for Tom Bradley. He was a real promoter of foreign trade. . . . He worked at it. [And] no question he was supportive of the airport."[75] Moore and Bradley worked especially closely together to build a new international terminal at LAX in preparation for L.A.'s hosting of the 1984 Olympic Games. As Bradley later recalled his role in this effort:

In fact, the international terminal at the airport was something which I recognized was important not only to that airport but to tourism. . . . And we were facing the Olympic Games coming to the city. . . . I was so persuaded that it was going to take a vigorous effort on our part that I either called or visited the airport every day just to see how the construction was going because I knew that if there was slippage anywhere we wouldn't make it. And we barely got in under the mark.[76]

In June 1984, just before the Olympics opened, the new Tom Bradley International Terminal was dedicated.

LAX had a major stimulative effect on the region's economy. In 1970, the airport pumped $3.3 billion into the Southern California economy, generating over one hundred thousand area jobs. By 1991, however, with mushrooming growth in international and air-cargo service, LAX claimed that it contributed $45 billion annually (in direct, indirect, and induced activity) to the region's economy (a 10 percent overall share), and created four hundred thousand jobs.[77] By 1992, LAX had become the world's fourth busiest airport, serving forty-seven MAP, up over 40 percent from 1980. Air cargo grew even faster, increasing 55 percent from 1980 to 1992, to nearly 1.4 million tons.[78] In the 1990s, in the increasingly acrimonious debate over LAX's future, supporters would stress the airport's role as a leading engine of regional development.

A New Environmental Regulatory Regime

The 1970s witnessed the creation of a new environmental regulatory regime that would profoundly affect the future of the region's global gateways. Key federal and state policies were the National Environmental Policy Act (NEPA) and the California Environmental Quality Act (CEQA); the federal Clean Air Act; and the California Coastal Initiative and California Coastal Act, which established the California Coastal Commission.

NEPA and CEQA

Both NEPA and CEQA were passed in 1970 with little fanfare or controversy. NEPA appeared to be an essentially procedural law that neither created a powerful new bureaucracy nor endowed existing agencies with new authority. This seemingly innocuous legislation committed the federal government to preserving the environment; but it required merely that federal agencies (or other entities under federal control or responsibility) undertaking environmentally sensitive projects assess their impacts via an Environmental Impact Statement (EIS). NEPA also created the Council on Environmental Quality (modeled after the Council of Economic Advisors) to develop guidelines and coordinate federal agencies. With similar language, CEQA was created as a mini-NEPA to govern California's public agencies. Declaring that the state must consider the environment in its decision-making process, CEQA merely required that state and local public agencies issue an Environmental Impact Report (EIR) as part of their project planning.[79]

The new laws vaguely prescribed a set of procedures that agencies had to follow to determine whether a given project was subject to an EIR/EIS and what issues a report needed to address (such as potential adverse environmental impacts); they also mandated a public-comment period. Yet the informational demand could be quite high. Under NEPA, agencies were required to provide a full list of mitigating measures and to determine "whether all practicable means to avoid or minimize environmental harm . . . have been adopted." However, there were no legal sanctions for failure to take mitigating actions as long as their lack of feasibility was explained. To date, the federal courts have not overturned agency mitigation decisions.[80]

Yet the courts soon became central participants in interpreting and implementing NEPA and CEQA. Because agency procedures and the contents of an EIR/EIS were not fully spelled out, the courts were called on to determine whether there was "full" and "reasonable" determination of the environmental issues and mitigation measures involved. While giving agencies needed flexibility, statutory ambiguity invited litigation. As John Ferejohn argues, such ambiguity may have been deliberate in that it allowed bureaucratic agencies to adjust their decision making on a case-by-case basis to reflect the changing balance of power between contending interests (the so-called "mirror principle").[81]

Nowhere has this ambiguity been more in evidence than with CEQA, which has become one of the most important forces shaping development in California. It has been aptly described as "something out of Alice in Wonderland—a paradoxical set of rules that is both more and less than it appears to be." CEQA was originally considered applicable only to actions taken directly by state or local governments. Yet in 1972 the California Supreme Court in the *Friends of Mammoth* case ruled that nearly all private development, because of state and local land-use regulations, was subject to CEQA. In the same year, the court asserted the right to review the sufficiency of CEQA compliance.[82]

For a growing number of critics, this was evidence that an out-of-control California state judiciary had overstepped its bounds. A blue-ribbon commission found CEQA a much-abused tool that encouraged individuals and groups to use "lawsuits to stall projects—not to protect the environment." The threat of blackmail became a growing concern, particularly with so-called "mitigated negative declarations," where adherence to specified conditions became the basis for not issuing a project an EIR/EIS.[83]

Because of their substantial environmental impacts and the deep pockets of sponsoring agencies, Los Angeles's mega-projects became inviting targets for neighborhood groups and environmentalists, who used the threat of EIR/EIS lawsuits. Both LAX master planning and regional-airport development (such as at Palmdale) soon were thwarted by environmental review. Because opponents also can delay projects (thus driving up completion costs), they can extract attractive side payments in exchange for foregoing legal action. For example, a 1972 environmental lawsuit against the Century Freeway project in Los Angeles resulted in both sizeable housing-replacement and job-training programs for affected residents. Of the project's record $2.2 billion cost (at $127 million per mile, more than any other freeway project in history), only half was spent on construction. Having transportation projects pay for social programs became a mantra for disaffected groups threatening to litigate L.A.'s other mega-projects.[84]

Federal Clean Air Act

The year 1970 also witnessed the passage of another federal environmental law that would affect L.A.'s global gateways and trade future. Congress in that year passed the federal Clean Air Act with the express purpose of attaining National Ambient Air Quality Standards (NAAQS) for "criteria air pollutants." These were defined as pollutants causing human health problems and included ozone, particulate matter, carbon monoxide, lead, nitrogen oxide, and sulfur oxide. The act originally called for NAAQS attainment by 1975. However, the act was amended in both 1977 and 1990, and deadlines were extended. Under the 1990 provisions, districts deemed to be in nonattainment of federal standards were given extensions based on the severity of the pollution. Southern California currently is the nation's only region deemed in extreme nonattainment. It is required to meet federal standards by 2010.[85] As Chapter Five details, the Clean Air Act would lead in the mid-1990s to a fierce battle that pitted federal regulators and environmental groups against the ports, shippers, and local business organizations.

The California Coastal Commission

The California Coastal Commission, a powerful regulatory body, was initially created by the 1972 Coastal Initiative (Proposition 20) and was given permanent status by the 1976 California Coastal Act. Its principal task was to "plan for and regulate land and water uses in the coastal zone consistent with the policies of the Coastal Act." The coastal zone extends seaward to the state's outer limit of jurisdiction and generally extends inland a thousand yards from the mean-high-tide line of the sea. A quasi-judicial agency, the commission (whose twelve voting members are appointed by the governor and the state legislature) has broad authority over all manner of development in the coastal zone, whether by private entities or state, local, and even federal agencies.[86]

The commission was authorized to review all port master plans and amendments for the state's commercial ports, such as Los Angeles and Long Beach. Port expansion projects needed commission approval. The commission's authority also extended to the issuance and certification of development permits, oversight of federally permitted/licensed/funded projects, and review of all local coastal programs. In the 1970s, both San Pedro Bay ports developed five-year master plans. Long Beach's plan easily passed commission scrutiny. But Los Angeles's proposal, requiring much more deep dredging, was rejected and delayed. As Chapter Five explains, the Port of Los Angeles's difficulties with the commission would extend into the 1990s.

A New State/Local Fiscal Regime

The late 1970s also witnessed the creation of a new state/local fiscal regime that would threaten the financing of L.A.'s mega-projects. The passage of Proposition 13 in 1978 and subsequent voter-approved initiatives dramatically altered both local- and state-government finances. "Ballot-box budgeting" produced a serious erosion of local government's historic "home-rule" fiscal autonomy, along with a reduction in state financial flexibility. Although 1980s-era prosperity masked the effects of California's new fiscal rules, the recessionary 1990s made Southern California's revenue-producing ports and airports tempting targets for raids by cash-strapped state and local governments.[87]

Proposition 13

The state's tax revolt did not occur in a vacuum. From the mid-1960s onward, inequities in California's property-tax system and the need for overhaul were evident. In the 1970s, rapidly escalating housing prices and tax assessments produced a huge fiscal surplus that was not returned as tax relief, thus fueling voter discontent. Proposition 13 promised substantial tax relief. It capped the property-tax rate at 1 percent of market value; limited yearly tax increases to no more than 2 percent except when property changed hands; required a two-thirds vote of the legislature for increases in state taxes; required two-thirds voter approval for any new local special taxes; and, importantly, gave the state the power to apportion a county's property taxes among competing local governments.

The measure eliminated nearly $7 billion in local property-tax revenues: $800 million for cities; $2.2 billion for counties; $3.5 billion for school districts; and $460 million for special districts. A local fiscal meltdown was averted by a massive infusion of state assistance to local governments coupled with a series of state buyouts of services previously provided by local governments. In all, $4.4 billion from the state surplus was returned to local government, reducing Proposition 13's immediate impact.[88] Yet the measure's effects were quickly felt at the Port of Long Beach when local voters in 1980 approved city-council authority to transfer up to 10 percent annually from the harbor revenue fund into the city's general fund.

Notwithstanding state assistance, a fundamental shift in the balance of state/local power was occurring. Local fiscal autonomy was threatened as own-source revenues were reduced. Counties lost 39 percent of their own-source revenue, while cities lost 6 percent. Proposition 13 eliminated one of the most flexible tools local governments had to make annual budgetary adjustments—the local property-tax rate. Once a local mainstay, the property tax now lay under state control. The state set every county tax at the maximum 1 percent—in effect creating a single statewide property-tax rate. Furthermore, the state now had the power to allocate locally collected property taxes among counties, cities, schools, and special districts. Ironically, this centralization of fiscal decision making was precisely the opposite of voter intentions as expressed in public opinion surveys.[89]

Other State Actions

Proposition 13 was only the first in a series of voter-approved initiatives that, in David Lyon's phrase, replaced home rule with fiscal rule.[90] Proposition 4 (1979) constrained state and local government expenditures. Propositions 62 (1986) and 218 (1996) required voter approval for new local-government general-fund taxes, special assessments, and fees. Initiatives also hamstrung state-government finances. For example, Proposition 98 (1988) required the state to allocate roughly 40 percent of its general-fund budget to K-14 education. Praised for protecting California's schools, the earmarked allocation created a claim on state funds and thus provided the legal basis for the state to shift local property-tax revenues from cities and counties to school districts.[91]

In the 1980s and early 1990s, new state laws compounded the municipal fiscal crunch by preempting local business-license taxes for financial institutions and shifting selected city revenues to counties. In 1992, with a state recession and budget crisis, Sacramento lawmakers created the Educational Revenue Augmentation Fund (ERAF) to meet the Proposition 98 school-funding requirement with local property-tax revenues rather than state general-fund outlays. Using Proposition 13's power to apportion the property tax, ERAF produced a dramatic $3.6 billion shift from California cities and counties to school districts. Although counties were hit hardest, cities lost nearly $500 million in property-tax revenue.

State actions such as ERAF created major shortfalls in local-government budgets. Thus, for 1993, the City of Los Angeles's general-fund budget faced a $200 million state-created deficit. Facing severe fiscal pressures, local governments responded by creating new revenue sources such as utility taxes, increased user charges and fees, transient-lodging taxes, and sales tax–generating retail development. As subsequent chapters reveal, charter cities such as Los Angeles and Long Beach also treated their revenue-producing port, airport, water and power departments as "cash cows" to balance their budgets. Yet such revenue diversions drove up the price of financing the region's ambitious mega-projects.[92]

As planning for Southern California's trade-infrastructure mega-projects went into high gear in the 1990s, they appeared to be on a direct collision course with these new regulatory regimes. The outcomes of close encounters in the 1990s between the local developmental state and the supra-local regulatory state over the region's port, trade-corridor, and airport-development plans are detailed in the following chapters.

Part Three   Mounting Challenges

The Riordan Years, 1993–2001

5 Weathering Storms at the Ports

In Los Angeles, the management of the port is now increasingly concerned that the historical autonomy is being undermined by actions of the state legislature and the city government. . . . If supervisory governments are able to continue dipping into the ports' discretionary reserves, it will make a sham of the ports' efforts to launch and sustain meaningful capital development programs.

—*Ezunial Burts, executive director, Port of Los Angeles, 1992*[1]

The Federal Implementation Plan (FIP), . . . designed to bring [the region] into attainment of national, health-based air quality standards for ozone and carbon monoxide pollution, . . . would have a significant and adverse economic impact on Southern California. . . . The FIP's largest impact would be on the Basin's transportation system. Restrictions and the imposition of higher costs on the Ports of Los Angeles and Long Beach . . . would divert the movement of goods to other hubs such as Ensenada, San Francisco/Oakland, Seattle, or Vancouver.

—*Los Angeles Area Chamber of Commerce, 1994*[2]

Of all the issues confronting Los Angeles' harbor area, one is paramount: the animosity toward City Hall that has triggered a secession movement in San Pedro and Wilmington. . . . As . . . city elections approach, that theme overrides all others. The [council] candidates talk about a lack of city services, a City Hall unresponsive to district needs, and how to end decades of tension between the fast-growing port and the neighboring residential areas of San Pedro and Wilmington. While the communities enjoy some benefits from the port, they also endure its worst side effects, such as air pollution, industrial eyesores, heavy truck traffic and terminal projects that consume neighborhoods and business districts.

—*Dan Weikel*, Los Angeles Times *reporter, 2001*[3]

This chapter and the next two examine key challenges—fiscal, environmental, governance, and community-based—to the region's trade-infrastructure mega-projects during the administration of L.A. Mayor Richard Riordan, 1993–2001, the city's first term-limited mayor. This chapter surveys port development during the Riordan years. For Long Beach, it focuses on the policies of Mayor Beverly O'Neill, elected in 1994 and reelected in 1998 and 2002. Chapter Six examines rail and highway trade-corridor projects during this era. Chapter Seven traces the uncertain path of airport development in

Southern California. Although port and rail projects successfully overcame such hurdles, international-airport projects such as the Master Plan for Los Angeles International Airport (LAX) and a proposed El Toro airport in Orange County did not. Failed airport projects were significant because the region's aspirations to be an export-based trade center rather than serving merely as the nation's leading gateway for Pacific Rim imports rested, in large measure, on its uncertain airport future.

The Riordan Years: New Challenges

In the early 1990s Los Angeles received an enormous triple hit to its economy. As the Cold War ended, military cutbacks cost the country's most defense-dependent economy two hundred thousand aerospace jobs between 1987 and 1994. The region's historically low unemployment rate soared, in 1993 reaching 9.2 percent—one-third higher than the national rate. As UC Berkeley Professor Stephen Cohen observed, "L.A. is the hole in the [national] bucket. Twenty-seven percent of the nation's entire 1990–92 job loss took place in Greater Los Angeles." [4] In the midst of the deepest downturn in the regional economy since the Great Depression, the 1992 Los Angeles riots erupted. The nation's worst twentieth-century urban disorder resulted in a three-day toll of fifty-five deaths, upward of $1 billion in property damage, over seven hundred businesses destroyed, and ten thousand jobs lost. Nature compounded these disasters with the costly 1993 Malibu fires and the 1994 Northridge earthquake, the nation's most costly temblor, which produced over $20 billion in property and infrastructure losses.

While this troika of disasters prompted *Forbes* magazine to drop Los Angeles from its list of the top ten places to conduct international trade, L.A.'s trade fortunes continued to boom. The 1990s marked the ascendancy of Southern California as one of the world's leading trade centers. In 1994, Los Angeles first surpassed New York as the nation's busiest trade hub.[5] L.A. benefited from the fast growing Asian Pacific economies as well as from recovery in the U.S. economy. It also profited from the region's substantial prior infrastructure investments. Between 1993 and 2000, merchandise trade through the L.A. Customs District grew by a robust 71 percent, from $166.5 billion to $284.7 billion, while New York Customs District trade grew by only 57 percent. Significantly, L.A.'s 1990s trade surge solidified its role as a trade entrepôt/transshipment center rather than as an export center. Imports (primarily shipped by vessel) accounted for three-quarters of L.A.'s robust, if lopsided, trade growth between 1993 and 2000.[6]

The 1990s also marked the ascendancy of trade in the local economy. As the five-county economy lost nearly a half million jobs from 1990 to 1993, direct employment in international trade continued to grow. Overall, between 1990 and 2000, trade employment accounted for 40 percent of the net increase of a half million jobs in the five-county economy. Whereas in 1990 trade jobs represented less than 80 percent of aerospace/high-tech employment in Southern California, by 2000 the booming trade sector employed well over twice as many people as did the aerospace/high-tech sector. Trade-infrastructure construction projects also aided recovery. In the 1990s the ports of San Pedro Bay spent $2 billion each on capital projects, and, in addition, the $2.4 billion Alameda Corridor rail project was launched. These mega-projects generated thousands of construction jobs.[7]

Notwithstanding the growing local importance of global trade, the Riordan administration had a contradictory set of policy priorities relative to the city's harbor and airports departments. On the one hand, Riordan declared that "international trade is arguably the most important part of the future of Los Angeles. We can be the most important international trade center in the world." Long Beach Mayor O'Neill also recognized the crucial role that trade played in the local economy.[8]

On the other hand, the L.A. mayor pursued a strategy of tapping deeply into the special revenue funds of L.A.'s "crown jewels"—its proprietary airports, harbor, and water and power departments. These funds would both pay for a massive buildup in the city's police force and close a burgeoning general-fund budget shortfall, estimated at $240 million in 1996, without raising taxes. In all, the Riordan administration's strategy of milking these "cash cows" netted over $550 million from 1994 to 1997. Yet revenue diversions had a long-term potential cost: a less competitive infrastructure unable to meet the challenges of a global marketplace. The costs of hefty revenue diversions would be borne in the form of higher user fees and project financing, resulting in reduced growth potential. Long Beach officials also sought port revenues to close a budget gap and finance other projects such as an aquarium.[9]

The Riordan years witnessed major regulatory and community/governance challenges to the three regional trade mega-projects launched during Tom Bradley's mayoralty: the 2020 port-development plan, the Alameda Corridor separated-grade rail project, and the LAX Master Plan. One such regulatory challenge was financial. The severe strain the deep recession placed on government budgets resulted in state and municipal raids on the revenue-producing proprietary harbor, airports, and water and power departments. California's post–Proposition 13 state/local fiscal regime was a key catalyst for revenue diversion. A second set of regulatory challenges arose from the federal and state environmental-policy regime created in the 1970s and 1980s. These challenges ranged from the draconian federal air-quality regulations and fines proposed for Southern California—which particularly threatened ocean shipping and air transportation—to stringent California Coastal Commission review and mitigation requirements for port projects.

A third set of challenges involved local governance and community relations. In the late 1990s two Los Angeles charter-reform commissions revisited municipal governance, including the once-vaunted independence of the proprietary departments. In addition there were community demands to control, block, or mitigate the mega-projects. Because substantial costs—traffic congestion, air pollution, and noise—were imposed on neighboring communities, the projects became ground zero for escalating conflicts between the forces of globalization and community. In the late 1990s, community activism took a new form. In the wake of secession fever in the San Fernando Valley, secession movements were launched in San Pedro and Wilmington, once-separate cities consolidated with Los Angeles in 1909.

This chapter examines the stormy weather concerning port development during the Riordan and O'Neill years. It considers the evolving character of the 2020 Plan; state and municipal revenue-diversion efforts; federal and state environmental/regulatory challenges and related community protests; and the twin governance challenges facing the Port of Los Angeles—charter reform and the harbor-area secession movement. It concludes with an assessment of the performance of the two ports in the 1990s.

The 2020 Plan: Differing Visions

While historically the ports of Los Angeles and Long Beach were fierce rivals, by the early 1980s cooperation began replacing competition. The focal point of joint action was the 2020 Plan, which was intended to solve land, terminal, and transportation problems well into the twenty-first century. The 2020 program was designed to develop new facilities that would meet a projected 250 percent cargo tonnage increase from 1990 to 2020. At an estimated cost of $4.8 billion, the plan was the nation's most ambitious port-development program. Though a comprehensive plan, 2020 was in reality a series of discrete projects that could be built in incremental fashion. Because projects could be prioritized, capital planning and financing were facilitated. Yet, because each project had to be reviewed separately, the environmental certification process became cumbersome.[10]

The project envisaged 2,400–2,500 acres of new landfill and 600 acres of development on existing land. The mega-project also envisioned thirty-eight or thirty-nine new marine terminals, seven miles of deep-water ship channels dredged fifty to eighty-five feet deep, and a significant new infrastructure of roadways, rail, intermodal container-transfer facilities (ICTFs), pipelines, and utilities. Major 2020 projects included the Pactex liquid bulk terminal and pipeline terminus project in Los Angeles, massive dredge-and-fill projects (Pier 300/400) in Los Angeles harbor, Pier J expansion in Long Beach, and large dredge-and-fill projects (Piers K and L) in Long Beach harbor.[11]

A New Long Beach Master Plan

In the early 1990s, Long Beach withdrew from the 2020 Plan when it concluded that the cost of dredge-and-fill expansion was too high. Long Beach's share of the 2020 Plan's cost was $2.3 billion, and federal financing was limited. As then-director of planning and environmental affairs, Long Beach's Geraldine Knatz observed, "Our main channel is sixty feet deep, which we recently dredged to between seventy-five and ninety feet. . . . If you already are a deep harbor, there is not much opportunity for federal funding for dredging." [12] According to Gordon Palmer, the port's then-manager of master planning, three factors contributing to Long Beach's withdrawal were the availability of private land for purchase and development, the possibility of a no-cost transfer of surplus Navy property, and the lack of environmental-mitigation projects, which were required in California for port dredging and landfill activities. [13]

In January 1993 Long Beach unveiled its new Facilities Master Plan based on updated cargo forecasts and revised port policies. The Board of Harbor Commissioners largely abandoned landfill projects in favor of those that redeveloped existing land. The new plan identified nine "near-term" development projects, such as a new container terminal on the 147-acre Pier J expansion, that were in the advanced stages of planning and could be completed in five years. As for remaining needs to the year 2020, the document outlined three approaches to long-range development: develop/improve available land and facilities; develop the Navy site; or create major landfills in the Southwest Harbor similar to those proposed in the 2020 Plan. [14]

Long Beach energetically pursued the first two alternatives. Port officials believed their "minimum-fill" strategy would save money and time. Existing land cost half as much to develop as the $1.2 million per acre needed to create landfill. Furthermore, surplus-military-property legislation allowed the Navy to transfer facilities to Long Beach at no cost. Port officials also claimed speed of project completion and lessened environmental review as additional advantages. Former port Executive Secretary Richard Aschieris observed:

> In 1991 we made a business decision not to engage in massive dredge-and-fill projects because we couldn't get an accurate handle on how long it would take to complete them and how long it would take to jump through various environmental hoops. We determined it would take around twenty years to create land for development, whereas existing land could be developed quicker. . . . With our ability to get these developments up and running faster than our competitors, we should be able to maintain our number one status for the long term. [15]

The port also had an aggressive program with respect to land acquisition. It purchased 725 acres of the old Wilmington oil field from Union Pacific Resources Company for $405 million. The parcel, which increased the port's size by 35 percent, would be developed with new container terminals and a neo/bulk terminal. This acquisition—and associated development costs of $230–270 million—drained the port's $500 million cash reserves, and it was then forced to borrow money for other capital projects.[16]

Although the former oil field had environmental problems—it was a state Superfund site—port officials contended that developing the property was cost-effective. According to port planner Knatz: "Not many people are willing to spend $405 million on a state Superfund site. From our perspective, its value is that it is existing land as compared with the difficulty of trying to get a major dredging land-fill permit through the environmental process. It's easier to clean up that property and reuse it than to get a permit and construction [on] landfill."[17]

Long Beach also planned to redevelop surplus Navy properties. The 1993 port Master Plan envisioned closure of the Naval Station, but assumed that the Naval Shipyard and Supply Center would remain in operation. The port planned to develop Naval Station lands on Terminal Island and the Navy Mole (the narrow pier extending south from Terminal Island). The Navy Mole could be used as a train-marshaling area and serve ancillary port-related purposes. As port officials worked though the Naval Station closure process, they encountered unexpected problems. The 1994 surplus-military-property legislation contained no implementation provisions. Port officials pressured Washington to put such regulations in place. Another issue involved the McKinney Act, which gave homeless groups first claim on closed military bases. A homeless group in Long Beach requested use of the entire Naval Station. Arguing that the port had few expansion options, Mayor O'Neill effectively lobbied in Washington to ensure that port-related uses had priority at the Naval Station.[18]

Long Beach's plans for Navy-site redevelopment underwent further revision. In its fourth round of military-base closings, the 1995 Defense Base Realignment and Closure Commission (BRAC) targeted the Long Beach Naval Shipyard, which employed thirty-one hundred civilian workers, for closure. Although port officials went on record as opposing closure, the port stood to benefit from BRAC's decision. Absent closure, the port's minimum-fill policy could meet only the year-2020 low-end cargo forecast. With closure, sufficient land would be available for developing the cargo-handling capacity needed to meet the high-end 2020 forecast. The port planned to build a container terminal on the property; the Naval Shipyard eventually closed in late 1997.[19]

After land acquisition, the port's highest priority was its transportation infrastructure. According to port planner Knatz, "Our train activity has doubled in the past year and we are having some operational difficulties just getting the trains in and out of the harbor. So infrastructure improvements are our highest priority." These improvements included $200 million for the

Alameda Corridor project to acquire the railroad rights-of-way and extend the corridor southward into the port; a $174 million project to double-track the port's rail system and construct highway overpasses so that truck traffic could flow above trains; and expansion and reconfiguration of the rail terminals on Pier J.[20]

Because of its minimum-fill approach, Long Beach did not anticipate major dredging and land filling—which would trigger costly habitat restoration—over the next five to ten years. There remained, however, one major dredging need. Because the port's main channel was much deeper than the approach channel outside the harbor, Long Beach asked the federal government to deep-dredge the approach for two miles outside the harbor. Because this was a navigational project, the Army Corps of Engineers agreed to do the dredging. None of the Corps's dredging models predicted the subsequent British Petroleum (BP) purchase of ARCO, whose tankers came into the port. Because BP used wider tankers, the Corps had to go back and widen the channel.

With Long Beach's withdrawal from the 2020 Plan, port officials claimed that they had moved ahead of Los Angeles in port development. Several of Long Beach's fast-track terminal projects soon went on line, earning revenue and easing port borrowing needs for future capital projects.[21]

Los Angeles's Pier 300/400 Implementation Program

While Long Beach chose a separate development path, Los Angeles stayed the 2020 course. It remained committed to dredge-and-fill expansion and its partnership with the Army Corps of Engineers because it had few alternatives. Though a deep-water port, Los Angeles's main channels are shallower than Long Beach's. The Port of L.A. had to deepen its main harbor channels in order to accommodate the larger ships that were being built to take advantage of economies of scale and to service the long routes from Asia to North America. Relative to Long Beach, Los Angeles was "landlocked" by non-port-related commercial, residential, and recreational development, which limited landside port development.

Renamed the Pier 300/400 Implementation Program, the new development program was essentially the first phase of the 2020 Plan. Comprising twenty-four discrete projects, Phase One included two new terminals on Pier 300—one container, one dry bulk—two new intermodal cargo terminals, new rail lines, six grade separations, and deep-water dredging for Pier 300 access. Approved in 1994, the $149 million dredging project was the nation's largest dredge-and-fill program. Completed in 1997, Phase One cost $800 million.[22]

Phase Two entailed completion of the planned 582-acre Pier 400 by dredging new harbor channels and deepening old channels created in Phase One.

There was some uncertainty, however, regarding mitigation for the Pier 400 project. The California Coastal Commission initially approved 395 acres of new landfill, basing its approval on the mitigation available from the Batiquitos Lagoon restoration project in northern San Diego County. The port then pursued additional mitigation credits to reach its goal of 582 acres. Pier 400 land-use plans called for additional cargo-handling space and liquid hazardous-materials facilities. Scheduled to be completed by 2010, Phase Two improvements are expected to cost $1.2 billion.[23]

Despite Long Beach's withdrawal from the 2020 Plan, the two ports continued to cooperate on projects of mutual benefit. Joint ventures included the 114-acre Southern Pacific intermodal container-transfer facility 2.5 miles north of the ports; double-stack train service; port highway-access demonstration projects; the sharing of pricing and marketing strategies; joint meetings of operational staff; combined lobbying before governmental bodies; joint forecasting; and a complex $100 million cost-sharing agreement covering six major infrastructure projects. However, the centerpiece of port cooperation is the Alameda Corridor project, which consolidated over ninety miles of rail lines and two hundred grade crossings into a single, uninterrupted, twenty-mile, high-speed, separated-grade rail system linking the two ports with the transcontinental rail yards located near downtown Los Angeles. Construction of the $2.4 billion project—with $400 million contributed by the two ports—began in 1995, and the corridor opened in April 2002.[24]

Revenue Diversion

In the early to mid-1990s, the ports faced—and ultimately overcame— two major regulatory challenges to their ambitious expansion plans: state-authorized port revenue diversion and stringent federal air-quality standards and emissions fines proposed for the region's shippers. Other regulatory challenges facing the ports—particularly Los Angeles—consisted of escalating municipal financial transfers and cumbersome Coastal Commission certification and habitat-mitigation procedures.

As noted, the $4.8 billion capital-development program, 1988–2020, for the ports of San Pedro Bay is the most ambitious in the nation's history. The twin ports' capital budget dwarfed those of their rivals. Table 5.1 displays capital-expenditure plans, 1993–97, for the ten leading U.S. ports. During this period, Los Angeles and Long Beach spent an estimated $1.8 billion— six times as much as the Port Authority of New York/New Jersey, more than three times as much as the Port of Seattle, and six times as much as the Port of Oakland. Capital outlays for the San Pedro Bay ports accounted for one-third of the $5.5 billion in capital spending, 1993–97, for the entire U.S. public port system.

Table 5.1   Capital-Expenditure Plans of Top U.S. Ports, 1993–1997
(in thousands of dollars)

Rank	Port	Planned Expenditures	% of U.S. Total
1	Port of Long Beach	1,099,900	19.9
2	Port of Los Angeles	703,489	12.7
3	Port of Seattle	577,264	10.4
4	Port of Oakland	302,989	5.5
5	Port Authority of New York/New Jersey	294,232	5.3
6	Port of Miami	279,730	5.1
7	Port of New Orleans	238,974	4.3
8	Port of Houston	217,663	3.9
9	Georgia Ports Authority	193,100	3.5
10	Port of Tacoma	170,028	3.1
	Top ten ports	4,077,369	73.8
	All U.S. ports	5,525,360	100.0

SOURCE: Data from U.S. Maritime Administration, *Public Port Financing in the United States* (Washington, D.C.: U.S. Department of Transportation, 1994), p. 21, Table 2.8.

Table 5.2   Capital-Expenditure Plans of Top U.S. Ports, 1997–2000
(in thousands of dollars)

Rank	Port	Planned Expenditures	% of U.S. Total
1	Port of Los Angeles	1,079,182	16.4
2	Port of Long Beach	866,200	13.2
3	Port of Oakland	520,000	7.9
4	Port Authority of New York/New Jersey	498,663	7.6
5	Port of Seattle	391,483	5.9
6	Port of Houston	291,628	4.4
7	Georgia Ports Authority	263,840	4.0
8	Maryland Port Administration	237,147	3.6
9	Port of New Orleans	226,260	3.4
10	Port of Tacoma	221,798	3.4
	Top ten ports	4,596,201	69.8
	All U.S. ports	6,584,238	100.0

SOURCE: Data from U.S. Maritime Administration, *A Report to Congress on the Status of the Public Ports of the United States 1996-1997* (Washington, D.C.: U.S. Department of Transportation, 1998), App. F, p. F-1.

Massive spending by the L.A.-area ports continued through the late 1990s. As Table 5.2 highlights, for 1997–2001, projected capital expenditures of $1.95 billion for Los Angeles and Long Beach again accounted for nearly one-third of the planned $6.6 billion in capital spending for all the nation's public ports.

The two Southern California ports financed their ambitious capital-development programs in two ways. Their first method was to spend cash reserves generated from port user fees such as tariffs and wharfage charges. Historically, capital projects at Los Angeles and Long Beach—the nation's most profitable ports—were financed in this way. To prepare for the 2020 Program, both ports built up substantial cash reserves. Thus, Long Beach's purchase of 725 acres from the Union Pacific Resources Company came from its $500 million discretionary reserve fund. The second method involved the issuance of revenue bonds and short-term commercial paper. Los Angeles used revenue bonds to finance its Pier 300/400 projects.[25]

The ports preferred pay-as-you-go financing. Yet their sizeable reserves of over a half billion dollars made the ports a tempting target in the early 1990s for cash-strapped supervisory governments trying to balance their budgets. The result was a series of raids on port funds. Revenue diversion took two forms: state legislation permitting port cities to tap into harbor reserves and city-charter provisions allowing the transfer of port funds.

SB 844

In September 1992, as a result of a severe state budget shortfall, Senate Bill (SB) 844 was passed to allow the five California chartered port cities—Los Angeles, Long Beach, Oakland, San Francisco, and San Diego—to tap into harbor "discretionary reserves" for two years in order to replace property taxes taken from the cities by the state. The legislation remained in effect until June 30, 1994. Engineered by Los Angeles–area lawmakers, the new legislation breached the historical independence and protection offered the ports by the California Tidelands Trust Act of 1911. Under the 1911 act, California's ports were granted control of the tidelands. All moneys generated by port operations are considered Tidelands Trust funds, to be dedicated to maritime-related uses involving commerce, navigation, and fisheries for the benefit of all California residents.

SB 844 permitted the port cities to transfer the greater of $4 million or 25 percent of the difference between total current assets and liabilities, up to an amount equal to the city's property-tax loss. The cap was inserted at the behest of Long Beach port officials, who faced the daunting prospect of $80 million annual transfer payments because of the port's $500 million accumulated reserves. Under the new law, the state's ports transferred a total of $140 million to their cities' general funds. Most of the transfers—$90 million—came from the San Pedro Bay ports. The Port of Los Angeles transferred $70 million, while the Port of Long Beach, benefiting from the cap, was able to limit its contribution to $20 million.[26]

What were the potential effects of SB 844 on the ports' finances and capital-development programs? The bond market sent the first signal. Standard & Poor's placed the California ports on credit watch, a special alert status that is generally a precursor to a lowered bond rating. As the Port of Long Beach's FY 1993 financial position worsened because of transfers and one-time expenses, its bond rating was downgraded, and the result was higher borrowing costs. At the Port of Los Angeles, outstanding debt went into technical default because the bond covenants had assured bondholders that debt service would have first claim on port revenues. The port quickly addressed these concerns through the cash defeasance of all outstanding revenue bonds.[27]

Port officials sent the second signal by lowering reserve-fund balances. As former Long Beach port finance officer John Kruse observed, "Rather than keep cash in the bank, we spend any savings quickly. That way the city won't look at it as a source of funds." With less money available for pay-as-you-go capital financing, the ports were forced to pursue more debt-intensive capital plans at an increased cost.[28] Port priorities and timetables also were restructured. As then-Port of Los Angeles Chief Financial Officer Jim Preusch noted, "We haven't been working on marginal projects in favor of the larger projects. Marginal projects which have public appeal but generate no revenue . . . have been deferred." Long Beach port planner Knatz concurred, noting that "we have been more cautious in terms of our development projects. . . . Some things have been put on the back burner, and we won't get to them for several years."[29]

Port officials expressed concern about the effects of revenue diversion on port users. As then-L.A. port director Ezunial Burts argued, "Customer credibility becomes a major concern in the present circumstances. . . . As a landlord port, WorldPort LA [as it was then called] has made an explicit pledge to the customers that the fees they pay the port will go back into port projects. Given this new circumstance . . . there is little a port can do to deter a customer from simply shifting business elsewhere."[30]

Attempts by cities to reenact port revenue sharing during the 1993–94 legislative session were unsuccessful. Then-Assistant L.A. Deputy Mayor David Cobb argued that Los Angeles chose not to pursue an SB 844 extension primarily because of the findings of the city's Nexus study, a joint project of the port, the mayor's office, and the city council. The Nexus study showed various ways the Harbor Department could contribute additional moneys to the city's general fund.[31]

Because of its short duration, SB 844 did not seriously impair the ports' capital-development programs. But port officials claimed that a reenactment would do so. According to Preusch, "If state revenue diversion is revived, the impact will come from the bond-rating agencies. Rating agencies like stability and predictability. A $30–50 million diversion each year would have a serious negative impact on port expansion plans and on retention of current tenants and users."[32]

Municipal Transfers

With the repeal of state revenue diversion, the cities of Los Angeles and Long Beach, facing continued budget deficits, used their charter authority to compel additional transfers from the ports. In L.A., newly elected Mayor Riordan appointed a blue-ribbon special advisory committee on fiscal administration to identify new revenues and efficiencies. The committee concluded:

> The most significant sources of potential additional revenues are the city's three largest business operations—the Department of Airports (primarily LAX), the Department of Water and Power and the Port of Los Angeles. . . . The amount of surplus revenues generated by these operations can be substantially increased through improvement in operations, and . . . if necessary, the city should aggressively seek legal authority through legislation, restructuring or otherwise to increase returns to the general fund from these entities.[33]

As a result, the city substantially increased its request for Harbor Department payments for city-provided services such as fire protection and personnel. Under the Tidelands Trust, the Harbor Department has historically paid for city services as a condition for maintaining the trust. For FY 1994, the last year of state revenue diversion, the port's payment for city services totaled $16.1 million. For FY 1995, the city significantly increased its payment request to $33.5 million. With the doubling of the charge, city services accounted for 34 percent of the port's FY 1995 operating budget.[34]

With the release of the Nexus study in July 1995, the city's transfer demands escalated. The Nexus study concluded that the port owed the city an additional $68 million in back fees—allegedly for underpayment for municipal services since 1977—and $12 million in current fees for police, fire, public-works, and other port-related services. These other services included a share of the cost of the convention center and of parks built on harbor property. In August 1995, the Board of Harbor Commissioners voted to pay the city $80 million in back and current fees over three or four years.[35]

The port revenue transfers captured the attention of the bond-rating agencies. Moody's Investors Service, for example, expressed concern about "the Port's ability to sustain the integrity of Port finances in the face of continuing city financial pressures." To reassure rating agencies and prospective bondholders, the port's 1995 $200 million revenue-bond indenture appeared to limit the transfers and contained a unique rate covenant that encompassed both transfers and debt service.[36]

Heightened revenue diversions beyond traditional city service charges posed a serious threat to the ports' capital programs. The ports of San Pedro Bay required prodigious amounts of capital—more than $3 billion by 2010. Long Beach planned to sell up to $400 million in new revenue bonds, adding significantly to its $600 million debt. Los Angeles, which sold $200 million in revenue bonds in early 1995, made a similar offering in spring 1996. According to the bond-rating agencies, the ports' credit ratings could suffer if transfers occurred in lieu of needed capital investments or hurt the port's competitive position. The rating agencies also considered threats by shippers to divert cargo to other ports because of the transfers. Concerned with the size and uncertainty of the new municipal charges, Standard & Poor's expressed growing alarm.[37]

In response, state regulators carefully scrutinized the legitimacy of the city's claims on port revenues. The State Lands Commission and the attorney general, the state's legal advisor, are charged with enforcing the Tidelands Trust Act. Although state officials historically construed their trust obligations in permissive fashion, they had serious questions about whether the Los Angeles Harbor Commission's $80 million transfer, based on the Nexus-study findings, violated the Tidelands Trust and the state constitutional prohibition against gifts of public moneys to municipal corporations.

The Nexus study raised two Tidelands Trust–related issues. The first was that many of the services for which the City of Los Angeles demanded reimbursement and annual payments were not located on trust lands and did not provide a direct benefit to the port. These services included the convention center, public parks, museums, and streets. The second issue involved the city's retroactive billing process for alleged underpayment of past services. The attorney general's office developed a set of criteria for appropriate service billing in order to avoid the problem of self-dealing created when the trustee provides municipal services. It argued that the city's transfer of $64 million for past fire services violated these standards: "It is not clear whether the charges properly relate to Harbor purposes, whether they are reasonable or whether the Harbor would have agreed to pay what the City is now seeking. Moreover, because tenants of the Harbor pay taxes, it would appear that Harbor tenants are being treated differently from other non-Harbor taxpayers within the City because these other non-Harbor taxpayers receive fire and police protection at no additional cost."[38]

The Nexus case also highlighted the growing conflict of interest among Los Angeles harbor commissioners between meeting their Tidelands Trust responsibilities and implementing the policy agendas of the mayor who appointed them. According to the Tidelands Trust Act, the ports' governing boards are supposed to use port revenues for maritime-related uses that benefit all Californians. Yet the politicized process for selecting port commissioners, exemplified in Los Angeles, encouraged a dereliction of trust duties. Los Angeles harbor commissioners were mayoral appointees (subject to city-council confirmation) who were chosen to implement the mayor's policy agenda. Though they served five-year terms, they could be removed by the mayor with city-council approval. Mayor Riordan's agenda involved diverting substantial port revenues to the city's general fund in apparent conflict with provisions of the Tidelands Trust Act.[39]

Charged with enforcing the Tidelands Trust, the State Lands Commission in 1996 sued Los Angeles to recover the $68 million that was transferred to the municipal treasury. State officials alleged the money was improperly diverted to pay for municipal services and projects unrelated to the port. In early 2001, a settlement was finally reached. Without admitting wrongdoing, the city agreed to repay the port $62 million over fifteen years in cash or credits against the bills the city sends the port for future services such as fire and emergency medical services.[40]

In contrast, Long Beach harbor commissioners, while not immune to local political pressures, serve six-year terms and are limited to two terms. Appointed by the mayor with council confirmation, members can be removed by the city council only "for cause." Charter protections tend to insulate Long Beach port commissioners from city policy agendas. Long Beach's council-manager system of government, which features a part-time council, also limits municipal political influence over port affairs.

But, facing budget deficits similar to L.A.'s, the City of Long Beach overrode these protections and also sought increased port revenue transfers. Historically, trade- and port-related city projects such as the convention center and the World Trade Center were funded by the port. Over the period 1990–95, the Board of Harbor Commissioners transferred more than $150 million to the city, including $90 million loaned for the convention center. Port officials cautioned that these transfers were made before plans had been made to purchase the Wilmington oil field and before the Alameda Corridor project was moving forward. They suggested that it would be difficult to make similar commitments in the future given their ongoing capital-investment program.[41]

Notwithstanding these concerns, at the behest of the mayor and the city council, the harbor board in mid-1995 agreed to a complex financing arrangement for an aquarium in downtown Long Beach. The port panel agreed to allow the city to divert hotel-bed tax funds (which had been pledged to repay the port's loans for the convention center) to help repay any future delinquencies on the aquarium bonds. The city charter also contained a provision allowing the city to transfer up to 10 percent of the port's net revenue for projects the city wanted funded in the tidelands area. This charter power (which apparently did not violate the Tidelands Trust) was not exercised until the end of state revenue diversion. For FY 1994, however, the city made a request—requiring harbor commission approval—for the full 10 percent of port net revenue.[42]

Long Beach port officials cautioned that the harbor was not the cash cow it once was. According to port planner Knatz, the port's net annual income was $25 million, down significantly from the past. Reduced revenues, which made the port a less tempting target for transfers, reflected the port's growing reliance on debt financing for capital projects. Principal and interest expenses rose from $32 million in FY 1994 to $73 million in FY 1998.[43]

Environmental Policy Challenges

Federal and state environmental regulatory policies posed the second challenge to port development. The ports of San Pedro Bay must comply with the environmental standards of seventy-two different federal, state, and local agencies. Although port officials complained that "this burden of accumulated regulations has resulted in process taking precedence over rational policy making,"[44] the two ports met the regulatory challenge during the 1980s. In the early 1990s, however, two major challenges were the tough, court-ordered federal antismog plan for the Los Angeles basin and the cumbersome California Coastal Commission review process for port-development projects.

The Federal Implementation Plan

The greatest regulatory threat to port operations and development was the proposed federal antismog plan for the Los Angeles basin. In 1987 local environmental groups brought suit against the federal Environmental Protection Agency (EPA) to force the region's compliance with National Ambient Air Quality Standards (NAAQS) for ground-level ozone and carbon monoxide under the 1977 Clean Air Act. The act gave the states primary responsibility for regulating sources of air pollution to meet federal air-quality standards. To comply, states were required to adopt a plan that showed how areas not in compliance with federal air-quality standards would attain them within a designated time period. Because California failed to develop adequate attainment plans for the South Coast basin and Ventura and Sacramento counties, the federal courts ordered the EPA to draw up a clean-air plan. The resulting 1994 Federal Implementation Plan (FIP) focused on emissions from ships, planes, trucks, and locomotives that operated in interstate and international commerce and thus are beyond the authority of the California Air Resources Board (CARB), which is responsible for developing the State Implementation Plan (SIP).[45]

The proposed FIP hit the shipping industry with particular force. The EPA found that ships using the ports were the "largest uncontrolled source of emissions of NOx [nitrogen oxides] and SOx [sulfur oxides] in California," accounting for "approximately 40% of all SOx emissions and 12% of NOx emissions from both mobile and stationary sources statewide." As a strategy to reduce ship nitrogen oxide emissions, the FIP included a stiff ship emissions-fee program that applied only to the ports of San Pedro Bay.[46]

San Pedro Bay port officials argued that the FIP's emissions-fee proposal was a formula for economic disaster. According to Long Beach's Knatz, "The impact [of the FIP] would be severe. We feel quite confident that we would lose 40% of our cargo business, including discretionary, intermodal cargo, that could easily go to the Pacific Northwest. If that happens, there would be no need for the Alameda Corridor project. The impact of job losses, lost tax revenue, we think it's pretty significant." [47]

In response to the EPA's request for analyses of the plan's economic effects, the ports of San Pedro Bay, the Chamber of Commerce, and industry groups conducted their own impact studies. The ports calculated the annual cost of the ship emissions fees at $309 million because of significant cargo diversion—up to 40 percent—to other ports. Cargo-diversion losses were estimated at fifty-seven thousand jobs and $2.5 billion in wages. Cargo diversion also threatened the prospects of financing port capital improvements. The Chamber of Commerce's study of the FIP's impact on the region's entire transportation system—ports, airports, trains, and trucks—estimated a $3 billion per year burden on the economy. [48]

Strenuous lobbying by California's elected officials and business groups resulted in the elimination of the FIP. Under the Clean Act Air, the South Coast Air Quality Management District (SCAQMD) and CARB were required to submit plans outlining how Southern California would meet federal air-quality standards. After heavy lobbying by Mayor Riordan, the SCAQMD removed stringent antismog measures for ships, airplanes, trucks, and trains from its proposed clean-air plan. Because international and interstate transportation falls under the EPA's sole jurisdiction, CARB's proposed antismog plan (or SIP), which was scaled back because of pressure from the oil and trucking industries, did not include regulations for ships and airplanes. [49]

State and local officials played significant roles in scaling back, delaying, and finally eliminating the FIP. Facing intense pressures from the governor and the mayor of Los Angeles, the EPA dropped the FIP's most criticized rules, such as the requirement for a ship emissions fee. The EPA then proposed a two-year delay in implementing the weakened FIP so that it could review an alternate clean-air plan crafted by state officials. Claiming that a delay was insufficient, Southern California representatives drafted legislation amending the 1990 Clean Air Act to eliminate the EPA's antismog plan for California. Congress and the president approved the smog exemption. [50]

Coastal Commission Review

Under the California Coastal Act of 1976, the ports are required to develop for Coastal Commission certification master plans that address the environmental, economic, and utilization impacts of proposed projects on the ports and surrounding regions. Under the California Environmental Quality Act of 1980, the ports are required to mitigate the adverse impacts of proposed projects. Habitat-mitigation projects require the approval of agencies such as the U.S. Environmental Protection Agency, the Fish and Wildlife Service, the National Marine Fisheries Service, the State Lands Commission, and the California Department of Fish and Game. To meet their future mitigation needs, the two ports are contributing $31 million apiece for Bolsa Chica wetlands restoration—which gives them 454 outer-harbor or 908 inner-harbor credits.[51]

Because of their different development strategies, the two ports have had divergent experiences with the California Coastal Commission. Long Beach has enjoyed a good working relationship with it. Under the Coastal Act, the commission pursues a minimization mandate—to limit the amount of fill to the minimum necessary and to minimize harmful project effects. Because of its minimum-fill approach to port development, which reduces the need for mitigation, Long Beach had little problem getting its Facilities Master Plan approved.[52]

Long Beach port officials argued that regulatory burdens shaped their approach to development. Former Executive Secretary Richard Aschieris explained that the port avoided landfill projects because of "the delaying effects of environmental hoops. We are basically being held hostage by the California Coastal Commission, the State Lands Commission, the Army Corps of Engineers, and the EPA." Mitigation also was a consideration: "The ironic thing is that we are a deep-water port, yet we are required to do wetland mitigation. It doesn't make any sense. Wetland restoration is much more costly, and the environmental impact of what we do as a deep-water port isn't nearly so extensive as to require this type of restoration."[53]

Forced to rely on dredge-and-fill development, the Port of Los Angeles experienced greater difficulty than Long Beach in meeting Coastal Commission certification standards. Although the commission certified the port's Master Plan in 1980, it retained permit authority over new landfills in the outer harbor south of Terminal Island. In 1991 the commission rejected the then-proposed 650-acre Pier 400 landfill because of "the lack of adequate alternatives analysis, the inherent level of uncertainty associated with the long-term economic and cargo forecasts which drive the landfill project, the adverse impacts on coastal resources associated with landfill construction, and the deficiencies associated with proposed marine resource mitigation projects."[54]

But L.A. persevered. Its revised 1992 Pier 300/400 Master Plan amendment allowed for 395 acres of landfill and expanded mitigation projects such as wetland restoration at Batiquitos Lagoon in San Diego County. The Coastal Commission approved the port's 1992 amendment but retained permitting authority for the remainder of Pier 400. When new mitigation credits became available, another Master Plan amendment was submitted to the commission

for approval to complete Pier 400. Because of the difficulties the port encountered with single-action commission approval of Pier 300/400, Los Angeles became committed to a phased-approval process.[55]

Operating in the port's favor was a provision of the 1976 Coastal Act that
declared that the Port of Los Angeles was one of four deep-water ports in the
state where the priority is commerce, not recreation. This provision restricted
the scope of the commission's review to the act's procedural and environmental requirements. The question remained whether the Coastal Commission applied the act uniformly to ports with different development needs.
Critics contended that the commission needed to examine whether its permitting system handicapped ports like Los Angeles and Oakland, which were
forced to rely on dredge-and-fill development.

Other Challenges

With the FIP and Coastal Commission battles apparently over, the ports
turned their attention to other looming environmental controversies. For the
Port of Los Angeles, the major issue involved habitat mitigation. The port pre-
vailed in several lawsuits filed by environmental groups to halt dredging in
Batiquitos Lagoon. And Los Angeles secured the additional mitigation credits needed for Pier 400 expansion through habitat restoration at the Bolsa
Chica wetlands. In the late 1990s, environmentalists and San Pedro/Wil-
mington community residents organized protests over a new coal-exporting
facility that included open-air storage of large coke piles, a feature opponents
claimed posed serious health hazards. In response, the port agreed to cover
the facility.

For the Port of Long Beach, major environmental issues in the mid- to late
1990s involved cleaning up the state Superfund site on the old Wilmington
oil field, securing additional habitat-mitigation sites, and resolving a lawsuit
over tainted storm-water runoff. The port's most serious concern was the
Superfund site. Officials were optimistic that their $40 million remediation
plan would work. The plan involved removing contaminated materials to
Terminal Island for treatment.[56]

But Long Beach's plans to build a $200 million, 145-acre cargo terminal
at the Naval Station for the China Ocean Shipping Company (COSCO), a
subsidiary of the Chinese military, were thwarted, mired in environmental
and political controversy. The project's opponents represented a crazy-quilt
coalition of environmentalists, conservatives, liberals, and preservationists.
Environmental groups strenuously objected to burying tons of contaminated
silt offshore in order to build the COSCO terminal. They claimed the proposed disposal method was untested and decried the project's threat to endangered species. Conservatives lobbied to block the deal because of national-

security concerns, while liberals were opposed because of Chinese human rights violations. Preservationists sought to halt the project out of concern for the historic value of the buildings on the fifty-five-year-old naval base. When Congress passed legislation forbidding COSCO's use of the former military base, COSCO agreed to stay in Long Beach. It took over and expanded a terminal vacated by Maersk Sealand (a merger in 2000 of the Maersk Line and Sealand), which was relocating to the Port of Los Angeles.[57]

L.A. Governance Challenges

The Port of Los Angeles faced two governance challenges that its Long Beach neighbor did not: charter reform and the threat of harbor-area secession.

Charter Reform

The city's constitution historically had provided the proprietary departments with considerable autonomy to pursue their capital-improvement programs. Yet, as noted in Chapter Four, from 1977 to 1995 a series of voter-approved charter amendments restricted the powers of the citizen commissions overseeing these once-independent agencies. The boards lost the authority to appoint and remove general managers, set departmental salaries, and act without city-council review and possible override of their decision making. These new charter provisions threatened to place Los Angeles at a competitive disadvantage relative to Long Beach and other rival West Coast ports.

Management of the L.A. Harbor Department thus became contested terrain, fought over by the commissioners, mayor, and city council. The mayor and council used their voter-granted charter powers to wrest authority from the commissions in appointing and removing general managers. The mayor could use an executive directive and the chief administrative officer to control the commissions' agendas and decisions. The city council could invoke Proposition 5 and employ the staff of the chief legislative analyst to review and override virtually every commission decision. The council invoked Proposition 5 review more often for the Harbor Department than for any other agency except the Department of Water and Power (DWP). As a result, proprietary departments and their general managers scrambled to meet the often conflicting demands of multiple political masters.

By the mid-1990s charter reform was becoming a serious issue in Los Angeles. The city faced a legitimacy crisis that stemmed both from the 1992 riots and from a brewing secession movement in the San Fernando Valley. Valley residents long had complained that they had little voice at City Hall, and they allegedly received few city services for their tax dollars. Both the city council and the mayor saw charter reform as a potent antidote for secession fever and civic malaise. By 1996, the aging 1925 charter had been amended over four hundred times and had expanded from fewer than one hundred pages to nearly seven hundred. Critics claimed that it was a cumbersome, inefficient, and ineffective document.[58]

The mayor and city council also saw charter reform as a way to gain institutional advantage over their rivals. A new charter could alter the balance of power between the municipal executive and the legislature. For the mayor, it could even shift the balance of power within the executive branch, particularly with respect to the city attorney's litigation powers and the remaining independence of both the proprietary departments and the Department of Public Works. By embracing charter reform, Mayor Riordan also could deprive potential rivals such as State Senator Tom Hayden of potent campaign issues in the 1997 mayoral race. Thus, the mayor and city council each had strong incentives to launch and guide their own charter-reform initiatives.

And launch they both did, making L.A. the only city in the nation with two separate charter commissions. The city council was the first out of the gate. In 1996, it established a twenty-one-member appointed commission selected by the city's elected officials to review and suggest revisions in the old charter. But the appointed board's recommendations required city-council approval before appearing on the ballot. Fearing that the city council would block comprehensive reforms and further safeguard its authority, the mayor then launched a successful voter-initiative campaign to create an elected charter commission whose recommendations would appear directly on the ballot.

For port officials and their shipping clientele, the fear was that a new charter would compromise the port's autonomy by handing greater control over its operations and ambitious capital-improvement program to a term-limited mayor with a short, eight-year career horizon. They also worried that a new charter might create neighborhood planning councils with NIMBY ("not in my backyard") attitudes that would be eager to halt port-development projects because of the negative impacts, such as air pollution and traffic congestion, on nearby communities.

The port also had to confront the threat of privatization. In 1993 mayoral candidate Riordan had campaigned on the promise of privatizing LAX. Later, as mayor, he launched a trial balloon to privatize DWP in preparation for the state's ill-advised experiment with electricity deregulation. The Reason Public Policy Institute (RPRI, formerly the Reason Foundation), a local free-market think tank, lobbied the two charter commissions for corporatization of the Harbor Department, the Airports Department, and DWP. Corporatization meant that the Harbor Department would be "an incorporated, for-profit business—with the government as its sole share-holder." The RPPI model for the proprietary departments involved privatization under government operation. Leadership by a strong (preferably private-sector) chief executive officer and business-oriented board of directors would enable these agencies to make profits and pay dividends to the city general fund. Although corporatization was not adopted, it was on the table for discussion.[59]

Yet charter reform also presented a unique opportunity for the Harbor Department. Less restrictive rules and oversight could improve port governance arrangements and thus lead to increased efficiency and competitiveness relative to rival West Coast ports vying for Pacific Rim trade. Port officials argued that Long Beach's charter better facilitated trade by giving port officials greater discretion in making contracting, leasing, and other key decisions. Complaining about Proposition 5 micromanagement and second guessing by the city council, port staff cited L.A.'s post-Proposition 5 (1992) loss of market share to the Port of Long Beach in tonnage, cargo value, and number of loaded containers.[60]

Citing burdensome charter provisions, Bill Stein, the then-director of port administration, gave as examples city-council approval requirements for tariffs, franchises, permits, long-term leases, and major contracts. Submitting items such as leases and purchases to the city council for approval meant going through fifteen separate steps that required 190 days to complete. For Stein, Long Beach's governance system was superior because it gave the port commission independent authority over such matters: "Current as well as prospective customers have told us that they do not understand why the Executive Director and the Board of Harbor Commissioners in Los Angeles are not able to finally sign off on an agreement as is the case in the Port of Long Beach."[61]

In the course of charter deliberations, the port also benefited in free-rider fashion from lobbying and testimony by organizations and individuals affiliated with the other proprietary departments. In particular, Los Angeles Water and Power Associates, a nonprofit civic organization whose board included many former top DWP officials, sent representatives to almost every meeting held by the two charter commissions. The group tirelessly educated the commissioners on the special needs of the proprietary departments as business entities and major economic engines. Executive Director Jack Driscoll of the Airports Department and General Manager David Freeman of the DWP highlighted similar competitive problems facing their departments. Their testimony strengthened the Harbor Department's quest for greater charter independence.[62]

The two charter commissions ultimately produced a unified charter proposal, which was approved by L.A. voters in June 1999. As Table 5.3 shows, the new charter changed port governance in a number of important ways. On balance, the new charter appeared to aid proprietary-department autonomy and could improve port governance. In particular, it increased the authority of departmental commissions by weakening the Proposition 5 provision for city-council review and veto of board decisions. The new rules required a two-thirds council vote to review and veto board actions (also see Table 2.1).

Table 5.3   L.A. Charter Reform and Port Governance

Issue	1999 Charter[a]	2000 Charter[b]
Harbor commissioner appointment	Appointees subject to no residency requirements (Section 72).	One harbor commissioner must reside within harbor district (Section 650).[c]
Harbor commissioner removal	Mayor removes, provided council majority confirms (Section 73).	Mayor removes, without consent or override by council (Section 502).
Harbor Department executive director	Appointed and removed by mayor, subject to confirmation by council (Section 79(c)). Mayor and council conduct merit-pay review annually; officer cannot be removed unless evaluated one year prior to notification of proposed removal (Section 79(d)).	Appointed by harbor commission, subject to confirmation by mayor and council. Removed by commission, with mayoral confirmation, unless two-thirds of council overrides within specified period (Section 604(a)). Harbor commission conducts merit-pay review annually, using council guidelines, but removal timing is not tied to review (Section 508(a), (b)).
Franchises, permits, and leases over five years	If council does not act to disapprove commission action in sixty days, it is valid (Section 140(e)).	If council does not disapprove commission action in thirty days, it is valid (Section 606(b)).
Industrial, administrative, and economic survey of proprietary departments every five years	Mayor and council initiate; council and commission receive copies of the report of the survey (Section 396).	Controller also initiates survey; mayor also entitled to copy of the survey's report (Section 266).
Debt accountability and major capital-improvement plan	No charter provisions.	Proprietary departments required to submit to mayor, council and controller biannually with their budgets (Section 610).
Hiring of outside legal counsel by proprietary departments	Approval of both city attorney and council required (Section 42(3)).	City attorney approval required only (Section 275).
Control of litigation, including client decisions over initiating litigation and approving settlements	Council makes all decisions; city attorney determines who is the client (Section 42(3)).	Commission control over litigation involving policies and funds under its control (Sections 272, 273).

Table 5.3   *(continued)*

Issue	1999 Charter[a]	2000 Charter[b]
Port police control	No charter provisions.	Controlled by Harbor Department (Section 657).
Civil service exemptions	Five positions for top-level management; ten additional positions, to be divided between harbor and airports departments. To be used in any city department: 150 positions for experts, with mayoral and council majority vote; up to 1 percent of city workforce with two-thirds council vote (Section 1001).	Four positions for top-level management. To be used in any city department, up to 150 positions for experts, with a cap of 75 on the number of managerial positions, with two-thirds council vote (Section 111).
Neighborhood councils	No charter provisions.	Department of Neighborhood Empowerment to help form advisory councils, equipped with early-notification system and ability to hold public hearings, monitor services, and submit annual budget priorities (Article IX).

NOTE: All 1999 and 2000 Charter provisions listed—except for those involving franchises, permits, and leases over five years-apply to the Airports Department as well.

[a] The 1999 charter is the 1925 charter, as amended through 1999.

[b] Approved by voters in June 1999, the new charter took full effect July 1, 2000.

[c] The new charter also increased the airport commission size from five to seven members and imposed residency requirements. One commissioner must reside near LAX and another near Van Nuys airport in the San Fernando Valley.

The council could no longer change board actions or substitute its own decisions. Department commissions were given back their previous authority to appoint and remove general managers, although now subject to mayor and council confirmation (or override). While the proprietary departments did not get back their original salary-setting authority, they were still protected against transfers of their powers. The new charter also gave the proprietary departments the authority to hire outside legal counsel and control litigation. Although city-council authority was weakened in these areas, the mayor's powers were enhanced in a crucial way. The mayor was given the power to remove commissioners unilaterally without council consent or override.

From the port's perspective, however, the new charter also heightened the risk of NIMBY interference with its development projects. It created a system of appointed, advisory neighborhood councils and equipped them with budgets and an early-notification system for pending city actions. Although they were not the elected and policymaking bodies sought by neighborhood activists, the councils had the potential for creating mischief for port projects. The new charter also imposed a local residency requirement for both the harbor commission (one member) and the airports commission (two members), thus recognizing the need for a local voice to represent residents and businesses disproportionately affected by these facilities.[63]

Harbor-Area Secession

The Port of Los Angeles faced one other major governance challenge: the threat of harbor-area secession. Much like the sprawling San Fernando Valley, San Pedro and Wilmington long had chafed under the rule of Los Angeles. In 1909 the two port communities had joined Los Angeles in part on the basis of a promise that L.A. would create New York City–style boroughs to give them a measure of self-government. The 1909 borough plan was thrown out by the courts as a violation of the state constitution. A later proposal for borough advisory boards was included in the 1925 charter at the behest of San Fernando Valley and Westside residents but was never implemented.

From the late 1950s to the mid-1970s local autonomy again became an issue in sprawling Los Angeles, particularly in distant, disaffected neighborhoods such as the Harbor district and the San Fernando Valley. Vincent Thomas, the harbor area's longstanding representative in the state legislature, explored the possibility of implementing borough government to give the area greater autonomy. But the L.A. city attorney forestalled action, claiming that the 1925 advisory boards violated the state constitution much as the 1909 borough plan supposedly had done.[64]

Despite L.A.'s district-representation system, many harbor residents believed their voices went unheard at City Hall. The area's 140,000 residents represented a bare majority in only one of the city's fifteen sprawling council districts. Persistent community complaints concerned air pollution, traffic, and the visual blight generated by the port, in addition to its languishing waterfront and commercial district. Residents feared that new port projects such as the 484-acre million-container terminal being built on Pier 400 would mean even greater pollution and traffic.[65]

The current harbor-area secession movement is a late outgrowth of long-simmering independence fever in Los Angeles neighborhoods, particularly in the San Fernando Valley. In the 1970s Valley residents—angered by forced school busing, the perceived flight of their tax dollars, and their seemingly weak voice at City Hall—began to work for secession. In 1975, according to journalist Phil Willon, "a handful of greenhorn political activists huddled in a restaurant on Ventura Boulevard to hatch a plot against the city of Los Angeles." They formed an organization known as CIVICC, the Committee Investigating Valley Independent City/County. CIVICC lasted a short three years, but the committee "revealed and inflamed Valley residents' sense that they were being slighted and ignored by the city of Los Angeles. That disenchantment reemerged in the mid-1990s in a new Valley secession effort led by Valley VOTE, a group of business leaders and homeowner associations." [66]

One of the problems faced by CIVICC was an unsympathetic California state legislature. The passage of the Cortese-Knox Local Government Reorganization Act (1985) made it more difficult than it had been for communities that were already part of incorporated cities to detach themselves and go their own way. Under pressure from Valley legislators, this law was eased. In October 1997, Governor Pete Wilson signed legislation repealing Cortese-Knox's provisions for a city-council veto on secession decisions. Yet restrictions still remained. The breakup of a municipal corporation had to be revenue neutral for both parties. This provision ensured that both new and old cities would be financially sound. In addition, secession still required a dual-majority vote for approval. Both the seceding area and the city as a whole had to agree to the breakup. With the bill's passage, Valley VOTE, the latest secession group, began gathering the needed 135,000 signatures. As Studio City attorney David Fleming aptly put it, "It [will be] the divorce of the century." [67]

But the Valley was not the only disaffected community in Los Angeles. Secession movements soon sprung up in the harbor area, Hollywood, Westchester, Venice, and South Central. In San Pedro/Wilmington, Andrew Mardesich, head of the secessionist Harbor Study Foundation, acknowledged a debt to the better-organized and well-financed Valley campaign: "We do realize we are a different area with different issues than the Valley, but we are going to follow the road they have carved out. Thank God for the Valley. Until they came along, this was all just a big dream." [68]

The various secession groups soon began coordinating their efforts in an attempt to overcome the dual-majority vote requirement. If the Local Agency Formation Commission (LAFCO), the local governmental entity given the authority to oversee the secession process under California law, were to place all the secession measures on the same ballot, the groups could assist each other in generating the majorities needed for breaking up Los Angeles.

In the harbor area, the economic stakes were particularly high. Who would control the Port of Los Angeles, one of the world's great trade facilities? Los Angeles was determined to keep control of the port, a facility in which it had invested a quarter-billion dollars. But Harbor VOTE, an organization leading the secession fight, also staked a claim to the port, pointing out that the state owned most of the harbor lands and waters and leased them to Los Angeles through a tidelands grant. The state could just as easily lease them to a separate harbor municipality. San Pedro/Wilmington then would have a greater say than it currently did in port plans through the permitting and environmental-review processes.[69]

For its part, the port claimed that it seriously tried to minimize the negative impacts of its projects on the local community. For example, the port used electric dredges in landfill operations to minimize pollution and expected a reduction of local truck traffic with completion of the Alameda Corridor project in 2002. It also funded a trolley line to link downtown San Pedro with other commercial areas around the harbor. Finally, Mayor Riordan sought to soothe secession fever by involving local citizens in planning for port projects. The mayor appointed a community representative "to resolve the long-standing differences between the port and the surrounding community[,] . . . to directly involve citizens in port projects, an unprecedented move, given the port's past insistence that it remain firmly in control of development on harbor land." Despite the mayor's efforts to give the community "a voice in what is done," secession leader Mardesich claimed that "there are lots of plans that have been shelved. The mayor's will be another one. This program is only window dressing."[70]

As the new millennium dawned, secession supporters faced additional hurdles besides the electoral requirements of ballot qualification and the need for a dual majority. One concerned the economic viability of a new "Harbor City." LAFCO's initial feasibility study concluded that a new city "would operate in the red" and that the "economic possibilities . . . would not be bright." In their rejoinder, secession backers offered a different financing plan that identified several revenue sources, from oil-pipeline fees to truck-permit charges, that it claimed were undercounted in the LAFCO study. Purportedly, "this plan presents a new harbor-area city that will be both vibrant and viable economically, and its transition will have minimal economic impact upon the remaining city of Los Angeles."[71]

Port supporters feared that a financially strapped Harbor City would opportunistically treat the port as a cash cow for budget-balancing and community-development purposes. Secessionist proposals gave credence to these concerns. Adopting as a model El Segundo—a South Bay city whose refinery generates sizeable municipal revenues—the pro-secession New Wilmington Committee planned to use port and refinery revenues for community-redevelopment and recreation projects.[72]

A second hurdle concerned the Tidelands Trust Act. Secession leaders had assumed they could simply take over the port. But, in fact, they had to get the approval of the State Lands Commission to include the state tidelands within the borders of the new city. The Harbor Study Foundation's Mardesich claimed that his group had trouble getting data from the city and other sources to complete its application to the state, and as a result any decision would be delayed. "Unfortunately, it's a very complicated, convoluted and difficult thing," Mardesich informed LAFCO.[73]

Yet the secessionists had overcome obstacles in the past, such as collect-

Table 5.4   Top Ten U.S. Container Ports, 1990 and 2000, Ranked by Year 1990
Container Traffic (in TEUs[a])

Port	1990	2000	Percentage Growth
Los Angeles	2,116,980	4,879,429	130
New York/New Jersey	1,898,436	3,050,746	61
Long Beach	1,598,078	4,600,787	188
Seattle	1,171,091	1,488,267	27
Tacoma	937,691	1,376,379	47
Oakland	817,480	1,776,922	117
Charleston	801,105	1,629,070	103
Houston	502,035	1,074,102	114
Savannah	419,079	954,382	128
Miami	373,851	868,178	132

SOURCE: 1990 data from *Containerisation International Yearbook, 1992*; 2000 data furnished by the individual ports.
[a] Twenty-foot equivalent units.

ing the requisite petition signatures to require LAFCO to study the feasibility of secession. Notwithstanding the twin defeats of Valley and Hollywood secession in 2002, if secessionists in the harbor area and other disaffected communities ever do succeed in splitting the city up, then Los Angeles could become the first California city broken up since Coronado left San Diego over a century ago.[74] If the harbor-secession movement had succeeded, Los Angeles ironically would have entered the twenty-first century as it did the twentieth—unable to control the port facilities that can so profoundly shape the region's destiny.

Clear Sailing?

Given these myriad financial, environmental/regulatory, and governance challenges, how did the San Pedro ports perform in the 1990s? Table 5.4 displays the growth in container traffic from 1990 to 2000 for the nation's ten leading ports. The San Pedro Bay ports successfully tacked in the face of stormy weather. Their ambitious expansion plans coupled with booming Pacific Rim trade and a bounding regional economy allowed them to capture a lion's share of West Coast trade. During this ten-year period, the two L.A.-area ports captured over three-quarters of the container-trade growth among the five major West Coast ports. As a result, their share of Pacific Coast container traffic rose from 56 percent in 1990 to 67 percent in 2000. By the turn of the century, the San Pedro Bay ports had realized their aspiration of becoming the nation's leading gateway for the Pacific Rim. Notwithstanding their large 1990 traffic base, the two Southern California ports outperformed the nation's other major ports during the decade. As Table 5.4 shows, their

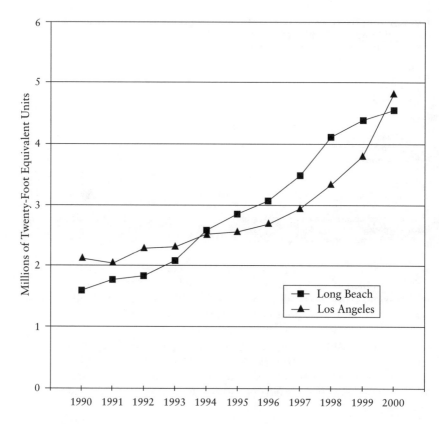

Figure 5.1. Trading Places: Port of Los Angeles and Port of Long Beach Container Traffic, 1990–2000.
Sources: Data from www.portoflosangeles.org and www.polb.com.

hefty TEU (twenty-foot equivalent unit) growth rates of 130 percent (Los Angeles) and 188 percent (Long Beach) met or exceeded those for other top ports. Overall, the two mega-ports' share of total U.S. container traffic grew from 25 percent in 1990 to nearly one-third in 2000.

During the 1990s, the two ports jockeyed fiercely for position in terms of the top ranking of U.S. container ports. Figure 5.1 shows year-by-year container traffic at the Port of Los Angeles and the Port of Long Beach from 1990 to 2000. Los Angeles led its rival until 1994, when Long Beach surged ahead, in large part because of its more expeditious landside expansion strategy. Relying on dredge-and-fill development, Los Angeles faced permitting and environmental-mitigation delays with its Pier 300/400 projects, delays that slowed container growth. Los Angeles also may have been hurt by revenue diversions and cumbersome charter-review provisions. But, with the opening of Pier 300 in 1997, L.A. container-traffic growth again accelerated. By 2000, Los Angeles had regained the top ranking among the nation's top container ports.

In early 2000 the intense, long-running competition between Los Angeles and Long Beach harbors took a dramatic tilt in favor of Los Angeles when Maersk Sealand, the world's largest shipping line and a prize Long Beach tenant for more than twenty years, signed a twenty-five-year lease with Los Angeles. Maersk Sealand now occupies the port's new Pier 400 container terminal, which will have the capacity to increase the port's annual volume of containers to well over the five million mark and thus will enable Los Angeles to maintain its ranking as the nation's busiest port.

Yet, at the beginning of the new century, the San Pedro Bay ports' reputation as the Pacific Rim gateway of choice was being tested in new ways. First, the higher shipping charges needed to finance their ambitious expansion programs also threatened their dominance over the nation's Pacific Rim trade. Competition for discretionary cargo was growing not only from West Coast rivals such as Seattle/Tacoma (a day's sail closer to Japan) but also from Houston and East Coast ports such as New York, Norfolk, and Charleston. It took Asian cargo three days longer to reach Houston than L.A. via the Panama Canal, but the price was $400 less per container. East Coast ports, which once dominated U.S. trade, also made a concerted effort to capture Asian shipping from Los Angeles and Long Beach. The ports of New York, Baltimore, and Boston dropped their cargo rates by as much as 30 percent, enough to encourage shippers to consider sending their Asian cargo through the Suez Canal to the East Coast.[75]

Second, the two ports faced growing labor and transportation challenges. The late 1990s saw labor disputes involving independent truckers and port pilots, limited hours of operation, and a massive dock and rail tie-up resulting from the Union Pacific's trouble-plagued takeover of the Southern Pacific railroad system. The tie-up, which led to up to thirty ships being diverted to other West Coast ports and threats by businesses to ship elsewhere, revealed a serious challenge facing the ports: a growing landside transportation bottleneck.[76] Thus, the Alameda Corridor project, designed to improve rail access to the ports, was integral to port-development plans. Chapter Six surveys the fate of the region's ambitious trade-corridor projects during the Riordan years.

6 Building Trade Corridors

> Seldom does an infrastructure project come around with as many social benefits as the Alameda Corridor. . . . [It] will provide a much needed boost to our local and national economy, and will benefit the environment in Southern California. . . . The project now faces perhaps its toughest hurdle on the road to completion—securing the $1.8 billion required to build the project.
>
> —*Congresswoman Jane Harman, 1994*[1]

> The Alameda Corridor is benefiting the world, but Compton isn't benefiting as much. We're concerned about traffic and its impacts. The economic picture isn't bright since construction jobs are only temporary employment. . . . We're just people in the way, and our concerns are not being heard.
>
> —*John Johnson, Compton assistant city manager, 1994*[2]

> The border land ports of entry and their supporting highway systems are a central component of the region's trade infrastructure. Despite progress on both the local and federal level, traffic congestion at the border remains a significant lag on the . . . region's global competitiveness.
>
> —*San Diego Dialogue, 2000*[3]

This chapter surveys the development of Southern California's major trade-corridor initiatives during the time Richard Riordan was mayor of Los Angeles (1993 to 2001); it focuses on the strategic environment and choices made regarding project planning, governance, and financing. Three rail megaprojects are examined: the Alameda Corridor (the nation's largest intermodal project), the Alameda Corridor–East (from the Union Pacific terminus of the Alameda Corridor to Colton Junction in San Bernardino County), and the Orange County Gateway (along the Burlington Northern Santa Fe main line). In regard to the Alameda Corridor initiative (considered a national model for innovative planning, governance, federal lobbying, and financing), my focus here is on the long, contentious planning phase, 1981–1998, which was fraught with discord and uncertainty relative to the shorter, fairly trouble-free construction period, 1998–2002. Because of the Port of Long Beach's involvement in the Alameda Corridor, I consider the roles of Long Beach officials such as Mayor Beverly O'Neill.

I also examine the development of major trade-related highway projects in Southern California during this period. These include the routes connecting the ports to downtown L.A. and to the fast-growing distribution and warehouse centers in the Inland Empire, as well as the increasingly important North American Free Trade Agreement (NAFTA) highways and commercial border crossings in San Diego and Imperial counties.

Regional Approaches

In the 1990s, the region's trade-corridor projects faced a unique set of challenges, particularly funding. The price tag for these projects would be steep. In all, the region would need $4.5 billion for rail projects, billions more for truck and goods-movement highway upgrades, and up to $2.3 billion for border-infrastructure improvements, according to the Southern California Association of Governments (SCAG) and the San Diego Association of Governments (SANDAG). With Proposition 13–era constraints on local-government finances, sluggish state and regional economic recovery, and limited federal and state transportation dollars, innovative financing strategies had to be devised. In addition, projects such as the twenty-mile long Alameda Corridor crossed multiple city boundaries and needed innovative governance mechanisms to secure cooperation from affected stakeholders. Yet trade-corridor initiatives, unlike port and airport projects, generally faced a supportive, not adversarial, regulatory environment because they promised environmental benefits such as reduced traffic congestion and less noise and air pollution.

Driving the flurry of high-priced regional trade-corridor projects were forecasts of robust trade growth and attendant increases in train and truck traffic, which threatened massive congestion and delays. Between 2000 and 2020, the value of port-of-entry merchandise trade through the L.A. Customs District (LACD) was projected to grow nearly 200 percent, from $230 billion to $661 billion. Containers through the San Pedro Bay ports were forecast to increase 175 percent, from 7 million loaded twenty-foot equivalent units (TEUs) in 2000 to 19.2 million TEUs in 2020.

Half these containers would be put on railcars for shipment to eastern destinations. On the two east/west rail corridors—the Burlington Northern Santa Fe (BNSF) and the Union Pacific (UP) railroad systems—the combined freight-train traffic was projected to grow by over 160 percent from 2000 to 2020. The projected growth was so dramatic that by 2020 the BNSF line through northern Orange County would see one train every ten minutes. Already, many trains, double-stacked with containers, were more than a mile long and caused major delays at grade crossings. Containers that were not put on trains were trucked to destinations in the huge Southern California market. By 2020, heavy-duty truck traffic in metropolitan Los Angeles was expected to grow by 65 percent relative to 1995 and could double on key routes such as Interstate I-710, which links the ports with downtown. Overall, travel times on freeways serving the airports and ports would likely double by 2020.[4]

At the same time, burgeoning NAFTA trade with Mexico (90 percent of it trucked across the border) created a new set of demands on the region's already-congested transportation system. California/Mexico trade, much of it generated by maquiladora manufacturers in Baja California, was projected to grow by 262 percent from 1996 to 2020—from $16 billion to $58 billion. Truck traffic crossing the border was forecast to grow similarly. Much of California's Mexican trade and truck traffic went through Los Angeles. In 1993, on the eve of NAFTA, the L.A. metropolitan area already accounted for nearly 60 percent of California origin-or-destination truck traffic crossing the Mexican border (compared with less than 20 percent for San Diego). For Greater L.A., NAFTA truck traffic with Mexico was projected to increase 300 percent between 1992 and 2015.[5]

In comparison with municipal port and airport projects, regional approaches to planning, governance, and finance were much more evident for trade-corridor projects (particularly rail initiatives). SCAG, the transportation-planning agency for metropolitan L.A., and SANDAG, the comparable agency for San Diego County, took the lead in regional freight-movement planning. The region's three major rail mega-projects—the Alameda Corridor and two successor projects from the downtown rail yards to the eastern fringes of the L.A. metropolitan area—featured innovative use of another regional mechanism: the joint-powers authority (JPA) for project financing and governance.

A JPA has the authority to issue revenue bonds and, by representing affected constituencies, potentially can resolve stakeholder conflicts. In the case of the Alameda Corridor, these conflicts involved disagreements between the ports and the communities along the route. The six county transportation commissions/authorities in Southern California, responsible for programming and funding transportation projects, were yet another set of regional entities concerned with freight-movement funding. Thus, the Los Angeles County Metropolitan Transportation Authority (LACMTA) served as a major funding partner for the Alameda Corridor.[6]

With a final price tag of $2.4 billion, the Alameda Corridor project linking the ports with the downtown rail yards was completed in April 2002. At the opening ceremony, U.S. Transportation Secretary Norman Mineta called it "one of America's most significant transportation projects[,] . . . a model of innovative financing, cooperation and good government."[7] Yet, as this chapter argues, this was not always so. In the mid-1990s, the project was beset with serious financing difficulties and conflicts between the ports and several corridor communities. Given the corridor's regional and national significance, I focus here on how these challenges were overcome with innovative financing and community-outreach strategies. Further, the Alameda Corridor project raises important questions concerning who benefits and who should pay. And corridor governance and policymaking raise serious questions regarding who should be represented (affected corridor communities versus resource constituencies like the ports and LACMTA) and who should bear responsibility for construction mitigation and community development.

While rail projects revealed the success of regional approaches, the same could not be said of highway and border-crossing projects. Here, regionalism largely ended with the planning process. These projects did not use a JPA for project governance and finance. In a much more decentralized political environment, sharp conflicts arose between project supporters and local communities and environmental groups over benefits and costs, and interjurisdictional battles among regional, state, and federal authorities took place over who should pay. As a result, highway and border projects were threatened with delays. Here I analyze major highway trade-corridor initiatives; the Inland Empire connecting freeways; and NAFTA initiatives involving Southern California's four land ports of entry to Mexico and key border highway projects.

The Alameda Corridor: "A Toll Road for Trains"

Early Planning and Design

By the early 1990s, railroads had become critical linchpins in the global transportation system. Panamax and post-Panamax cargo ships—those too large to pass through the Panama Canal—called on fewer ports and relied on rail transport to distribute cargo to inland and transcontinental destinations. Railroads now handled over one-quarter of total U.S. trade. Nowhere was this more true than in Los Angeles, owing to its status as the leading transshipment center for Pacific Rim imports. By 1996, the railroads shipped nearly 50 percent of the LACD's $152 billion in waterborne commerce to midwestern, eastern, and Gulf Coast destinations such as Chicago, New York City, and Houston.[8]

The weak link in the nation's railroad system was the seaport connection. Throughout the country, ports were choked by poor railroad connections. Problems ranged from too few tracks to too many bridges or tunnels blocking the best routes to too many at-grade highway crossings. The 1990s trade boom at the nation's largest ports placed an enormous strain on a rail infrastructure that had not been significantly expanded in fifty years because of slim profit margins on containerized cargo. At the San Pedro Bay ports, a growing rail bottleneck loomed as the major challenge to port development. Figure 6.1 shows the ports' preeminent role by the late 1990s in the nation's intermodal rail system. Handling one-third of the nation's international

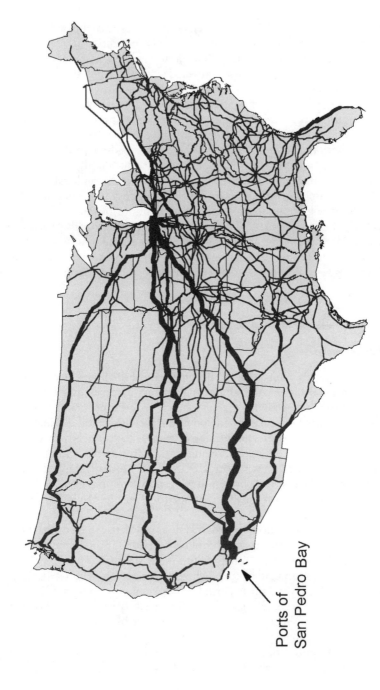

Ports of
San Pedro Bay

Figure 6.1. Rail Intermodal Flows, 1998 (freight density in relative tonnage).
Source: Federal Highways Administration Office of Freight Management and Operations, *Multi-Modal Freight Analysis*, 2000.

waterborne commerce and shipping half of its enormous container volume inland, the two ports and their transcontinental rail connections served as the country's premier gateway for Pacific Rim imports.[9]

Foreseeing such a bottleneck, port and regional planners took the lead in developing the Alameda Corridor initiative. Figure 6.2 is a map of the project. The purpose was to facilitate rail and truck access to the ports of San Pedro Bay while mitigating such adverse aspects of port growth as traffic congestion and air pollution. Port traffic initially was projected to grow from twenty-nine trains per day in 1991 to ninety-seven trains in 2020—a 234 percent increase.[10] The project would consolidate over ninety miles of rail lines intersected by two hundred at-grade road crossings into a single, uninterrupted, twenty-mile, high-speed, grade-separated rail system linking the ports of San Pedro Bay with the transcontinental rail yards located near downtown Los Angeles. The double-track corridor would be built along what was formerly the Southern Pacific's San Pedro branch right-of-way adjacent to Alameda Street. The ports would purchase the right-of-way for use by the two merged railroads serving the ports—the BNSF and the UP lines.

South of State Route SR-91, the proposed rail corridor would be at grade, with overpasses constructed for cross streets. North of SR-91, the railroad corridor would be depressed to 25th Street in a trench approximately thirty-five feet deep and forty-seven feet wide. The main cross streets would bridge the trench. Plans included a continuous at-grade parallel drill track to serve local industries. They also provided for the widening and improving of Alameda Street, which parallels the rail corridor, to expedite port truck traffic.[11]

The origins of the Alameda Corridor can be traced to 1981, when SCAG created the Ports Advisory Committee (PAC) in response to growing concerns about the ground-transportation system's ability to handle the increasing levels of highway and rail traffic accompanying port expansion. PAC's membership included local, state, and federal elected officials and representatives of the two ports, the California Department of Transportation (Caltrans), the Army Corps of Engineers, the Los Angeles County Transportation Commission (predecessor to the Metropolitan Transportation Authority), and representatives from the railroads and the trucking industry.[12]

The committee commissioned two sets of port-access studies. The first, completed in 1982, dealt with highway issues such as state-route realignments and street widening. A $58 million federal highway demonstration grant helped build the recommended improvements. The second study, completed in 1984, looked at rail access and focused on the impacts of projected train traffic on the communities north of the ports. After considering three alternative routes, the study recommended consolidating all freight-train traffic on an upgraded route using the then-Southern Pacific's San Pedro Branch right-of-way.

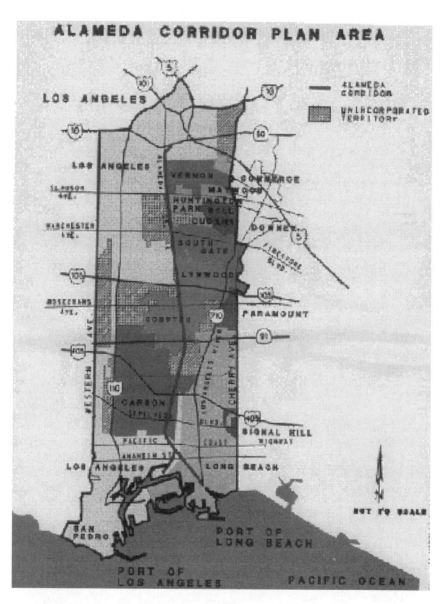

Figure 6.2. Alameda Corridor Rail Project.
Source: Alameda Corridor Transportation Authority, at www.acta.org.

The study also recommended creating a task force to analyze the myriad issues—legal, financial, design, and environmental—associated with planning and building the rail-corridor project.[13] In response, in 1985 SCAG created the Alameda Corridor Task Force (ACTF), whose membership was similar to that of PAC, with the addition of the cities along the corridor and the California Public Utilities Commission, which has regulatory powers over rail projects. The ACTF proposed creating a JPA to oversee the project's development. The need for it was buttressed by a 1988 port study that analyzed the effects of trends in global trade and freight handling on the region's rail system. Based on containerization growth and the development of near-dock and on-dock rail yards, the report recommended that the ports buy the railroad rights-of-way and conduct the needed rail-capacity, engineering, and environmental studies.[14]

By 1989 the cities of Los Angeles and Long Beach had agreed to use their joint-powers authority to create a consolidated rail-corridor agency—now called the Alameda Corridor Transportation Authority (ACTA). The sixteen-member ACTA Governing Board included representatives from the cities of Los Angeles and Long Beach, the ports of Los Angeles and Long Beach (two each), Caltrans, the Los Angeles County Board of Supervisors, the Los Angeles County Metropolitan Transportation Authority, SCAG (ex-officio), and the cities of Vernon, Huntington Park, South Gate, Lynwood, Compton, and Carson. In early 1993, with the preferred alternative plan chosen, the ACTA Governing Board unanimously approved the project's Environmental Impact Report (EIR). Because of promised environmental benefits, there were few legal challenges to the EIR. In early 1995 ACTA filed an Environmental Impact Statement (EIS) with the Federal Highway Administration and the Federal Railroad Administration, and it was approved.[15]

The project passed early regulatory muster because its environmental benefits appeared substantial. Traffic delays at grade crossings would be reduced by 90 percent as highway-railroad conflicts were eliminated at nearly two hundred grade crossings. Train noise would be cut by 90 percent as a result of the depressed railway design and consolidation of rail traffic. Train delays and stoppages would also be reduced by 75 percent. Because of on-dock facilities and containerization, truck-traffic growth would be cut by nearly one-quarter. Finally, the corridor would reduce air pollution through reduced hours of locomotive operation, lessened highway congestion, and fewer train and vehicle delays. Locomotive emissions (mostly nitrogen oxides) would be cut by 28 percent. A major environmental challenge would come later—the need to mitigate construction-related discharge of contaminated groundwater.[16]

Strategies for Negotiating with the Railroads

It took longer to acquire the railroad property than was originally antic-ipated. In 1993–94, negotiations with the railroads stalled over the rights-of-way purchase and operating agreements. The ports had the Southern Pacific's San Pedro Branch right-of-way appraised at $100 million. Because of alleged loss of competitive advantage, the railroad demanded much more. Thus, Southern Pacific's initial asking price was $500 million—later reduced to $275 million, then $260 million—for its property and loss of competitive ad-vantage. The L.A. Board of Harbor Commissioners, appointed by Mayor Ri-ordan, seemed not to care what the port paid; but when Long Beach's panel held firm for the lower price, negotiations ceased.[17]

Lobbied by city and port officials, the state then exerted pressure on the railroads. When Caltrans was given the power to acquire the Southern Pa-cific's right-of-way through eminent domain, railroad officials feared that the condemnation rate would be much lower than their asking price. The State Board of Equalization estimated the value of the property (but not the loss of competitive advantage) at only $78 million. Pressured back to the bargaining table, the Southern Pacific agreed to a lower sale price of $235 million (plus the sweetener of another $60 million for construction of a drill track). A new agreement was also reached on the costs of the property's clean up, estimated at between $7 million and $28 million.[18]

Then it was the UP's turn to play hardball in hopes of a windfall. The rail-road balked at the $30-per-container fee that the corridor authorities planned to charge the railroads for using the new line. The proposed fees, though, were crucial to the corridor's overall funding. Fully $700 million (and ultimately more) of the $2-plus billion price tag was to be financed by revenue bonds paid off by rail user and wharfage fees. After months of tough negotiations, with the sweetener of a higher price for its own right-of-way (as an overflow route), the UP signed an operating agreement. The last holdout was the BNSF, which had already sold its right-of-way to LACMTA for $50 million. When L.A. negotiators were willing to give BNSF another windfall, Long Beach again held the line, with a small sweetener eventually sealing the deal. The pro-tracted railroad negotiations delayed the project's completion by a full year.[19]

Financing Strategies

With the railroad agreements finalized and most environmental hurdles overcome, the project's chief challenge in the mid-1990s was finding needed funding. The corridor faced an $800 million shortfall—33 percent of its final cost—because of uncertain federal and state funding prospects. Conflicts be-tween the ports and several cities along the corridor complicated the funding quest and threatened further project delays. Indicative of the tensions among

ACTA's stakeholders were two lawsuits filed by some corridor cities against the ports. Here I explore the interrelated challenges of project financing and port/community conflicts—and the innovative strategies devised for overcoming both of them.

Experiencing delays, ACTA revised the project's cost estimate to $2-plus billion. The new figure included all engineering and construction costs, acquisition of rights-of-way, inflation, contingencies, and project reserves. Although ACTA's then-General Manager Gill Hicks believed this was a reasonable estimate, he acknowledged that it was based on an engineering design that at the time was less than 10 percent completed. More detailed design was delayed until the railroad right-of-way agreement was finalized. Begun in early 1995, the detailed analysis yielded a more accurate—and higher—estimate of actual project costs.[20]

As of early 1996 project officials had identified $1.4 billion—nearly 60 percent of the project's then-estimated total cost—in funding sources exclusive of new federal or state funding. Nearly all the early funding commitment came from local sources. The San Pedro Bay ports spent more than $400 million for project design, environmental review, and railroad right-of-way acquisitions. LACMTA quickly became a major financial partner. It would spend $8 million for engineering work and early on committed $129 million from the $350 million it pledged to the project in its Long Range Plan. As for private funding, $711 million in construction costs (later increased to $866 million) would come from revenue bonds, with debt service paid by container and wharfage fees charged to the railroads and the steamship companies. Another $8 million came from railroad matching funds. In sharp contrast, only $127 million—6 percent of the project's then-estimated cost—had by then come from the state and federal governments. The state committed $80 million in Proposition 116 transportation funding. The federal government authorized $47 million in funds from the Intermodal Surface Transportation Efficiency Act of 1991 and the Economic Development Administration.[21]

Facing an $800 million shortfall, ACTA crafted a financing strategy that relied primarily on the federal government. Two factors dictated this choice. First, other funding sources were limited. In regard to private financing, user fees to support a growing variety of financial instruments—bonds, loans, credit lines—could be raised only so much before competitive hardships became evident. Privatization was considered as a funding option, but project officials labeled it "tricky" and in need of "substantially more research." As then-L.A. Harbor Commissioner Jon Thomas argued, "Privatization could be problematic. For example, as part of our federal funding effort, we are doing everything we can to seek a tax exemption for debt issued by ACTA. If we were to privatize the Corridor, making it owned and operated by the railroads and other private parties, there would be zero chance of receiving tax exempt status." Tax exemption could lower project borrowing interest rates by up to two percentage points.[22]

State funding opportunities also appeared limited. The California Transportation Commission (CTC) initially delayed consideration of ACTA funding because of the lack of "a financial plan which maximizes the uses of revenues generated from users (ports, railroads and trucks)." ACTA's financial plan, in turn, was delayed because it took two and a half years to negotiate the railroad agreements. Even with signed agreements and a financial plan, ACTA was able to secure only limited state funding because of recession-induced funding shortages in the State Transportation Improvement Plan (STIP). As the CTC informed the legislature in late 1994, "State transportation programs are currently facing serious funding shortages. The 1994 STIP, as programmed through 1999, was $4.5 billion underfunded, resulting in immediate cash flow problems, significant delays in building programmed projects, and the inability to add new projects to the 1994 and 1996 STIPs—[the result is] no new programming before 2003."[23]

CTC officials also pointed to programmatic barriers to public funding of freight-rail projects. As then-CTC Chairperson Mary Berglund observed, "Private freight railroads cannot now receive state funding—public money diverted to private use. Even when owned by the ports, rail projects cannot access State Highway Account [SHA] funds, as this is considered inequitable. The SHA funds are technically user fees collected from truckers and private autos for highway use and should not be diverted to rail use."[24]

There appeared to be few other state funding options. Recession-weary California voters were in no mood to approve new spending. In 1994, voters defeated Proposition 185, which earmarked $350 million for the Alameda Corridor. The California Infrastructure Bank, created in 1994 to lend money to cities for needed projects, was another potential vehicle for corridor financing. However, the bank's initial funding depended on a $200 million ballot measure, which was defeated, and, throughout the 1990s, there was no state funding for the infrastructure bank.[25]

A second key factor dictating ACTA's decision to seek federal funding was the corridor's national economic benefits. A 1994 ACTA study, based on conservative forecasting, suggested that at least 185,000 new jobs could be generated nationwide by 2020 if the corridor were built. Less conservative forecasting suggested that the full national job impact could be up to twenty times greater—3.7 million jobs. To aid its congressional lobbying efforts, ACTA borrowed a page from defense-procurement funding stratagems and developed estimates of the project's trade, employment, and government-revenue benefits for every congressional district.[26]

Project officials believed that credibility in Congress would be enhanced by showing that all other funding possibilities had been exhausted. According to L.A. Harbor Commissioner Thomas, "The goal is to squeeze every drop out of local, regional and State sources and then to seek the balance from the Federal government. . . . We don't want to be in a situation where the federal government says we haven't explored all our local funding opportunities."[27] Critical to this negotiating strategy were contributions from the project's major stakeholders—the ports. Although port officials claimed they were contributing all they could, heightened port-revenue diversions—for example, those recommended in Los Angeles's Nexus study—appeared to undercut their efforts.

Another ACTA federal lobbying strategy involved demonstrating widespread regional and statewide support for the project. Despite growing disunity on the ACTA Governing Board between the ports and the corridor cities —Assemblywoman Martha Escutia called them "one big happy dysfunctional family"—there was an impressive display of bipartisan support from local, state, and federal officials. The Riordan administration, which initially viewed the project as a white elephant, was converted into one of its biggest champions. In early 1994, Riordan, California's two U.S. senators, and a dozen other local, state, and congressional elected officials lobbied the House public-works subcommittee for corridor funding. Long Beach Mayor O'Neill also entered the lobbying fray.[28]

Project advocates saw state support as critical to federal funding success, particularly for the White House and Senate. At their behest, the governor's office, the CTC, Caltrans, the Public Utilities Commission, and the Assembly Transportation Committee's Task Force on the Alameda Corridor Project lobbied Washington. The governor's office claimed the Alameda Corridor was a top priority. Caltrans included it among the state facilities to be made part of the National Highway System. State Senator Betty Karnette, representing the port area, also lobbied in Washington. The CTC and State Assembly both urged the president and Congress to provide the corridor full federal funding.

Until the 1994 congressional elections and Republican victory, ACTA had focused its efforts on securing federal grant money. In 1993, it sought $170 million—one-fifth of the project's funding gap—from a National Highway System (NHS) bill, with the remainder to be made up by future grants. Congress, though, did not allocate any new project money. Prior federal demonstration matching grants totaling $53 million (mostly City of L.A. highway projects delayed by intrajurisdictional squabbles) were escrowed but were not yet spent. As a result, ACTA got only $9 million in the House, while the Senate zeroed the project out because it wanted a so-called clean bill. The conference committee could not resolve the differences, so the NHS bill—and ACTA's measly $9 million—was carried over to the next Congress.[29]

In early 1995, ACTA's advocacy team faced a new, conservative Congress. Lobbyists had to fight a defensive battle to keep the $53 million already allocated but not yet spent. In a strong budget-cutting mood, Congress voted to rescind unspent transportation funds. Working closely with the region's lawmakers on both sides of the aisle, ACTA's lobbyists succeeded in restoring the project's unspent funding. Responding to the new political realities, the advocacy team then crafted a revised funding plan around four areas of "legislative potential": (1) full authorization and prioritization of the Alameda Corridor as a "nationally significant corridor" in NHS designation legislation; (2) innovative, leveraged finance mechanisms such as a proposed line of credit program in Department of Transportation appropriations bills; (3) tax-exempt status for the Alameda Corridor, which would lower financing costs for construction-related funding of the project; (4) supporting legislation— the "Truth in Budgeting Act"—to place transportation trust funds "off-budget" in order to release $1 billion in surplus funds being held because of current budgetary ceilings.[30]

The advocacy team also worked closely with federal transportation officials to ensure effective implementation of these proposals should they pass. Looking beyond FY 1996, project lobbyists sought a potential funding earmark for the corridor in the president's FY 1997 budget. The centerpiece of "legislative potential" was inclusion in the NHS bill, which was signed into law. Under this bill, the project became eligible for Federal Highway Administration (FHWA) funds. Previously, FHWA funds were not available because ACTA lacked revenues such as gas taxes. Without such assets, ACTA was beholden to local transportation agencies willing to serve as funding vehicles.[31]

ACTA's strategy was clear: to find as many federal funding options and ways of lowering project costs as possible. At the behest of ACTA's lobbyists, the NHS bill also amended the Intermodal Surface Transportation Efficiency Act (ISTEA) to add the Alameda Corridor to its list of high-priority corridors. The inclusion in ISTEA not only authorized the project but provided access to a variety of funding mechanisms such as loan guarantees and letters of credit. Although there was no funding earmark for FY 1996, the project's fortunes soon improved. Reflecting California's importance in an election year, both the president and Congress approved a $400 million Department of Transportation loan guarantee in 1996.[32]

A growing local fiscal crisis, created by the recession and the post-Proposition 13 state fiscal regime, also threatened corridor financing. LACTMA had become a major source of corridor funding as it had pledged $350 million—primarily in federal transportation money—for the project. Yet, in 1995, the state legislature approved the transfer of $150 million in LACMTA funds to aid fiscally strapped Los Angeles County. The bailout sent ACTA officials scrambling for assurances that previously awarded transit moneys were safe. Transfers interfered with LACMTA's ability to make a long-term commitment to the corridor. Even though the Bill Clinton administration later pledged $364 million in federal aid to assist Los Angeles County's health-care system, transfer pressures on LACMTA remained intense. Reflecting such uncertainties, the U.S. General Accounting Office concluded in 1998

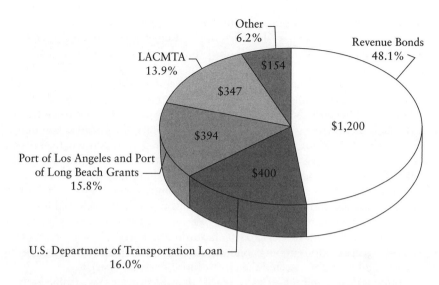

Figure 6.3. Alameda Corridor Funding Sources (in millions of dollars).
Source: Data from Alameda Corridor Transportation Authority at www.acta.org.

that the project's short- and long-term costs were uncertain, while its financing arrangements (particularly with LACMTA) still remained incomplete.[33]

Finally, by early 1999, the project had cobbled together an innovative and firm financing package. Sponsors claimed that the "Alameda Corridor is essentially a toll road for trains." Eighty percent of the project's $2.4 billion final cost would be covered by revenue bonds (backed by container fees and wharfage charges), federal loans (similarly backed), and port contributions (funded by tariff and wharfage charges). In contrast, less than one-fifth of the project was funded by federal and state transportation grants (funneled primarily through LACMTA). Figure 6.3 furnishes a detailed breakdown of project funding sources.[34]

Resolving Port/Corridor-City Conflicts

From its inception the Alameda Corridor project created tensions between the ports and the corridor cities. The conflict was rooted in different conceptions of the project's purpose and in differing assessments of its benefits and costs. Then-L.A. port Executive Director Ezunial Burts expressed the difference succinctly. For the ports, he argued, "this is a transportation project, not an economic development project. The cities see it as economic development. The ports do not."[35] Because the project promised to reduce rail and truck congestion—looming ground-access barriers to port development —the ports were its primary beneficiaries and chief financial stakeholders. They contributed nearly $400 million to purchase the railroads' rights-of-way and paid for the project's initial design and engineering work. In addition, user fees would finance $1.2 billion in revenue bonds.

The corridor cities were concerned about the project's concentrated costs and dispersed benefits. Because the project sent the ports' rail and truck traffic through their business districts and neighborhoods, the corridor communities believed they bore most of the costs, ranging from construction disruptions to train noise and vibrations, air pollution, and increased truck traffic. The City of Compton was the most vocal about negative impacts. As Reginald Tabor, then-special assistant to the Compton city manager, noted, "We're concerned about back-ups, truck traffic on adjacent roads and how it will impact street maintenance in terms of increased tonnage on city streets. We're concerned about trucks carrying hazardous materials." [36] Compton officials also were anxious about economic disruptions during construction because the rail corridor bisected the city's central business district.

Many of these communities also feared that the project was insufficiently attentive to their economic-development needs. Located in southeast Los Angeles County—a once-vibrant manufacturing and residential area economically hollowed out by recession, deindustrialization, and defense downsizing —they had large black and Latino populations with high unemployment and poverty rates. By the late 1990s, their unemployment and underemployment rates were as high as 34 percent compared with a 6 percent overall jobless rate in the county. For them, economic development was a primary policy concern, and they looked to the corridor project for economic salvation. Yet they feared this relief would not be forthcoming because of the project's focus on creating national, but not local, jobs.[37]

ACTA tried to assuage their concerns. ACTA's Contracting Policies and Plan Review Committee, with representatives from four of the six corridor cities, was given responsibility for construction hiring. Economic development became a more salient item on the agenda of ACTA's Governing Board. A review of the board's minutes from January 1993 to May 1994, for example, revealed only ten references to project impact or economic development relating to the corridor cities. Most of the queries came from corridor-city representatives. Between May 1994 and December 1994, after the corridor cities filed a lawsuit against the Port of Long Beach, ACTA board discussion of economic development along the corridor increased significantly.[38]

Fearing further project delays, ACTA, regional planners, and public officials worked feverishly on plans to promote corridor-city revitalization. While ACTA General Manager Hicks acknowledged that port expansion would not necessarily create permanent jobs in the corridor cities, ACTA's Economic Development Committee labored to establish goals for business and employment development associated with construction of the Alameda Corridor and growth of the ports. SCAG developed a subregional strategy for southeast Los Angeles County—part of its Regional Comprehensive Plan—which highlighted the Alameda Corridor's role as a local economic stimulus.[39]

Assemblywoman Escutia played a role in revitalization planning for the corridor cities. She created a community self-help program—the Southeast Community Development Corporation—to enhance the input of the small corridor cities into project design and job creation. The model was the Century Freeway project, which featured extensive community outreach. Long Beach port planner Geraldine Knatz counseled the corridor cities to take full advantage of state and federal stimulus programs. Long Beach served as a model. The city had the area extending east to the 605 freeway designated as a state enterprise zone, which gave tax incentives for business expansion and for hiring and training designated local residents. Similarly, the City of Long Beach took the initiative and was awarded a $2 million federal Economic Development Administration engineering planning grant for the Alameda Corridor. As a result, Assemblywoman Escutia introduced a bill that designated the corridor cities as an enterprise zone.[40]

Yet conflict persisted over the ports' responsibilities regarding corridor-city economic development. Kofi Sefa-Boakye, a Compton development official, argued that "port officials must channel revenue from user fees and other port activities into a special trust fund to foster the economic revitalization and infrastructure improvements of the impoverished corridor communities." In contrast, David Hauser, a former member of the Long Beach Board of Harbor Commissioners and ACTA's Governing Board, argued that the ports already had made a substantial investment of $400 million and had "agreed to run almost 10 miles of the corridor rail line in a trench almost 30 feet below ground level through [Compton] and three [four] others [cities] for environmental mitigation at a cost which is expected to add almost $300 million to the total project."[41]

As a result of their concerns, the corridor cities filed lawsuits against the ports and ACTA to mitigate the adverse impacts of port expansion and to ensure greater community control over project decision making. The first lawsuit, filed in 1994, concerned the Port of Long Beach's expansion plans. The cities of Compton, Lynwood, South Gate, and Vernon sued Long Beach over its EIR for the Pier J reconfiguration project. When completed, the project would generate additional train and truck traffic through these cities. They were concerned that the port had not made a strong enough commitment, as expressed in the EIR, to having the Alameda Corridor serve as mitigation for terminal expansion. The cities sued to commit the port to building the rail project as a mitigation measure; if the suit were successful, Long Beach alone would have to make up the project's $700–800 million shortfall. After the port pulled out of the corridor project, effectively bringing it to a halt for a month, and then agreed to a minor change in the EIR, the cities dropped their lawsuit.[42]

The second lawsuit involved control over project financial decisions. The backdrop was the controversial third amendment to ACTA's joint-powers agreement. As Burke Roche, then L.A. County's representative on ACTA's Governing Board, explained, "The ports were getting very antsy with the corridor cities. The ports proposed a third amendment [to the joint-powers agreement] to transfer powers to a newly created Finance Committee. Any decision about money is in the power of the Finance Committee. The ports control the committee and have disenfranchised other key member cities. The ports exerted their power since they are allocating so much money to finance this project."[43] The seven-member Finance Committee, approved at the October 1993 ACTA board meeting with only two dissenting votes, consisted of representatives from the two ports, the cities of Los Angeles and Long Beach, Los Angeles County, Caltrans, and one member from the corridor cities.

Claiming the third amendment had disenfranchised them, Compton, South Gate, Lynwood, and Vernon in early 1995 sued the two ports and the cities of Los Angeles and Long Beach to disband the Finance Committee and transfer its powers back to the ACTA Governing Board. As Long Beach's Knatz explained, "The third amendment returns financial decision making to the financial investors. . . . The imbalance between the financial investors and the six local governments whose communities will be impacted by the corridor has developed into a tenuous, often emotional relationship. The lawsuit reflects this imbalance."[44] Complicating settlement was LACMTA's demand to be seated on the Finance Committee because of its $350 million long-term commitment to the project. In the final settlement, the courts stripped the corridor cities of their ACTA representation. The ACTA Governing Board was reduced to just seven members representing the major local financial stakeholders: the ports (two representatives each), the cities of L.A. and Long Beach, and LACMTA. Yet the settlement also yielded corridor-city payoffs. The ports pledged millions of dollars in economic-development moneys to lawsuit cities, such as Compton, and even to nonlawsuit cities, such as Carson.

Even if they had won the lawsuits, the corridor cities would have been at a major disadvantage in dealing as equals with Los Angeles and Long Beach port and city officials on ACTA's board. These small cities—many with disadvantaged minority populations and limited financial resources—did not have the staff or technical expertise to take full advantage of available grants and programs. Their elected officials served part-time, experienced high turnover, had little staff, and frequently were unavailable for meetings on short notice. The crucial October 1993 vote on the third amendment illustrated the problem of corridor-city representation. Of the six corridor cities, only one— Vernon (joined by LACMTA)—voted against the amendment. As then-ACTA board member Roche observed, "As a representative of L.A. County, I objected to this amendment. However, I had no support from the corridor cities. The cities had no idea of what was going on. They actually voted themselves out of the decision-making process." [45]

Notwithstanding the lawsuit financial settlements, ACTA officials remained concerned that the frustrations of some corridor cities could lead to project delays. Cities had substantial leverage because they controlled the construction permitting process and approved project design elements that affected local facilities and public services. ACTA also feared that conflicts between the corridor cities and the ports could undermine the "united front" thought essential for successful lobbying of federal and state officials for needed project funding. As ACTA's Hicks argued, the project needed "to strengthen its coalitions with . . . many interest groups and have one unified voice." [46]

The negative effects of ACTA board disunity were mitigated by the impressive bipartisan united front shown by the region's state and federal lawmakers in support of the project. Another key mitigating factor was the less-than-united front among the corridor cities in opposition to port plans. The corridor cities of Carson—racially mixed and middle class—and Huntington Park—heavily Latino and working class—were sympathetic to the project. They were conspicuously absent from the two lawsuits. Tom Jackson, then-chair of ACTA's Governing Board and a councilperson in Huntington Park, criticized the lawsuits as "counterproductive" and called "unrealistic" the development hopes of some corridor cities. Working in favor of a united front on the ACTA board were the project's potent fund-raising opportunities for sympathetic local officials. One corridor-city councilman, for example, celebrated his appointment to the ACTA board with a $1,000-a-table fund-raiser designed to solicit funds from the project's contractors and lobbyists. [47]

To assuage local concerns and further compensate the corridor cities for their loss of ACTA board representation, ACTA created ambitious programs for minority contracting, local job training, and construction mitigation. In 1998, ACTA's Governing Board took a major step forward by voting to award 22 percent of contract value (more than double the federal requirement) to minority- and women-owned businesses. ACTA also called for job training for a thousand residents and for local residents to secure 30 percent of total work hours on mid-corridor projects. Project officials estimated that construction ultimately would require ten thousand workers. According to Dennis Rockway, senior counsel with the Legal Aid Foundation of Long Beach, "This is the largest local hiring plan of any public works project in the history of the United States." ACTA's policies paved the way for training neighborhood residents for construction and trade-related jobs. [48]

Businesses in the construction zone, ranging from manufacturing plants to warehouses and small industrial-support firms, feared that impeded access during the four-year construction period would drive away customers and disrupt crucial shipping and receiving schedules. In response, ACTA spent millions on a mitigation plan to limit construction disruptions. Yet knotty community-development issues still remained. The 1999 Alameda Corridor Industrial Reclamation Act authorized the L.A. County Community Development Commission to develop a revitalization task force and program for the area. With a multifaceted plan, backed by a commitment from the region's civic entrepreneurs, the corridor potentially could serve as an economic-development magnet for manufacturers, cargo consolidators, and warehousing and distribution companies, especially given the shortage of suitable property near the ports. L.A.'s designation in the mid-1990s as a federal empowerment zone offered further assistance. Yet few financing mechanisms were available for such key tasks as acquiring older "brownfields" industrial land along the corridor and performing cost-effective environmental cleanup.[49]

ACTA may have unwittingly oversold the economic benefits to the corridor communities and thereby created unrealistic expectations. The Alameda Corridor did offer real potential for local economic benefits beyond temporary construction contracts and hiring. In the long term, by substantially reducing traffic congestion and delays, the project made it possible for businesses—particularly those valuing proximity to the ports and rail system—to locate nearby without worrying that their employees and trucks would spend hours at congested rail crossings. But, in the end, the corridor was essentially a transportation project, not an economic-development project. An important lesson for future projects is to explain early and honestly to community residents what the local benefits and associated time horizon likely will be; such explanations can reduce the potential for disappointment and backlash.

Other Rail Projects: The Alameda Corridor–East and the Southwest Passage

Although the Alameda Corridor was designed to improve the capacity and efficiency of the rail system from the ports to the downtown rail yards, it did nothing for freight traffic from the rail yards continuing inland via the main UP and BNSF rail lines through the San Gabriel Valley, northern Orange County, and San Bernardino and Riverside counties. Beyond the Alameda Corridor, the main lines had another 141 highway/rail at-grade crossings needing separation (via trench or overpass) and other safety improvements. With train traffic from the San Pedro Bay ports and other intermodal train traffic projected to grow by 160 percent from 2000 to 2020, additional grade-improvement projects appeared to offer myriad benefits, including reduced vehicle congestion and delays, enhanced safety, improved air quality, and possibly greater goods-movement efficiency.

In the mid- to late 1990s, local officials in the San Gabriel Valley and

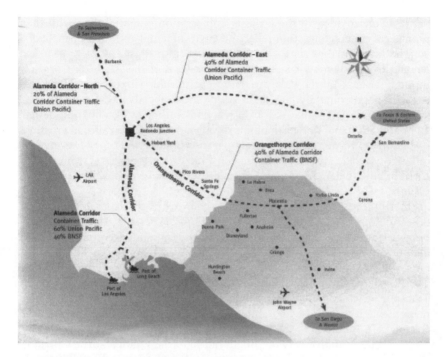

Figure 6.4. Southern California Rail Corridors.
Source: OnTrac Joint Powers Authority, *Orange County Gateway* (Placentia, Calif.: OnTrac JPA, 2000), p. 8.

northern Orange County launched two ambitious "Alameda Corridor–East" rail initiatives designed to streamline freight-rail movement through the entire metropolitan region at an estimated cost of $3 billion. Figure 6.4 shows the two projects—the Alameda Corridor–East and the Orangethorpe Corridor—in relation to the Alameda Corridor.

Although borrowing governance mechanisms and funding strategies from the Alameda Corridor, the two extension projects had different origins and grassroots relations. Here, initiative came not from the ports but from affected communities concerned with the negative effects of port and rail-traffic growth. The ports, already saddled with their own multi-billion dollar development projects and $400 million Alameda Corridor funding, made it clear that they lacked the wherewithal to be major financial stakeholders. The ports also saw the projects largely as grade-separation initiatives: they would reduce local vehicular-traffic delays but would provide only modest benefits in freight-throughput capacity compared with the Alameda Corridor. But grassroots tensions were reduced because these were middle-class communities less concerned with the projects' job-creation potential than with their promise of traffic-congestion relief and environmental and safety benefits.

The first initiative was the Alameda Corridor–East (ACE) Project, extending from downtown L.A. (the northern end of the Alameda Corridor) through the San Gabriel Valley to the San Bernardino County line. Here, borrowing a page from the Alameda Corridor, local officials spearheaded the creation of a new JPA—the ACE Construction Authority—to finance, design, and build $900 million worth of improvements at fifty-five railroad crossings (including up to twenty-one grade separations) along the thirty-five-mile UP rail corridor. The authority's board consisted of representatives from the five corridor cities where major improvements were planned as well as from L.A. County.[50]

In 1998, project advocates scored a coup when the federal Transportation and Equity Act for the 21st Century (TEA-21) designated ACE as a high-priority trade corridor with an initial $136 million funding earmark. TEA-21 high-priority corridor and funding status later were extended to the main lines in San Bernardino and Riverside counties and to northern Orange County. The San Bernardino Association of Governments and the Riverside County Transportation Commission developed their own rail-crossing improvement plans through to the desert communities of Barstow and Indio at an estimated cost of $575 million.[51]

A second initiative was the BNSF rail line (the Orangethorpe Corridor) through northern Orange County. (On a daily basis, more BNSF freight trains traversed the Orangethorpe Corridor than were expected to use the Alameda Corridor because the downtown-L.A. Hobart Intermodal Facility added even more freight trains.) The City of Placentia took the lead in creating the $476 million Orange County Gateway (OCG) Project to build a rail-lowering trench under eight BNSF grade crossings (plus two standard underpasses and one street closure) and thus eliminate traffic conflicts. Here too the Alameda Corridor served as a model. In 2000, the City of Placentia and its Redevelopment Agency formed a JPA—called OnTrac (the Orange North-American Trade Rail Access Corridor)—to fund and build the OCG Project. Alameda Corridor staff helped lower OnTrac's learning curve. As Christopher Becker, OCG Project executive director, noted: "We are working with Gill Hicks and the Alameda Corridor team. They're providing some counsel on how to put together internal policies for the OnTrac Board so that we'll be in good standing with State and Federal requirements for processing future grants and meeting Disadvantaged Business Enterprise requirements for small and minority- or women-owned firms."[52]

The OCG/OnTrac Project also emulated the Alameda Corridor's federal funding strategy. The project would demonstrate its national significance (and funding attractiveness) by showing its trade and job benefits in various regions and congressional districts. Its supporters hoped to have federal environmental certification completed before the next reauthorization of the federal transportation bill in 2003. OCG officials commissioned a cost/benefit analysis, which revealed that the project's environmental, safety, and economic benefits were more than twice its construction costs. With funding, construction could begin as early as 2005 and end two years later.[53]

The "Southwest Passage" strategy was an even more ambitious rail/trade-corridor initiative; it was launched in the late 1990s. This SCAG-sponsored initiative was designed to transform east/west rail and highway routes along the U.S./Mexico border into a seamless freight-transportation system from Southern California to Texas. The UP's Sunset route, the BNSF rail line, and the I-8 and I-10 highways, which link Southern California to Arizona and other southwestern states, would serve as a mini-land bridge linking the San Pedro Bay ports with the ports of Houston and Corpus Christi. Thus, the Los Angeles/Long Beach ports would be able to maintain their dominance over Pacific Rim trade, while Asian imports destined for Europe would be shipped over the land bridge and placed on vessels in Houston and Corpus Christi. The strategy also called for strengthening north/south rail and highway links in the four southwestern border states to capture greater Mexican trade.[54]

Collectively, these grade-separation initiatives faced key challenges. First, they needed railroad support. Cooperation was made difficult by state policy requiring the railroads to pay 10 percent of project costs. Both the UP and the BNSF remained officially neutral in regard to both proposals. Second, financing remained uncertain. TEA-21 provided only limited grade-separation funding. Hence, the ACE received only a small funding earmark. TEA-21 did designate the ACE projects and the California portion of the Southwest Passage as high-priority trade corridors, and they were thus eligible for further federal funding. Yet, by 2001, only one-quarter of the $3 billion-plus four-county ACE plan was funded. The Southwest Passage received only token funding for initial planning.[55]

Southern California's other freight-rail initiative in the 1990s involved the San Diego/Baja California border region. That region's manufacturers and two small ports (San Diego and Ensenada) lay at competitive disadvantage because they lacked direct rail connections to national and international markets. Instead, San Diego and Tijuana rail cargo was shipped via a BNSF spur line through Los Angeles for transshipment, with resulting delays of one to three days and higher freight charges for local shippers. Baja California's maquiladoras, heavily dependent on trucking, lacked direct rail links to the United States or to the interior of Mexico. San Diego transportation planners proposed reopening and modernizing the San Diego and Arizona Eastern (SD&AE) line. The SD&AE—a 134-mile-long rail link, 44 miles of which ran through Mexico—was severed in 1983 by a tunnel collapse. If restored, it would provide the region with a direct rail connection to the east via the UP's Sunset line in Imperial County.

Political wrangling on both sides of the border stalled the rechristened

"NAFTA train." Despite strong support from the local congressman, a rival legislator, fearing that the railway would be a magnet for illegal immigrants and drug dealers, blocked an Alameda Corridor–like federal loan guarantee. Although TEA-21 contained $10 million to build a port rail yard in San Diego, nothing was pledged toward the $100 million-plus needed to repair and modernize the SD&AE system. Mexico's auction of the rail concession for the forty-four-mile Tijuana-to-Tecate portion of the line was repeatedly delayed because of legal and financial difficulties with privatization. Moreover, the project's economic prospects hinged on two unlikely developments: growth of marine cargo at the Port of San Diego and an eventual rail link to the Port of Ensenada, located seventy miles south of Tijuana. For the foreseeable future, San Diego and Tijuana/Tecate rail cargo would continue to be routed through Los Angeles.[56]

Highway Trade Corridors

Regional Challenges

By the mid- to late 1990s transportation planners and policymakers in Southern California confronted a new set of choke points in the goods-movement system: highways congealed with truck traffic. One emerging bottleneck involved the freeways connecting the San Pedro Bay ports to downtown Los Angeles and to the fast-growing distribution/warehouse complex in the Inland Empire in western San Bernardino and Riverside counties. Fully half the containers unloaded at the ports were placed on trucks for transportation and distribution to the huge Southern California market. Port studies found that 60 percent of port truck traffic initially came to rest off I-710; only 5 percent went directly to the Inland Empire.[57]

Spurred by NAFTA, a second bottleneck was emerging at California's border crossings with Mexico. With 90 percent of the state's NAFTA trade transported by truck and 60 percent originating in or destined for metropolitan Los Angeles, the commercial ports of entry and connecting highways experienced mounting congestion and delays. Given NAFTA's state and national trade benefits, there was growing regional debate, resulting in project delays, over who should pay for border highway improvements.

The already-crowded Southern California highway system faced the daunting challenge of a dramatic increase in truck traffic with inadequate funding for needed improvements. With nine thousand lane-miles of freeways and fifteen thousand lane-miles of principal arterial streets, Southern California has one of the nation's most extensive and complex highway systems. This network serves the region's ports and airports, its manufacturing, intermodal, distribution, and warehousing facilities, and connects to the U.S. hinterland, Mexico, and Canada via the interstate highway system.[58]

Driven by a projected 65 percent rise in regional freight tonnage by 2020, the combined increase in truck and automobile traffic threatened to paralyze the highway system. The most affected routes were those serving the ports, airports, and railroad and truck warehousing/distribution/transfer facilities. By the late 1990s, these trade arteries handled 30–45 percent of the region's total truck traffic. In particular, I-710 (the ports), I-5 (the major north/south thoroughfare), I-15 (the east/west thoroughfare), and SR-60 and SR-91 to the Inland Empire were likely to suffer the most acute truck congestion. For example, the I-710 freeway linking the ports with downtown L.A. could see a 250 percent increase in truck traffic by 2020, leading to substantial traffic congestion, delays, and accidents during peak periods as trucks competed with passenger vehicles for shrinking freeway space.[59]

As truck tonnage and traffic grew regionally and nationally, public highway funding did not keep pace. Passed by Congress in 1991, ISTEA gave the states $155 billion from 1992 to 1997 to develop a national intermodal transportation system that was economically and energy efficient, environmentally sound, and globally competitive. Yet, once touted as a harbinger of new highways, ISTEA effectively heralded the end of expansion of the interstate highway system. It merely closed existing freeway gaps and completed the interstate network as highway management and operational efficiencies replaced freeway building. In the 1990s, Southern California saw the completion of only one major freeway.[60]

Despite all these hurdles, economic recovery and temporary budget surpluses were hopeful signs in the late 1990s. Under TEA-21, federal highway funding increased. For 1998–2004, $167 billion would be spent improving and extending the nation's highway system. Sponsored by California Senator Barbara Boxer, in response to growing Southern California border-traffic concerns, TEA-21 also earmarked $700 million for border infrastructure and trade-corridor projects. TEA-21's new trade-corridor orientation was paralleled in California with the designation of two new high-priority state highway networks. In 1995, the Intermodal Corridors of Economic Significance system was established to improve trade corridors deemed critical to the California economy, such as I-5, I-8, and I-15 in Southern California. One year later, Caltrans created the NAFTA Network/International Border Trade Corridor program to improve the state's border crossings with Mexico and the connecting highway system. In the late 1990s, the state also decentralized transportation planning and funding, reserving 75 percent of state funding for local projects and furnishing 25 percent for interregional projects. This change produced a tug of war over who should pay—the local governments or the state—for border highway improvements.[61]

In response to growing congestion and limited public resources, private trucking companies in the 1990s began using complex information technology (IT)–based logistics systems, which were designed to improve inventory control, communications, transportation, and distribution. For example, just-in-time delivery was designed to enhance timely, coordinated, and dependable transportation and material handling. Yet a logistics revolution by itself could not overcome the looming capacity crisis facing Southern California's already-congested highway system.

Notwithstanding public-funding constraints, in the 1990s SCAG embarked on an ambitious goods-movement planning program. Two promising SCAG planning initiatives were truck-only lanes for major trade corridors—I-5, I-15, I-710, and SR-60—and a low-cost, high-impact IT-based "Jump Start" program to improve access to intermodal facilities and relieve traffic congestion at at-grade rail crossings through the use of "intelligent" transportation systems, signal synchronization, and safety improvements. Dedicated truck lanes would be established along the outer perimeter of existing freeways. SCAG determined that truck lanes were feasible for SR-60 and recommended further multimodal corridor analyses. A more controversial initiative was SCAG's proposed $6.2 billion high-speed rail system to serve the region's airports. As of 2002, SCAG's regional trade-transportation projects still remained in the planning stages, and funding was uncertain.[62]

NAFTA Highways and Border Crossings

With the implementation of NAFTA, the Southern California/Mexico border quickly became a new bottleneck in the region's trade-transportation system. In 1996, Southern California's four commercial land ports-of-entry—Otay Mesa, Tecate, East Calexico, and Andrade—handled 1.5 million trucks, a 67 percent increase over 1993. Projections to 2020 were for robust NAFTA-induced growth in border truck traffic—to 4.3 million trucks, a nearly 200 percent increase over 1996. Regional planners in San Diego County estimated that their border transportation improvements would cost upward of $1.5 billion. By 2000, local, state, and federal agencies had cobbled together only a $1 billion funding package.[63]

Maquiladora manufacturers in Baja California generated much of the cross-border trade and truck-traffic growth. Between 1978 and 1998, maquiladoras along the California border grew from 178 to 1,017—a nearly 500 percent increase. Their ability to get their products to market depended heavily on the Southern California highway system. For maquiladoras to manufacture commercial electronics products such as television sets, component parts from Asia were trucked in from the Los Angeles/Long Beach port complex. Finished products then were trucked back across the border to consumer markets, primarily those within a seven-hundred-mile radius—San Diego, Los Angeles, the Bay Area, Phoenix, and Las Vegas. The border crossings quickly became clogged with truck congestion, which threatened the smooth flow of maquiladora products. Strains also were placed on the region's highways, with the accompanying increase in warehousing and related services in the San Diego region. Truck traffic became a growing problem for

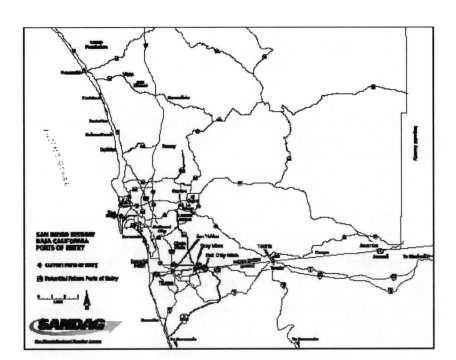

Figure 6.5. San Diego Region/Baja California Ports of Entry, 2000.
Source: San Diego Association of Governments, *2020 Regional Transportation Plan* (San Diego: SANDAG, April 2000), p. 212.

San Diego's local streets and highways because of the lack of direct connections from the border crossings to the state and interstate highway systems.[64]

In the period 1993–2001, regional planners proposed four major border improvement projects. Figure 6.5 displays the border ports of entry and highway projects in the San Diego/Baja California area. First (and foremost), the $250 million SR-905 freeway project was touted as a vital new link from San Diego's Otay Mesa commercial border crossing to the I-805 and I-5 freeways and the Southern California market. However, the project quickly experienced delays because of disagreements over who should fund it.

Although SANDAG, the local planning agency, claimed in 1994 that SR-905 was "vital to meet the region's need for an adequate transportation system to serve the demand brought about by the strong economic activity in the border area," it initially did not make it a high-priority funding item. It argued that such NAFTA-related projects were of statewide, not merely local, significance and benefit and hence should be funded out of the 25 percent of the state funds reserved for interregional projects rather than the 75 percent allocated for local projects. In 1998, with local Congressman Bob Filner as the project's champion, TEA-21 broke the local/state funding logjam by ear-marking $54 million in federal border-corridor funding for SR-905. The project also relied on strong lobbying support from local business organizations.[65]

In 1999, SR-905 was given added impetus by California Governor Gray Davis, who made border-infrastructure improvements part of his campaign to repair California-Mexican relations. With a state budget surplus, new funding was made available. Also, the creation of a new border-infrastructure authority allowed tax growth from within a three-mile-wide border zone to be redirected to infrastructure projects such as SR-905. As a result, by 2000 combined federal, state, and local project funding climbed to $175 million— or 70 percent—of the $250 million needed. Successfully completing environmental reviews, the project had its target date for becoming a four-lane expressway moved up to 2005 from 2015, with a subsequent expansion to six lanes programmed. Together with tax incentives under state enterprise-zone and foreign trade zone legislation for businesses in the border region, SR-905 was considered a vital catalyst for Otay Mesa's future as a center for high-tech and biomedical research and manufacturing.[66]

A second proposed border link was SR-125, a nine-mile tollway and two-mile state connector financed with $400 million in private capital and $130 million in regional and federal funds. This eight-lane north-south route would connect the Otay Mesa border crossing with the regional interstate highway system. SR-125 also was integral to Baja California's proposal for a new commercial border crossing two miles east of the Otay Mesa port of entry that would link up with a Mexican highway running through the heart of the maquiladora district. But SR-125 encountered environmental opposition. In 1999, the Preserve South Bay group filed a lawsuit to block construction. The cynosure of the dispute was the Quino checker spot butterfly, which was placed on the federal endangered species list in 1997 because of the decline of its vernal pool habitat. In response, Caltrans developed an elaborate plan to mitigate habitat loss. Opponents also voiced fears of adverse traffic impacts ranging from increased noise and air pollution to the contamination of a nearby reservoir to the degradation of a regional park. Notwithstanding such concerns, the project's EIR/EIS was approved in 2000. With anticipated private construction financing, an initial four-lane highway could be opened in 2004.[67]

Third, in the Tecate region, thirty-five miles east of San Diego, vocal op-position by rural residents seeking to limit truck traffic stalled proposals for widening SR-94 (a mountainous highway serving the Tecate border crossing) and for renovation and enlargement of the Tecate port of entry. Here, cross-border traffic threatened to substantially worsen, from seven thousand vehicles per day in 1996 to fifty thousand per day by 2002. With the area's hundred-plus maquiladoras driving traffic growth, trucks experienced three-hour waits for a three-minute inspection as they queued in a single, primitive, truck-inspection lane that contrasted with the five truck lanes and nearly one hundred inspection docks at Otay Mesa. One proposed solution was a new port of entry at Jacumba/Jacumé, in the mountainous region east of Tecate and sixty miles from San Diego. Yet here too local opposition, led by the Back Country Coalition, warned of more trucks and worsening hazardous conditions on already-overtaxed rural highways.[68]

Finally, a new Calexico border crossing built in the 1990s in Imperial County, equipped with advanced vehicle-inspection and drug-search technologies, made Mexicali increasingly competitive with Tijuana as a cross-border manufacturing center. Breaking another local/state funding logjam, TEA-21 accelerated the industrial development of Calexico-Mexicali by allocating $6 million to begin construction of SR-7 from the new border crossing to I-8 near El Centro. But the Calexico port of entry's economic future also hinged on completion of the so-called Tijuana Loop—a private-venture Mexican toll road connecting the Otay Mesa crossing with the Ensenada toll road, Tijuana, Tecate, and Mexicali—which remained on the drawing board because of lack of funds.[69]

Cross-border trade-infrastructure development increasingly depended on binational cooperation between San Diego and Baja California. Here, there were promising signs as SANDAG developed an extensive planning program with its Mexican counterparts. In 1996, SANDAG and several other Southern California agencies signed an agreement with the State of Baja California and its five municipalities to develop a joint border transportation plan. Similarly, Caltrans crafted cooperative agreements with Mexican federal and state transportation agencies for cross-border transportation planning. It still remained to be seen whether binational planning cooperation could be translated into joint action on border-infrastructure development.[70]

Thus, at the dawn of the new millennium Southern California's major trade-corridor projects had a mixed track record. During the 1990s, both rail and highway projects embodied regional planning approaches, but with different governance and development trajectories. Rail initiatives utilized the JPA, which facilitated grassroots conflict resolution and innovative public/private funding partnerships. As a result, rail projects enjoyed considerable success. In contrast, highway projects featured more decentralized institutional arrangements, involving a host of regional, state, and federal agencies. Beset with local opposition and funding conflicts and lacking coordination mechanisms, highway improvements experienced delays.

7 International-Airport Development

At Stall Speed

Key to Los Angeles' role as a leading global city is Los Angeles International Airport—LAX. Demand for access to Los Angeles via LAX is outstripping the airport's capacity. LAX must modernize or the Los Angeles region risks losing its competitive advantage in the world marketplace. . . . [But] the airport is surrounded by vital communities like Westchester, Inglewood, El Segundo, and Hawthorne. What happens next at LAX must meet the needs of the future, and be compatible with these communities' futures as well.

—*City of Los Angeles Department of Airports, 1997*[1]

My constituents [around LAX] are saying—quite appropriately—that they have had enough. We've been promised for decades now that each expansion at LAX was the last, and we've been lied to.

—*Los Angeles City Councilwoman Ruth Galanter, 1998*[2]

The regional politics around aviation are dismal. . . . El Toro [in south Orange County] may never be built, and San Diego voted against airport expansion. . . . Local politicians . . . promote Palmdale, but it's a joke. . . . The LAX Master Plan in the short-term is *dead.*

—*Daniel P. Garcia, former president, L.A. Board of Airport Commissioners, 2000*[3]

This chapter examines international-airport development in Southern California during L.A. Mayor Richard Riordan's administration, 1993–2001. In contrast to port and trade-corridor projects, airport expansion projects remained largely stalled. A key question explored here is why airports threatened to become the Achilles' heel of L.A.'s trade future. Paradoxically, the era began with high airport hopes. The long-delayed LAX master planning process was restarted, a terminal-expansion program was launched at L.A.'s Ontario airport, and the potential for a major commercial airport at Palmdale was explored. Further, the federal government handed over four military air bases in Southern California—El Toro in Orange County and three Inland Empire facilities—that could be turned into commercial airports. This "peace dividend"—the silver lining of a deep local recession induced by defense cutbacks—offered an unparalleled opportunity to help solve the region's pressing international- and cargo-airport needs.

New airport capacity was needed to handle the region's projected dramatic growth in aviation demand, particularly for international travel. In the six-county Southern California Association of Governments (SCAG) planning region, passenger air travel was forecast to nearly double between 1993 and 2015, from 66 million annual passengers (MAP) to 123 MAP. Air cargo, much from the Pacific Rim, was projected to grow at a much faster rate: from 1.5 million tons in 1995 to 4.8 million in 2010. Subsequent projections to 2025 forecast even more explosive growth—to 167 MAP and 9.5 million air-cargo tons. Absent new runways, by the early twenty-first century the region's five metropolitan commercial airports (LAX, Ontario, John Wayne, Burbank, and Long Beach) would experience a serious physical-capacity shortfall (exacerbated by noise and air-quality policy constraints) relative to burgeoning demand.[4]

Failure to resolve this looming shortfall, particularly for international service, threatened the city's and region's future as a global export center. In 1995, well over half of regionally produced exports (by value) were shipped by air. Airborne exports added more in value to the local economy than did waterborne exports. High-technology, high value-added manufactured products were especially conducive to air shipment. Airborne exports also included services, which accounted for one-fifth to one-quarter of total trade activity. In Southern California service exports were especially important in rapidly growing industries such as tourism, entertainment, and professional/business services. International airports were potent economic catalysts. In 1994, LAX claimed to generate $43 billion in regional economic activity—roughly 10 percent of the region's then total output—and nearly four hundred thousand jobs. Implementation of the Master Plan by 2015 promised to double LAX's economic contributions. By 2010, a proposed twenty-eight MAP international airport at El Toro could create $15 billion in new economic activity and more than one hundred thousand additional jobs.[5]

Yet airport development also imposed substantial environmental costs (such as traffic congestion, noise, and air pollution) on neighboring communities. As a result, "not-in-my-backyard" (NIMBY) community opposition presented a major challenge to airport projects. By 2001, fierce community resistance forced Mayor Riordan to support limited LAX growth. In south Orange County, it threatened to scuttle plans for the proposed El Toro airport.

This chapter traces the arc of regional airport development from 1993 to 2001, from grandiose plans to downsized expectations. It focuses on the fierce battles over international-airport development at LAX and El Toro. The major concern here is with the beleaguered LAX Master Plan and the competing strategies of airport-expansion supporters and opponents. I also examine LAX's much-criticized efforts at regional airport planning.

Three major challenges to LAX expansion are explored. The first was financial. Given L.A.'s municipal budget crisis of the early 1990s and the high priority the Riordan administration placed on public safety, LAX became another tempting "cash cow" for revenue diversion to the city's general fund, thereby threatening capital-improvement financing. Yet Riordan's diversion plans—ranging from an early privatization initiative to sharply increased landing fees and municipal transfers—encountered strong opposition from the airlines and federal officials. I analyze their strategic interaction.

The second and gravest threat involved intense community opposition. I explore the policy tensions undermining LAX's public-outreach efforts and examine the political strategies of antiexpansion leaders such as L.A. City Councilmember Ruth Galanter and El Segundo Mayor Mike Gordon. LAX critics claimed to embrace regional approaches, and in order to encourage airport development elsewhere they constructed a powerful areawide coalition of cities, agencies, and local congresspersons from the South Bay (the coastal communities south of LAX) to the Inland Empire.

The third challenge was environmental policy. I examine LAX environmental issues and mitigation efforts, the morass of airport environmental regulation, the Master Plan Environmental Impact Report (EIR)/Environmental Impact Statement (EIS) process and lawsuits, and the environmental-justice movement in minority communities such as Inglewood (beneath the LAX flight path), which received a disproportionate share of airplane noise and air pollution.

Besides LAX expansion controversies, this chapter focuses on the escalating battle in Orange County in the 1990s over building a new international airport at El Toro. Called Orange County's "civil war," the airport plan pitted a generally supportive north county against strong opposition in south-county communities near the airport. I analyze the competing visions and political strategies of airport advocates and foes. I also consider the largely unsuccessful efforts to attract business to the new Inland Empire airports—the closed/realigned Norton, March, and George military bases. Whereas trade-corridor projects demonstrated the success of regional approaches, airport development revealed the failure of regional cooperation and solutions. I conclude by analyzing this crucial policy malfunction.

Downsizing LAX Expansion

The Regional Airport System

In 2000, Southern California had one fully international airport—LAX—plus limited global service at Ontario International Airport and San Diego's Lindbergh Field. LAX was the world's third-busiest passenger airport and air-cargo facility. By the 1990s it had become the nation's leading Pacific Rim air gateway, capturing one-third of the Asian passenger market and over one-quarter of its cargo market. Although LAX's market dominance was not as great as that of the San Pedro Bay ports, in 2001 it still handled 45 percent of total West Coast global air cargo by value (see Table 1.3). Los Angeles World Airports (LAWA, formerly the Department of Airports), a municipal proprietary department like the Harbor Department, operated LAX and Ontario as well as Van Nuys (general aviation) and Palmdale regional airports. Elsewhere, John Wayne, Burbank, and Long Beach airports provided short- and medium-haul domestic service. With the Cold War's end, new airport capacity became available at four closed/realigned military bases: El Toro, March, George (renamed Southern California Logistics), and Norton (San Bernardino). Figure 7.1 shows existing and proposed commercial airport sites for the L.A. region in 2000.

Southern California also faced severe subregional imbalances in aviation demand and service, with the greatest deficiencies concentrated in Orange and San Diego counties. These were among the fastest growing areas in Southern California, with a heavy emphasis on high-tech manufacturing, tourism, and international trade. Yet their needs for international passenger service and air-freight service were met primarily by LAX. In all, LAX accounted for three-quarters of total regional air-cargo shipments—domestic as well as international—while Ontario handled nearly 20 percent.

Because of the long history of LAX expansion, Orange and San Diego counties had strong incentives to be free riders rather than to expand their own undersized, five-hundred-acre airports. Both areas enjoyed convenient freeway access to LAX and Ontario airports. As a result, small John Wayne Airport never needed to expand to provide international and long-haul domestic air service. Half of Orange County travelers used LAX and Ontario airports. Further, John Wayne handled only 5 percent of the area's air-cargo shipments; the rest were trucked to LAX and Ontario.

San Diego's cramped Lindbergh Field, with few possibilities for expansion, also offered limited international service, primarily to Mexico and Canada. It could handle only one-third of San Diego's air-cargo shipments; the rest were trucked up to LAX or Ontario. Indeed, in 2001 Lindbergh Field handled only $153 million in international air cargo—minuscule compared with LAX's $64 billion (see Table 1.3). Because of San Diego's air-service deficiencies, nearly ninety daily commuter flights went from San Diego airports to LAX. One-third of the area's air passengers traveled to L.A.-area airports, and they placed additional strains on an already-burdened LAX.

The Master Plan Process

The previous LAX Master Plan had been produced in 1971–72; it projected a maximum capacity of forty MAP—a figure surpassed in 1986. As demand for passenger and cargo facities at LAX grew, officials struggled to

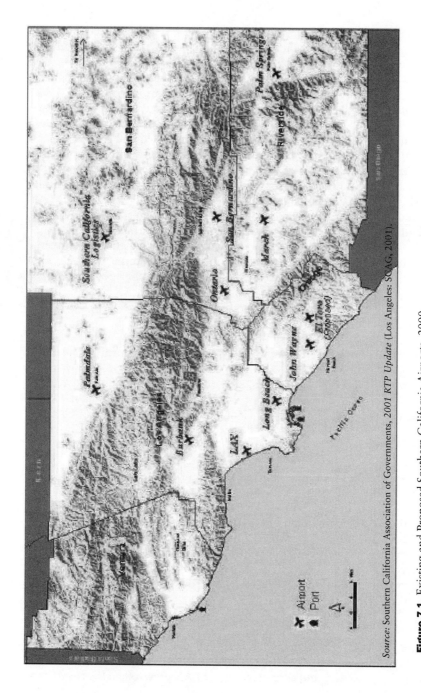

Figure 7.1. Existing and Proposed Southern California Airports, 2000.
Source: Southern California Association of Governments, *2001 Regional Transportation Plan Update* (Los Angeles: SCAG, 2001).

keep up. Begun in 1989, a new master planning effort soon became trapped in political infighting between the mayor and Councilwoman Galanter, who represented LAX and adjoining Westchester. For two years, an interdepartmental task force (led by the City Planning Department) laboriously developed a set of goals that eventually would become the Master Plan's scope of work. Mayor Riordan, elected in 1993, returned planning responsibility to a nervous airports department. As newly appointed Airports General Manager Jack Driscoll observed, "Because LAX is growing at a rate of about a million passengers a year, we should have been doing this Master Plan about five or six years ago. The Bradley Terminal for international flights is completely overwhelmed and overburdened. We need more gates for international traffic and more space for customs."[6]

Although the Master Plan focused on LAX, airport officials acknowledged the need to address planning from a regional perspective. As a result, LAWA resurrected a then-moribund expansion project at Ontario Airport. The fast-tracked $250 million project created a new twenty-four-gate terminal complex and major ground-access improvements, ready for operation in late 1998. In addition, LAWA studied Palmdale's feasibility as a major airport. LAX planners also included other regional airports such as Burbank, Long Beach, and John Wayne—not part of the city's airport system—in their aviation forecasts and sought to determine whether El Toro had commercial potential. Yet critics later would charge that LAWA did not seriously examine other potential airport sites. As described later in this chapter, this criticism became a rallying cry for a potent regionwide anti-LAX coalition ranging from the South Bay to the Inland Empire. As Driscoll later recalled ruefully, regional planning "is an issue that I believe did jump up and bite LAX. . . . What we missed were the 'wanna-be's' [from areas wanting new airports] joining with the 'NIMBY's' [around LAX] and creating a joint [anti-LAX] effort."[7]

The LAX Master Plan process consisted of three phases. Phase I, completed in late 1995, developed long-term aviation forecasts and economic assessments. Forecasts to the year 2015—which used 1994 as the base year—showed dramatic passenger and air-cargo growth. By 2015, LAX, which was nearing capacity by the mid-1990s, would need to serve ninety-eight MAP, a 90 percent increase over 1994. Global travel would generate over two-thirds of this growth. For 1994–2015, air cargo was estimated to jump from 1.7 million to 4.1 million annual tons—a 150 percent increase—with international freight accounting for over half of the projected growth. LAWA also began building the economic case for a larger LAX, which would be used to solicit political, business, and labor support. With growth, by 2015 an additional $37 billion in regional economic output (direct, indirect, and induced) and 367,000 jobs could be generated.[8]

Phase II, begun in early 1996 and completed in mid-1998, developed design alternatives to accommodate projected demand. Thirty proposals were considered. The most controversial envisaged expanding the airport into Santa Monica Bay; this plan was similar to those for expensive airport land-fill projects in Japan, South Korea, and Hong Kong. The economic bene-fits here appeared enormous, boosting LAX's economic impact from $52 bil-lion to $112 billion annually, with a half million new jobs created. But critics claimed that the environmental consequences, ranging from ocean pollution to threats to endangered species, would be catastrophic. Faced with the threat of litigation delaying expansion for a decade or more, LAX officials shelved this grandiose plan.[9]

Four alternatives were chosen for public review and feedback. Two sce-narios called for six runways; a third proposed five. A final option kept the original four runways and proposed using nearby Hawthorne airport for re-gional commuter flights (such as from San Diego), with a transit connection (buses or a people mover) to LAX. Commuter flights were a major bottle-neck. They accounted for one-third of LAX flight operations but only 5 per-cent of the passenger load, producing serious operational inefficiencies. Small commuter turboprop aircraft took longer to land than a 747 jet. However, Hawthorne officials rejected this plan.[10]

Starting in mid-1997, LAWA initiated formal public meetings to evalu-ate the alternatives and define the scope of the EIR/EIS. Based on community feedback, airport planners narrowed the design options to two. Alternative One, for ninety-three to ninety-five MAP, consisted of adding a fifth runway to the north. Alternative Two, for ninety-four to ninety-six MAP, consisted of adding two new runways, one north and one south. Both sought to enhance airfield capacity by adding a third arrival stream and separating smaller com-muter aircraft from the larger aircraft fleet. Common features also included a new west entrance and terminal (with eighty to one hundred additional aircraft gates) and major transportation improvements such as direct mass-transit service to LAX, a direct freeway connection and airport ring road, and a people mover connecting the terminals.[11]

Phase III, begun in late 1998, involved choosing a preferred design alter-native, completing an EIR/EIS, and securing necessary approvals from the city council and the Federal Aviation Administration (FAA). The draft EIR/EIS was delayed by California Environmental Quality Act (CEQA) amend-ments as well as by a new airport-expansion alternative. In 1998, Mayor Ri-ordan returned from an East Asia trade mission highly impressed with Hong Kong's new airport. Finally focusing on LAX expansion and upset with well-organized community resistance, he fired Dan Garcia, president of the airport commission, who had spearheaded the master planning effort. Later, a frus-trated Driscoll resigned as LAWA's executive director. Bowing to commu-nity pressure, the mayor then proposed a modest eighty-nine MAP alterna-tive featuring no new runways. The mayor's new plan, designed to encourage international service and discourage short commuter flights, became the staff recommendation in the draft EIR/EIS finally released in January 2001. A lengthy six-month public-comment period then began, which newly elected L.A. Mayor James Hahn, an expansion opponent, further extended.[12]

Expansion hopes were dealt a further blow in spring 2001 when SCAG— the region's transportation-planning agency, which also handles regional aviation—bowed to LAX critics and capped proposed expansion at seventy-eight MAP. Only 16 percent above the sixty-seven MAP handled by LAX in 2000 (and well below the ninety-eight MAP originally considered necessary), the new limit was inadequate relative to projected demand. SCAG's action threatened LAX's federal and state transportation funding if a larger airport were constructed. As Chapter Eight details, after the September 11th terrorist attack, Mayor Hahn directed LAWA to develop a modest, seventy-eight MAP design focused on modernization and security rather than new capacity.[13]

Revenue Diversion: Strategies and Resistance

During the Riordan years, three major challenges to LAX expansion arose— revenue diversion, community opposition, and environmental review. At an estimated $8–12 billion, LAX expansion promised to be the nation's most expensive airport capital-improvement program. Its financing was threatened by the Riordan administration's relentless revenue-diversion efforts. Similar to his treatment of the Harbor Department, the mayor throughout his first term (1993–97) sought to transfer revenues from the Department of Airports to the municipal general fund to balance the budget and help pay for additional police. His schemes, however, encountered strong opposition from the airlines and their federal-government allies. Only in his second term (1997– 2001), as revenue diversion faltered, would the mayor belatedly focus on LAX expansion.

Ironically, the Tom Bradley administration in its waning days had paved the diversionary way. Beset with a burgeoning fiscal crisis because of the deep recession and a state-mandated property tax shift from cities and counties to school districts, Mayor Bradley and the city council desperately searched for new revenue. The Department of Airports and its nearly $250 million annual budget was an inviting target. Thus, in mid-1992, Bradley's appointees on the airport board commissioned an LAX valuation study that estimated the city could receive annual lease payments of $60 million to $130 million if the facility were privatized. Councilwoman Galanter then sponsored an "airport revenue and mitigation reform package." It included proposals to increase landing fees, reduce municipal and federal restrictions on using airport revenue for other municipal purposes, permit LAX leasing, and control airport growth.[14]

During the 1993 mayoral campaign Riordan, a former venture capitalist, endorsed privatizing LAX. His supporters claimed that the airport was a "mismanaged, bureaucratically bungled department" headed by globe-trotting junketeers. Large lease payments could be used to pay for more needed municipal services. The Reason Foundation, a local pro-privatization think tank, estimated that a thirty-year lease could initially generate annual municipal payments of $100 million, which would rise to $850 million at the lease's end. Once elected, Mayor Riordan found his privatization plans stymied by powerful foes ranging from the airline industry to influential members of Congress to local labor unions and their city-council allies. Also thwarted were the hopes of Lockheed Air Terminal, the nation's largest private airport operator, which had contributed $158,000 to lobby L.A. city officials for LAX privatization.[15]

Undaunted, the Riordan administration then pursued a dual strategy of supporting hefty airport landing-fee increases and lobbying Congress to ease federal restrictions on the use of airport revenues for nonairport purposes. In its final meeting before Riordan took office, Bradley's airport commission endorsed Councilwoman Galanter's proposal for higher landing fees. Negotiated in the early 1950s, the old fees were among the nation's lowest. The airport panel voted to triple landing fees (based on a "cost-of-service" rather than a "residual" calculation), making them comparable to those levied at other major airports. Riordan strongly supported the board's action; upon taking office, he quickly installed attorney/developer Ted Stein as airport board president to wring still more money out of LAX. The new administration pledged to reverse Bradley's alleged policy of giving the airlines "sweetheart" deals.[16]

Stung by the steep LAX fee rise and fearing that other airports might follow suit, forty airlines filed a lawsuit to block the city's action and refused to pay the new fees pending the outcome of litigation. Riordan countered with a high-stakes game of chicken by threatening to ban nonpaying airlines from LAX. After tense negotiations brokered by the U.S. Transportation Secretary Federico Peña, the airlines yielded and paid the fees under protest while challenging their legality. By 1995, the courts and federal agencies had largely upheld the city's methodology and approved over 80 percent of the fee increase. Encouraged, the airport panel then hiked LAX's fees by another 32 percent.[17]

The Riordan administration also lobbied Congress to ease federal restrictions on airport-revenue uses. Of particular interest were LAX's lucrative concessions, which were bringing in more than $100 million annually. LAX pursued a "Wolfgang Puck" strategy of upgrading its restaurant, food, and beverage services in order to increase concession revenues potentially transferable into the general fund. Yet, lobbied hard by a powerful airline industry, Congress actually strengthened, not weakened, federal antidiversion rules. Under federal airport laws and grant assurances, airports like LAX (which had not earlier shared revenue but which had later accepted federal grants) would be barred from diverting revenues for twenty years. In 1994, LAX stopped taking federal grants to permit future revenue transfers. As a result, from 1994 to 2001 LAX lost $117 million, which could have been used for capital improvements and mitigation.[18]

Facing $200–300 million annual budget deficits, the Riordan administration also embarked on a "benchmarking" strategy involving audits of the city's proprietary departments to find new budget-balancing revenues. Leading that effort was Deputy Mayor (and later Chief Operating Officer) Michael Keeley, a former business associate of the mayor. Audits by the grand jury and the city attorney identified a host of new, potentially divertible LAX revenues. City Hall forced air-terminal developers to pay street-improvement fees, secured the transfer of $54 million in airport land-sale funds to the general fund, and sought reimbursement for early airport loans and emergency services—the cost of which had allegedly ballooned to $350 million—that supposedly never were repaid. Overall, airport-revenue diversions tripled during Riordan's first two years.[19]

A GOP-controlled Congress, the FAA, and the airlines were not amused. Congressional displeasure heightened when LAWA hired President Bill Clinton's former associate attorney general, Webster Hubbell (then under investigation for fraud), to lobby for LAX revenue diversion. In a rancorous battle extending throughout 1996, the FAA and Congress both demanded that L.A. return $31 million siphoned from the airport fund allegedly to repay an ancient loan. Playing another high-stakes game of chicken, the Riordan administration refused. Pressed by the airlines, an angry Congress threatened to discontinue funding the L.A. County Metropolitan Transportation Authority (LACMTA) until the $31 million was repaid. This move would have imperiled LACMTA funding for the Alameda Corridor—a pet Riordan project. This time L.A. yielded; City Hall reluctantly returned the money to the airport fund. The airlines also succeeded in getting the U.S. Department of Transportation to further restrict airport-revenue diversions. According to the Air Transport Association, the industry's chief lobbying group, this restriction was "the direct result of shenanigans" at LAX.[20]

Despite Riordan administration assurances that revenue transfers would not affect LAX's costly capital-improvement program, there was reason to believe otherwise. Transfers reduced pay-as-you-go financing and increased the amount of debt needed to fund Master Plan improvements. Debt reliance increased with the airport board's 1994 decision not to accept new federal grant money for LAX improvements. This loss was counterbalanced by increased landing fees. But the fee hike, coupled with diversion attempts, angered the airlines and made them less willing partners than they had been in LAX expansion.

In an indication of this new adversarial relationship, American Airlines called off a $77 million renovation of its LAX terminal when Riordan's airport board threatened not to approve the project unless the airline agreed to revenue sharing. United was similarly threatened and put a hold on its own terminal plans. After years of standoff, the Riordan administration finally caved in, and the airlines restarted their projects. In a further bow to the airlines, LAWA lowered LAX landing fees but implemented a new $3 passenger facility fee to pay for soundproofing residential homes near the airport. Absent federal airport-improvement money, airport officials hoped to finance capital improvements with revenue bonds (leveraging landing fees and capital lease agreements) and tenant-sponsored terminal financing. These sources would be supplemented with federal and state transportation grants to pay for $2–3 billion in ground-access improvements.[21]

Community Opposition

Public Outreach

LAWA conducted a valiant but ultimately ineffective public-outreach campaign that failed to stem mounting community opposition to LAX expansion. Airport commissioner Garcia, a chief architect of the Master Plan, and LAWA Executive Director Driscoll led the effort with minimal involvement from Mayor Riordan. Nearly three hundred public and private meetings were held with business, labor, civic, and community organizations and leaders before the formal EIR/EIS public scoping meetings even began. LAWA officials focused on neighboring Westchester, whose city council representative, Galanter, would play a pivotal role in the approval process. Airport manager Driscoll personally met with forty to fifty Westchester leaders over a two-year period. LAWA also held nearly two hundred meetings with elected officials and groups in El Segundo, Manhattan Beach, Hermosa Beach, Redondo Beach, Torrance, and Inglewood. In addition, LAWA officials met with the region's leading business, labor, and civic organizations, as well as with newspapers such as the Los Angeles Times, the suburban weeklies, and business journals.[22]

LAWA's message to nearby communities was twofold. First, an expanded airport was critical to their future economic health. LAWA stressed the local economic benefits of expansion, claiming that 40 percent of the 63,500 direct LAX-related jobs were located within ten miles of the airport; 80 percent could be found within twenty miles in the South Bay, West L.A., Central L.A., and the San Fernando Valley. Second, LAWA adopted a "good-neighbor policy" dedicated to mitigating environmental impacts. Unlike the situation in the 1960s, when the airport's controversial expansion was based on property condemnations, LAWA publicly committed itself not to acquire homes unless they were offered by residents. It also vowed not to expand LAX beyond its current layout except to the east toward the 405 freeway and north toward

Manchester Boulevard. The airport's north side would be developed for community benefit, with recreational, commercial, and educational facilities.[23]

LAWA's goodwill overtures were largely dismissed by the people they were supposed to benefit. Community outreach was hampered by the long history of animosity between the airport and its neighbors. Since the late 1950s and early 1960s, when the jet age and airport expansion collided with suburban development, LAWA had had an acrimonious and litigious relationship with neighboring communities such as Westchester and Playa Del Rey. To one close observer, battles over noise abatement and land condemnation produced a relationship not unlike that between the English and Irish or the Israelis and Palestinians—one so fraught with misperception and mistrust that the slightest misstep was quickly blown out of proportion.[24]

Major policy tensions further constrained and compromised the public-outreach effort. First, LAWA had difficulties in determining the permissible extent of advocacy and lobbying relative to neutrally providing public information. LAWA initially wanted as many supporters signing on the dotted line as possible. Thus, early outreach was directed toward this end rather than toward simply informing community groups of airport plans and engaging them in dialogue. As a result, LAWA had great success in getting business and labor groups on board; they provided over one hundred Master Plan endorsements. These groups were an easy sell, particularly when the substantial economic benefits of LAX expansion were made clear.[25]

Although mobilizing core supporters first is an understandable strategy, it had the unintended consequence of increasing community mistrust and opposition. According to critics, local residents perceived their concerns as being neglected so that LAWA could support its "real" clientele—business and labor. LAX foe Robert Pinzler, then a Redondo Beach city councilman, decried the public-outreach effort as merely a "sales job": local communities were "negligibly engaged in the planning process and heavily engaged by the selling process."[26] When L.A. Councilwoman Galanter complained, LAWA was largely forced to halt its support-building efforts. In response, airport commissioner Garcia formed LAX 2000 (renamed LAX 21), a private-sector group, to build political and financial support for LAX expansion in the larger business community (particularly among minority businesses) and the region's powerful unions. This effort failed when the mayor, in a power struggle with the ousted airport commissioner, asserted his control over the group and then did little.[27]

The second tension with the public-outreach process was that LAWA had to start it well before anyone knew what expansion would look like. As a result, area residents complained about the absence of specific information regarding LAWA's intentions and wondered why airport officials weren't more forthcoming with crucial Master Plan details. Looking back, former airport commissioner Garcia observed:

The challenge here was immense and time consuming. . . . It took six months to finish the regional forecast. It took another year to develop the first broad matrix of options. No one has ever demolished and rebuilt a sixty MAP airport on 3,000 acres and kept it operational throughout—especially in an ecologically fragile and traffic burdened location. But we couldn't wait two to three years with no public participation. So we chose to open a dialog which was general as a result. LAWA sounded vague about its plans and hence the criticism and lack of focus. But it was a Hobson's choice—start early and be vague or start late and be resented for hiding facts from the public. . . . I guarantee you no matter which avenue you choose you'd be blasted.[28]

The third crucial tension involved the mayor's participation. What was the appropriate role for the mayor in the master planning process? In the early 1980s, Bradley, a hands-on mayor, had successfully guided LAX expansion. Riordan's involvement with the airport (except for revenue diversion), however, was late coming and muddled. Given the acrimonious history between LAX and nearby communities, LAWA needed early, strong leadership from the mayor's office, which was not forthcoming. Despite pleas from LAWA officials, the mayor preferred to delegate responsibility. As one prominent LAX supporter exclaimed with wonderment and frustration, "Here is one of the most important projects to the entire region, and two [airport] commissioners and the head of LAWA are left to do it." [29] Riordan's lack of early engagement seriously hurt the expansion cause. His silence left Councilwoman Galanter—a vocal and effective expansion critic—as the highest-ranking public official regularly speaking out on the issue. Critics like Galanter and El Segundo Mayor Mike Gordon were able to frame the expansion debate.

Neither the mayor nor his staff ever developed a coherent political strategy to build support for LAX expansion. Riordan went from apathy in his first term to complete control in the second term, his main contribution being to hire a public relations firm to organize a media blitz. When he finally focused, he wanted the project done fast but spent little time understanding the complexity of the issues or playing a meaningful and effective role.

The mayor's frenetic last-minute efforts were inept. He was ineffective when finally meeting with L.A. County officials. In another instance, Riordan, expecting an endorsement, brought a newspaper reporter with him to a meeting with influential African American Congresswoman Maxine Waters, who represented constituents under LAX's flight path. The congresswoman was furious, resenting such apparent arm twisting. By this action alone, the mayor brought about her active opposition, which would weigh heavily in the 2001 mayoral campaign. Riordan also squandered the opportunity to work with officials from other municipalities such as El Segundo and Inglewood and thus allowed Councilwoman Galanter to cultivate these communities, which later joined the antiexpansion ranks. Thus, Riordan avoided the real work of coalition building: community-by-community arm wrestling and interest-group-by-interest-group negotiation. Such an effort would test the endurance and courage of any politician, let alone a political neophyte such as Riordan. According to one close participant, the mayor "blew his opportunity by inaction and laziness and then used Dan Garcia as a scapegoat."[30]

Finally, LAWA could do little to mediate conflicts among expansion supporters. As a result, an airline labor dispute cost substantial union support for the Master Plan. One of the major carriers awarded its security contract to a low-bidding nonunion firm that refused to pay the so-called living wage required of municipal contractors. Despite pressure from the service workers union's Living Wage Coalition, the airline refused to intervene, claiming the dispute was between the coalition and the subcontractor. As Garcia later recalled, "I had all Unions on board at the beginning of this process. . . . [But] the standoff resulted in a withdrawal of union support . . . in order to put pressure on the airlines for a master plan, which they supported. Weak mayoral attempts to help were useless. Union support for the master plan then ended because of a dispute over . . . wages. What a country!"[31]

Oppositional Strategies

Effective counter strategies developed by elected officials in neighboring Westchester and El Segundo also thwarted the Master Plan and outreach efforts. In classic NIMBY fashion, foes contended that LAX expansion would produce unmitigable traffic congestion and noise and air pollution and thus threaten property values. Yet their chief contribution was to regionalize the debate, claiming that outlying airports such as Palmdale, Ontario, and El Toro, in areas projected to grow rapidly, could serve the region's future aviation needs better than LAX could.[32]

Leading the initial antiexpansion effort was Councilwoman Galanter. Her contributions were several-fold. First, she regionalized the issue by relentlessly pressing the case for remote Palmdale as the alternative to LAX as an international hub airport. Starved for growth, Palmdale-area public officials, businesses, and residents aggressively lobbied for airport development. Their willingness to promote a much larger airport was used by Master Plan opponents, who contended that there was little need to expand LAX while Palmdale continued to be underutilized. Galanter downplayed the market, location, and ground-access problems associated with Palmdale. Instead, she pointed to the site's strengths: it had plenty of available land, was in a sparsely populated area welcoming airport development, and was already part of the LAWA system. Following Galanter's lead, L.A. county supervisors representing Palmdale and LAX breathed life into the moribund Southern California Regional Airport Authority (SCRAA) to push LAWA for less LAX expansion and more Palmdale development.[33]

To LAX supporters, Palmdale was a politically expedient ruse, not a viable airport alternative. They claimed that the Palmdale market was too small and the location too remote. The airlines, for whom market accessibility was key, resisted going there because, as one Master Plan proponent pointed out, "airlines go to markets, not airports." Furthermore, the Antelope Valley, in which Palmdale is located, was poorly served by freeways in and out of L.A. Already-congested Highway 14 (the only existing route to L.A.) was incapable of handling twenty to thirty million air passengers and related cargo a year. By 2020, the average peak-period sixty-mile commute from downtown L.A. to the Antelope Valley would be three hours or more. High-speed rail (HSR) was an alternative but required voter approval of a multi-billion dollar bond measure. HSR also posed a "reverse commute problem," making urban airports like LAX more accessible than Palmdale to residents of the Antelope and Santa Clarita valleys. Other liabilities involved the combination of high altitude and hot thermal conditions, which offset passenger loads and safety, and a flight path that also served as an Air Force supersonic test corridor.[34]

Second, Councilwoman Galanter, a former community planner and organizer, used her skills to organize political opposition in neighboring communities, from West L.A. to the South Bay. In particular, she played a critical role in enlisting El Segundo elected officials in the antiexpansion campaign. Here, LAX growth was a double-edged sword. Although El Segundo residents feared greater traffic and lowered property values, much of the town's economic base depended on the airport.

Galanter passed the baton to El Segundo's Mayor Gordon, who was first elected to the city council in 1996. In 1998, Gordon persuaded his colleagues to spend $1.5 million in city funds to hire a consultant to develop a strategy to fight LAX expansion. He then painstakingly assembled a regionwide coalition of over a hundred cities, counties, and public agencies. In March 1999 this broad coalition of public officials, ranging from representatives of the South Bay and Westside (seeking to curb LAX growth) to leaders from the Inland Empire and Palmdale (seeking airport expansion and associated economic benefits in outlying areas), unveiled a blueprint for the region's air-transportation future that spread out its growth rather than concentrating it at LAX. The group, dubbed by critics the "NIMBYs and wannabes," favored smaller LAX expansion, to only seventy MAP; construction of a twenty-four MAP Orange County international airport at El Toro; and relatively modest growth at ten other regional airports. Gordon used SCAG's Aviation Task Force as a key platform for promoting the coalition's objectives. His group also threatened lawsuits should L.A. approve the LAX EIR/EIS. Later, a bipartisan coalition of twelve local congresspersons, led by Congresswoman Jane Harman representing LAX and the South Bay, joined the burgeoning anti-LAX movement.[35]

Beleaguered Master Plan supporters discerned an opposition cycle on the part of elected officials that they claimed was politically motivated. As one participant cynically concluded:

> It is interesting to note that it was quiet for some time in the early stages of the Master Plan effort and is currently (early 2000) quiet. All the opposition mounted and became vocal during the elections. Elected officials from every city in the South Bay were up for election during this time. The County Board of Supervisors was having elections, the State Assembly and Senate seats were contested, and the Congressional seat was vacant. The Master Plan became the horse everyone was riding.[36]

LAWA did in fact make concessions, which critics saw as driven by political expediency. Opponents claimed that LAWA was pursuing the twin strategies of cobbling together the minimum coalition necessary for approving expansion (a strategy that resulted in greater benefits for fewer stakeholders) and seeking to divide and conquer the opposition. For example, opponents pointed to a late 1998 LAWA plan to shift a proposed new runway from the north to the south. Although this change addressed the concerns of north-side residents living in Westchester, who were L.A. voters and could influence LAX expansion, it appeared to be at the expense of south-side El Segundo residents, who didn't vote in city elections. Later, the City of Los Angeles entered into a "cooperation agreement" with the City of Palmdale to encourage the long-term development of Palmdale Regional Airport. An elated Councilwoman Galanter saw this as a "real breakthrough" but then challenged "the mayor and LAWA to produce a serious investment plan for Palmdale, including service commitments from the airlines." In the biggest concession of them all, Mayor Riordan agreed to a smaller eighty-nine MAP LAX expansion with no new runway.[37]

Environmental Policy Challenges

Like the ports, the region's airports in the mid-1990s successfully fought the Federal Implementation Plan (FIP), the stiff air-quality regulations and fines proposed for Southern California, which threatened air transportation as well as ocean shipping. That battle was detailed in Chapter Five. Here I consider the major environmental problems at LAX and the airport's mitigation policies; the complex regulatory morass hampering LAX planning and public outreach; the Master Plan's EIR/EIS process and legal challenges; and opposition based on environmental-justice considerations.

Environmental Mitigation

With LAX flight operations, passengers, and cargo increasing regardless of what happened at other regional airports, the question increasingly became whether expansion was going to be planned—and mitigated—or un-planned—and unmitigated. Although LAWA officials acknowledged the need to spend $2–3 billion or more on mitigation measures—more than virtually any other airport in the world—airport critics demanded that LAWA mitigate existing environmental concerns before expansion occurred. Operating a major international airport like LAX in a densely populated urban area created a host of interwoven environmental problems, especially jet noise, air pollution, and traffic congestion. Jet noise was the preeminent airport environmental problem the world over. During peak hours, planes took off and landed at LAX every two minutes; 85,000 people resided in the airport's sixty-five-decibel noise contour, qualifying them for federal/airport soundproofing assistance.

Air quality also was a growing public health concern. By the 1990s, LAX was the third largest source of smog in Southern California, much of it from jet engines. LAX generated roughly 75 percent of the air pollution coming from the area's fourteen oil refineries. According to 1993 South Coast Air Quality Management District (SCAQMD) data, aircraft and airport-related ground vehicles in the region were responsible for emitting thirty-one tons of hydrocarbons and nitrogen oxides daily. These two pollutants react in sunlight to form ozone, the main component of smog. Aircraft engines accounted for half of such pollutants, with the remainder generated by parking-lot shuttles, vans from rental-car firms, and taxis. (The SCAQMD data did not include the millions of cars, shuttles, and trucks transporting LAX passengers and cargo.) SCAQMD estimated that LAX expansion to ninety-eight MAP could result in 50 percent more air pollution by 2010, much due to the growing number of jets. Anti-airport activists claimed that the increased incidence of local respiratory ailments and cancer cases was aircraft-generated, a result of excess fuel dumped on neighborhoods and carcinogens emitted by jet engines.[38]

Traffic congestion in and around the airport, which surfaced as an issue in the 1960s, was another pressing problem. On-site parking structures often were filled to overflow, leading to frequent gridlock on LAX's inner arterials. Freeway access became a major problem as traffic congestion on I-405, already the slowest freeway in the region, steadily worsened. SCAG projected a significant increase in freeway travel times to LAX by 2020. Because the light-rail system did not directly serve LAX, only 5 percent of air passengers took mass transit.[39]

LAWA officials appeared to understand the environmental problems their operations caused for surrounding communities. LAWA spent hundreds of millions of dollars attempting to mitigate the worst impacts on its neighbors, particularly noise. In 1996, LAWA more than doubled its annual contribution for residential soundproofing, from $5 million to $12 million. Over the life of this program, LAWA spent nearly $300 million to insulate more than twenty-one thousand affected dwelling units. The airport also acquired Manchester

Square, a nearby area of 2,500 units and 450 single-family houses, when owners decided to sell rather than soundproof. This effort was the nation's largest airport property-acquisition program.[40]

But LAX's soundproofing program was beset by legal squabbles. The airport alienated residents by requiring avigational easements (air navigation rights of way) as a condition for receiving airport financial assistance. Under a federal program, the FAA provided 80 percent of the soundproofing cost. LAWA offered to pick up the remaining 20 percent contingent on homeowners signing an easement forfeiting their right to sue the airport. In 2001, LAWA signed an agreement with Inglewood not to block lawsuits by occupants of soundproofed homes. LAWA also adopted a number of "green" air-quality measures such as employee ride-share programs and the use of alternative fuels and zero-emission vehicles in its nonaircraft operations. It became a world leader in encouraging the shift to quieter Stage 3 aircraft and created more efficient aircraft flows on the airfield to reduce taxiing and idling.[41]

The Regulatory Morass

The Master Plan and public-outreach efforts were hampered by the regulatory morass surrounding aviation environmental issues. LAX was one of the largest generators of smog in the region. Yet aircraft in the Los Angeles area were not subject to SCAQMD's regional rules. Instead, they were governed by global standards, which were set by the International Civil Aviation Organization (ICAO). In 1999, the ICAO endorsed cutting nitrogen oxide emissions from newly designed aircraft engines by 16 percent as of 2003. The United States initially refused to approve the tougher standard because of airline industry and FAA opposition. Later, the United States relented and accepted the modest proposal, which only codified existing technology, excluded existing engine designs, and was applied less stringently to larger engines. The new standard then was incorporated into federal Environmental Protection Agency regulations, to be enforced by the FAA. Thus, the airline industry was subject to no "technology-forcing" pollution-control regulations such as the ones the California Air Resources Board imposed on the auto industry with great success. As a result, U.S. aircraft remain largely exempt from air-pollution rules.[42]

This broad exemption limited LAX to ground-side antipollution efforts. Here, LAX could do little except provide clean generators for runway operations and ask the airlines to use cleaner aircraft and fuel. As for existing jet engines, Pratt & Whitney introduced a retrofit kit that allowed its JT8D-200 engine (used mainly with MD-80s operated by American and Delta airlines) to meet the new standards. Although the technology was cost effective, the airlines had few incentives to install it. Cash-starved airlines resisted reengineering, wanting to keep old engines as long as possible. They claimed that cutting pollution by 35–45 percent—an amount less than regional mandates already facing oil refineries, power plants, and other Southland industries—would cause the elimination of half of their LAX flights. In 1995, American Airlines voluntarily offered to bring only its cleanest-running planes to LAX but backed off when other airlines refused, claiming that doing so would create a scheduling nightmare.[43]

Failures to reduce jet emissions penalized other generators of air pollution in the region, who came under increased pressure from SCAQMD to balance out the emissions coming from aircraft. Although virtually every factory, utility, business, and motorist in Los Angeles has had to comply with stringent environmental regulations in an effort to clean up the nation's worst smog, aircraft remain largely exempt. Because airplanes are one of the region's only major uncontrolled sources, aircraft emissions in the future threaten to become an even larger portion of the local air-pollution inventory as air traffic grows.[44]

LAWA faced another regulatory quagmire with noise reduction. The airport has little control over its airspace, which falls under the FAA's jurisdiction. Earlier, noise concerns heightened when the FAA lowered the flight ceiling for jets departing from LAX by 20 percent. The FAA also widened the flight area in which departing planes could turn to the south (a ruling that brought the planes closer to the shoreline and residential areas such as El Segundo). In response to mounting local pressure, FAA officials in late 1997 announced the formation of a task force to address community noise concerns in the Los Angeles basin. Its first project involved early aircraft turns and community overflights at LAX. In early 1999, the FAA proposed altering LAX flight routes and altitudes to dampen noise. The FAA also sets limitations on the number of flights. Critics feared that the FAA's dual responsibilities—to ensure safety in the air and to promote the airline industry—would work at cross-purposes where LAX expansion was concerned.[45]

Because the FAA is such a crucial player in airport operations affecting the quality of life of nearby communities, its apparent lack of early direct involvement in the LAX Master Plan was a particular source of frustration for local residents. As Roy Hefner, a local activist involved with LAX issues since 1965, observed: "The FAA repeatedly denies that they're involved with the Master Plan and [claim] that they will evaluate the plan once it's submitted, . . . conveniently ignoring the fact that they are in charge of what happens with the runways and thus are critical to every other aspect of the LAX Master Plan, including environmental and community issues."[46]

Thus, there was considerable confusion regarding which agencies were responsible for mitigating particular airport-related environmental impacts. One seasoned veteran of the airport wars proclaimed that "nobody is in charge" of mitigation. LAWA's lack of regulatory authority hampered community outreach. Repeated claims by airport officials that LAX operations were exempt from SCAQMD standards appeared callous to local residents. And blaming other agencies—such as the ICAO and the FAA—for air-quality and noise problems made airport officials seem ineffectual.[47]

EIR/EIS Challenges

In Phase III of the Master Plan, the airport prepared its first environmental-impact assessment in over twenty years, despite steady growth beyond the forty MAP ceiling adopted in 1978. Since then, there had been steady but incremental expansion of facilities at LAX (without environmental-impact studies) to meet burgeoning passenger and cargo demand. Critics charged that the airport had deliberately chosen incremental expansion to avoid the high costs of environmental compliance. They claimed that "creeping expansion" violated environmental laws. Hence, El Segundo filed a lawsuit in late 1999 challenging six LAX improvement projects that airport officials had claimed were sufficiently small to be exempt from CEQA requirements. Mayor Gordon, joined by Congresswoman Waters, claimed that LAWA was deliberately side-stepping the Master Plan process in order to expedite expansion projects bogged down by community opposition. El Segundo dropped its lawsuit in early 2001, contending that it had forced LAWA into environmental compliance. LAX supporters retorted that its chief purpose had been to delay the process beyond Mayor Riordan's term of office in the hopes that his successor would be more skeptical of LAX expansion.[48]

With the growing threat of legal action against the Master Plan, critics charged that LAWA was using the EIR/EIS public scoping process to prepare its legal defense. Appearing to rigidly adhere to the formal scoping requirements, airport staff allegedly was using the process to gauge, rather than respond to, public reaction. As one close observer noted, "LAX expansion is going to court, and if there is any value now to LAWA in their outreach program, it's to find out what the attacks will be so that in court they can anticipate them and respond."[49]

Environmental Justice

As the EIR/EIS process slowly wrapped up, a new challenge presented itself: environmental justice. Under a 1994 federal executive order, airports seeking FAA funding had to consider the environmental and health effects on nearby communities and had to ensure that expansion did not unduly harm minority neighborhoods. Failure to do so could result in lawsuits and loss of federal funding. Starting in late 1999, antiexpansion and environmental groups opened a new front by raising environmental-justice concerns about the effects of LAX expansion on minority areas under the flight path, such as

Inglewood and Lennox. For LAWA officials, environmental justice was a real concern and was regularly discussed and referred to. They convened a task force to consider the matter and hired environmental and civil rights attorneys and consultants to analyze the issue, devise mitigation measures, and incorporate them into the draft EIR/EIS. Yet when the draft EIR/EIS was released in early 2001, lawyers for L.A. County criticized as inadequate both the analysis of expansion effects on minority communities and the offsetting mitigation measures. The movement suffered a legal setback in spring 2001, when the U.S. Supreme Court ruled that plaintiffs not only had to show discriminatory impact but also had to meet the more difficult standard of proving discriminatory intent.[50]

Critics further complained that LAWA outreach to minority communities was inadequate because it relied primarily on limited, personal contacts with local minority leaders rather than on full-fledged community outreach, education, and economic-development programs. Although airport commissioner Garcia personally met with African American L.A. County Supervisor Yvonne Braithwaite Burke and other minority leaders to try to stimulate interest in LAX-related economic development and job training, there was little LAWA follow-up. A job-training program on the table since the beginning of the Master Plan never got off the ground. Such inaction lent credence to minority activists' claims that the airport engaged in selective outreach. They alleged that LAWA paid more attention to wealthier, organized communities such as El Segundo and Redondo Beach at the expense of poorer, less-organized communities of color such as Inglewood, Lennox, and Hawthorne.[51]

With the early 2001 release of the twelve-thousand-page draft LAX Master Plan EIR/EIS, which recommended the mayor's no-new-runway alternative, antiexpansion foes sought variously to extend the public-comment process beyond Riordan's term of office (ending June 30th) in the hopes of dealing with a more sympathetic successor; to pressure the leading mayoral candidates to oppose LAX expansion; or if all else failed, to sue. The denouement, examined in Chapter Eight, involved newly elected Mayor James Hahn's rejection of LAX expansion in favor of modernization and security.

The Battle over El Toro: Competing Visions and Strategies

In the early 1990s an intense new airport battlefield opened at El Toro Marine Corps Air Station in south Orange County. As part of the federal military-base closure and reuse process, four Southern California military bases were slated for closure/realignment and possible civilian conversion: El Toro, March, Norton, and George. SCAG regional aviation studies consistently showed that El Toro had greater potential for serving passengers than any proposed new airport, including Palmdale. Originally developed during

World War Two, El Toro became encircled by suburban development as the county's postwar population exploded from 130,000 in 1945 to 2.8 million in 2000. Scheduled for closure in 1999, the forty-seven-hundred-acre El Toro facility (larger than LAX) had become expendable as encroachment threatened its military mission.[52]

Regional aviation planners hailed El Toro's potential to relieve LAX. Unlike remote Palmdale, El Toro was located in the middle of the nation's eleventh largest metropolitan economy, with $130 billion in regional output. With Orange County's small, five-hundred-acre John Wayne Airport capped by a noise-settlement agreement at 8.4 MAP and offering minimal air-cargo service, the region was highly underserved. Fifty percent of Orange County passengers and over 95 percent of its air cargo traveled to other airports, primarily LAX and Ontario. El Toro also could assist the underserved San Diego market.[53]

Yet El Toro quickly became the epicenter of the biggest and most expensive land-use conflict in California. Orange County's "civil war" pitted a generally pro-airport north county against a vehemently anti-airport south county. Airport supporters included the County (a narrow three-to-two pro-airport majority on the board of supervisors), the City of Newport Beach (seeking to limit growth at nearby John Wayne Airport), leading business organizations such as the Orange County Business Council, and a group of nine north-county cities organized as the Orange County Regional Airport Authority.

Airport opponents included a powerful, well-organized NIMBY coalition of seven south-county cities (led by the City of Irvine), organized as the re-constituted El Toro Reuse Planning Authority (ETRPA), which was concerned with noise, traffic congestion, and property values. Environmental groups and some south-county business firms with quality-of-life concerns later joined the coalition. Over a nine-year span (1994–2002), the conflict spawned four ballot measures, numerous lawsuits, and full-time employment for a cadre of lawyers, consultants, and pollsters. In arguably the nation's foremost example of ballot-box planning, the two sides spent $90 million in public moneys to determine the future of El Toro through voter initiatives, lawsuits, and environmental reviews.[54]

Airport politics made for strange bedfellows. In the pro-airport camp, conservative, affluent Newport Beach residents joined with immigrant, working-class, Democratic north-county residents. On the anti-airport side, conservative south-county Republicans joined with liberal environmentalists. The contest also featured political spillover from LAX expansion battles; public officials such as Mayor Riordan and anti-LAX activists lobbied Orange County officials and SCAG in favor of an El Toro airport in order to more equitably share the region's burden. SCAG consistently endorsed El Toro, calling in 2001 for a twenty-eight MAP El Toro airport while urging that LAX be capped at seventy-eight MAP.[55]

At base, the El Toro conflict featured competing visions of Orange County's future. For airport supporters, the area's future was as a high-tech, world-trade center and high-end resort destination. An Orange County International Airport (OCX) would serve as a crucial catalyst for continued diversification of the county's economy into high-tech, knowledge-based research and manufacturing, professional services, and tourism. Thus, a twenty-eight MAP OCX promised to be a major pillar of the region's economy, generating by 2020 an estimated $14–18 billion in economy activity, representing 7–10 percent of the area's projected economic output. A large share of the high-tech jobs would be near the airport and would thus benefit south county.[56]

Appealing to Orange County fiscal conservatism, supporters stressed that this "once-in-a-lifetime" opportunity featured low start-up costs (initially estimated at $1.4 billion) because much of the necessary infrastructure, such as runways, was already in place. Moreover, local taxpayers' bank accounts and public treasuries would not be drained because airports were self-financed. Supporters also stressed the value of self-sufficiency. Orange County air travelers and shippers faced risks and uncertainties by continuing to rely on embattled LAX, which likely would become more expensive, congested, and inaccessible to future air travelers from Orange County; travel times on the region's already-clogged freeways threatened to double by 2020.[57]

In contrast, the opponents stressed suburban quality-of-life and environmental concerns. They made classic NIMBY arguments about unfairly bearing the burden of airport noise, air pollution, and traffic congestion. They also stressed that other uses for El Toro—a large park, college campus, stadium, or mixed residential and commercial development—were more compatible with south county's suburban lifestyle. For them, an international airport conjured up images of LAX and a feared "Los Angelesization" of the area, with attendant smog, congestion, and crime. They also proffered political arguments about local self-determination, claiming that affected communities had been unfairly locked out of the airport decision-making process.[58]

To frame the public debate and shape the final outcome, the two sides crafted sophisticated political strategies. Supporters faced the more formidable task. Airport benefits (primarily economic) were diffuse and unnoticed, while airport environmental impacts, real or imagined, were highly concentrated and visible and thus produced intense opposition in affected communities. These different impacts created much stronger incentives for airport opponents rather than supporters to mobilize. The initial reuse planning mechanism gave a strong voice to south-county communities, where NIMBY pressures would be greatest. After President Clinton signed the base-closure order, Orange County, in late 1993, abdicated land-use authority over El Toro and created the original nine-member ETRPA, composed of the five county supervisors (two from south county), three city councilmembers from

Irvine (which was adjacent to El Toro and lay largely in unincorporated territory), and one councilmember from nearby Lake Forest. The federal government recognized ETRPA as El Toro's local redevelopment authority.

Given that county government seemed fairly committed to an airport from the beginning, airport advocates had incentive to restack the deck to create a county-controlled planning process. Supporters also saw value in framing reuse only as an airport and fast-tracking airport planning before the opposition could mobilize. Hence, airport advocates turned to the ballot box. Appearing on the November 1994 ballot, Measure A mandated a commercial airport at El Toro (if no "fatal flaw" were found) by amending the county's general plan and zoning the site for airport use. This measure would effectively take El Toro planning out of ETRPA's hands and give it to the more sympathetic Board of Supervisors. The campaign was underwritten by wealthy local developer/businessman George Argyros, who saw as his legacy an international airport that would transform the region into a world-trade center. In all, Argyros would spend over $3 million of his own money on airport initiatives.

Aiding Measure A was the still-weakened state of the local economy; job creation remained a potent lure. Also, placing the measure on the general-election (rather than primary) ballot ensured higher turnout from sympathetic working-class Democratic voters in north county. Still, the airport measure passed only narrowly—51 to 49 percent—with a pronounced north/south voting split. In 1996, Argyros financed a successful campaign to defeat Measure S (which would have repealed Measure A) as foes also resorted to the ballot box.[59]

But the pendulum soon swung in the other direction. As the economy recovered, job creation lost its appeal. With low unemployment coupled with soaring housing prices, opponents now warned that an airport would exacerbate a growing jobs/housing imbalance. South-county residents viewed Measure A as a deliberate act of disenfranchisement in that it removed the most affected stakeholders from the decision-making process. They also decried a seemingly closed county planning process that failed to seriously examine nonairport alternatives. Here, opponents capitalized on the massive voter distrust toward the Board of Supervisors caused by the December 1994 county bankruptcy, the largest municipal default in the nation's history. The opposition also became better organized and financed. In 1995, seven south-county cities reconstituted themselves as a new ETRPA, pooling their ample financial resources to push for a different redevelopment plan for the base. However, their initial forays were ineffective. They filed an unsuccessful legal challenge to Measure A and then lost the Measure S election, in which they secured only 40 percent of the vote.[60]

Notwithstanding such setbacks, opponents benefited from supporters' tactical errors. In August 1996, the El Toro EIR and Community Reuse Plan were released. The recommended alternative called for a large, thirty-eight MAP passenger/cargo airport (well over half the size of LAX). Although the attorneys spearheading the plan believed that the big-airport proposal would create bargaining leverage, this tactic backfired when it angered local residents and environmentalists. In response, a chastened Board of Supervisors in December 1996 approved a passenger/cargo airport EIR with a Master Plan capped at twenty-five MAP. They also mandated that the Master Plan investigate curfews, preferential runways, and other mitigation measures. In early 1997, ETRPA filed a successful lawsuit challenging the airport EIR. Because of county mismanagement, it took nearly four years to complete a second EIR. This was a key strategic error because it allowed opponents time to become organized and vocal. Foes capitalized on public anger with a seemingly opaque airport planning process and a controversial 1999 decision by the supervisors to endorse a twenty-nine MAP airport in direct violation of their 1996 promise.[61]

In addition to filing environmental lawsuits, opponents crafted a multifaceted political strategy to kill airport plans. First, the City of Irvine (leading the anti-airport drive) launched a well-financed campaign to annex El Toro and remove the base from county planning. However, such a move required both the approval of the obscure Local Agency Formation Commission (LAFCO) and a tax-sharing agreement with the county. Both proved difficult. Four of the seven LAFCO board members were from south county; the county supervisors altered this delicate balance of power by appointing a pro-airport supervisor to the commission to replace an anti-airport colleague. Further, the pro-airport county-board majority failed to approve a tax-sharing agreement.[62]

Second, with the supervisors blocking annexation and ostensibly scheduled to vote in early 1999 on an airport master plan, opponents sought to alter the precarious balance of power on the Board of Supervisors. With three of five seats up for grabs in the 1998 elections, anti-airport candidates entered the fray. Yet, in one of the costliest elections in county history, with heavy and unreported last-minute spending by "independent expenditure committees," pro-airport forces were able to maintain their narrow 3-to-2 board majority. In 2000, anti-airport forces attempted to unseat another pro-airport supervisor but failed to do so.[63]

Third, airport foes pursued a "fatal-flaw" line of attack. A provision in Measure A allowed supervisors to scuttle the airport if a federal or state agency found a "fatal flaw" or if a citizens advisory committee recommended that the airport was unworkable. As a result, airport foes (and supporters) heavily lobbied officials at the Pentagon, at the FAA, and on Capitol Hill. Opponents sought to convince relevant federal agencies that the airport was fatally flawed because of safety or environmental concerns (including cleanup costs). The Navy had to decide whether it was cost effective to hand over the land to the county. The FAA had to make a final determination about whether El Toro could safely become an airport, with critics voicing major runway and air-corridor safety concerns. Foes believed that any adverse finding would give them significant leverage with the county board.[64]

Finally, airport foes returned to the initiative process, but with a more Machiavellian strategy. The two previous initiatives had essentially been yes-or-no votes regarding an airport as the preferred land use. In 1999, ETRPA launched a new initiative campaign that would make it more difficult to build a commercial airport. Measure F, which appeared on the March 2000 ballot, required two-thirds voter support in a public referendum before an airport, large jail facility, or hazardous-waste landfill could be built. Significantly, the measure also prohibited the county from spending any money "promoting" an airport, jail, or landfill without a prior vote of the people. Advocates chose a low-turnout March primary election when high-propensity, affluent Republican voters in solidly anti-airport south county would be out in force relative to pro-airport, working-class Democratic voters in north county. This "LULU" (locally unwanted land use) strategy worked brilliantly. The measure passed by a two-to-one majority notwithstanding Argyros's contribution of $1.2 million to defeat the initiative.

With anti-airport propaganda continuing to hammer out the message that El Toro was "unwanted, unneeded, and unsafe," the measure effectively silenced the county's pro-airport public relations campaign. But borrowing a page from the opposition playbook, airport supporters then filed a lawsuit to overturn Measure F. In December 2000 the anti-airport initiative was thrown out as an impermissible usurpation of the supervisor's planning and land-use authority.

Undaunted, ETRPA and the City of Irvine launched yet another initiative effort—this time seeking to recast the choice. Instead of simply giving voters a thumbs-up-or-down choice on an airport, Measure W (the "Great Park" initiative) offered voters the opportunity to rezone El Toro for an assortment of popular nonairport uses, such as a large park. Although pro-airport groups legally challenged Measure W's signature-gathering process, it was approved for the March 2002 ballot. With public opinion polls showing strong support for Measure W, a beleaguered county board responded by capping the airport at eighteen MAP as a last-ditch effort to save the plan.

El Toro had once held considerable promise as the region's second major international airport. Through the missteps of supporters and the adroit moves of opponents, it had been downsized to a medium-sized domestic airport with limited international service. Yet, even this plan was jeopardized. Chapter Eight discusses the outcome of the Measure W campaign, which would kill any plans for a commercial airport at El Toro.

The Failure of Regionalism

Despite the apparent bounty of airports in the Los Angeles region, the effective options for expansion at existing or newly converted airports were surprisingly limited. LAX would remain the region's chief airport, particularly for international service, for the foreseeable future. The short-haul domestic market was shifting to Burbank, Long Beach, John Wayne, and Ontario airports. Yet three of the regional airports (Burbank, Long Beach, and John Wayne) had little or no room for expansion because physical limits, noise curfews, and legally enforceable limits on operations (the product of sharp conflicts with their neighbors) severely constrained both the number of flights and the hours of operation.

With El Toro's apparent demise, the main international-airport alternative to LAX became LAWA's Ontario Airport, which had undergone a major terminal-expansion program. Ontario was the region's second largest airport for domestic-passenger and air-cargo service; it could expand to twenty MAP if state air-quality ceilings on flight operations were relaxed. In 2001, it resumed international air service to Mexico. Remote Palmdale, once touted as the region's next international airport, likely would be a small commuter airport absent an unlikely multi-billion dollar investment in infrastructure and high-speed-rail access to populated areas.[65] Other expansion possibilities were offered by three recently closed or realigned military bases in the Inland Empire: March (renamed March Inland Port), Norton (San Bernardino International), and George (Southern California Logistics). These sites suffered from the same market and transportation difficulties as Palmdale. As a result, they initially billed themselves as industrial airports serving cargo, corporate, and charter aviation needs.

Local boosters embraced the chimera of high-speed-rail connections to urban centers. In the 1990s, two HSR initiatives were launched. California's Intercity High Speed Rail Commission recommended a statewide network 676 miles long, including a Palmdale/Los Angeles link. Public funding, requiring difficult-to-obtain voter approval, would be needed for the $20–30 billion in estimated construction costs. SCAG proposed its own HSR system to serve the region's airports. At a projected cost of $6.2 billion, magnetic-levitation trains would connect LAX, Ontario, and March airports on an elevated track. The public sector would provide the right-of-way, and the private sector would finance, construct, and operate the system. But this unproven technology failed to find willing investors. Federal demonstration-project funding also was lacking for SCAG's proposal.

As a result, Southern California airport planners faced a frustrating paradox. While demand for passenger and air-cargo service was expected to double or triple by 2020, there was little regional consensus regarding where to place new airports. The airline industry favored a massive expansion of

LAX and development of a new international airport at El Toro. Located in densely developed areas, these sites were attractive to the airlines because they were near housing and job centers. Yet plans for LAX and El Toro growth were placed on hold because of determined opposition from nearby residents, who argued that new airport capacity should be located in the fast-growing periphery of the region. Although communities around Palmdale, March, Norton, and George welcomed airports as potent development tools, the airlines were opposed to these remote sites, where demand had not yet reached critical mass. As Neil Bennett, western regional director of the Air Transport Association, observed, "It's a Catch-22. In order to have demand, you have to have population density. And when you have population density, you have conflict." [66]

The region's public officials and community activists strongly agreed about the need for greater coordination among the region's airports. Those interested in international trade cited the need for coordination in order for the region to be competitive in the global marketplace. Those concerned with quality-of-life issues supported regional planning as a means of diffusing the adverse environmental and health impacts of airports. [67]

Yet few institutional mechanisms were available to resolve the region's looming capacity shortfall. LAWA could make decisions only for its own airport system. A constrained LAX and a market- and ground-access-challenged Palmdale left Ontario as the only near-term expansion possibility. Although SCAG was the lead agency for regional transportation planning (including aviation), it lacked the land-use and financial authority needed to develop and operate airports. SCAG excelled in technical studies and provided a useful voluntary forum for elected officials to debate regional airport issues. But its decision-making process could be politicized. For example, it was commandeered by anti-LAX forces in 2001 to force growth elsewhere, particularly at El Toro. But south Orange County public officials and voters had other ideas. While SCAG saw air-cargo possibilities for the three Inland Empire ex-military bases, it could offer few incentives for air service there.

The promise of the Southern California Regional Airport Authority (SCRAA), created in 1983 and revived in 1999, remained largely illusory. Notwithstanding the appearance of real authority, it functioned as a voluntary association comprising the City of Los Angeles and the counties of L.A., Orange, San Bernardino, and Riverside, with SCAG participating as a non-voting member. Under state law, SCRAA appeared to have the authority to own, acquire, construct, and operate commercial airports. In theory, it also had the powers of eminent domain and revenue-bond financing. Yet, when Orange County finally joined SCRAA in 1992, it did so on the condition that each member had contractual veto power over the authority's decisions. Veto power severely limited the agency's regional-airport development authority. Chronically underfunded, SCRAA was reactivated by several L.A. county supervisors only as a bargaining chip to give them greater say over the LAX Master Plan, including alternatives such as Palmdale.

Local public officials had few incentives to create a veto-free regional airport authority. The combination of concentrated environmental costs (imposed on airport neighbors) and diffuse economic benefits (for the region) created a political milieu in which no politician wanted to risk the ire of highly motivated opponents for promises of support from more passive proponents. Also, there was the structural problem of a privileged status quo. Any existing airport operator who felt its interests threatened by a regional authority would have an incentive to keep local veto power in place.

Strong pressures continued for LAX growth relative to other sites. Since airline deregulation in 1978, the airline industry's preference has been to concentrate air service at a single, well-located hub. Air passengers' airport choices (shaped by perceptions of travel times, relative convenience, and the availability, frequency, and price of flights to preferred destinations) also favored large facilities like LAX—even when they were not necessarily the "optimal" available choice. Another driver was convenient transportation to and from various airport sites.

SCAG's regional aviation models suggested that even if all existing airports in the region (including Palmdale) were expanded to capacity—considering only physical limitations and disregarding legal and political restrictions—and, further, if all potential sites at existing military bases were converted to civilian aviation uses, demand at LAX still would increase. An international airport at El Toro would take some passenger and cargo traffic away from LAX, but the load at LAX would still grow. Yet constraints on LAX expansion would ultimately result in an uncompetitive airport, with higher fares, fewer flight options, and greater delays.

The failure of international-airport development in Southern California threatened to have serious consequences. At the dawn of the new millennium, the region faced a growing airport capacity crisis that imperiled its trade future, with few institutional mechanisms to help resolve it. The combined land size for the region's five commercial airports (7,900 acres) was only slightly larger than Chicago/O'Hare Airport (7,700 acres) and was dwarfed by Dallas/Fort Worth (18,000 acres) and Denver International Airport (34,000 acres). Absent new runways, by 2025 the region would experience a 50 percent capacity shortfall—the greatest among the nation's major metropolitan areas. L.A.'s nearest rivals—the Bay Area, Phoenix, and Las Vegas, all with ambitious airport-expansion projects—were poised to capture a growing share of its global business. Airports were becoming the Achilles' heel of Southern California's global engagement.

Part Four The New Millennium

At the Global Crossroads

8 Rethinking Global Los Angeles

New Challenges and Formulas

> Toto, I've got a feeling we're not in Kansas any more.
>
> —*Dorothy in* The Wonderful Wizard of Oz,
> *quoted in Edward W. Soja,* Thirdspace *(1996)*[1]

> International trade is one of the driving forces in the Southern California economy and
> one of the main contributors to the region's enormous growth over the past 25 years.
>
> —*Abraham F. Lowenthal, L. Thomas Best Jr., and Michael Browrigg (1996)*[2]

> The slump in international trade flows in 2001 was a splash in the face of cold water for
> the Southern California economy. Not only were there the recessions in both the U.S.
> and Asia, but the September 11th attack introduced a whole new operational dynamic
> to the business of international trade. . . . [The region's] international trade infrastruc-
> ture remains under stress.
>
> —*Los Angeles County Economic Development Corporation, 2002*[3]

This chapter examines the current status and uncertain future of Southern
California as a major trade and transportation center. I consider developments since the election of L.A. Mayor James K. Hahn in June 2001 and
particularly since the September 11, 2001, terrorist attacks in New York
and Washington. As the new millennium began, Greater Los Angeles lay at a
global crossroads. In 2001, after twenty-plus years of surging gains, two-way
trade flows through the L.A. Customs District (LACD) registered a decline.
Driven by a sharp drop in global air-cargo shipments, the overall value of
LACD merchandise trade (by district of unlading) fell 5 percent from the previous year—to $270 billion.[4]

Despite a modest increase projected for 2002, L.A.'s trade future grew
ever more uncertain. After the September 11th terrorist attacks, L.A.'s trade
and infrastructure faced new security challenges. Local secession threats also
took their toll. As a result, under the new mayor port and airport expansion
took a back seat to community, environmental, and security concerns. Given
a looming infrastructure impasse, particularly with respect to international-
airport development, the region scrambled to find new global formulas.

Contributing to the current rethinking of the region's global engagement, this chapter is divided into four parts. The first section considers how the analysis of trade and infrastructure in this book squares with the leading perspectives on L.A. globalization: the so-called L.A. School and what might be called the New Boosterism. The second section assesses L.A.'s global performance by looking at the benefits and costs of being a major trade and transportation center. The third section examines the new challenge of providing security against terrorism, both nationwide and regionally. The concluding section explores L.A.'s uncertain global future. I examine the policies of L.A.'s new mayor, address the growing regional debate concerning trade and infrastructure development, and assess new formulas being advanced.

In Search of Global L.A.

At the start of the twentieth century, L. Frank Baum, author of *The Wonderful Wizard of Oz* (1900), his classic parable about "the money power" in the tornadic age of American industrialization, completed the sequel while wintering in sparsely settled Southern California. The region then was home to only three hundred thousand residents, many of them recent transplants from Kansas, Iowa, and other midwestern states. As the twenty-first century begins, Los Angeles has moved far beyond these modest midwestern roots. In the span of a century, Southern California has developed into one of the world's largest and most ethnically diverse metropolises. No longer Kansas West, the region today is star witness to another tornadic age: that of globalization. How does this story of trade and infrastructure development relate to current debates concerning global restructuring in Southern California? How might we better understand Los Angeles's supposed emergence as what Edward Soja calls "the capital of the twentieth century"? [5]

"Life is green; theory is gray," or so said Goethe. This was certainly the case throughout most of the twentieth century in Los Angeles, where, despite well-watered lawns, there was little cultivation of serious theorizing about L.A. in either national or global perspective. There were a few great nonfiction books about Los Angeles, notably Carey McWilliams's *Southern California: An Island on the Land* (1946), Robert M. Fogelson's *The Fragmented Metropolis: Los Angeles, 1850–1930* (1967), and Reyner Banham's *Los Angeles: The Architecture of Four Ecologies* (1971). Yet these classics did not dislodge the conventional popular and academic wisdom that L.A. was an exception or an "antitype": the nesting ground of religious cults, crackpot politics, and an invertebrate mass of "60 suburbs in search of a city." [6]

Since the mid-1980s, L.A. has ceased being treated as terra incognita. Once-neglected Los Angeles, long considered the great exception to urban-development patterns as portrayed by the famous Chicago School, now serves as harbinger of new urban spatial forms and social relations. Los Angeles is considered archetypal of "cities without suburbs"; it shows how annexation can dramatically expand city limits and ensure continued growth and prosperity. Sprawling L.A. serves as the quintessential "edge city" of multiple urban cores—an example of how all metropolitan areas now supposedly evolve. Once the most WASPish of American cities, Los Angeles also is being studied anew for its transformation into the nation's new Ellis Island. Rapidly growing Latino and Asian Pacific immigrant communities now constitute a majority of the city's and county's population—a key element of L.A.'s globalization.[7]

Two rival interpretations—one by Soja and the L.A. School; the other by Joel Kotkin and what may be termed the New Boosters—have emerged to chart global economic restructuring in the region. I consider these two perspectives on L.A. globalization, one rooted in postmodernism and the other in free-market ideology, as they relate to the questions explored here: the rise of L.A. as a major trade center, the development of the region's huge trade-transportation complex, and the local state's role in promoting both.

The L.A. School—the Many Faces of the "Postmetropolis"

Not until the mid-1980s did a school of urbanists—the L.A. School— emerge that was dedicated to exploring the development of Los Angeles in theoretical and global context. A loose congeries of planners, geographers, sociologists, and historians based primarily at UCLA, the L.A. School has as its collective postmodern manifesto Soja's "it all comes together in Los Angeles." For them, L.A. embodies how the late twentieth-century urban landscape has been radically altered by a multifaceted global-restructuring process—the "hollowing out" and redevelopment of downtown, the abandonment of the inner city and minorities, the decay of older suburbs, the decentralization of industry, the emergence of information-age "edge cities," and the hypermobility of international capital and labor flows. Soja likens Los Angeles to "the Aleph," the place "where all places are" in Jorge Luis Borges's famous short story of the same name.[8] He argues:

> One can find in Los Angeles not only the high technology industrial complexes of the Silicon Valley and the erratic Sunbelt economy of Houston, but also the far-reaching industrial decline and bankrupt urban neighborhoods of rustbelt Detroit or Cleveland. There is a Boston in Los Angeles, a Lower Manhattan and a South Bronx, a Sao Paulo and a Singapore. There may be no other comparable urban region which presents so vividly such a composite assemblage and articulation of urban restructuring processes. Los Angeles seems to be conjugating the recent history of capitalist civilization in virtually all its inflectional form.[9]

Drawing on the work of Allen Scott and Mike Davis, Soja does not offer an integrated theory of postmodern urbanization but instead presents six overlapping images of simultaneous "urban transformation" in "postmetropolitan" Los Angeles:[10]

1. Peripheralization: Los Angeles broke with the pattern of concentric zones radiating from a central point, a pattern that, according to the Chicago School, was the hallmark of modern urban growth. By decentralizing population, manufacturing, and retailing but then reconcentrating them on the metropolitan periphery, decentered, polynucleated Los Angeles became the prototypical "Exopolis" or "city turned inside out."[11]

2. Post-Fordism: L.A. became the first "post-Fordist" metropolitan economy as large-scale, assembly-line manufacturing, characteristic of "the Fordist era," receded, small-scale craft production (of apparel, furniture, and jewelry) grew, and expanding suburban "technopoles" provided information and business services.[12]

3. Multiculturalism: Los Angeles became a "heteropolis"—or heterogeneous cultural microcosm made up of a multiplicity of ethnic subcommunities composed of people from around the world—as it experienced an unprecedented immigrant influx. Observers differed, however, on whether the result would be L.A.'s cultural decline into "a third-world megalopolis" or its elevation into a paradigm of multicultural progress.[13]

4. Repolarization: L.A. became "the fractal city"—fractured along class as well as ethnic lines—as the lower and upper classes found themselves separated by a widening divide.[14]

5. Repression: Los Angeles became "the carceral city" as social splintering undermined social control and caused a resort to new high-tech modes of policing and surveillance.[15]

6. Manipulation: L.A. became the model for "simcities" everywhere, marketing "simulacra," or re-creations, of experiences that never really occurred but were more commercially palatable than the genuine article. Recreation-oriented theme parks for the young (Disneyland) and not-so-young (Leisure World) metastasized across the region, and foreign tourists visiting Universal Studio's CityWalk could enjoy simulations of Los Angeles without ever actually walking down its "mean streets."[16]

*The New Boosterism—Marrying Pacific Rim Diversity
to Digital Technology*

Joel Kotkin, Senior Fellow at Pepperdine University's Institute for Public Policy and Research, and journalist David Friedman, Senior Fellow at the New America Foundation, offer their own multifaceted vision of global Los Angeles, a vision that differs significantly in tone as well as substance from that of the L.A. School. Kotkin and Friedman are unapologetic cheerleaders for L.A.'s aspirations to become the preeminent Pacific Rim trade entrepôt and high-tech metropolis.[17] As Kotkin argues:

> By 1997, well over a third of Los Angeles's businesses were minority-owned, contributing greatly to the area's unexpected economic resurgence. Newcomers . . . had expanded into a number of highly specialized, classically urban niches, including apparel, textile, light manufacturing, and international trade. . . . [The] transformation of immigrant-favored cities into centers of global trade has been accelerated by technological change[,] . . . which has seen the price of transoceanic calls fall by over 90 percent, the cost of air travel by 80 percent, and ocean freight charges by half. With the rise of the Internet and other communications technologies such as satellites, global trade-related activities will become ever more important and accessible.[18]

The New Boosters cheer on insurgents and innovators, especially immigrant entrepreneurs, though their ethnic pantheon has shifted considerably with the times. In the 1980s, it was expatriate Japanese bankers who, "like financial Jesuits around the globe," were making Los Angeles "Tokyo's twenty-fourth ward" and facilitating what "has been labeled 'transpacific integration' tying the economic fates of Asia and America inextricably together." During the recession of the early 1990s, as Japanese investment capital ebbed, the overseas Taiwanese, known as *tai kung fei jen,* or "spacemen," for their circuit around trans-Pacific venues, emerged as "super immigrants" combining New World risk taking with home-country "*guanxi* or connections."[19] More recently, the New Boosters' vision of global L.A. as the latest "universal city"—successor to ancient Alexandria, the first of the great international business centers—has showcased the contributions of immigrant entrepreneurs from the Middle East—Israelis, Iranians, Lebanese, and Armenians—whose number of business start-ups in the L.A. metropolitan area is comparable to those of Taiwanese and Korean immigrants.[20]

The New Boosters are populists who celebrate small business but only if it is up-to-date and plugged into the global economy. Kotkin's vision of L.A.'s economic future has two tracks: "midlopolitan" marketplaces—older suburbs revitalized by manufacturing and commercial enterprises that globally market such items as toys, textiles, and food products—and peripherally located "nerdistans," whose information-age businesses include electronics, computer software, professional services, and multimedia. These two tracks are linked by the pervasive involvement in both of immigrant entrepreneurs or engineers and by the new digital technology connecting both to Pacific Rim trade.[21]

Kotkin argues that just as transportation innovations such as railroads and interstate trucking sped the movement of goods nationally during the era of the industrial city, telecommunications innovations are revolutionizing global commerce in the era of the postindustrial city. Production of goods will be much less place-bound than in the past, and business locational decisions will be shaped by the lifestyle preferences of high-tech managers and professionals regarding the kinds of communities in which they want to live and work.[22]

Yet the dot.com bubble of the late 1990s raised warning signals, especially in Friedman's mind, about the "pragmatism" of local development policies favoring "new-economy" industries over a "full-spectrum" development strategy encouraging a more diversified economic base. Friedman still looks to Southern California for an ideal type of future economic development, but his model now is the low- to medium-tech Inland Empire rather than high-tech Ventura County. Kotkin continues to have faith that the "best of both worlds" is possible if "high-tech nerdistans" on the metropolitan periphery abandon attempts at isolation and enthusiastically embrace global Los Angeles's pluralistic culture and economy.[23]

Mooring the Global Metropolis

Despite their differences, the L.A. School and the New Boosterism share major analytical deficiencies that this study seeks to correct. The L.A. School does not give sufficient attention to trade's key role in the region's economic restructuring. And although the New Boosters recognize trade's importance, they choose to highlight the catalytic role of telecommunications, not transportation, infrastructure. Neither seriously considers the local state's role in promoting trade and infrastructure development.

Soja and his associates are best known as critics of capitalist culture and urban form, yet the central anomaly that inspired their rethinking of Los Angeles concerned economic development. During the 1970s and 1980s, while other cities and regions were emptied of manufacturing employment, L.A. continued to thrive as a production center. Its losses in "Fordist" factory employment were exceeded by gains in "post-Fordist" jobs in small-scale manufacturing and light industry. Soja argues that Los Angeles's periodic "restructurings" over the course of the twentieth century were largely a response to "surges" of social crises—beginning with the labor strife of the Progressive Era, continuing with the military-industrial demands of World War Two and the Cold War, and culminating in the racial upheavals of 1965 and 1992. Unfortunately, he offers no consistent, detailed elaboration of this nexus between social crises and economic restructuring.[24]

Nor are Soja's invocations of "internationalization" as an explanation for recent economic trends ever linked with a systematic analysis of either Los Angeles's growing share of Pacific Rim trade or its world-class trade-transportation complex. Major public investments in trade infrastructure are discussed only in connection with the early twentieth-century "takeoff era," when San Pedro harbor was developed; subsequent infrastructure developments do not receive requisite attention. Soja does mention the critical importance of current plans "for the largest direct public financial stimulus ever given to any metropolitan region," but his reference is to mass transit rather than to trade-related plans to invest in port, rail, and airport development.[25] "Aerospace Alley"—the airport-to-port high-tech complex ranging from Santa Monica to Long Beach—is classified by Soja as one of L.A.'s "exopolitan" districts. Yet his discussion emphasizes not its expanding role in international trade but its declining status as "probably the . . . largest concentration of the American military-industrial complex." Soja also highlights the significance of "a continuous sequence of public and private sector partnerships" in L.A. not as having contributed to trade and economic development, but rather as having "directly or indirectly induced the most violent interracial conflagrations that have occurred in any U.S. city."[26]

Historian Mike Davis provides a partial exception to the L.A. School's failure to offer a cogent explanation of L.A.'s trade development. Davis has a coherent theory of the "internationalization" of Los Angeles's economy. The theory can be summarized in this way. Cheap imports from Japan flood the U.S. market, eliminating manufacturing jobs; the Japanese reinvest their trade surplus in speculative downtown real estate, underwriting redevelopment policies that uproot inner-city populations; and the void is filled by an influx of destitute immigrants, primarily from Mexico, who toil in the new "sweatshops." Co-opted by foreign capital, City Hall vastly expands port facilities and, until late in the day, strives to keep down landing fees at LAX in the interest of "megabanks and technology monopolies" headquartered across the Pacific.[27]

With a mixture of horror and admiration, Davis recognizes the "Bismarckian municipal will" (in Kevin Starr's words) of modern L.A.'s early twentieth-century founding fathers, who "created the world's biggest man-made port, aqueduct and inter-urban electric railroad system" at the same time that they "smashed the labor movement." By the late twentieth century, however, the local state and "power structure," in his account, have shrunk to minimalist stature. They can no longer shape L.A.'s destiny. Davis's provocative marriage of history and theory, however, appears to purchase consistency at the price of conspiratorialism, ignores the regional benefits flowing from trade, entrepreneurialism, and innovation, and reduces the complex impacts of globalization to predatory speculation by the rich and the concomitant immiserization of the poor.[28]

The New Boosters, it need hardly be added, have an antithetical vision of the global economic transformation of Los Angeles.[29] Rather than being cast as the villain of the L.A. economy, "the booming trade sector" is viewed as its salvation. Hence, according to Kotkin: "Much like Renaissance Venice, the sprawling industrial region around downtown Los Angeles has developed a series of specialized industrial districts tied to the processing, warehousing, and trading of global products. . . . In Los Angeles, trade-related activities have spawned the growth of more than 100,000 jobs during the past decade and today sustain a larger number of jobs than aerospace, previously the region's bellwether industry."[30]

Ironically, however, perhaps because of their populist suspicion of government, the New Boosters are reticent about the high-profile involvement by local government in L.A.'s global economic-development process. The government-assisted renovation of "unglamorous and underappreciated assets," such as local warehouses to service small manufacturers, is at the top of their priority list, but major public investments in port, rail, and airport improvements receive only pro forma endorsements.[31]

In global cities that successfully compete, economic restructuring goes hand in hand with state restructuring, without which it cannot succeed. Both the L.A. School and the New Boosters ignore the creative role that local governments in Southern California have played in trade, infrastructure, and economic development. As these pages argue, the "hollowing out of the state" at the national level has actually created openings for the entrepreneurial local state at city and regional levels to play a vital role in shaping the transportation and telecommunications infrastructures critical for global competitiveness.[32]

Gauging L.A.'s Global Performance

Trade's Regional Effects

What have been the benefits, costs, and tradeoffs of Greater Los Angeles's becoming a major trade and transportation center? Trade has complex direct and indirect effects on the economy. The few existing regional-level trade-impact studies narrowly focus on goods exports to the exclusion of service exports and imports. Yet Southern California is a poster child for a broader conceptualization of trade performance, which helps dispel its image as a trade underachiever. Here, service exports such as motion-picture production and tourism are as important as merchandise exports. As Cynthia Kroll and colleagues argue in a study of foreign trade and California's economic growth, trade is reshaping the state's job opportunities away from blue-collar manufacturing and toward white-collar service jobs. Nowhere is this truer than in Southern California.[33]

Further, even imports can generate gains in domestic employment. Although import competition can result in direct job losses in the manufacturing sector, mitigating factors may counteract this effect. One such factor is the expansion of overall demand as import competition encourages both greater efficiency and lower prices from domestic manufacturers. Imported inputs also can promote expansion of domestic production and employment. Thus, computer-industry imports encourage domestic job growth in related service-sector industries. Finally, and of paramount importance to Southern California, the warehousing and transshipment of large volumes of imports can produce significant employment in the burgeoning logistics industry.[34]

How has global trade (broadly defined) transformed the Southern California economy? In 2001, upward of one-quarter (or $160 billion) of the Greater Los Angeles $650 billion economy depended on global trade, up from 13 percent in 1972. International trade has become two distinct industries in the region. The first involves the production of goods and services for export. Here, L.A.'s export profile is different from that of other leading trading regions. Unlike "export-monoculture" regions with a dominant export industry, such as Seattle, the Bay Area, and Detroit, Southern California has a highly diversified manufacturing base. Its exports reflect that diversity. The region's most export-dependent sectors are located at opposite ends of the technological spectrum, from high value-per-unit computer equipment and aerospace components to low-value primary metals, wastepaper, petrochemicals, and leather products.[35]

Compared with Seattle or the Bay Area, Los Angeles exports fewer manufactured goods, such as aircraft or computer parts, but generates unusually large service exports (up to half of the region's exports, compared with one-quarter nationwide) in globally oriented local industries such as entertainment, engineering, international tourism, and software development. According to the best estimates, goods and services exports directly and indirectly generate 15–20 percent of L.A.-area economic activity and employment.[36]

The second trade-related industry is logistics, the distribution and transportation of cargo moving into and out of the region. This is an underappreciated engine of regional job growth. Although imports usually are conceived of as the cause of domestic job losses (nationally in the automobile, steel, and shoe industries, and in Southern California in import-sensitive sectors such as apparels and canning), the jobs created in the distribution and transshipment of imported goods can generate sizeable regional economic benefits. Such may be the case for the Inland Empire, which has been transformed into a major warehouse/distribution center serving the entire Southwest. However, balanced against these regional benefits are costs: a welter of low-paying warehouse jobs, inefficient land uses, and growing truck-generated traffic congestion and air pollution.[37]

Southern California has become one of the world's great trade entrepôts: a gigantic warehouse, distribution, logistics, and transportation complex of port- and airport-related industries and users, ranging from freight forwarders to local distributors who receive foreign goods for resale. According to the best estimates, freight handling likely generates directly or indirectly another 5–8 percent of overall regional economic activity. This appears to be a much higher share of gross regional product than for near-pure trade entrepôts such as Buffalo and New Orleans, where only a small fraction of exports are locally produced and, similarly, few imports are locally consumed. Although the region's massive domestic market, sizeable Asian Pacific and Latino communities, and strategic Pacific Rim location all have contributed to L.A.'s rapid rise as a trade mecca, its extensive port, rail, airport, and highway network has played a significant, albeit underrecognized, catalytic role.[38]

Foreign direct investments also have propelled L.A.'s growth. Such investments are closely linked to trade. They can function as a form of direct or indirect trade substitution, as when a foreign exporter invests in locally based production. The Chinese, Japanese, Koreans, Filipinos, Dutch, British, and Canadians have invested significantly in L.A. manufacturing, real estate, wholesale trade, and entertainment. Mainland China has become so heavily invested in L.A. that, should U.S./Chinese relations deteriorate into a military confrontation, local economists joke that "Los Angeles is the last city they would strike because they've got so damned much money invested here."[39]

But balanced against sizeable regional trade and related benefits are claims of trade-induced job displacement and wage losses. In particular, the North American Free Trade Agreement (NAFTA) has sparked a sharp debate about potential dislocations in Southern California. NAFTA's impact on the local jobs balance sheet remains hotly contested. The Economic Policy Institute puts California's net job loss at eighty thousand-plus (presumably over half located in Southern California). Of the twelve L.A. firms applying for NAFTA trade-adjustment assistance, nine (more than for any other region) were certified to meet the combined criteria of regional concentration, import penetration, and declines in both employment and real wages. Eight of the nine firms reported production shifts to Mexico. Especially hard hit were smaller firms (employing minority workers in low-wage jobs) in electronics (experiencing sharp drops in both employment and wages) and apparel manufacturing (suffering wage declines though maintaining its jobs base). In contrast, after earlier pessimistic assessments, UCLA's North American Integration and Development Center estimates NAFTA's national impact at more than one hundred thousand jobs in the plus column, with California garnering a significant share.[40]

NAFTA's regional balance sheet also appears to have a positive side. Imports frequently enter market niches that complement domestically produced goods. Compensating job increases have been concentrated in high-end, high-tech jobs, especially among firms specializing in exports of intermediate goods to the maquiladoras in Mexico. Even in the low-end manufacturing sector, improvements accelerated the region's economic recovery. Rebuilding its manufacturing base in the 1990s, Southern California shifted from high-wage, high-skilled jobs in large aerospace firms to high-wage jobs in design-based industries (medical instruments, automobiles) as well as to lower-wage jobs in small shops producing clothing, furniture, and other nondurable products. By the late 1990s, over fifty thousand regional jobs depended on exports to Mexico. Mexican trade (as well as the Central and South American markets to which it is the gateway) took on added regional importance as an "insurance policy" against Asian downturns. Overall, there was no evidence of significant NAFTA-induced job loss in Southern California, although the trade pact was not the panacea touted by its supporters.[41]

Trade's Distributional Effects

Besides these aggregate trade impacts, the intraregional distribution of trade benefits and costs needs to be considered. In a provocative study of L.A. trade winners and "strugglers," Manual Pastor Jr. argues that globalization may well exacerbate regional racial and economic inequalities. Analyzing the industry export shares of and the wages in fifty-eight subregions of L.A. County from 1988 to 1993, he ranks subregions on a relative (not absolute) scale as trade winners, neutrals, or strugglers. Pastor finds that Anglo neighborhoods, such as L.A.'s affluent Westside, were trade winners (having gained the most in exports and wages from international trade), while impoverished minority communities, such as the Alameda Corridor cities, were strugglers, gaining the least. For Pastor, the Alameda Corridor rail project was emblematic of growing equity struggles. He argues that the corridor cities' 1995 lawsuit had its origins in local concerns over the lack of long-term benefit from the project.[42]

Pastor's otherwise admirable analysis is incomplete. In considering trade as an industry, it does not examine the logistics industry, the region's fastest growing sector in the 1990s. In analyzing the impact of trade on industry, it excludes Southern California's burgeoning service export sector. It thus substantially underestimates the positive value of trade to the region's economy.

Further, there is little evidence, nationally or regionally, that trade is the major factor in the widening income divide. Nationally, trade competition at best may explain up to only 20 percent of the rising wage gap. Technology appears to be a far greater culprit. Regionally, industrial restructuring and widening inequalities have been caused by a host of non-trade-related factors such as branch-plant closures, recession, and defense downsizing. The Alameda Corridor communities (now identified as L.A.'s "rust belt") suffered a hollowing out of manufacturing that preceded increased globalization. During the 1990s, with heightened trade competition, the Alameda Corridor's manufacturing base performed the best of the six major manufacturing regions in L.A. County. Between 1991 and 2001, the North Gateway (Alameda Corridor) area saw only a 7 percent drop in manufacturing employment, compared with a 27 percent overall regional decline. Because of defense downsizing, there was a steep 47 percent manufacturing job loss in Long Beach/Lakewood and a 33 percent drop in the South Bay/LAX area. Casting further doubt on trade's role in local inequalities, Pastor finds that Latinos and Asian Pacific Americans who found work in Southern California's export-oriented manufacturing sector scored greater income gains that either Anglos or African Americans.[43]

Left unanswered is an all-important question: How would minority and working-class income levels look had the region not plugged into the global economy? In the early 1990s, fast-growing global trade was a major reason why the effects of the region's sharp economic downturn were not more severe. As the Cold War ended, military cutbacks decimated the country's most defense-based regional economy. With L.A. County alone losing two hundred thousand aerospace jobs, the region's historically low unemployment rate climbed to 50 percent above the national average. During the 1990–93 recession, as Stephen Cohen observed, "L.A. [was] the hole in the [national] bucket." Twenty-seven percent of the total U.S. job loss took place in the five-county metropolitan area.[44]

International trade helped revitalize, restructure, and rebuild a shattered economy. Between 1990 and 2001, the five-county region gained more international trade jobs than it had lost in aerospace/high-tech employment. By 2001, international trade (defined as moving commodities in and out of the customs district, but not including manufacturing) directly employed 441,000 persons in the region compared with 194,000 for aerospace/high tech. Minorities and low-income workers found new job opportunities as logistics specialists, office workers, warehouse workers, and truck drivers.[45]

In regard to community struggles over infrastructure projects, the Alameda Corridor cities successfully used lawsuits to secure tangible concessions (such as economic-development funds and project training and hiring guarantees). With the settlement, the project was completed without further delay. To the extent that the Alameda Corridor reduces local rail and traffic congestion, it makes affected communities more economically competitive. Again, one wonders what the costs to minorities and low-income workers would have been if the rail project had not been built. The harbor and corridor-city areas might be strangling in traffic while losing business and jobs to rival ports and trading regions.

The gravest threats to the region's mega-projects and global future now may come from affluent Anglos, not poor minorities. The region's export future (particularly high valued-added, high-tech industries) depends on airport projects rather than port/rail development. Affluent Westside and South Bay residents (deemed by Pastor trade winners or neutrals) led the successful fight against LAX expansion. In Orange County, affluent Anglo residents living in the export-oriented, high-tech south-county area led the winning battle against an international airport at El Toro. The region's infrastructure challenge involves building project consensus not only among job-conscious minorities but also among affluent, quality-of-life-oriented Anglos. If one compares the successful completion of the Alameda Corridor rail project with the region's two major airport-expansion failures, this NIMBY challenge appears far greater because affluent residents don't want projects built/expanded nearby and are largely indifferent to side payments (whether economic or even environmental).

Infrastructure's Regional Impacts

L.A.'s global performance can be approached in yet another way: by gauging the effects of the region's massive trade-infrastructure investments. On the economic side, the global gateways serve as major engines of regional development. By 1994 the two ports claimed to support five hundred thousand regional jobs and 7 percent of local economic activity. That same year LAX's direct benefits were estimated at $43 billion in regional economic activity (10 percent of the region's then-total output) and four hundred thousand jobs. These benefits were in the areas of air transportation, passenger spending (consumption), and cargo-related production of goods and services. Critics, however, charged that these estimates were inflated because they did not include substitution effects—shipping through other ports and airports should those L.A. facilities not have been built. However, such effects are mitigated by the capacity constraints of and L.A.'s distance from other West Coast ports and airports. San Diego's diminutive port and airport system could not readily pick up the L.A. slack without major expansion. The Bay Area's facilities—the Port of Oakland and San Francisco International Airport—have greater capacity but are already overburdened and are located nearly five hundred miles away.[46]

Regarding the Alameda Corridor, a conservative 1994 study (which included substitution effects) suggested that, at a minimum, 185,000 new jobs would be generated nationwide as a direct or indirect result of tandem port and rail development by the year 2020. However, the full impact could be twenty times greater—3.7 million jobs. There has been no separate analysis of port/corridor projected impacts for the five-county region. This is a crucial omission. Much of the local policy debate concerns the extent and geographical distribution of corridor economic benefits within Greater Los Angeles. The corridor cities, for example, were fearful that the economic benefits would bypass them while they absorbed the bulk of the project's construction costs. Extrapolating from the project's national analysis, combined port/rail development could yield as few as thirty-five thousand regional jobs and as many as seven hundred thousand. A reasonable estimate probably lies somewhere on the lower end—perhaps one hundred thousand new regional jobs.[47]

Unconstrained expansion of L.A.'s major international port, rail, and airport projects would likely have generated roughly one-quarter of the five-county area's employment increase, between 1994 and 2020, in its seven-sector core economic base: professional services, transportation and wholesale trade, diversified manufacturing, high-tech manufacturing, tourism and entertainment, defense-related employment, and resource-related industries. The Southern California Association of Governments (SCAG) estimates that regional employment in the core base would have increased from 6.6 million jobs in 1994 to 10.6 million in 2020. Of the four million new jobs added, roughly one million would likely have been trade related.[48]

However, the failure to build a new international airport at El Toro that could handle thirty million annual passengers (MAP) and the sizeable down-sizing of LAX expansion from ninety-eight MAP to seventy-eight MAP place a major crimp in these regional forecasts. With unconstrained expansion, these two airports likely would generate over $50 billion in new regional out-put and over five hundred thousand new jobs by 2020. Even with substitu-tion effects (such as greater utilization of other regional airports like On-tario), the El Toro no-build scenario and constrained LAX expansion at the very least threaten to cost the region well over $15 billion in new economic activity and up to 150,000 jobs. Much of the loss is tied to international-trade and trade-related employment.[49]

Balanced against their regional economic benefits are the very real nega-tive effects of L.A.'s global gateways: significant air and water pollution, traf-fic congestion, and noise. The ports of San Pedro Bay are the region's worst polluter. Vessels entering and leaving the two ports add more to smog than any other local site, but they have been little regulated by regional agencies because of lack of jurisdiction over foreign-flagged ships and local fears of losing trade. Heavy diesel train and truck traffic at the port further contrib-utes to air pollution. Neighborhoods in the harbor area bear the brunt of die-sel exhaust. A South Coast Air Quality Management District study shows that diesel exhaust around the ports subjects local residents to a significantly greater cancer risk than is experienced by people living elsewhere in the South-land. Yet there are hopeful signs. In 2001 local residents and environmental groups brought a lawsuit against the Port of Los Angeles that challenged the approval of a 174-acre terminal for China Shipping Group Co. In 2003, a $60 million settlement agreement required the port to take significant steps to reduce diesel emissions. As a result, L.A. may become the nation's first port to provide cargo ships with electricity so that their diesel engines can be turned off while they are in port.[50]

Similarly, LAX is the region's third largest smog source, much coming from jet engines. Jet noise is another major LAX problem. But possible new, more stringent federal environmental standards for ships, locomotives, air-planes, and trucks may mitigate these problems. In addition the ports and LAX are plagued with heavy traffic congestion. The fact that all these envi-ronmental costs are concentrated while the economic benefits are dispersed produces a political dynamic that encourages opposition voices to better or-ganize and be more vocal.[51]

Finally, terrorist attacks threatened grave harm to the region's trade economy. In the aftermath of September 11th, SCAG estimated that aviation-related losses (in air transportation, exports, tourism, and aircraft manufacturing) cost the region 145,000 to 171,000 jobs and over $6 billion in lost income. Attacks on the region's trade "crown jewels" could be far more costly. The San Pedro Bay ports and LAX were at the top of the state's list of potential terrorist targets in California. In 2003, the war in Iraq resulted in additional security measures, costs, and concerns.[52]

State and National Benefits

Any cost/benefit calculus of L.A.'s global gateways also needs to include the trade activity and job growth they facilitate outside the metropolitan area. These nonregional economic benefits are substantial. For example, the Los Angeles/Long Beach port, rail, and airport system serves as the Pacific Rim trade/transportation hub for San Diego and Imperial counties and for northern Baja California. L.A.'s precocious overbuilding of regional infrastructure encouraged the rest of Southern California, including San Diego, to act as free riders and not expand their own facilities. As a result, San Diego's inadequate airport, port, and rail systems force that region (at $113 billion, the world's thirty-seventh largest economy, larger than Israel's) into heavy reliance on L.A.'s superior facilities.

Because of severe physical constraints (525-acre size, a single, 9,400-foot runway) Lindbergh Field is unable to meet up to one-third of San Diego's air-passenger demand and two-thirds of its air-cargo demand. Hence, LAX meets much of San Diego's international-passenger needs and nearly all of its global air-cargo demand. Further, over 90 percent of the vessel cargo shipped to and from the cross-border region goes through the ports of San Pedro Bay rather than through the small, niche Port of San Diego, which suffers from severe capacity and expansion constraints. Until NAFTA's new rules of origin took effect in 2001, Baja California's maquiladora industry had its component parts shipped from East Asia primarily through the L.A./Long Beach ports; the parts were then transported by truck to border plants.[53]

One can argue that to date the cross-border region's reliance on the Los Angeles port, rail, and airport system has been efficient. These world-class facilities offer a breadth of service unavailable locally. Accessible to the cross-border region, L.A.'s facilities have reduced the need for sizeable local capital investments in port, rail, and airport facilities. Also avoided are the associated environmental costs. Yet this strategy is not without trade-offs. By piggy-backing on L.A. facilities and uncertain expansion plans, San Diego and Tijuana forfeit a measure of control over their economies. Lindbergh Field's international-passenger and air-cargo deficiencies cost the region's economy an estimated \$4–5 billion annually in high value-added activity and hinder San Diego's aspirations to become a leading export-based high-tech center. That opportunity cost will only grow in the future.[54]

San Diego offers an intriguing test of the trade/infrastructure connection. Like L.A., it has sought to create an export-oriented high-tech economy since the early-1990s collapse of its defense-based economy. Unlike L.A., it is an infrastructure underachiever. Compared with their L.A. counterparts, San Diego businesses are forced to pay higher transportation costs (including travel time and reliability concerns) to ship through L.A. global gateways to overseas markets. Despite apparently impressive merchandise export growth in the 1990s, San Diego's economy remains more insulated from the global marketplace than other West Coast regions with superior trade infrastructure. Global exports (both goods and services) appear to account for only 8–10 percent of San Diego economic activity, compared with 15–20 percent for the Los Angeles area, and over one-quarter for the export-oriented, high-tech Bay Area and Seattle economies.[55]

Finally, the ports of San Pedro Bay confer substantial nationwide trade and related economic benefits. One-third of the country's international waterborne commerce courses through the twin ports. Further, half of the inbound container twenty-foot equivalent units are transported by rail to other markets. Thus, 60 percent of the imported goods shipped into the Chicago area pass through the L.A.-area ports. Table 8.1 shows for 2000 the national trade benefits of the two ports by region of the country. The twin ports shipped nearly \$200 billion in two-way merchandise trade between the U.S. and overseas trade partners. While half of this huge trade flow served the southwestern states, almost one-third served the Atlantic Seaboard and Great Lakes markets.

A New Challenge: Security Against Terrorism

Notwithstanding international trade's major contribution to Southern California's economy and the national benefits conferred by L.A.'s global gateways, the region (as indeed the nation as a whole) soon faced a daunting new challenge: protecting its trade, infrastructure, and economy from terrorist attack. The long-term implications of the new mantra—"The world changed on September 11, 2001"—were not immediately clear. It was clear, however, that the trend toward globalization, which had propelled Los Angeles into preeminence as a leading Pacific Rim metropolis, had been undermined. Unlike the sporadic, occasionally violent antiglobalization protests—most notably during the World Trade Organization meetings in Seattle in 1998—systemic terrorism threatened to slow or even halt international trade. The same properties that made global supply chains so valuable—the swift, seamless, intermodal connection of goods and people across continents and oceans—

Table 8.1   National Trade Benefits: Year 2000 Two-Way Merchandise Trade
Between U.S. Regions and Overseas Trade Partners Shipped via
the San Pedro Bay Ports

Region	Billions of Dollars
Northwest (Washington, Oregon, Montana, Idaho, Wyoming)	2.2
Southwest (California, Nevada, Arizona, Utah, Colorado, New Mexico)	98.0
Great Plains (North Dakota, South Dakota, Nebraska, Kansas, Minnesota, Iowa, Missouri)	8.6
South Central (Texas, Oklahoma)	12.1
Southeast (Arkansas, Alabama, Georgia, Florida, Louisiana, North Carolina, South Carolina, Tennessee, Mississippi)	16.0
Great Lakes (Illinois, Wisconsin, Michigan, Indiana, Kentucky, Ohio, West Virginia)	25.0
Atlantic Seaboard (Connecticut, Delaware, Maine, Maryland, Massachusetts, New Hampshire, New Jersey, New York, Pennsylvania, Rhode Island, Vermont, Virginia)	34.4
Total	196.3

SOURCE: Data from OnTrac Joint Powers Authority, "OnTrac Trade Impact Study," Placentia, Calif.: OnTrac JPA, Dec. 2002, p. vii.

also made them vulnerable. Airports and ports—linchpins in the supply chain—were tempting targets because of the potential to inflict enormous economic damage.

As transportation security expert Stephen Flynn observed, "The hallmarks of the post-Cold War world—open societies, liberalized economies, and new technologies—also provide potential adversaries and sophisticated criminals with incentives and opportunities to target or exploit America's transportation networks." The looming question was whether a borderless world with free flows of goods and services could survive transnational terrorist movements that exploit that same openness. Almost overnight, the national security state of the Cold War era was revived to protect the nation's airports, ports, and borders. National Guard troops patrolled airports and the Coast Guard boarded all vessels entering the nation's ports. Customs and Immigration and Naturalization Service (INS) border inspections increased dramatically under heightened alert.[56]

Aviation

The airlines were hardest hit. With the attacks, commercial aviation came to a temporary halt. Fears of terrorism and stringent new airport security measures dramatically reduced air travel; the results were airline layoffs of eighty thousand workers, flight cutbacks of 20 percent, 16.5 million fewer revenue passenger miles (disproportionately in overseas travel), and at least

$5 billion in losses (soon covered by federal emergency relief) during the months after September 11th. By November 2001, security at the nation's 429 commercial airports had been federalized. To screen 670 million passengers and one billion checked bags, the new Transportation Security Administration (TSA) would be allocated $4 billion. This represented more than twenty-five times what the Federal Aviation Administration (FAA) had spent on security in 2001. But the TSA's takeoff was bumpy as critics carped about delays in hiring baggage screeners and securing sufficient explosives-detection machines to meet a December 31, 2002, implementation deadline.[57]

Airports also were severely affected. The estimated cost of September 11th to the nation's 429 commercial airports was placed at $4 billion because of increased security, less passenger traffic (which reduced federal funding), and lost concession revenues. To meet new federal mandates, airports would need to shoulder significant new security costs. At LAX, the cost was estimated at $120 million. Like other major airports, LAX experienced a sharp drop in passenger traffic and revenues. Between January and June of 2002, LAX traffic fell nearly 20 percent relative to the same period one year earlier. The precipitous passenger decline threatened the airport's finances. LAX officials feared a $100 million-plus revenue loss from parking lots, concessions, and landing fees for the fiscal year. As a result, a nervous Wall Street placed major international and hub airports like LAX on credit watch for a possible downgrade of their ratings, which could increase borrowing costs. Like the airlines, airports also saw their "war-and-allied-perils" insurance coverage canceled. Instead, insurers offered airports and airlines drastically reduced liability coverage at high premiums.[58]

LAX was a prime terrorist target. Already, in December 1999, an Algerian trained in Osama bin Laden's Afghan camps had fortuitously been caught crossing from Canada to Washington State in a car loaded with bomb-making materials. He and his confederates intended to blow up LAX during the millennium celebrations. Yet it took September 11th to end the working assumption among regional airport planners that LAX was "a no threat theater of operations." In the wake of the attacks, LAX instituted the most stringent controls on vehicular traffic of any major airport in the country. Strictly applying the FAA's restrictions on parking within three hundred feet of airline terminals, the airport initially closed the access road and all nearby parking structures. After weeks of protests from laid-off aviation workers and concessionaires, the airport board finally agreed (with FAA approval) to reopen the garages and roadway in the central terminal area. LAX security concerns heightened once again in mid-2002 when an Egyptian-born immigrant opened fire at the El Al Israel Airlines ticket counter, killing two and wounding several others before being killed himself.[59]

Airlines and airports also faced daunting challenges protecting air-cargo shipments. While the federal government focused primarily on screening passengers and luggage, the risk increased of a terrorist bomb in air cargo. Studies warned that "cargo is likely to become—and may already be—the primary threat vector in the short term." The FAA's post-September 11th forty-eight-hour ban on air-freight traffic had national and international ripple effects. After the ban was lifted, shippers' compliance with costly new documentation and tracking rules delayed handling. Canceled routes and heightened security measures (such as the new "known-shipper" rule restricting walk-in business to regular customers) further reduced shipping options and increased costs and delays. Air-freight costs increased on average between 5 and 12 percent because of "war-risk" surcharges that cost the airlines over $1.5 billion. The cumulative negative effects of September 11th threatened to reduce worldwide annual air-cargo growth over the next decade from 5 percent to 3 percent. At LAX, air-cargo tonnage fell 8 percent from January to June of 2002 relative to one year earlier.[60]

After September 11th, Southern California's estimated four hundred air-freight-forwarder companies, forced to pay higher shipping charges, also saw their survival threatened by the increase in the time needed to get a package on an international jet—from between two and four hours to twenty-four hours. Orange County's Western Digital Corporation (WDC), a maker of computer disk drives, demonstrated the adverse effects of tightened security procedures on local firms dependent on swift global air shipments. Prior to September 11th, WDC was the beneficiary of the Customs Service's "paperless-release" program at LAX, which permitted low-risk trans-Pacific shipments to clear customs immediately. Afterward, it took up to two days for clearance of WDC's imported Malaysian components, with the resulting risk of a plant shutdown. A troubling irony was that increased delays resulting from new safety rules meant that shipments were parked for longer periods in relatively insecure off-airport warehouses in cities like Inglewood and Carson.[61]

Maritime, Shipping, and Freight Industries

The maritime, shipping, and freight industries were also significantly affected by September 11th, though less so than air freight. Seaborne traffic through the nation's 361 seaports accounts for 90 percent of U.S. imports and exports (in tons). Yet containerization of cargoes—a prerequisite of the supply-chain management revolution—has proven to be an economic triumph but security nightmare. Stretched thin, the Customs Service was able before September 11th to inspect only 2 percent of the seven million containers arriving annually. Five agents needed three hours to inspect a single container. Even with the aid of new high-tech sensors, the 10,600 front-line customs agents could not provide systematic inspections. In fact, it was standard practice to allow containerized cargo entering U.S. ports and then linked intermodally to truck or rail carriers to be hauled around the country for up to thirty days without any declaration of contents, specification of contents, or identification of final destination.[62]

After September 11th, the Coast Guard began inspecting all arriving vessels, checking manifests and crew lists. The new antiterrorism focus came at the expense of the agency's other duties, such as drug interdiction. All ships entering U.S. ports also were required to provide twenty-four-hour notification of their pending arrival, including identification of all those aboard. At the Los Angeles and Long Beach ports, the Coast Guard instituted round-the-clock patrols to board and inspect cruise liners, container ships, and tankers. All inbound vessels had to wait at anchorage pending inspection. Tightened security resulted in a loss of eight hours (or one stevedoring shift) in getting vessels to berth. Led by local Congresswoman Jane Harman, whose district included the L.A. port, federal and local officials demanded a vulnerability assessment and even more security because initial procedures were only "a work in progress." Yet, despite the economic doldrums of 2001, trade surged in 2002 at the ports of San Pedro Bay, with increased consumer spending, a rebound in demand from U.S. trading partners, and the looming threat of a West Coast dockworkers' strike.[63]

At the federal level, the Hollings-Graham Port and Maritime Security Act, a sweeping regulatory measure, slowly moved out of the legislative limbo and toward final passage in late 2002. Senator Ernest "Fritz" Hollings, the chief sponsor, called the ports "perhaps the most vulnerable link in our transportation system." Reflecting concern that containers could be used to transport weapons or terrorists, the legislation required federal agencies to develop a cargo-container identification and screening system and authorized U.S. security sweeps of foreign ports. Ports would be obliged to create comprehensive security plans and to conduct background investigations on port employees. The bill authorized $1.1 billion for new customs agents, security training, and the purchase of high-tech screening and detection machines. Further, the bill created a $3.3 billion loan-guarantee program for local port agencies to finance needed security improvements. Passage was delayed by opposition from shipping and port interests (fearing its costs and effects on commerce) and by the powerful International Longshore and Warehouse Union (which was opposed to background checks).[64]

The terrorist attacks also shook up the shipping industry (already in the doldrums because of the sagging global economy) as well as businesses dependent on global supply chains. Shipping costs and times rose as insurers imposed "war-risk" premiums on coverage, while security checks slowed cargo movements. Within the shipping industry talk turned to mergers and even bankruptcies. Even though the complex global supply chain appeared to return to near normality within weeks of the terrorist attacks, many companies began rethinking just-in-time delivery systems and lean inventories. Initial estimates of U.S. business costs included $18 billion to carry additional inventory and $2 billion for heightened security by shippers, including truckers. Together, they constituted a 2 percent add-on to the nation's annual freight-hauling bill.[65]

The nation's railroad and trucking industries, linked intermodally to the ports and airports, were affected in turn. After September 11th, U.S. railroads stepped up security around bridges, tunnels, freight offices, and telecommunications facilities. Further, they contemplated new electronic control systems (at a projected cost of $1.2 billion) to take automatic control of a runaway or hijacked train. Such measures may be the only way to save rail projects such as the Alameda Corridor from being derailed by a collision between the imperatives of efficiency and security. Trucking companies installed new screening, training, and identification systems for truckers. Also being explored were satellite tracking systems, such as the online truck-matching service and the Global Positioning Systems, which provide near real-time ability to track rigs and trailers. Intermodal shippers, whether using trains or trucks, were under increasing pressure to pay for new technology to embed "transparent" tracking features in their systems that would make it possible to monitor the progress of shipments all the way from points of origin, where goods were loaded, to points of entry, where deliveries were made.[66]

Border Crossings

After September 11th, the nation's Canadian and Mexican borders became dramatic, albeit temporary, choke points. The Big Three U.S. car makers buy parts from Canadian suppliers and take delivery within six hours of an order's placement. An unanticipated border-inspection queue can result in an assembly-line shutdown costing $1 million per hour. On September 11th, the Detroit Windsor Tunnel was shut down, and all incoming traffic to the United States was suspended. Although the shutdown was short-lived, it was replaced by lengthy security inspections. Two weeks after the terrorist attacks, delays at seventeen U.S.-Canadian border crossings were down from an initial twenty hours to between eight and nine hours (compared with the average delay of one hour or less before September 11th), enough to still threaten the smooth operation of just-in-time assembly operations.[67]

After the attacks, an Alert Level 1, calling for "sustained intensive anti-terrorism operations," also was imposed on the U.S.-Mexico border. Customs Service and INS (including Border Patrol) officers stepped up inspections of all traffic crossing the two-thousand-mile-long border. At the San Diego–Tijuana border, vehicular wait times worsened as new bomb checks aggravated an average delay that had already tripled since 1997. Border businesses were particularly hard hit, as northbound traffic declined by 30 percent. A local congressman pleaded with the president and the governor of California to declare a border state-of-economic-emergency and thereby make affected businesses eligible for low-cost loans. Cross-border trade further declined as the U.S. economic downturn caused Mexican maquiladora manufacturing output to drop significantly. Responding to growing complaints, the federal government substantially increased spending for border security and tightened the visa entry system. The new legislation was designed to speed up border flows while enhancing security.[68]

Balancing the efficient movement of commerce with the security needs at the nation's airports, ports, and borders would be a formidable challenge. The choices made would have major repercussions for global trade and the economy. The terrorist attacks resulted in a significant increase in federal responsibility for protecting the nation's vital trade infrastructure. The new Transportation Security Administration, the Coast Guard, the Customs Service, and the INS (including the Border Patrol) were all slated to be housed in the new federal Department of Homeland Security. Yet local officials in places such as Los Angeles still retained major responsibilities for the nation's ports and airports—potent but now vulnerable sites for trade and regional development. In the wake of September 11th, they too struggled to find the appropriate balance between commerce and security. For former L.A. Mayor Richard Riordan, the new antiterrorism duties of local officials sent a signal: "City Hall goes to war." In 2003, with the war in Iraq, additional infrastructure security measures further taxed local resources.[69]

At the Global Crossroads

In Southern California, the 2001 terrorist attacks on New York City and Washington occurred in the midst of a local trade slump and mild economic downturn. At the same time, secession pressures in Los Angeles encouraged a go-slow policy with respect to infrastructure development. As Los Angeles lurched toward the November 2002 citywide votes on breakaway bids by the San Fernando Valley and Hollywood, civic leaders struggled to keep L.A. whole. Looking for a winning formula in the campaign for the hearts and minds of L.A. voters, they championed popular neighborhood and environmental concerns at the expense of infrastructure development. The twin secession bids failed decisively at the polls. At the same time, the September 11th attack contributed to new security-focused infrastructure plans. Here I examine the policies of new L.A. Mayor Hahn, who took office in July 2001, and the growing regional debate about trade, infrastructure, and L.A.'s global future.

Mayor Hahn's Policies

Initially preoccupied with the threat of secession, the new L.A. mayor championed community and environmental priorities at the expense of port and airport expansion. Work continued on the L.A. port's massive Pier 400 project (scheduled for completion in 2004) and on Long Beach's $1.9 billion Pier G mega-terminal, but many other capital projects were put on hold. San Pedro/Wilmington secession hopes were dashed (or at least delayed) by a LAFCO ruling in mid-2001 that they would not be economically feasible as a city. Yet the new mayor (a San Pedro resident, as is his sister Janice Hahn, the new councilwoman representing the area) and his harbor-panel appointees genuflected to community sentiment. Three of the five new harbor board members came from still-restive San Pedro. The localistic board made neighborhood recreational and educational projects its top priority.[70] The mayor and his appointees also pledged no net increase in port emissions as diesel pollution became a pressing environmental concern. Further, Hahn shifted power to neighborhood councils by ordering quarterly meetings with departmental general managers. After the September terrorist attacks, the mayor's watchword became security. He convened a security task force (composed of local and federal public officials and business, labor, and community leaders) to devise measures to protect the ports of San Pedro Bay. It proposed controversial background checks of port workers.[71]

In regard to the airports, Mayor Hahn became actively involved in the post–September 11th national security discussion in his role as chair of the U.S. Conference of Mayors task force on airport security. Regionally, a dramatic decline in post–September 11th air-travel demand played into the hands of airport critics. Traffic at LAX fell nearly 20 percent in the first half of 2002 relative to 2001. With reduced expansion pressures, the mayor (a foe of LAX expansion along with the other leading mayoral candidates in the 2001 elections) unveiled in mid-2002 a new, $9.6 billion LAX Master Plan; the plan focused on security and modernization while offering only limited growth (to seventy-eight MAP). Hahn's scheme envisaged a remote parking and check-in facility. Terminal and airfield upgrades would be made to accommodate the next generation of super jumbo-jets, such at the Airbus A380. Yet, the financially strapped airlines complained about the huge bill (which they would largely foot) relative to the small airport capacity increase. They also were concerned about added inconvenience to their customers. Skeptics saw the plan as a political stratagem to placate LAX's vocal community and environmental critics, especially high-propensity Westside voters.[72]

Observers wondered whether the plan, with cumbersome security checks and little room for growth, was actually designed to discourage passengers from using LAX. In effect, the mayor appeared to be trying to shift the regional burden (particularly for short-haul flights) elsewhere. Unfortunately, Burbank, Long Beach, and John Wayne airports all had limits on their ability to grow. Hahn strongly supported airport expansion at city-managed Ontario and Palmdale airports, both outside L.A. city limits, and called for the creation of a regionwide airport system.[73]

Yet Hahn's regional vision was dealt a severe setback. With the terrorist attacks eroding airport expansion support everywhere, Orange County voters in March 2002 strongly supported Measure W, which rezoned El Toro for parkland, open space, and institutional uses rather than as an international airport. Only lawsuits kept slim airport hopes alive. LAX felt the squeeze of El Toro's demise. Farther to the south, San Diego watched unfolding developments at LAX and El Toro with growing alarm. The new countywide San Diego Regional Airport Authority was created to operate cramped Lindbergh Field and to find a site for a new international airport. With SCAG estimating that the September 11th attack had merely pushed regional demand projections back by two to three years, airports indeed had become the Achilles' heel of Southern California's global engagement.[74]

The new mayor appeared to make international trade a high priority. Unlike Tom Bradley, who had seen L.A. as the "gateway for the Pacific Rim," Hahn initially saw the region's (and his own) fortunes tied to Mexico. The new L.A. city charter gave the mayor more power than his predecessors had over the region's development in a globalized economy (particularly over appointments to municipal and regional boards). Hahn used his control of the city's airport system to build bridges to the Mexican American community, which had strongly supported his opponent, Antonio Villaraigosa, in the hard-fought 2001 mayoral campaign. In late 2001, Hahn returned from his inaugural trade mission to Mexico with promises of daily international flights from Mexico to Ontario airport. (After secession failed in late 2002, the mayor headed a trade and tourism mission to China, Japan, South Korea, and Taiwan that resulted in an agreement for air-cargo flights from Taiwan to Ontario.)[75]

On his initial cross-border sojourn, Hahn met with Mexican President Vicente Fox; the visit continued a tradition of L.A. mayors being treated as veritable heads of state. Previously, Riordan had met with the Chinese premier on his Asian trade mission, while Bradley frequently met with East Asian chiefs of state. Harking back to the Bradley City Hall, Hahn opened up an international-trade division within the mayor's office. In contrast to Bradley's Asian focus, Hahn's bureau concentrated initially on Mexico. Only later would the Mexican trade desk be joined by Asian and European desks. An intriguing Hahn initiative was the International Small Business Development Strategy, which encouraged immigrants to reach out to country-of-origin home-town associations and small-business networks. The hope was that these immigrant contacts could be developed into viable trade and investment opportunities.[76]

Hahn's policies, though, appeared to continue the dubious practice begun in the Riordan years of placing short-term political expediency ahead of the region's long-term prosperity. Both Hahn and Riordan displayed little interest in port and airport expansion—the veritable "crown jewels" of Bradley's global vision. Significantly, these were the first L.A. mayors with term limits, which shortened policy horizons to eight years. Thus, Riordan relentlessly milked the "cash cows" to pay for his police buildup and budget balancing. Trade development also languished under Riordan. While the businessman-turned-mayor touted Los Angeles as the "jewel of the Pacific Rim, a leader in the global marketplace," he largely scuttled Bradley's international initiatives except for a few high-profile trade missions to Asia and belated lobbying for the Alameda Corridor and LAX Master Plan projects.[77]

In contrast, Bradley's international vision had included a vigorous quest for tandem infrastructure and trade development. Serving as mayor for twenty years, he could make long-term policy commitments to ensure the region's future. Yet Bradley also began the questionable practice of reining in the once-independent proprietary departments—the real engines of Southern California's precious twentieth-century growth. In earlier days, when the proprietary departments enjoyed considerable autonomy, port and airport officials had been at the center of trade efforts: innovative infrastructure development, trade missions, global advertising. Mayors and city councilmembers went on high-profile trade missions but otherwise limited their involvement. In the pre-Bradley era, port and airport commissioners acted more as independent trustees than as instructed delegates.[78]

For Bradley, commissioners were mayoral emissaries. Riordan and Hahn also embraced the emissary model, but without Bradley's strong global vision and commitment to infrastructure. For their commissioners, facility expansion took a back seat to short-term fiscal, community, and environmental priorities. The open question was whether the region could ever expect term-limited public officials to make enormous, expensive, and controversial long-term infrastructure commitments.

New Global Formulas

By the late 1990s a growing chorus was urging new directions in L.A.'s international role. Many questioned the region's historic reliance on physical infrastructure and public-sector leadership. Although heretofore an acknowledged infrastructure leader, Los Angeles appeared to be a laggard with respect to other trade-development efforts, perhaps partially as a result of its infrastructure advantages. Because L.A.'s superior facilities served as a ready trade magnet, they lessened the incentive to devise other programs. Los Angeles County Economic Development Corporation (LAEDC) Chief Economist Jack Kyser voiced a growing concern that "Southern California needs to move beyond viewing international trade in terms of infrastructure. The reality is that trade is based on global connections and creative people, things which the region has in abundant amounts. Thus, an innovative new approach is required."[79]

Several new global formulas for the region have been advanced. One involves greater private-sector trade and infrastructure participation, not only from leading business organizations but also from the region's trade community. A second approach, advanced by Pastor, recognizes the advantages of the area's superior trade infrastructure but calls for better utilization of the region's renowned ethnic diversity and greater equity in expanding trade and infrastructure opportunities. A third direction, championed by New Boosters such as Kotkin, would capitalize on L.A.'s ethnic diversity but also would emphasize investments in cutting-edge telecommunications infrastructure for L.A.'s high-tech future.[80]

There is much to commend in these approaches. With term limits, enhanced mayoral powers over the proprietary departments, and new fiscal and environmental regulatory pressures, the ports and airports can no longer easily perform their traditional developmental roles. Term-limited public officials no longer have the luxury of making difficult long-term project commitments whose benefits cannot be captured within their short terms of office but whose costs are quickly evident. The local business community, which had supplied strong support for early port and airport development, faltered in the postwar era as corporate stalwarts disappeared. Given palpable present-day constraints on public-sector initiatives and leadership, business might be able to reclaim its traditional leadership role. In addition, given political bottlenecks in public-sector infrastructure development, private-sector resources might be marshaled for telecommunications investments in order to provide global connections for the region's high-tech industries.

L.A.'s vaunted diversity also might help trade performance. With the realization growing that ethnic networks can shape trading patterns, the area's immigrants held promise as trade promoters, as in Mayor Hahn's "hometown" initiative. In particular, the area's large Asian Pacific American and Mexican American communities could facilitate trade with their home countries. Already, there is growing immigrant participation in international trade, especially among Koreans and Chinese in the garment and toy industries.[81]

Although promising, these strategies needed careful scrutiny. Organizing the fractured L.A. business and trade communities would not be easy. L.A.'s economy was no longer dominated by large corporations, and once-powerful business organizations such as the L.A. Chamber of Commerce had lost much of their clout. Instead, the region's new economy was dominated by small- to medium-sized businesses. New ethnic, minority, and female entrepreneurs reflected the area's demographic diversity. Yet many of the new players were unable or unwilling to assume regional leadership roles because of the press of operating businesses, an interest in industry-specific concerns rather than in regional matters, and lingering cultural differences with larger organizations. This economic and social diversity aggravated the region's collective-action problem with respect to trade development.[82]

A babel of voices also hindered the mobilization of the area's diverse international-trade community, which, compared with its West Coast rivals, had done a poor job of articulating its interests. Lacking major corporations to set the trade agenda, the region became home to over seventy-five trade-related organizations sharply divided along ethnic and industry lines. Many were parochial, weak, and poorly funded, more preoccupied with survival than with trade promotion. In Seattle, in contrast, two active and influential umbrella organizations for trade actively promoted the region's interests via business missions, trade delegations, trade-related assistance, and a targeted, international marketing campaign. L.A.'s highly diverse trade profile—a large import sector and a smaller, but growing, export sector—further complicated the task of organizing a regional trade constituency.[83]

Recognizing this lacuna, in the late 1990s the region's two major business organizations launched their own trade-development initiatives. The LAEDC, the area's leading business-assistance organization, joined with the World Trade Center Association-Los Angeles, Long Beach (WCTA LA-LB) in a clearinghouse for trade information, to pool and leverage resources to facilitate regional trade. WCTA LA-LB has launched an ambitious trade-match program, designed to help foreign-based companies find local business partners. The Greater Los Angeles Chamber of Commerce created LATRADE, an export-promotion and trade-assistance program. The question remains whether these private-sector initiatives will bear significant fruit, particularly in facilitating regional exports, tapping into the fast-growing NAFTA market, and marketing the L.A. brand overseas.[84]

There are other private-sector initiatives. The LAEDC has created the Critical Infrastructure Council (composed of regional business leaders) to provide private-sector input into infrastructure development, to educate the business community about the importance of infrastructure, and to provide policy analyses of trade and transportation issues. The council has participated in debates concerning the LAX Master Plan and regional high-speed rail proposals. In the wake of September 11th, the LAEDC, Mayor Hahn, and the L.A. County supervisors convened the Economic Action Summit to prioritize the region's needs and avoid an economic downturn. Business leaders claim that they are laying the foundations for a strong local economy: better workforce education and training, smoothly functioning transportation and communications systems, and a business-friendly tax and regulatory environment. Given the growing crisis of public-sector leadership, there are pressures for further private-sector efforts.[85]

A major role can also be played by organized labor, a powerful force in municipal and regional politics and policymaking. Although still skittish of free trade, Southland labor has strongly supported big-ticket infrastructure projects, for both construction jobs and long-term regional benefit. Labor is a crucial stakeholder and potential broker for a broader regional trade formula that would embrace diversity and equity. Notwithstanding its trade performance, L.A. appears to be a serious racial- and income-equity laggard. L.A. labor, with the skills it has already exhibited in organizing low-wage service workers and securing a living-wage ordinance, can play a pivotal equity brokering role. Looming labor challenges include organizing immigrant port truckers (currently independent contractors) as well as workers in trade-sensitive local sectors such as the garment and toy industries. Here, labor confronts new ethnic/class cleavages involving Asian American business owners and Mexican immigrant workers.[86]

In 2002, labor's trade focus was on the docks, where the West Coast dockworkers' union was engaged in tough contract negotiations with the shippers over new labor-saving technologies and job security. After talks failed, a ten-day management-ordered lockout of dockworkers affected global supply chains and resulted in billions of dollars in business losses. Over two hundred ships were idled off the Southern California coast, and shippers and retailers were forced to begin rethinking shipping and transportation routes. With federal intervention, a new contract was finally signed; it guaranteed existing union jobs and benefits while allowing for the introduction of new information technologies. The agreement ensures a period of labor peace at the West Coast ports.

The local equity discussion involves more than class, race, and ethnicity. It also concerns geography. An increasingly acrimonious debate in Southern California revolves around the subregional benefits and burdens of trade and infrastructure. Ground zero for the burden-sharing controversy has shifted from the Alameda Corridor to the Inland Empire and Orange County. The fast-growing Inland Empire, a major warehouse and distribution center, sees itself as unduly burdened by port truck and rail congestion. It seeks a modicum of port financing for its grade-separation rail projects. Denying culpability, the ports claim that little port truck traffic goes directly to the Inland Empire. Given the national benefits of the San Pedro Bay ports, growing sentiment in the region favors having the federal government pay for Inland Empire transportation improvements.

The fairness issue in Orange County involves airports. With El Toro's defeat, most Orange County air travelers and cargo will continue to access airports elsewhere (particularly LAX and Ontario), further exacerbating local traffic congestion and air pollution. To encourage a fairer sharing of the region's aviation burden, SCAG supported state legislation making equity (for example, county burden sharing and environmental justice) a "guiding policy" of regional aviation planning. Although punitive provisions such as the withholding of state transportation funding were removed from the bill, Orange County was put on notice that it needed to do more with cramped John Wayne airport.[87]

The New Boosters' prescriptions also deserve careful examination. Like Pastor, Kotkin sees ethnic diversity as a critical linchpin in the area's large trade sector. Yet, unlike Pastor, Kotkin is much more interested in high-flying ethnic entrepreneurs than in low-wage immigrant workers. Kotkin now pins the region's global hopes on the Chinese, who might attract new capital and trade from one of the world's fastest-growing economies and L.A.'s soon-to-be leading trading partner. Yet ethnic entrepreneurs are only beginning to be involved in the region's trade-development efforts. Regarding Kotkin's new-economy infrastructure agenda, there now is a worldwide as well as a regional glut in telecommunications capacity. Yet export-oriented, high-tech economies also require international-airport capacity and access, which are in increasingly short supply in Southern California.[88]

W(h)ither Infrastructure?

In this swirling policy debate, L.A.'s global gateways remained a firm bedrock of regional trade-development efforts. Should trade flows be uninterrupted, port-of-entry international trade in Southern California was projected to nearly triple between 2000 and 2020, from $230 billion to $661 billion. With blockages, trade growth could diminish substantially. As of early 2003, with federal military priorities, a growing national budget deficit, and a massive state budget crisis, the region could expect limited help from Washington and Sacramento for its trade-infrastructure projects. The political challenge was to assemble powerful regional, state, and national goods-movement coalitions to press for scarce federal transportation dollars for needed projects. California's Global Gateways Development Program was just such a statewide effort; it involved major stakeholders (seaports, airports, shippers, receivers, carriers, and local public agencies). Regionally, the L.A. County Metropolitan Transportation Authority and the L.A. Chamber of Commerce launched a similar coalition-building effort.[89]

At the ports, the issue was no longer system capacity but achieving greater operating efficiency. Yet port modernization involving labor-saving technologies was a controversial subject for the unions—and the core of several labor disputes. With ongoing port expansion and related rail projects on schedule, the major transportation bottleneck was the Long Beach Freeway (I-710) and other highways serving the ports. Already, I-710 carried 15 percent of the total U.S. seaborne container volume. Proposed improvements such as truck-only lanes could cost more than $4 billion and take a dozen years to complete. But scarce financing and community and environmental opposition threatened to delay Long Beach Freeway improvements for years.[90]

Gateway airports were a graver regional concern than the ports. With the downsizing of LAX growth and the demise of El Toro, the region's air future appeared headed to the Inland Empire. If Ontario Airport (subject to air-quality operations ceilings and needing a second runway) and the inland area's former military bases could expand, export-oriented and high-tech businesses had incentive to move inland. In the future, Inland Empire communities, rather than coastal areas (tied to LAX), could be the region's trade winners. Besides airport proximity, inland lures included relatively inexpensive commercial real estate and affordable housing. Should San Diego not solve its airport problems, it too could lose some of its high-tech future to Riverside and San Bernardino counties. There were hopeful signs of cooperative airport planning. Although the underfunded Southern California Regional Airport Authority appeared headed toward extinction, the City of Los Angeles pledged to coordinate its Ontario master planning with that of other Inland Empire airports. However, should NIMBY and environmental opposition inhibit airport development there, Southern California's global future could be profoundly affected.[91]

International trade has become the driving force of the Southern California economy, and timely infrastructure investments remain essential to regional development and to global competitiveness. Of all the region's ambitious trade mega-projects, airport development is the furthest behind schedule, faces the greatest challenges, and yet offers the greatest regional benefits in facilitating high value-added goods and service exports. Southern California's aspirations to become a leading export-based world trade center (rather than merely the nation's top Pacific Rim's import gateway) rest, in large measure, upon its uncertain airport future.

Notes

Preface

1. Clarence H. Matson, *Building a World Gateway: The Story of the Los Angeles Harbor [BAWG]* (Los Angeles: Pacific Era, 1945), p. 82.
2. "Beery Wisecracks," *San Diego Sun*, August 16, 1928, p. 3.
3. "Futureville," *The Economist*, February 3, 1996, p. 20.

Chapter One

1. Tom Bradley interview, 1995.
2. Richard Riordan, "The New Los Angeles—Strategies for Economic Growth" (transcript of speech, Office of the Mayor, Los Angeles), March 6, 1996, p. 4.
3. According to Xandra Kayden, "The big story about the Los Angeles region and the impact of globalization is its people." Xandra Kayden with Jennifer Resnik, "The Impact of Globalization on Los Angeles" (draft, Pacific Council on International Policy [PCIP], Los Angeles), 2001, p. 14. Also see Michael Clough, *Can Hollywood Remain the Capital of the Global Entertainment Industry?* (Los Angeles: PCIP, September 2000); Gregory F. Treverton, *Making the Most of Southern California's Global Engagement* (Los Angeles: PCIP, June 2000); Abraham Lowenthal et al., "International Linkages," in Michael J. Dear, ed., *Atlas of Southern California*, vol. 1 (Los Angeles: Southern California Studies Center [SC2], University of Southern California, 1996), pp. 27–33; and Steven P. Erie, "Southern California's Trade Future: Facing the Challenges of Expanding the Region's Global Gateways" (draft, PCIP, Los Angeles), March 2003.
4. See Steven P. Erie, "Los Angeles as a Developmental City-State," in Mi-

chael J. Dear, ed., *From Chicago to L.A.: Making Sense of Urban Theory* (Thousand Oaks, Calif.: Sage, 2002), pp. 133–59. On the weaknesses of Southern California's regional institutions, see William Fulton, *The Reluctant Metropolis: The Politics of Urban Growth in Los Angeles* (Point Arena, Calif.: Solana Press Books, 1997); Scott A. Bollens, "Fragments of Regionalism: The Limits of Southern California Governance," *Journal of Urban Affairs* 19:1 (1997), pp. 105–22.

5. Jameson W. Doig, *Empire on the Hudson: Entrepreneurial Vision and Political Power at the Port of New York Authority* (New York: Columbia University Press, 2001). Regarding organizational roles, see Charles Perrow, *Complex Organizations: A Critical Essay*, 3d ed. (New York: McGraw-Hill, 1986).

6. See, for example, Margaret E. Crahan and Alberto Vourvoulas-Bush, eds., *The City and the World: New York's Global Future* (New York: Council on Foreign Relations, 1997); San Diego Dialogue, *The Global Engagement of San Diego/Baja California: Final Report* (San Diego: San Diego Dialogue, November 2000); Richard Feinberg with Gretchen Schuck, *San Diego, Baja California and Globalization: Coming from Behind* (Los Angeles: PCIP, October 2001); Treverton, *Making the Most of Southern California's Global Engagement*; Earl H. Fry et al., *Mapping Globalization Along the Wasatch Front* (Los Angeles: PCIP, January 2002); S. L. Backman, *Globalization in the San Francisco Bay Area: Trying to Stay at the Head of the Class* (Los Angeles: PCIP, January 2003); Frederic A. Morris, *Boeing and Beyond: Seattle in the Global Economy* (Los Angeles: PCIP, January 2003); H. V. Savitch and Paul Kantor, *Cities in the International Marketplace: The Political Economy of Urban Development in North America and Western Europe* (Princeton, N.J.: Princeton University Press, 2002).

7. Paul R. Krugman, *Geography and Trade* (Cambridge, Mass.: MIT Press, 1990). Also see Helzi Noponen, Julie Graham, and Ann R. Markusen, eds., *Trading Industries, Trading Regions* (New York: Guilford Press, 1993).

8. See Richard L. Florida, *The Rise of the Creative Class* (New York: Basic Books, 2002); Robert D. Putnam, *Making Democracy Work* (Princeton, N.J.: Princeton University Press, 1993); John F. Helliwell and Robert D. Putnam, *Education and Social Capital* (Cambridge, Mass.: National Bureau of Economic Research, 1999); Emily Eakin, "The Cities and Their New Elite," *New York Times*, June 1, 2002, pp. A15, A17. On the economic importance of local public infrastructure investments, see David C. Perry, ed., *Building the Public City: The Politics, Governance, and Finance of Public Infrastructure* (Thousand Oaks, Calif.: Sage, 1995); and Alan Altshuler and David Luberoff, *Mega-Projects: The Changing Politics of Urban Public Investment* (Washington, D.C.: Brookings Institution Press, 2003).

9. Regarding local trade-development programs, see the National League of Cities, *American Cities in the Global Economy: A Survey of Municipalities on Activities and Attitudes* (Washington, D.C.: National League of Cities, April 1997), Table 20, p. 43, on municipal involvement in eighteen trade-related activities; and Earl H. Fry, *The Expanding Role of State and Local Governments in U.S. Foreign Affairs* (New York: Council on Foreign Relations Press, 1998), pp. 84–88.

10. Los Angeles County Economic Development Corporation [LAEDC], *International Trade Trends & Impacts: The Los Angeles Region 2001 Results and 2002 Outlook* (Los Angeles: LAEDC, June 2002), p. 20; U.S. Bureau of the Census, *Highlights of U.S. Import and Export Trade 1972–1987*, FT990 Series (Washington, D.C., 1988); U.S. Bureau of the Census, *U.S. Merchandise Trade: Selected Highlights 2000*, FT920 Series (Washington, D.C., 2001); Evelyn Iritani, "L.A. Surpasses New York City as Top Trade Hub in 1994," *Los Angeles Times*, March 17, 1995, pp. D1, D3.

11. For transshipment hubs such as Los Angeles, district-of-unlading measures are better than port-of-entry data in accounting for the impact of trade on a region's transportation system and economy. Thus, for 2001, the LACD handled $213 billion in port-of-entry merchandise trade versus $270 billion in district-of-unlading trade—a 27 percent difference. Here I use the FT920 merchandise trade data. Export values are f.a.s. (free alongside ship, or without shipping charges), while import values are by district of unlading. For a discussion of why district-of-unlading data are more useful than port-of-entry data for L.A. regional transportation planning, see Southern California Association of Governments [SCAG], *SCAG Regional Economic Profile* (Los Angeles: SCAG, December 1990), pp. 56–58. The LACD includes the ports of Los Angeles and Long Beach (also called the San Pedro Bay ports), LAX, Ventura County's Port Hueneme, and Las Vegas's McCarran Field. Nearly all LACD trade (over 90 percent) goes through the ports of San Pedro Bay and LAX.

12. SCAG, Economic Analysis Division, "RTP Input for JIT Manufacturing and the Region as a Trade Center" (draft memo), November 13, 1996; Abraham F. Lowenthal et al., *Strengthening Southern California's International Connections: Trade and Investment Aspects* (Los Angeles: SC2, University of Southern California, 1996), p. 1.

13. LAEDC, *International Trade Trends & Impacts* (2002), pp. 9–17, 29–35.

14. Lisa M. Grobar, "Export-Linked Employment in Southern California," *Contemporary Economic Policy* 17:1 (January 1999), p. 98; and LAEDC, *International Trade Trends & Impacts* (2002), pp. 10, 38. Exporter Location data should be used with caution because the exporter of record often is the seller, not the goods producer. Origin of Movement data more closely indicate the actual manufacturing site; however, they are not available at the local level.

15. For the relationship between local transportation systems and global competitiveness, see David J. Keeling, "Transport and the World City Paradigm," in Paul L. Knox and Peter J. Taylor, eds., *World Cities in a World-System* (New York: Cambridge University Press, 1995), pp. 115–31; Nigel Harris, "The Emerging Global City: Transport," *Cities* 11:5 (October 1994), pp. 332–36; John D. Kasarda, "Transportation Infrastructure for Competitive Success," *Transportation Quarterly* 50:1 (Winter 1995), pp. 35–50.

16. Roger Keil, "Globalization Makes States: Perspectives of Local Governance in the Age of the World City," *Review of International Political Economy* 5:4 (1998), pp. 616–46; Dennis A. Rondinelli, James H. Johnson Jr., and John D.

Kasarda, "The Changing Forces of Urban Economic Development: Globalization and City Competitiveness in the 21st Century," *Cityscape* 3:3 (1998), pp. 72, 85, 87. For the private-sector and public-sector roles in goods movement, see "Building Freight Capacity Through Better Operations: Defining the National Agenda" (briefing paper prepared for the Federal Highway Administration Freight Operations Conference, Long Beach, Calif., July 26–27, 2001).

17. Morris, *Boeing and Beyond*, p. 12.

18. Tony Robison with Stephen Buckmelter, "Cowtown Goes Global: Denver in the World System" (paper presented at the 1996 Annual Meeting of the Western Political Science Association, San Francisco, March 14–16, 1996), pp. 24–28; Bachman, *Globalization in the San Francisco Bay Area*; Feinberg, *San Diego, Baja California and Globalization*. Also see Bay Area Economic Forum, *Air Transport and the Bay Area Economy: Phase Two* (San Francisco: Bay Area Economic Forum, 2000), p. 14. On the positive two-way correlation between infrastructure investment and regional economic growth, see David Arsen, "Is There Really an Infrastructure/Economic Development Link?" in Richard D. Bingham and Robert Meier, eds., *Dilemmas of Urban Economic Development* (Thousand Oaks, Calif.: Sage, 1997), pp. 82–98.

19. California Department of Transportation, *California Trade and Goods Movement Study* (Sacramento, Calif.: Caltrans, 1996).

20. Five-year capital budgets provided by Los Angeles, Long Beach, San Francisco, Oakland, Seattle, Tacoma, and New York/New Jersey port and airport planning, budget, and financial offices.

21. SCAG, *Draft Regional Transportation Plan: Task Forces—Aviation* (Los Angeles: SCAG, February 2001), p. 1.

Chapter Two

1. Nigel Harris, "The Emerging Global City: Transport," *Cities* 11:5 (October 1994), pp. 332, 336.

2. David J. Olson, *Governance of U.S. Public Ports: A Preliminary Survey of Key Issues* (Washington, D.C.: Marine Board Port Governance Roundtable, November 1992), pp. 21–22.

3. Since the terrorist attacks of September 2001, one also may discern a new security regime for airports and ports that is being fashioned in Los Angeles and elsewhere; these measures drive up the costs of both transportation and trade. This new system is examined in Chapter Eight.

4. World Trade Organization, "Merchandise Export, Production, and Gross Domestic Product, 1950–2000," www.wto.org. For the pre-1980 period, see International Monetary Fund, *Direction of Trade* (Washington, D.C.: International Monetary Fund, 1994), "Total World Exports."

5. World Trade Organization, "Merchandise Trade by Region," www.wto.org. Also see Paul R. Krugman and Maurice Obsfelt, *International Economics: Theory*

and Policy, 3d ed. (New York: HarperCollins, 1994), pp. 212, 239–47; James Foreman-Peck, *A History of the World Economy: International Economic Relations Since 1850* (New York: Harvester Wheatsheaf, 1995), pp. 235, 242, 268–70; Jagdish Bhagwati, "Threats to the World Trading System," *Journal of International Affairs* 48:2 (Summer 1994), pp. 279–85; Paul R. Krugman, "The Uncomfortable Truth About NAFTA—It's the Foreign Policy, Stupid," *Foreign Affairs* 72:5 (November/December 1993), pp. 13–19; Sylvia Ostry, "The NAFTA: Its International Economic Background," in Steven J. Randall, ed., *North America Without Borders?* (Calgary: University of Calgary Press, 1992), pp. 21–29. Despite robust NAFTA trade growth, by 2001 full-scale economic liberalization still had not taken place. See James Mann, "International Outlook: Those Embarrassing Political Views," *Los Angeles Times*, August 16, 2001, pp. A1, A5.

6. In 1993, Mattel's then-CEO Jill Barad warned that, without most-favored-nation status for China, duties on Chinese-manufactured toys would rise from 12 to 70 percent, an increase that would threaten her firm's survival; see James Mann, *About Face: A History of America's Curious Relationship with China, from Nixon to Clinton* (New York: Vintage Books, 1998), pp. 106–7, 229–33, 262–81; Zhang Jialin, *U.S.-China Trade Issues After the WTO and the PNTR Deal—A Chinese Perspective*, Hoover Essay in Public Policy (Stanford, Calif.: Hoover Institution, August 2000).

7. John D. Kasarda, "Transportation Infrastructure for Competitive Success," *Transportation Quarterly* 50:1 (Winter 1995), pp. 35–50; and John D. Kasarda, "Emerging Industrial Trends and Business Strategies" (unpublished manuscript), August 1998.

8. David Luberoff and Jay Walder, "U.S. Ports and the Funding of Intermodal Facilities: An Overview of Key Issues," *Transportation Quarterly* 54:4 (Fall 2000), pp. 23–45; John Gulick, "'It's All About Market Share': Competition Among U.S. West Coast Ports for Trans-Pacific Containerized Cargo," in Paul S. Ciccantell and Stephen G. Bunker, eds., *Space and Transport in the World-System* (Westport, Conn.: Greenwood Press, 1998), p. 61.

9. Kasarda, "Emerging Industrial Trends and Business Strategies," pp. 6–7.

10. For the importance of air cargo to the Southern California economy, see Southern California Association of Governments [SCAG], Economic Analysis Division, "RTP Input for JIT Manufacturing and the Region as a Trade Center" (draft memo), November 13, 1996, p. 4; John D. Kasarda and Dennis A. Rondinelli, "Innovative Infrastructure for Agile Manufacturers," *Sloan Management Review* 39:2 (Winter 1998), pp. 73–82; Dennis A. Rondinelli, James H. Johnson Jr., and John D. Kasarda, "The Changing Forces of Urban Economic Development: Globalization and City Competitiveness in the 21st Century," *Cityscape* 3:3 (1998), pp. 71–105. Export data from U.S. Bureau of the Census, *U.S. Merchandise Trade: Selected Highlights*, FT920 Series (Washington, D.C., 2002).

11. Steven P. Erie, John D. Kasarda, and Andrew M. McKenzie, *A New Orange County Airport at El Toro: An Economic Benefits Study* (Irvine, Calif.: Or-

ange County Business Council, 1998), pp. 3-13 to 3-15; Steven P. Erie, John D. Kasarda, Andrew M. McKenzie, and Michael A. Molloy, *A New Orange County Airport at El Toro: Catalyst for High-Wage, High-Tech Economic Development* (Irvine, Calif.: Orange County Business Council, 1999), pp. 2-5 to 2-7; Kenneth Button and Roger Stough, *The Benefits of Being a Hub Airport City: Convenient Travel and High Tech Job Growth* (Fairfax, Va.: Institute of Public Policy, George Mason University, November 1998). On the marriage in Charlotte, North Carolina, of high-tech industries to aggressive trade- and transportation-infrastructure development (including an international airport and inland foreign trade zone), see Manuel Pastor Jr. et al., *Regions That Work* (Minneapolis: University of Minnesota Press, 2000), p. 141.

12. John Friedman, "The World City Hypothesis," *Development and Change* 17:1 (January 1986), pp. 70–79. Also see John Friedman and Goetz Wolff, "World City Formation: An Agenda for Research and Action," *International Journal of Urban and Regional Research* 6:3 (1982), pp. 309–93. Michael Storper, although sympathetic to the Friedman-Wolff approach, criticizes the world-city hypothesis in reference to Los Angeles. He argues that for L.A.'s multinationals the shift toward world markets was more effect than cause in that it was initiated by core expansion and locally acquired expertise. Michael Storper, *The Regional World: Territorial Development in a Global Economy* (New York: Guilford Press, 1997), pp. 233–36.

13. Saskia Sassen, *The Global City: New York, London, Tokyo* (Princeton, N.J.: Princeton University Press, 1991). Storper (*Regional World*, pp. 223–30) points out that the shift toward financial and producer services extends to many more cities than Sassen's big three. For an application of the world-city model to Los Angeles, see Roger Keil, *Los Angeles: Globalization, Urbanization and Social Struggles* (New York: Wiley, 1998).

14. Carl Abbott, "The International City Hypothesis," *Journal of Urban History* 24:1 (November 1997), pp. 28–52. Also see Nestor Rodriguez and Joe Feagin, "Urban Specialization in the World System," *Urban Affairs Quarterly* 22 (December 1986), pp. 187–220; Peter Karl Kresl, "Gateway Cities: A Comparison of North America with the European Community," *Ekistics* 58 (September 1991), pp. 351–56; Peter Karl Kresl, "Montreal's Place in the North American Economy," *American Review of Canadian Studies* (Autumn 2000), pp. 283–314. Scott Campbell mordantly terms Los Angeles's and Seattle's gateway status "more accurately . . . Asia's gateway into American markets." Scott Campbell, "Increasing Trade, Declining Port Cities: Port Containerization and the Regional Diffusion of Economic Benefits," in Helzi Noponen, Julie Graham, and Ann R. Markusen, eds., *Trading Industries, Trading Regions* (New York: Guilford Press, 1993), p. 220. For the importance of goods transportation to a region's global competitiveness, see David J. Keeling, "Transport and the World City Paradigm," in Paul L. Knox and Peter J. Taylor, eds., *World Cities in a World-System* (New York: Cambridge University Press, 1995), pp. 115–32.

15. For an early critique of the factor-abundance approach, see Wassily Leontieff, "Domestic Production and Foreign Trade: The American Capital Position Re-Examined," *Proceedings of the American Philosophical Society* 97 (1953), pp. 331–49. Also see Harry Bowen et al., "Multicountry, Multifactor Tests of the Factor Abundance Theory," *American Economic Review* 77 (December 1987), pp. 791–809. For the newer approach to modeling imperfect competition, see Avinash Dixit and Joseph Stiglitz, "Monopolistic Competition and Optimum Product Diversity," *American Economic Review* 67 (June 1977), pp. 297–308.

16. J. A. Brander and B. J. Spencer, "Export Subsidies and International Market Share Rivalry," *Journal of International Economics* 18 (1985), pp. 83–100; Paul R. Krugman, *Rethinking International Economics* (Cambridge, Mass.: MIT Press, 1990). The location of initial breakthrough innovations in an industry—such as the first marketable silicon chip at Fairchild Semiconductor—often determines the durable location of core agglomerations. Such initial innovations confer "first-mover" advantages on the firms and regions in which they are situated. See Storper, *Regional World*, p. 69; Allen J. Scott, *Regions and the World Economy* (New York: Oxford University Press, 1998), p. 95; and Michael Porter, *Competitive Advantage of Nations* (New York: Free Press, 1990).

17. Paul R. Krugman, *Geography and Trade* (Cambridge, Mass.: MIT Press, 1990); Storper, *Regional World*, pp. 134–69. See also AnnaLee Saxenian, *Regional Advantage: Culture and Competition in Silicon Valley and Route 128* (Cambridge, Mass.: Harvard University Press, 1994); and Edward L. Glaeser et al., "Growth of Cities," *Journal of Political Economy* 100 (1992), pp. 1126–52.

18. Krugman, *Geography and Trade*; Walter Christaller, *Central Places in Southern Germany* (Englewood Cliffs, N.J.: Prentice-Hall, 1966). See also Peter Dicken and Peter E. Lloyd, *Location in Space* (New York: Harper & Row, 1972), pp. 180–82.

19. Hideo Konishi, "Formation of Hub Cities: Transportation Cost Advantages and Population Agglomeration," *Journal of Urban Economics* 48 (2000), pp. 1–28; Masahisa Fujita, Paul R. Krugman, and Anthony Venables, *The Spatial Economy of Cities: Regions and International Trade* (Cambridge, Mass.: MIT Press, 1999), pp. 129–31; Masahisa Fujita and Tomoya Mori, "The Role of Ports in the Making of Major Cities: Self-Agglomeration and Hub-Effect," *Journal of Development Economics* 49 (1996), pp. 93–120. A growing number of studies attest to the facilitating trade role of transportation infrastructure. See, for example, Spiros Bougheas, Panicos O. Demetriades, and Edgar L. W. Morgenroth, "Infrastructure, Transport Costs and Trade," *Journal of International Economics* 47:1 (February 1999), pp. 169–89.

20. Kenichi Ohmae, *The End of the Nation State: The Rise of Regional Economies* (New York: Free Press, 1995); Neal R. Peirce, *Citistates: How Urban America Can Prosper in a Competitive World* (Washington, D.C.: Seven Locks Press, 1993); Rosabeth Moss Kanter, *World Class: Thriving Locally in the Global Economy* (New York: Simon & Schuster, 1995). See also Peter Karl Kresl and Gary Gappert,

eds., *North American Cities and the Global Economy: Challenges and Opportunities* (Thousand Oaks, Calif.: Sage, 1995); and William R. Barnes and Larry C. Ledebur, *The New Regional Economies* (Thousand Oaks, Calif.: Sage, 1998).

21. Abraham F. Lowenthal et al., *Strengthening Southern California's International Connections: Trade and Investment Aspects* (Los Angeles: Southern California Studies Center, University of Southern California, 1996), pp. 1, 8, 16.

22. John J. Kirlin, "Citistates and Regional Governance," *National Civic Review* 82 (Fall 1993), pp. 371–79; Allan D. Wallis, "Regions in Action: Crafting Regional Governance Under the Challenge of Global Competitiveness," *National Civic Review* 85 (Spring/Summer 1996), pp. 15–24; Theodore Hershberg, "Regional Cooperation: Strategies and Incentives for Global Competitiveness and Urban Reform," *National Civic Review* 85 (Spring/Summer 1996), pp. 25–30; Peirce, *Citistates*, pp. 322–25; Kanter, *World Class*, pp. 174–97.

23. Thomas W. Bonnett, *Competing in the New Economy: Governance Strategies for the Digital Age* (published by the author, Brooklyn, N.Y., 2000), p. 105. Also see Susan E. Clarke and Gary L. Gaile, *The Work of Cities* (Minneapolis: University of Minnesota Press, 1998), pp. 80, 86, 161, 204; and August E. Grant, "Telecommunications Infrastructure and the City," in James O. Wheeler et al., eds., *Cities in the Telecommunications Age: The Fracturing of Geography* (New York: Routledge, 2000), pp. 102–3.

24. Candace Howes and Ann R. Markusen, "Trade, Industry, and Economic Development," in Helzi Noponen, Julie Graham, and Ann R. Markusen, eds., *Trading Industries, Trading Regions* (New York: Guilford Press, 1993), pp. 17–19. Howes and Markusen favor more dynamic state intervention. See Markusen's concluding essay, "Trade as a Regional Development Issue," in Noponen, Graham, and Markusen, *Trading Industries, Trading Regions*, p. 300, where she criticizes the advocates of industrial clustering for their policy prescription limiting government to fostering a favorable climate for innovation and positive spillovers; she contends that such a restricted role is insufficient in depressed areas suffering from deindustrialization and other development blockages.

25. Peter Evans, *Embedded Autonomy: States and Industrial Transformation* (Princeton, N.J.: Princeton University Press, 1995); Peter Evans, "Predatory, Developmental, and Other Apparatuses: A Comparative Political Economy Perspective on the Third World State," *Sociological Forum* 4:4 (1989), pp. 561–87. Regarding government/market interactions in the context of East Asian development, see R. Wade, *Governing the Market: Economic Theory and the Role of Government in East Asian Industrialization* (Princeton, N.J.: Princeton University Press, 1990).

26. Peter K. Eisinger, *The Rise of the Entrepreneurial State: State and Local Economic Development Policy in the United States* (Madison: University of Wisconsin Press, 1988).

27. See Robert A. Caro, *The Power Broker: Robert Moses and the Fall of New*

York (New York: Random House, 1974); and Jameson W. Doig, *Empire on the Hudson: Entrepreneurial Vision and Political Power at the Port of New York Authority* (New York: Columbia University Press, 2001).

28. For an elaboration of this argument, see Steven P. Erie, "Los Angeles as a Developmental City-State," in Michael J. Dear, ed., *From Chicago to L.A.: Making Sense of Urban Theory* (Thousand Oaks, Calif.: Sage, 2002), pp. 131–59.

29. Charles Oliver, "Why Los Angeles Doesn't Work," *Investor's Business Daily*, December 9, 1994; City of Los Angeles, *2000–2001 Budget Summary* (Los Angeles: City Clerk, 2000). Also www.lacity.org/cao/econdemo.htm, Table 37, "Net Debt City of Los Angeles as of March 1, 2001," p. 39.

30. Olson, *Governance of U.S. Public Ports*, Appendices II and III, pp. 35–39. As of 2000, the nation's fifteen largest cities were New York, Los Angeles, Chicago, Houston, Philadelphia, San Diego, Phoenix, San Antonio, Dallas, Detroit, San Jose, San Francisco, Indianapolis, Jacksonville, and Columbus. Governance data compiled from city websites.

31. Statistics compiled from the Airports Council International, city and local airport websites: www.airports.org.

32. Michael Denning, "Structure, Policies and Performance: Public Ports as Public Enterprise" (paper presented at the Annual Meeting of the American Political Science Association, New Orleans, Louisiana, 1985). Also see Campbell, "Increasing Trade, Declining Port Cities," pp. 212–55, esp. pp. 212–15 and 249–51.

33. Olson, *Governance of U.S. Public Ports*, pp. 21–29; David J. Olson, "Public Port Accountability: A Framework for Evaluation," in Marc J. Hershman, ed., *Urban Ports and Harbor Management: Responding to Change Along U.S. Waterfronts* (New York: Taylor & Francis, 1988), pp. 307–33; Alan V. Tucker, "The Politics of Airport Expansion in Denver and St. Louis" (paper presented at the Annual Meeting of the American Political Science Association, New York, September 1–4, 1994), pp. 8–12. Regional authorities can also be politicized. Richard Leone, former chairman of the Port Authority of New York/New Jersey, argues that while governors of the two states complained for decades about the agency's independence, they have now taken over: "Today the agency is ruled by reliable political allies of the governors, former lieutenants and campaign fundraisers. Rather than functioning as an independent force for the interests of the region, it is more often just a place where bistate interests are brokered." Richard Leone, "The Port Authority's Role in the World Trade Center," *New York Times*, August 6, 2002, p. A19.

34. Gulick, "'It's All About Market Share,'" pp. 61–83; Herman L. Boschken, *Strategic Design and Organizational Change: Pacific Rim Seaports in Transition* (Tuscaloosa, Ala.: University of Alabama Press, 1988), p. 196.

35. Gordon L. Clark and Michael J. Dear, *State Apparatus: Structures and Language of Legitimacy* (Boston: Allen & Unwin, 1984), esp. pp. 131–52; and Carl Brent Swisher, *Motivation and Political Technique in the California Constitutional Convention of 1878–79* (New York: De Capo Press, [1930] 1969).

36. E. P. Oberholtzer, *The Referendum in America* (New York: Scribner, 1912); and Lance W. Lancaster, "State Limitations upon Local Indebtedness," in *The Municipal Year Book*, vol. 3 (Chicago: International City Managers Association, 1936), pp. 313–27. Regarding the early importance of local public financing for cities, see Eric Monkkonen, *The Local State: Public Money and American Cities* (Stanford, Calif.: Stanford University Press, 1995).

37. Ray A. Billington, *America's Frontier Heritage* (New York: Holt, Rinehart and Winston, 1966).

38. See Francis M. Carney, "The Decentralized Politics of Los Angeles," *Annals of the American Academy of Political and Social Science* 353 (May 1964), pp. 107–21; Edward C. Banfield, *Big City Politics* (New York: Random House, 1965); Charter of the City of Los Angeles, 1889 (as amended to 1911), 1925, 2000; and Burton Hunter, *The Evolution of Municipal Organization and Administrative Practice in the City of Los Angeles* (Los Angeles: Parker, Stone & Baird, 1933), pp. 109, 125, 209.

39. Long Beach City Charter, 1907, 1915, 1921, 1999; and Charter of the City of Los Angeles, 1925 (as amended up to 1999), 2000.

40. See Elaine B. Sharp, "Voting on Citywide Propositions: Further Tests of Competing Explanations," *Urban Affairs Quarterly* 23 (1987), pp. 233–48; and Winston W. Crouch, "The Initiative and Referendum in Cities," *American Political Science Review* 37 (1943), pp. 491–504.

41. Martin Shefter, "Regional Receptivity to Reform: The Legacy of the Progressive Era," *Political Science Quarterly* 98 (1983), pp. 459–83; and C. R. Woodruff, "Of What Does Municipal Advance Consist?" *National Municipal Review* 3 (1914), pp. 1–12.

42. Regarding the debate concerning political control versus autonomy of the federal bureaucracy, see Mathew D. McCubbins, Roger Noll, and Barry Weingast, "Administrative Procedures as Instruments of Political Control," *Journal of Law, Economics, and Organization* 3 (1987), pp. 243–77; Mathew D. McCubbins and Thomas Schwartz, "Congressional Oversight Overlooked: Police Patrol Versus Fire Alarms," *American Journal of Political Science* 28: 1 (February 1984), pp. 165–79; Terry Moe, "The Politicized Presidency," in John E. Chubb and Paul E. Peterson, eds., *The New Directions in American Politics* (Washington, D.C.: Brookings Institution, 1985), pp. 235–72; Terry Moe, "Congressional Control of the Bureaucracy: An Assessment of the Positive Theory of 'Congressional Dominance'" (paper presented at the Annual Meeting of the American Political Science Association, New Orleans, Louisiana, 1985); and Daniel Carpenter, *The Forging of Bureaucratic Autonomy* (Princeton, N.J.: Princeton University Press, 2001).

43. See Steven P. Erie and James W. Ingram III, "History of Los Angeles Charter Reform," in Kevin F. McCarthy, Steven P. Erie, Robert E. Reichardt, and James W. Ingram III, *Meeting the Challenge of Charter Reform* (Santa Monica, Calif.: RAND, 1998), pp. 58–81.

44. Ibid.; and Committee on Improving the Delivery of City Services, *Report*

on the Proprietary Departments (Los Angeles: Elected Los Angeles Charter Reform Commission, May 26, 1998), pp. 13–14.

45. See Task Force on Civil Service/Personnel, *Report, Part II: Civil Service and the Personnel Department* (Los Angeles: Elected Los Angeles Charter Reform Commission, November 16, 1998).

46. Matthew A. Crenson, "Urban Bureaucracy in Urban Politics: Toward a Developmental Theory," in J. David Greenstone, ed., *Public Values and Private Power in American Politics* (Chicago: University of Chicago Press, 1982), p. 212.

47. Steven P. Erie, "How the Urban West Was Won: The Local State and Economic Growth in Los Angeles, 1880–1932," *Urban Affairs Quarterly* 27:4 (June 1992).

48. For an analysis of the evolution of the Port of Los Angeles's pricing strategies, see Michael Denning and David J. Olson, "Comparative Analysis of West Coast Ports" (University of Washington), 1988, pp. 98–100.

Chapter Three

1. Los Angeles Board of Harbor Commissioners [LABHC], *The Port of Los Angeles: Its History, Development, Tributary Territory, Present and Prospective Commerce, and Relation to the Panama Canal* (Los Angeles: Board of Harbor Commissioners for the City of Los Angeles, 1913), p. 60.

2. Harry W. Krotz, "Long Beach in Path of New Trade Line," *Daily Telegram*, April 15, 1922, sec. 2, p. 1.

3. Quoted in Judge Peirson "Pete" Hall oral history, May 18, 1977, Public History—Airport file, Collection 2113, box 3, Department of Special Collections, UCLA Library.

4. David L. Clark, "Improbable Los Angeles," in Richard M. Bernard and Bradley R. Rice, eds., *Sunbelt Cities: Politics and Growth Since World War II* (Austin: University of Texas Press, 1983), pp. 268–308; Martin J. Schiesl, "Airplanes to Aerospace: Defense Spending and Economic Growth in the Los Angeles Region," in Roger W. Lotchin, ed., *The Martial Metropolis: U.S. Cities in War and Peace* (New York: Praeger, 1984), pp. 135–49. More generally, see James E. Rauch, "Bureaucracy, Infrastructure, and Economic Growth: Evidence from U.S. Cities During the Progressive Era," *American Economic Review* 85:4 (September 1995), pp. 968–79. In 1880, Orange County was still a part of Los Angeles County; it would become a separate jurisdiction in 1889. In 1893, Riverside County was created from portions of Los Angeles and San Diego counties.

5. See Robert Fogelson, *The Fragmented Metropolis: Los Angeles, 1880–1930* (Cambridge, Mass.: Harvard University Press, 1967); Steven P. Erie, "How the Urban West Was Won: The Local State and Economic Growth in Los Angeles, 1880–1932," *Urban Affairs Quarterly* 27:4 (June 1992), pp. 538–47; Martin J. Schiesl, "Politicians in Disguise: The Changing Role of Public Administrators in Los Angeles, 1900–1920," in Michael H. Ebner and Eugene M. Tobin, eds., *The Age of Re-*

form: *New Perspectives on the Progressive Era* (Port Washington, N.Y.: Kennikat Press, 1977), pp. 108–16; and Theodore J. Lowi, "Machine Politics—Old and New," *Public Interest* 9 (Fall 1967), pp. 83–97.

6. See Gordon L. Clark and Michael J. Dear, *State Apparatus: Structures and Language of Legitimacy* (Boston: Allen & Unwin, 1984); Terrence J. McDonald, "The Burdens of Urban History: The Theory of the State in Recent American Social History," *Studies in American Political Development* 3 (1989), pp. 3–29.

7. For a revisionist account noting the pluralism of L.A. politics by the 1920s, see Tom Sitton, "Did the Ruling Class Rule at City Hall in 1920s Los Angeles?" in Tom Sitton and William F. Deverell, eds., *Metropolis in the Making: Los Angeles in the 1920s* (Berkeley: University of California Press, 2001), pp. 302–18.

8. Stephen L. Elkin, *City and Regime in the American Republic* (Chicago: University of Chicago Press, 1987); and Todd Swanstrom, *The Crisis of Growth Politics: Cleveland, Kucinich, and the Challenge of Urban Populism* (Philadelphia: Temple University Press, 1985).

9. Anna G. Wiggs, "The History of Los Angeles City Government Under the Second Charter, 1889–1925" (master's thesis, University of Southern California, 1928); Lola I. Kassel, "A History of the Government of Los Angeles, 1781–1925" (master's thesis, Occidental College, 1929); and Charter of the City of Los Angeles, 1889.

10. Winston W. Crouch and Beatrice Dinerman, *Southern California Metropolis* (Berkeley: University of California Press, 1963), pp. 149–79.

11. Charles F. Queenan, *The Port of Los Angeles: From Wilderness to World Port [POLA]* (Los Angeles: Los Angeles Harbor Department, 1983), pp. 18–22, 27–41.

12. Boyle Workman, *The City That Grew* (Los Angeles: Southland Publishing Company, 1935), p. 159; Remi Nadeau, *City-Makers: The Men Who Transformed Los Angeles from Village to Metropolis During the First Great Boom, 1868–1876* (Garden City, N.Y.: Doubleday, 1948), p. 85; and Remi Nadeau, *Los Angeles: From Mission to Modern City* (New York: Longman Green, 1960), pp. 64–67.

13. See Stuart Daggett, *Chapters on the History of the Southern Pacific* (New York: Ronald Press, 1922); Spencer C. Olin Jr., *California Politics, 1846–1920: The Emerging Corporate State* (San Francisco: Boyd & Fraser, 1981), pp. 30–41; and Kevin Starr, *Inventing the Dream: California Through the Progressive Era* (New York: Oxford University Press, 1985), p. 230.

14. See Erie, "How the Urban West Was Won," Tables 1 and 2, pp. 527–29; Daggett, *Chapters on the History of the Southern Pacific*; and George E. Mowry, *The California Progressives* (Berkeley: University of California Press, 1951).

15. On the land boom, see Glenn S. Dumke, *The Boom of the Eighties in Southern California* (San Marino, Calif.: Huntington Library, 1944). Also see Joan Didion, "Letter from Los Angeles," *New Yorker* (February 26, 1990), pp. 87–97; Robert Gottlieb and Irene Wolt, *Thinking Big: The Story of the Los Angeles Times, Its Publishers and Their Influence on Southern California* (New York: Putnam, 1977).

16. On DWP political prowess, see Vincent Ostrom, *Water and Politics: A Study of Water Policies and Administration in the Development of Los Angeles* (Los Angeles: Haynes Foundation, 1953).

17. Mowry, *California Progressives*; Donald R. Culton, "Charles Dwight Willard: Los Angeles' 'Citizen Fixit,'" *California History* 57:2 (June 1978), pp. 158–71; and William Issel, "Citizens Outside Government: Business and Urban Policy in San Francisco and Los Angeles, 1890–1932," *Pacific Historical Review* 57 (1988), pp. 112–31.

18. Mowry, *California Progressives*, pp. 43, 91. For the history of the L.A. reform movement, see Albert H. Clodius, "The Quest for Good Government in Los Angeles, 1890–1910" (Ph.D. diss., Claremont Graduate School, 1953). Also see Mowry, *California Progressives*; Spencer C. Olin Jr., *California's Prodigal Sons: Hiram Johnson and the Progressives, 1911–1917* (Berkeley: University of California Press, 1968).

19. Fogelson, *The Fragmented Metropolis*, pp. 43–62.

20. Daggett, *Chapters on the History of the Southern Pacific*, pp. 125–31; Queenan, *POLA*, p. 70.

21. William F. Deverell, *Railroad Crossing: Californians and the Railroad, 1850–1910* (Berkeley: University of California Press, 1994), pp. 100–118; Ernest Marquez, *Port Los Angeles: A Phenomenon of the Railroad Era* (San Marino, Calif.: Golden West Books, 1975), p. 87. The classic contemporary account of the harbor battle remains Charles D. Willard, *The Free Harbor Contest at Los Angeles* (Los Angeles: Kingsley-Barnes & Neuner, 1899).

22. William F. Deverell, "The Los Angeles 'Free Harbor Fight,'" *California History* 70 (1991), pp. 12–29; and Gottlieb and Wolt, *Thinking Big*.

23. See G. Allen Greb, "Opening a New Frontier: San Francisco, Los Angeles and the Panama Canal, 1900–1914," *Pacific Historical Review* 47:3 (1978), p. 407.

24. D. A. Shotliff, "San Pedro Harbor or Los Angeles Harbor? Senator W. H. Savage and the Home Rule Advocates Fail to Stem the Tide of Consolidationism, 1906–1909," *Southern California Quarterly* 54 (1972), pp. 127–54. Also see James W. Ingram III, "L.A.'s Long Platonic Affairs with Neighborhood Councils," *Los Angeles Times*, November 2, 1997, p. M6.

25. California Legislature, Joint Committee on Harbors, *California Harbors: Report and Recommendations* (Sacramento: State Printing Office, 1908); Queenan, *POLA*, p. 70.

26. Fogelson, *The Fragmented Metropolis*; and Clarence H. Matson, *Building a World Gateway: The Story of the Los Angeles Harbor [BAWG]* (Los Angeles: Pacific Era, 1945), pp. 217–19.

27. Matson, *BAWG*, pp. 83–89, 116–18, and 122–25; Harbor Bond Campaign Committee, *Harbor Bonds Vote Yes: Develop Our Commerce and Industry* (Los Angeles: Harbor Bond Campaign Committee, 1919).

28. The DWP fared much better at the ballot box when going it alone. From 1904 to 1932, when only water and power bonds appeared on the ballot, nearly 80 percent of the offerings secured the necessary two-thirds voter approval. For an

analysis of DWP bond referenda from 1904 to 1931, see Erie, "How the Urban West Was Won," Table 5, pp. 542–43.

29. Matson, *BAWG*, pp. 188–206.

30. LABHC, *Annual Report of the Board of Harbor Commissioners, 1913* (Los Angeles: LABHC, 1913), p. 35; LABHC, *Annual Report, 1915*, pp. 71–79; LABHC, *Annual Report, 1924*, p. 35; and James W. Ingram III, "Building the Municipal State: Coalitions and Infrastructure Development in Los Angeles, 1889–1939" (paper presented at the Annual Meeting of the American Political Science Association, New York City, September 1–4, 1994), p. 21.

31. Municipal League, *Bulletin*, vols. 1–5 (n.d.); and Los Angeles Chamber of Commerce, *Bulletin*, 7:14 (October 31, 1932).

32. See Ronald M. Ketcham, "Voting on Charter Amendments in Los Angeles," in *Studies in Local Government*, no. 3 (Los Angeles: Bureau of Governmental Research, UCLA, 1940), Table I, p. 5. In a study of fifty Los Angeles elections held over thirteen years, Ketcham found that turnout averaged 31 percent for special municipal elections, nearly 40 percent in regular municipal elections, and over 75 percent for state general elections.

33. Matson, *BAWG*, pp. 177–81; LABHC, *Annual Report, 1916*, pp. 15–194; LABHC, *Annual Report, 1917*, p. 12; and LABHC, *Annual Report, 1919*, pp. 10–11.

34. LABHC, *Port of Los Angeles*, pp. 15–22; and Greb, "Opening a New Frontier."

35. U.S. Army Corps of Engineers, *Los Angeles–Long Beach Areas Cultural Resource Survey* (Washington, D.C.: Government Printing Office, 1978), p. 57.

36. LABHC, *Annual Report, 1930*, pp. 24–31.

37. Frank L. Beach, "The Transformation of California: The Effects of the Westward Movement on California's Growth and Development in the Progressive Period" (Ph.D. diss., University of California, Berkeley, 1963), pp. 219–20.

38. Erie, "How the Urban West Was Won," pp. 534–38; LABHC, *Annual Report, 1930*, p. 66; Queenan, *POLA*, p. 70; and Matson, *BAWG*, p. 13.

39. Matson, *BAWG*, p. 82.

40. Matson, *BAWG*, pp. 37–39, 157, 161; LABHC, *Annual Report, 1918*, pp. 10–11; and Clarence H. Matson, *The Port of Los Angeles* (Los Angeles: Department of Foreign Commerce and Shipping, Chamber of Commerce, 1935), p. 11.

41. Haynes Collection, 1937, box 136, Department of Special Collections, UCLA Library. Also see Schiesl, "Politicians in Disguise."

42. See Richard DeAtley, *Long Beach: The Golden Shore: A History of the City and the Port [LBTGS]* (Houston, Tex.: Pioneer, 1988).

43. See Charles F. Queenan, *Long Beach and Los Angeles: A Tale of Two Ports [LBLA]* (Northridge, Calif.: Windsor, 1986), pp. 30–33; Walter H. Case, *Long Beach Community Book [LBCB]* (Long Beach, Calif.: Arthur H. Cawston, 1948), pp. 50, 179–80; Larry L. Meyer and Patricia Larson Kalayjian, *Long Beach: For-*

tune's Harbor [LBFH] (Tulsa, Okla.: Continental Heritage Press, 1983), pp. 37–42.; and DeAtley, *LBTGS*, pp. 31–35.

44. See Deverell, *Railroad Crossing*, for the role of the LATR. As Case notes in *LBCB*, the LATR later became part of the Union Pacific system (p. 180). Also see Queenan, *LBLA*, pp. 46, 50.

45. Queenan, *LBLA*, p. 61; Case, *LBCB*, p. 65.

46. Case, *LBCB*, pp. 64–65; Meyer and Kalayjian, *LBFH*, p. 64.

47. Meyer and Kalayjian, *LBFH*, p. 64; Case, *LBCB*, pp. 64–66; DeAtley, *LBTGS*, p. 56.

48. See Case, *LBCB*, pp. 66–67; and Queenan, *LBLA*, p. 81. See also Crouch and Dinerman, *Southern California Metropolis*, pp. 246–48.

49. DeAtley, *LBTGS*, pp. 37, 57; Case, *LBCB*, p. 124; Queenan, *LBLA*, pp. 65, 70.

50. Case, *LBCB*, p. 126; Queenan, *LBLA*, pp. 65–67.

51. See Case, *LBCB*, pp. 124–127; and Walter H. Case, *History of Long Beach [HOLB]* (Long Beach, Calif.: Press-Telegram Publishing Co., 1935), pp. 53–54.

52. Loretta Berner, "A Shipyard for Long Beach," in *A Step Back in Time* (Long Beach, Calif.: Historical Society of Long Beach, 1990), p. 47; Queenan, *LBLA*, pp. 65–68; DeAtley, *LBTGS*, pp. 57, 76; Meyer and Kalayjian, *LBFH*, p. 69; Case, *HOLB*, p. 54; and Case, *LBCB*, pp. 125–26, 133–34.

53. Ingram, "Building the Municipal State."

54. See Charter of the City of Long Beach, 1907; and Los Angeles City Charter, 1905.

55. Charter of the City of Long Beach, 1914; DeAtley, *LBTGS*, p. 67; and Queenan, *LBLA*, p. 79.

56. See Case, *HOLB*, p. 70; DeAtley, *LBTGS*, p. 67; Meyer and Kalayjian, *LBFH*, p. 72; Queenan, *LBLA*, pp. 79–81, 92.

57. See Robert P. Farrington, "The Evolution of Long Beach City Government Culminating in the City Manager Plan" (Long Beach Public Library, Long Beach, Calif.), 1933, p. 9. See also Charter of the City of Long Beach, 1921, Article IV, Section 36; Article VI, Section 48; Article XXI.

58. DeAtley, *LBTGS*, p. 68; *Long Beach Press*, October 1–21, 1921, and *Long Beach Daily Telegram*, April 13–19, 1922. Henderson would go on to succeed Windham as city manager. See Walter H. Case, "Charles S. Henderson," in *History of Long Beach and Vicinity*, vol. 2 (Chicago: S. J. Clarke, 1927), pp. 582–86. Also see *Long Beach Press*, May 7, 1924; Case, *LBCB*, pp. 126–27; and Elections History Folder, Long Beach City Clerk.

59. See Charter of the City of Long Beach, 1925, and 1929, Article XXI; Los Angeles City Charter, 1911, 1913, 1925; Long Beach Board of Harbor Commissioners, *75th Anniversary, 1911–1986* (Long Beach, Calif.: Board of Harbor Commissioners, 1985); and Charter of the City of Long Beach, 1931, section 108 and Article XXI. The port manager now served at the pleasure of the Board of Harbor Commissioners. Discretionary control over the harbor revenue fund was trans-

ferred from the city council to the board. On Craig's harbor-commission service, see Case, *LBCB*, pp. 130–31.

60. See Charter of the City of Long Beach, 1921, 1925, 1929, 1931, Article XXI; DeAtley, *LBTGS*, p. 76; and Case, *LBCB*, p. 58.

61. Farrington, "Evolution of Long Beach City Government," pp. 15–20. See also DeAtley, *LBTGS*, p. 76; Case, *HOLB*, pp. 88; Queenan, *LBLA*, pp. 92–94.

62. As early as the mid-1920s, Long Beach was beginning to take business away from Los Angeles. See "Long Beach Drawing Business away from Los Angeles Harbor," *Long Beach Press Telegram*, July 21, 1926, sec. 2, p. 1; and Queenan, *LBLA*, p. 92.

63. Paul David Friedman, "Fear of Flying: The Development of Los Angeles International Airport and the Rise of Public Protest over Jet Noise" (master's thesis, University of California, Santa Barbara, 1978), pp. 17–18; Clifford Henderson oral history, January 9, 1977, Public History—Airport file, Collection 2113, box 3, Department of Special Collections, UCLA Library. Henderson was the first director of the L.A. airport. Also see Greg Hise, *Cities and Flight: Aviation and Western Metropolitan Development*, Lusk Center Research Institute Working Paper LCRI-95-06P (Los Angeles: Lusk Center Research Institute, University of Southern California, September 1995).

64. Tom Moran, *Los Angeles International Airport: From Lindbergh's Landing Strip to World Air Center [LAIA]* (Canoga Park, Calif.: CCA, 1993), pp. 19–21; Ford Ashman Carpenter, "Preliminary Report on the Airports or Landing Fields of Los Angeles County: Prepared for the Los Angeles Chamber of Commerce," n.d., Los Angeles World Airports Archives [LAWAA].

65. Lloyd to Ford Motor Co., June 17, 1927, LAWAA; Moran, *LAIA*, p. 20.

66. "Program Agenda for meeting with Jack Maddux," June 30, 1927, and George Cleaver to Edsel Ford, January 21, 1928, LAWAA. Moran, *LAIA*, pp. 17–21.

67. Frank Parent to Crawford, July 15, 1927; Cleaver to Ford, January 21, 1928; Mayo to George Cleaver, February 2, 1928; and Harry Culver to George Cleaver, December 1, 1927; all in LAWAA.

68. "Report of the Finance Committee on Airport Sites to the City Council of Los Angeles," March 16, 1928, LAWAA.

69. Hall oral history. Earlier, Hall, a lawyer, had worked on oil leases in the Owens Valley and had closely studied the operations of the Los Angeles DWP, the largest property owner in Inyo and Mono counties. In the process, he became a strong champion of municipal ownership.

70. Moran, *LAIA*, pp. 22–23; Hall oral history; Harry Wetzel, "Why the Municipal Airport (Mines Field) Was Chosen for the 1928 National Air Races," n.d., LAWAA.

71. See Greg Hise, *Magnetic Los Angeles: Planning the Twentieth-Century Metropolis* (Baltimore: Johns Hopkins University Press, 1977), p. 128. Hise notes that Douglas and North American both established bridgeheads at Mines Field in

the late 1920s, even though the city's lessee status was an impediment. See also "Report of the Finance Committee to the Los Angeles City Council, Los Angeles," n.d., LAWAA.

72. Sheldon Warren Stahl, "The Los Angeles International Airport—An Economic Analysis" (Ph.D. diss., UCLA, 1964), pp. 22–24. Hall oral history; Friedman, "Fear of Flying," p. 26. On early airport governance, see Fred G. Crawford, *Organization and Administrative Development of the Government of the City of Los Angeles During the Thirty-Year Period July 1, 1925 to September 30, 1955* (Los Angeles: School of Public Administration, University of Southern California, 1955), pp. 173–74.

Chapter Four

1. Los Angeles Board of Harbor Commissioners [LABHC)], *The Port of Los Angeles: Annual Report, 1982* (Los Angeles: LABHC, 1982), p. 5.

2. Port of Long Beach, *Harbor Handbook* (Long Beach, Calif.: Port of Long Beach, 1991), pp. 1, 2.

3. Clifton Moore interview, 1995.

4. Data tabulated by the Southern California Association of Governments [SCAG] Community and Economic Development staff and from the Los Angeles Department of Airports, the Port of Los Angeles, and the Port of Long Beach.

5. Regarding public entrepreneurship, see Jameson W. Doig and Erwin C. Hargrove, eds., *Leadership and Innovation: Entrepreneurs in Government* (Baltimore: Johns Hopkins University Press, 1990).

6. Michael Denning and David J. Olson, "Comparative Analysis of West Coast Ports" (University of Washington), 1988, p. 98; Los Angeles City Clerk to Harbor and Water and Power Commissions, June 15, 1934, File 3185 [1934], Central File 424.100, "LAHD Revenue Bonds, 1925/58," Los Angeles Harbor Department [LAHD]; Board of Economic Survey of the Port of Los Angeles, "Revenues and Expenditures, 1912–1932" and "Operating Expenses, 1912–1932," Central File 424.100, "LAHD Revenue Bonds, 1925/58," LAHD; LABHC, *Annual Report, 1930*, pp. 14–16; LABHC, *Annual Report, 1934*, pp. 83–85; and LABHC, *Annual Report, 1937*, pp. 9, 65–67.

7. LABHC, *Annual Report, 1938*, p. 7; LABHC, *Annual Report, 1939*, p. 81. Regarding Long Beach oil development, see Richard DeAtley, *Long Beach: The Golden Shore: A History of the City and the Port [LBTGS]* (Houston, Tex.: Pioneer, 1988), p. 87. Also see David J. Olson, "California Ports" (University of Washington), 1980, p. 49.

8. Stephen T. Sato, *San Pedro Bay Area* (Northridge, Calif.: Windsor, 1990), pp. 56–62; DeAtley, *LBTGS*, pp. 80, 92–93; and LABHC, *Annual Report, 1941*, pp. 77–82.

9. Port of Los Angeles, *1994 Shipping Handbook* (Los Angeles: Los Angeles Harbor Department, 1994), p. 33; DeAtley, *LBTGS*, p. 91.

10. Charles F. Queenan, *Long Beach and Los Angeles: A Tale of Two Ports* *[LBLA]* (Northridge, Calif.: Windsor, 1986), pp. 115–117.

11. LABHC, *Annual Report, 1951*, p. 22; LABHC, *Annual Report, 1954*, p. 6; City of Los Angeles, *Los Angeles Year Book 1949* (Los Angeles: Bureau of Printing, 1949), p. 29; and Queenan, *LBLA*, p. 126.

12. DeAtley, *LBTGS*, pp. 90–91, 96; and http://www.polb.com/html/1_about/1940.html.

13. Queenan, *LBLA*, pp. 125–26.

14. LABHC, *Annual Report, 1952*, p. 12; LABHC, *Annual Report, 1958*, p. 7.

15. LABHC, *Annual Report, 1957*, p. 7; LABHC, *Annual Report, 1959*, pp. 6–7; Abraham J. Falick, "The Twin Ports of Los Angeles/Long Beach" (master's thesis, University of California, Los Angeles, 1967), p. 74.

16. Steven P. Erie and James W. Ingram III, "History of Los Angeles Charter Reform," in Kevin F. McCarthy, Steven P. Erie, Robert E. Reichardt, and James W. Ingram III, *Meeting the Challenge of Charter Reform* (Santa Monica, Calif.: RAND, 1998), pp. 78–79.

17. Denning and Olson, "Comparative Analysis," p. 94. In a 1995 interview with the author, Bradley claimed that although he didn't remember asking for such letters, it "was a practice that was used by Sam Yorty, who preceded me. . . . I know in that first wave of appointments we did not. . . . Generally, if you asked for someone's resignation, you would get it."

18. Eloi J. Amar obituary, *Long Beach Independent*, May 28, 1963, pp. B4-5; Queenan, *LBLA*, p. 125; Long Beach Harbor Department, *Port Book 1940* (Long Beach, Calif.: Long Beach Sun, 1940), p. 5; Associated Property Owners of Long Beach, "Tax Consciousness" (mimeographed newsletter), 1948.

19. Larry L. Meyer and Patricia Larson Kalayjian, *Long Beach: Fortune's Harbor* *[LBFH]* (Tulsa, Okla.: Continental Heritage Press, 1983), p. 140; DeAtley, *LBTGS*, pp. 99–100.

20. Olson, "California Ports," pp. 49–50; DeAtley, *LBTGS*, 96–101; Walter H. Case, *Long Beach Community Book [LBCB]* (Long Beach, Calif.: Arthur H. Cawston, 1948), pp. 151–54; Meyer & Kalayjian, *LBFH*, p. 144.

21. Denning and Olson, "Comparative Analysis," pp. 121–22; Olson, "California Ports," pp. 18–23.

22. LABHC, *Annual Report, 1958*, pp. 6, 10; LABHC, *Annual Report, 1962*, p. 7; LABHC, *Annual Report, 1963*, p. 7; LABHC, *Annual Report, 1969*, p. 7; Charles F. Queenan, *The Port of Los Angeles: From Wilderness to World Port* *[POLA]* (Los Angeles: Los Angeles Harbor Department, 1983), pp. 103–5.

23. DeAtley, *LBTGS*, p. 124; also see Queenan, *LBLA*, p. 128.

24. Sato, *San Pedro Bay Area*, p. 72; DeAtley, *LBTGS*, pp. 105–6, 123–25; Queenan, *LBLA*, p. 104; also see the Port of Long Beach website's historical timeline at http://www.polb.com.

25. Denning and Olson, "Comparative Analysis," pp. 126, 143.

26. Queenan, *LBLA*, p. 137.

27. Falick, "Twin Ports," p. 87.

28. Samuel Yorty, "Ask the Mayor," 1987, UCLA Oral History Program, pp. 163–64; *Los Angeles Times*, January 29, 1967, pp. B1, B3.

29. Quoted in DeAtley, *LBTGS*, p. 106, emphasis in the original.

30. Thomas J. Thorley, "The Port of Long Beach: Its Development and Growth," Long Beach Collection, Long Beach Public Library, September 1974, p. 8; see also Queenan, *LBLA*, p. 137; DeAtley, *LBTGS*, p. 106; Meyer and Kalayjian, *LBFH*, p. 167.

31. LABHC, *Annual Report, 1981*, p. 11; Queenan, *POLA*, pp. 113–15; Queenan, *LBLA*, p. 143.

32. Information in this paragraph comes from www.polb.com/html/1_about/history.html.

33. LABHC, *Annual Report, 1981*, pp. 6–7, 11; Queenan, *POLA*, p. 118.

34. Denning and Olson, "Comparative Analysis," pp. 98–99; DeAtley, *LBTGS*, p. 123; Meyer and Kalayjian, *LBFH*, p. 167. Also see Willis H. Miller, "The Port of Los Angeles–Long Beach in 1929 and 1979: A Comparative Analysis," *Southern California Quarterly* 65:4 (Winter 1983), pp. 341–78.

35. Denning and Olson, "Comparative Analysis," pp. 127–28; Port of Long Beach, *Interport: 1988 Annual Report* (Long Beach, Calif.: Port of Long Beach, 1988), p. 19; Long Beach Harbor Commissioners, *Annual Report, 1993* (Long Beach, Calif.: Long Beach Harbor Commissioners, 1993); DeAtley, *LBTGS*, p. 124.

36. Tom Bradley interview, 1995.

37. LABHC, *Annual Report, 1975*, pp. 17–18; LABHC, *Annual Report, 1976*, p. 19; LABHC, *Annual Report, 1979*, p. 11; LABHC, *Annual Report, 1983*, p. 5; Queenan, *LBLA*, p. 149; and Port of Long Beach website's historical timeline at http://www.polb.com (quote).

38. Denning and Olson, "Comparative Analysis," p. 129.

39. Steven P. Erie, *International Trade and Job Creation in Southern California: Facilitating Los Angeles/Long Beach Port, Rail, and Airport Development* (Berkeley: California Policy Seminar, 1996), pp. 35–52.

40. Meyer and Kalayjian, *LBFH*, p. 169; DeAtley, *LBTGS*, p. 123; Queenan, *LBLA*, pp. 155–56.

41. Alameda Corridor Transportation Authority, *The Alameda Corridor: A National Priority* (Huntington Park, Calif.: Alameda Corridor Transportation Authority, February 1993), pp. 1–2, 9–10.

42. WorldPort LA, *1993 West Coast International Trade Market Share Analysis* (Los Angeles: Port of Los Angeles, September 1994), pp. 32, 68.

43. Ibid., pp. 14, 69; Denning and Olson, "Comparative Analysis," pp. 8–9.

44. Temple, Barker & Sloane, Inc., *The Economic Impact of the Ports of Los Angeles and Long Beach* (Lexington, Mass.: Temple, Barker & Sloane, Inc., October 1989), p. 6; DeAtley, *LBTGS*, p. 106. Also see SCAG, *The Port of Long Beach and Its Impact on the Southern California Economy* (Los Angeles: SCAG, 1987).

45. Los Angeles Department of Airports [LADOA] Director, "To the Mayor

and Members of the City Council," 1937, Los Angeles World Airports Archives [LAWAA].

46. Ray Jones in absence of the mayor, KFWB, 1937, LAWAA.

47. Paul David Friedman, "Fear of Flying: The Development of Los Angeles International Airport and the Rise of Public Protest over Jet Noise" (master's thesis, University of California, Santa Barbara, 1978), pp. 3–4, 31–34; Sheldon Warren Stahl, "The Los Angeles International Airport—An Economic Analysis" (Ph.D. diss., UCLA, 1964), pp. 26–28; Greg Hise, *Magnetic Los Angeles: Planning the Twentieth-Century Metropolis* (Baltimore: Johns Hopkins University Press, 1997), pp. 123–27.

48. Harry Hopkins to the Honorable Frank L. Shaw, May 29, 1937; Ray Jones to Bob Pritchards, September 22, 1938, both in LAWAA. Also Friedman, "Fear of Flying," pp. 15–17, 35–37.

49. Tom Moran, *Los Angeles International Airport: From Lindbergh's Landing Strip to World Air Center [LAIA]* (Canoga Park, Calif.: CCA, 1993), pp. 42–43.

50. Philip S. Klatchko, "Los Angeles International Airport: Conception—Development—Maturity" (University of Southern California), 1970, pp. 3–4, 6; Hopkins to Shaw, May 29, 1937, LAWAA.

51. Winston W. Crouch, *Metropolitan Los Angeles: A Study in Integration* (Los Angeles: Haynes Foundation, 1954), p. 50. After the war, the federal subsidy, although still sizeable, was reduced by almost one-half. For 1947–62, the federal share of LAX expansion costs was 28 percent. See Stahl, "Los Angeles International Airport," pp. 8, 31–32, 46; Hise, *Magnetic Los Angeles*, pp. 137–49; Martin J. Schiesl, "Airplanes to Aerospace: Defense Spending and Economic Growth in the Los Angeles Region," in Roger W. Lotchin, ed., *The Martial Metropolis: U.S. Cities in War and Peace* (New York: Praeger, 1984), pp. 135–49; Carl Abbott, *The Metropolitan Frontier* (Tucson: University of Arizona Press, 1993), pp. 11, 68–78.

52. LADOA, *Master Plan for Los Angeles International Airport* (Los Angeles: LADOA, March 1953), p. 7; "LAX: The Center of So Cal Aviation," *Airliners: The World's Airline Magazine* 46 (1996), p. 5, in LAWAA.

53. Carl Blume, "Los Angeles High-Activity Airport," *Aero Digest* (July 1949), in LAWAA.

54. LADOA, *Master Plan*, pp. 6–8; Los Angeles Chamber of Commerce, Aviation Committee, "Summary of a Report on the Master Plan of Airports for the Los Angeles County Regional Planning District," n.d., LAWAA; Hise, *Magnetic Los Angeles*, pp. 117–52.

55. LADOA, "Fiscal History—LADOA," June 1956, LAWAA; Los Angeles City Council, Ordinance 61923, Los Angeles City Archives; and Stahl, "Los Angeles International Airport," pp. 33, 76–77.

56. Young to De Silva, February 4, 1949, LAWAA.

57. Mayor Bowron to Los Angeles City Council, January 13, 1947, LAWAA; Friedman, "Fear of Flying," p. 37; Moore interview; Moran, *LAIA*, pp. 43, 48.

58. Norris Poulson, "Who Ever Would Have Dreamed?" 1966, UCLA Oral History Program, pp. 203–4, 302–3.

59. Klatchko, "Los Angeles International Airport," pp. 9–10; "LADOA Historical Review," May 1995, p. 8, LAWAA; Stahl, "Los Angeles International Airport," pp. 55–64, 88–98; Moore interview.

60. Francis T. Fox oral history, July 20, 1977, Public History—Airport File, Department of Special Collections, UCLA Library.

61. LADOA, "Brief History of Los Angeles International Airport and the City's Regional Airport System," September 1990, LAWAA. Also see Steven P. Erie, Thomas P. Kim, and Gregory Freeman, *The LAX Master Plan: Facing the Challenges of Community, Environmental and Regional Airport Planning* (Los Angeles: Southern California Studies Center, University of Southern California, 1999), p. 10.

62. Information available at www.lawa.org.

63. Peggy G. Hereford, LADOA Director of Public Relations, "For Immediate Release," n.d.; LADOA, "Statement of Policy," May 20, 1964; Francis T. Fox, "Statement for the Highway and Transportation Joint Assembly and Senate Committees," n.d.; all in LAWAA.

64. Hereford, "For Immediate Release"; LADOA, *What About Tomorrow? Let's Face It Today!: Master Plan Development* (Los Angeles: LADOA, 1967); LADOA, "Land Acquisition Summary, Los Angeles International Airport," January 24, 1989, LAWAA; and Fox oral history.

65. Fox oral history; Peggy Hereford, former LADOA Director of Public and Community Relations, oral history, April 14, 1977, Public History—Airport File, Department of Special Collections, UCLA Library.

66. LADOA, *Annual Report, 1976*, p. 6, and LADOA, "Brief History," LAWAA.

67. "Comprehensive Report on the Master Plan of Airports for the Los Angeles Department of Airports County Regional Planning District," sponsored by the Aviation Committee, Los Angeles Chamber of Commerce, and the Los Angeles County Regional Planning Commission, 1940, p. 10, LAWAA.

68. LADOA, *Regional Airport Study Committee* (Los Angeles: LADOA, July 31, 1960); Stanford Research Institute, *Southern California Regional Airport Study* (South Pasadena, Calif.: Stanford Research Institute, 1964); "A New Regional Airport Authority?" *Town Hall Reporter* (July 1984); LADOA, *What About Tomorrow?*, p. 3.

69. Fox oral history.

70. LADOA, "Board of Airport Commissioners Resolution No. 4168"; LADOA, *Annual Report, 1967*, p. 12; LADOA, "Fact Sheet: Palmdale Regional Airport," n.d., all in LAWAA; Moore interview.

71. LADOA, "Fact Sheet"; Moore interview.

72. LADOA, *Study of a Proposal to Establish a Regional Airport Authority* (Los Angeles: LADOA, 1976); LADOA, *Annual Report, 1976*, p. 5.

73. William E. Pereira to Clifton Moore, April 7, 1976, LAWAA, emphasis in original.

74. Moore interview.

75. Ibid.

76. Bradley interview.

77. LADOA, *Annual Report, 1976*, p. 12; Wilbur Smith Associates, *The Economic Impact of Los Angeles International Airport* (Los Angeles: Wilbur Smith Associates, March 1992), pp. 1–6.

78. Information available at www.lawa.org.

79. L. K. Caldwell, "Implementing NEPA: A Non-technical Political Task," in Ray Clark and Larry Canter, eds., *Environmental Policy and NEPA: Past, Present, and Future* (Boca Raton, Fla.: St. Lucie Press, 1997), pp. 25–50. Also see Otis Graham Jr., ed., *Environmental Politics and Policy: 1960s–1990s* (University Park: Pennsylvania State University Press, 2000); and Robert B. Olshansky, "The California Environmental Quality Act and Local Planning," *Journal of the American Planning Association* 62:3 (Summer 1996), pp. 313–30.

80. National Environmental Policy Act (1970), Section 1505.2; and K. S. Weiner, "Basic Purposes and Policies of the NEPA Regulations," in Ray Clark and Larry Canter, eds., *Environmental Policy and NEPA: Past, Present, and Future* (Boca Raton, Fla.: St. Lucie Press, 1997), p. 61.

81. W. M. Cohen and M. D. Miller, "Highlights of NEPA in the Courts," in Ray Clark and Larry Canter, eds., *Environmental Policy and NEPA: Past, Present, and Future* (Boca Raton, Fla.: St. Lucie Press, 1997), pp. 181–92; John A. Ferejohn, "The Structure of Agency Decision Processes," in Mathew D. McCubbins and Terry Sullivan, eds., *Congress: Structure and Policy* (Cambridge: Cambridge University Press, 1987), pp. 441–61.

82. William Fulton, "The Environmental Push and Pull," *California Lawyer* 5:3 (March 1985), p. 51; also John D. Landis et al., *Fixing CEQA: Options and Opportunities for Reforming the California Environmental Quality Act* (Berkeley: California Policy Seminar, 1995), pp. 17, 29; and Debra M. Van Alstyne, "Environmental Decision-Making Under CEQA: A Quest for Uniformity," *UCLA Law Review* 24:4 (1977), pp. 838–76.

83. Landis et al., *Fixing CEQA*, p. 3; William A. Fischel, *Regulatory Takings* (Cambridge, Mass.: Harvard University Press, 1995), pp. 246–48; Olshansky, "California Environmental Quality Act," p. 315. Also see Robert B. Olshansky, "Evaluation of the California Environmental Quality Act," *Environmental Management* 20:1 (January/February 1996), pp. 11–23; and R. Catalano and R. Reich, "Local-Government Law and EIR—California Experience," *Urban Lawyer* 9:1 (1997), pp. 195–206.

84. *Keith v. Volpe*, 352 F. Supp. 1324 (1972); and Bill Kisliuk, "Appeals Court Gives Colleague Cold Shoulder," *Recorder*, July 15, 1997.

85. 1990 Amendment to the Clean Air Act, Title I, Section 103; also see the South Coast Air Quality Management District's website: www.aqmd.gov.

86. California Coastal Act, Chapter 4, Article 3, Section 30330, and California Coastal Commission website, www.coastal.ca.gov.

87. See Fred J. Silva and Elisa Barbour, *The State-Local Fiscal Relationship in California: A Changing Balance of Power* (San Francisco: Public Policy Institute of

California, 1999); Frank Levy, "On Understanding Proposition 13," *Public Interest 56* (Summer 1979).

88. Jeffrey Chapman, *The Continuing Redistribution of Fiscal Stress: The Long Run Consequences of Proposition 13* (Cambridge, Mass.: Lincoln Institute of Land Policy, 1998), pp. 20–21.

89. Gregory D. Saxton, Christopher W. Hoene, and Steven P. Erie, "Fiscal Constraints and the Loss of Home Rule: The Long-Term Impacts of California's Post-Proposition 13 Fiscal Regime," *American Review of Public Administration* 32:4 (December 2002), pp. 423–54; Jack Citron and Frank Levy, "From 13 to 4 and Beyond: The Political Meaning of the Ongoing Tax Revolt in California," in F. Kaufman and K. Rosen, eds., *The Property Tax Revolt* (Cambridge, Mass.: Ballinger, 1981); Silva and Barbour, *State-Local Fiscal Relationship*, p. 32; Chapman, *Local Government Fiscal Autonomy*, p. 29.

90. David Lyon, *From Home Rule to Fiscal Rule in California* (San Francisco: Public Policy Institute of California, 2000).

91. See Jon Sonstelie and Peter Richardson, eds., *School Finance and California's Master Plan for Education* (San Francisco: Public Policy Institute of California, 2001); and Michael A. Shires, *Patterns in California Government Revenues Since Proposition 13* (San Francisco: Public Policy Institute of California, 1999), p. 8.

92. Keith Comrie, Los Angeles City Administrative Officer, "Restoration of Home Rule Protection for Local Government" (Office of the City Administrative Officer, Los Angeles), October 29, 1993; Paul G. Lewis and Elisa Barbour, *California Cities and the Local Sales Tax* (San Francisco: Public Policy Institute of California, 1999), pp. 3–8; Silva and Barbour, *State-Local Fiscal Relationship*, p. 47; Shires, *Patterns in California Government Revenues*.

Chapter Five

1. Ezunial Burts, "Remarks," *Port Governance Roundtable* (Washington, D.C.: Marine Board, National Research Council, November 10, 1992), pp. 9–11.

2. Los Angeles Area Chamber of Commerce, *Economic Impact of the U.S. Environmental Protection Agency's Federal Implementation Plan on the South Coast Air Basin* (Los Angeles: Los Angeles Area Chamber of Commerce, August 29, 1994), pp. ii, 3.

3. Dan Weikel, "Key Issue in Harbor Area Is Secession from City," *Los Angeles Times*, April 2, 2001, p. B1.

4. Stephen Cohen, "L.A. Is the Hole in the Bucket," *Los Angeles Times*, March 7, 1993, p. M1.

5. Evelyn Iritani, "L.A. Surpasses New York City as Top Trade Hub in 1994," *Los Angeles Times*, March 17, 1995, pp. D1, D2. These rankings are based on port-of-entry merchandise trade.

6. U.S. Bureau of the Census, *U.S. Merchandise Trade: Selected Highlights*,

1989–2000, FT920 Series (Washington, D.C., 2001). Import figures are based on port of unlading (where goods actually are unloaded) rather than port of entry (where the customs papers are filed).

7. Los Angeles County Economic Development Corporation [LAEDC], *International Trade Trends & Impacts: The Los Angeles Region* (Los Angeles: LAEDC, May 2001), Table 19, p. 42. The LAEDC estimates direct international-trade employment on the basis of allocated shares of communications, transportation, wholesale-trade, financial-services, and professional-services employment.

8. Jim Newton, "Major Economic Projects Could Define the L.A. of 21st Century," *Los Angeles Times*, December 14, 1997, p. A1 (Riordan quote).

9. Jean Merl, "City Reliance on Profitable Departments Threatened," *Los Angeles Times*, March 25, 1996, pp. B1, B3; Steven P. Erie, "Balancing a Budget at the Expense of L.A.'s Future," *Los Angeles Times*, May 23, 1993, pp. M1, M6; Steven P. Erie, "A Budget That Pays Today's Bills with L.A.'s Future Growth," *Los Angeles Times*, May 19, 1996, p. M6.

10. Wharton Econometric Forecasting Associates–Manalytics, *San Pedro Bay Cargo Forecasting Project 2020* (Bala Cynwyd, Pa.: Wharton Econometric Forecasting Associates–Manalytics, 1987).

11. WorldPort LA, *The 2020 Program* (Los Angeles: Port of Los Angeles, 1991); San Pedro Bay Ports of Los Angeles and Long Beach, *2020 OFI [Operations, Facilities and Infrastructure] Study Summary* (Oakland, Calif.: Vickerman, Zachary, Miller, April 1988), pp. 1–15.

12. "Port of Long Beach: A Vision and Capital Plan for 2020," *Metro Investment Report* II:3 (August 1994), p. 9; Geraldine Knatz interview, 1994.

13. Gordon Palmer interview, 1995; Michael Denning and David J. Olson, "Comparative Analysis of West Coast Ports" (University of Washington), 1988, p. 132.

14. Port of Long Beach, *Facilities Master Plan* (Long Beach, Calif.: Port of Long Beach, January 1993), pp. 1–5, 9.

15. Knatz interview; Palmer interview; Richard Aschieris interview, 1995.

16. Palmer interview.

17. Quoted in "Port of Long Beach," p. 12.

18. Port of Long Beach, *Facilities Master Plan*, pp. 10–11; Palmer interview; Knatz interview; "Port of Long Beach," p. 9.

19. Richard A. Serrano, "Long Beach Yard, 32 Other Bases Targeted to Close," *Los Angeles Times*, March 1, 1995, pp. A1, A16; James Flanigan, "A Port in a Storm: Will Long Beach Turn the Corner?" *Los Angeles Times*, April 12, 1995, pp. D1, D13; "Council Decides on Port Plan for Long Beach Shipyard," *Los Angeles Times*, July 4, 1996, p. B4; Port of Long Beach, *Facilities Master Plan*, pp. 10–11.

20. Knatz quoted in "Port of Long Beach," pp. 1, 9; Port of Long Beach, *1994 Annual Report* (Long Beach, Calif.: Port of Long Beach, 1994), p. 17; Palmer interview.

21. "Port of Long Beach," p. 9; Palmer interview; Knatz interview.

22. WorldPort LA, *2020 Program*; "A New Perspective on WorldPort LA's Plans & Priorities," *Metro Investment Report* II:5 (October 1994), pp. 1, 11–12, 15, 17; Ezunial Burts interview, 1994; Dick Wittkop (former 2020 program officer) interview, 1995.

23. Port of Los Angeles, *Port Master Plan Amendment Piers 300/400: 1993 Update* (Los Angeles: Port of Los Angeles, November 1993).

24. Steven P. Erie, *International Trade and Job Creation in Southern California: Facilitating Los Angeles/Long Beach Port, Rail, and Airport Development* (Berkeley: California Policy Seminar, 1996), pp. 11–33; Denning and Olson, "Comparative Analysis," p. 143; "Port of Long Beach," p. 18.

25. Jim Preusch interview, 1995; Aschieris interview; Palmer interview.

26. Aschieris interview.

27. Preusch interview; John Kruse interview, 1995.

28. Kruse interview; U.S. Maritime Administration, *Public Port Financing in the United States* (Washington, D.C.: U.S. Department of Transportation, 1994), p. 80.

29. Preusch interview; "Port of Long Beach," p. 16.

30. Burts, "Remarks," pp. 11–12.

31. Aschieris interview; David Cobb interview, 1994.

32. Preusch interview.

33. Mayor's Special Advisory Committee on Fiscal Administration, *Final Report* (Los Angeles: City of Los Angeles, February 24, 1994), p. 12.

34. Moody's Investors Service, *Moody's Municipal Credit Report: Los Angeles Harbor Department (Port of Los Angeles), California* (n.p.: Moody's Investors Service, January 11, 1995), pp. 3, 10.

35. Ernst & Young, "City of Los Angeles Harbor Nexus Study," June 1995; David M. Griffith & Associates, "City of Los Angeles: Costs of City Services to the Harbor Department," December 15, 1994; Jeff Leeds and John Cox, "L.A. Harbor Panel Votes to Pay City $80 Million in Fees," *Los Angeles Times*, August 25, 1995, p. B3.

36. Moody's Investors Service, *Moody's Municipal Credit Report: Los Angeles Harbor Department*, pp. 3, 10.

37. Bill Mongelluzzo, "Transfer of Funds Threatens Ports' Ratings," *Journal of Commerce*, August 24, 1995, p. 1B. Approximately 50 percent of the cargo passing through the Southern California ports was destined for the East and could go through competing West Coast ports. The Steamship Association of Southern California, which represents the carriers using the ports, sharply criticized the Nexus study's methodology and findings. Leeds and Cox, "L.A. Harbor Panel Votes," p. B3.

38. Nancy A. Saggese, Deputy Attorney General, "Memorandum to State Lands Commission re Los Angeles Harbor Department Nexus Study," August 11, 1995, pp. 1–5.

39. Robert C. Hight, Executive Officer, State Lands Commission, to Board of Harbor Commissioners, Port of Los Angeles, re Port of Los Angeles/Nexus Study,

August 15, 1995; State Lands Commission to Los Angeles City Council and Board of Harbor Commissioners, Port of Los Angeles, November 3, 1995; Roderick E. Walston, Chief Assistant Attorney General, to Michael Keeley, Chief Operating Officer to Mayor Richard Riordan, Re: Tidelands Trust Revenues, February 15, 1996; Roderick E. Walston to James Hahn, City Attorney, City of Los Angeles, March 15, 1996.

40. Dan Weikel, "City to Repay $62 Million to Port of L.A.," *Los Angeles Times*, January 20, 2001, pp. B1, B7.

41. "Port of Long Beach," pp. 12, 16; Palmer interview.

42. Mongelluzzo, "Transfer of Funds Threatens Ports' Ratings," p. 1B; Palmer interview. Under the aquarium agreement, the city would issue $100 million in revenue bonds to be paid back by project revenues, the city's transient-occupancy tax, and if a shortfall existed, the city's Tidelands Trust fund.

43. Knatz interview; Moody's Investors Service, *Moody's Municipal Credit Report: Long Beach (Port of Long Beach), California* (n.p.: Moody's Investors Service, September 27, 1993), p. 8.

44. Burts, "Remarks," p. 12.

45. U.S. Environmental Protection Agency, Region IX, *Federal Implementation Plans in California: 1994 Notice of Proposed Rulemaking* (Washington, D.C., 1994); James Flanigan, "Deals in Smoke-Filled Rooms Could Help Clear the Region's Air," *Los Angeles Times*, November 11, 1994, pp. D1, D7.

46. U.S. Environmental Protection Agency, "Proposed Rules," *Federal Register* 59:86 (May 5, 1994), pp. 23377–84.

47. "Port of Long Beach," p. 16.

48. Port of Los Angeles and Port of Long Beach, *Control of Ship Emissions in the South Coast Air Basin: Assessment of the Proposed Federal Implementation Plan Ship Emission Fee Program* (Los Angeles and Long Beach: Port of Los Angeles and Port of Long Beach, August 1994), p. ES-4; Los Angeles Area Chamber of Commerce, *Economic Impact of the U.S. Environmental Protection Agency's Federal Implementation Plan*, p. ii; Marla Cone, "Anti-Smog Plan Would Hobble Transit and Shipping, Industries Say," *Los Angeles Times*, July 19, 1994, pp. A3, A10; Marla Cone, "Smog Plan Would Harm Economy, L.A. Chamber Says," *Los Angeles Times*, August 30, 1994, pp. A3, A20.

49. Marla Cone, "Mayor Asks Delay on Smog Rules," *Los Angeles Times*, August 10, 1994, pp. A1, A24; Marla Cone, "L.A. Gains Concession on Anti-Smog Rules," *Los Angeles Times*, September 7, 1994, pp. A3, A16; Marla Cone, "Smog Agency Bows to L.A., Defers Some Stricter Limits," *Los Angeles Times*, September 10, 1994, pp. A1, A20; Marla Cone, "State Scales Back Clean-Air Plan in Bow to Oil, Trucking Industries," *Los Angeles Times*, November 10, 1994, p. A16.

50. Marla Cone, "EPA Gives State 2-Year Reprieve on Smog Rules," *Los Angeles Times*, January 13, 1995, pp. A1, A29; Faye Fiore, "EPA Bends on State Anti-Smog Plan," *Los Angeles Times*, February 3, 1995, p. A3; Marla Cone, "U.S. Unveils Scaled-Back Clean-Air Plan," *Los Angeles Times*, February 15, 1995, pp. A3, A18; Faye Fiore, "Clinton Expected to OK Smog Exemption," *Los Angeles Times*,

April 8, 1995, p. A18; Donald Rice (former director of environmental management, Port of Los Angeles) interview, 1994.

51. "Good-Looking Deal for Wetlands 'Gem,'" *Los Angeles Times*, July 11, 1995, p. B8.

52. Palmer interview.

53. Aschieris interview.

54. Larry Simon, Coastal Commission Ports Coordinator, to Sid Robinson, Director of Planning and Research, Port of Los Angeles, February 14, 1991, in Port of Los Angeles, *Port Master Plan Amendment Piers 300/400* (Los Angeles: Port of Los Angeles, November 1992); Greg Krikorian, "Harbor Expansion Plans Face Sea of Opposition," *Los Angeles Times*, January 4, 1991, p. B4.

55. Port of Los Angeles, *Port Master Plan Amendment Piers 300/400: 1993 Update*; U.S. Army Corps of Engineers and Los Angeles Harbor Department, *Final Environmental Impact Statement/Environmental Impact Report Deep Draft Navigation Improvements, Los Angeles and Long Beach Harbors, San Pedro Bay, California* (Los Angeles: U.S. Army Corps of Engineers and Los Angeles Harbor Department, September 1992); Greg Krikorian, "Coastal Panel Staff Urges Approval of Dredging Plan," *Los Angeles Times*, October 14, 1992, p. B7.

56. Knatz interview.

57. Regarding the Naval Station reuse controversy, see Jeff Leeds, "Coastal Commission Oks Permit for Long Beach Port Terminal," *Los Angeles Times*, January 9, 1997, p. B3; Jeff Leeds, "Long Beach Base Conversion Draws Protest," *Los Angeles Times*, March 13, 1997, pp. B1, B3; Jeff Leeds, "Long Beach Port Plan Faces Rising Tide of Criticism," *Los Angeles Times*, March 24, 1997, pp. B1, B3; and Knatz interview.

58. Kevin F. McCarthy, Steven P. Erie, Robert E. Reichardt, and James W. Ingram III, *Meeting the Challenge of Charter Reform* (Santa Monica, Calif.: RAND, 1998).

59. Robert W. Poole, Jr., "Reforming Municipal Enterprises: Turning LA's Proprietary Departments into World-Class Competitors" (typescript of speech to Elected L.A. Charter Reform Commission, Reason Public Policy Institute, Los Angeles), May 6, 1998, esp. p. 2.

60. In a March 23, 1998, letter to the Elected L.A. Charter Reform Commission, Larry Keller, executive director of the Port of Los Angeles, argued that "the length of time it takes for approval of Harbor Department contracts and leases is a Charter imposed competitive barrier faced by the department. A recent comparative study of west coast ports shows that it takes approximately 180 days to receive final approval in Los Angeles versus 45 to 60 days in other jurisdictions. The Charter . . . should be designed to enable the port to be more competitive with other ports, in particular, the Port of Long Beach." Also, Port of Los Angeles, *1996 West Coast International Trade Market Share Analysis* (Los Angeles: Planning & Research Division, Port of Los Angeles, 1997), pp. 7–8 and fact sheets.

61. Bill Stein, reply to "Los Angeles Elected Charter Reform Commission, Questionnaire re: Contracts, Leases Franchises, Procurements," September 22,

1998. Also see Jonathon P. "Pat" Nave to Elected L.A. Charter Reform Commission, February 17, 1998, with attachments. Nave was an assistant city attorney for the Harbor Department who advised the commission during its work.

62. David Freeman, "Streamlining DWP Governance," May 6, 1998, and David Freeman, "Recommendation of the General Manager of the Los Angeles Department of Water and Power to the Charter Commissions," September 4, 1998; Jack Driscoll, presentation to the joint charter committees, May 6, 1998.

63. Ed Farrell, who served as chief counsel for the Harbor Department from 1966 to 1971 (and held similar positions with the Department of Airports and DWP), argued that because the harbor and airports departments disproportionately affect a single area of the city, councilmembers from the area ought to be more involved than they are in the "process by which projects are developed and implemented" by the department. Edward C. Farrell, "Memorandum to Committee on Improving Financial and Managerial Accountability, Los Angeles Elected [sic] Reform Committee," March 16, 1998.

64. James W. Ingram III, "L.A.'s Long Platonic Affair with Neighborhood Councils," *Los Angeles Times*, November 2, 1997, p. M6.

65. Jean Merl, "Though Overshadowed by the Valley's Breakaway Effort, a Drive by San Pedro and Wilmington to Leave Los Angeles Could Lead to a Fight over Control of the Port," *Los Angeles Times*, May 31, 1999, p. B1; Gordon Smith, "San Pedro Blues," *San Diego Union-Tribune*, December 3, 2000, pp. C1, C4.

66. Phil Willon, "Valley Secession Effort's Roots Go Back to the '70s," *Los Angeles Times*, Valley Edition, August 16, 1998, p. A1.

67. Quoted in ibid. The legislation (AB 62) applied generally throughout the state of California and was not specifically tailored to the needs of the San Fernando Valley or other communities wanting to break away from L.A. See Nancy Hill-Holtzman, "Governor Signs Secession Bill," *Los Angeles Times*, Valley Edition, October 13, 1997, p. A1; Hugo Martin, "Money, Message Keys for Valley Secession Group," *Los Angeles Times*, February 10, 1998, p. A1.

68. Eric Malnic and Miguel Bustillo, "Secession Backers Get Necessary Signatures," *Los Angeles Times*, July 29, 1999, p. B1. See also Merl, "Though Overshadowed by the Valley's Breakaway Effort."

69. Malnic and Bustillo, "Secession Backers Get Necessary Signatures," p. B1; Smith, "San Pedro Blues."

70. Dan Weikel, "Riordan Seeks to Soften Harbor Area Secession Sentiment," *Los Angeles Times*, December 15, 2000, p. B3.

71. Patrick McGreevy, "New Slant on Harbor Area Bottom Line," *Los Angeles Times*, June 10, 2001, p. B1; Patrick McGreevy, "Harbor Cityhood Found Infeasible," *Los Angeles Times*, April 26, 2001, pp. B1, B9.

72. Deborah Belgum, "A Return to an Independent Wilmington," *Los Angeles Times*, December 15, 1997, pp. B1, B6.

73. Patrick McGreevy, "DWP Tangle Could Impede Secession of Valley, Harbor," *Los Angeles Times*, August 24, 2000, p. B3.

74. Martin, "Money, Message Keys for Valley Secession Group," p. A1.

75. Steven P. Erie and Edward Rodriguez, *Facing the Challenges of Expanding Southern California's Global Gateways* (Los Angeles: Pacific Council on International Policy, 2000), pp. 9–13; Evelyn Iritani, "Business Surges at L.A. Ports," *Los Angeles Times*, January 22, 1997, p. D1.

76. Assembly Transportation Committee Hearing, Los Angeles, California, December 12, 1997; Jeff Leeds, "Long Beach, L.A. Ports Face Crisis in Labor Dispute," *Los Angeles Times*, May 8, 1996, pp. A1, A11; James Flanigan, "Striking Costs," *Los Angeles Times*, July 16, 1997, pp. D1, D11; Richard Simon and Jim Newton, "Rail Backlog Strands Cargo at L.A.–Area Ports," *Los Angeles Times*, November 4, 1997, pp. A1, A20; Evelyn Iritani, "Ports Must Chart New Course in '98," *Los Angeles Times*, December 28, 1997, pp. D1, D4.

Chapter Six

1. Jane Harman, "Alameda Corridor a Funding Priority for Delegation," *Metro Investment Report* I:8 (January 1994), pp. 1, 10.

2. John Johnson interview, 1994.

3. San Diego Dialogue, *The Global Engagement of San Diego/Baja California: Final Report* (San Diego: San Diego Dialogue, November 2000), p. 12.

4. Alameda Corridor–East Construction Authority [ACECA] et al., *Alameda Corridor–East Trade Corridor Plan: Draft Report* (Irwindale, Calif.: ACECA, March 2001), Table 3 (p. 13), Table 4 (p. 16), p. 35; Los Angeles County Metropolitan Transportation Authority [LACMTA], *Southern California Freight Management Case Study* (Los Angeles: LACMTA, February 2002), pp. 6–7. Also see Southern California Association of Governments [SCAG], *2001 Regional Transportation Plan* (Los Angeles: SCAG, April 2001), p. 91. Year 2020 regional-trade, container, and train forecasts furnished by the Los Angeles County Economic Development Corporation.

5. San Diego Association of Governments [SANDAG], *State Route 94 Corridor Tecate Port of Entry: Trade and Truck Traffic* (San Diego: SANDAG, July 1997), Table 14; Caltrans District 11, *California Border Briefing* (San Diego: Caltrans District 11, July 1999); SCAG, *The NAFTA Transportation Impacts in SCAG Region Study: Final Report* (Los Angeles: SCAG, July 1996), fig. 21, p. 42, and fig. 22, p. 43.

6. LACMTA, *Southern California Freight Management Case Study*, pp. 14–25.

7. Quoted in Louis Sahagun, "Politicians Toot Horns at Rail Corridor Opening," *Los Angeles Times*, April 13, 2001, p. B3.

8. Daniel Machalaba, "Cargo Hold: As U.S. Seaports Get Busier, Weak Point Is a Surprise: Railroads," *Wall Street Journal*, September 9, 1996, pp. A1, A10; Daniel Machalaba, "A Long Haul: America's Railroads Struggle to Recapture Their Former Glory," *Wall Street Journal*, December 5, 1997, pp. A1, A6.

9. Steven P. Erie, *International Trade and Job Creation in Southern California:*

Facilitating Los Angeles/Long Beach Port, Rail, and Airport Development (Berkeley: California Policy Seminar, 1996), pp. 35–52; Machalaba, "Cargo Hold."

10. Alameda Corridor Transportation Authority [ACTA], *The Alameda Corridor: A National Priority* (Huntington Park, Calif.: ACTA, February 1993).

11. Ibid., pp. 1–2; Gill Hicks (then-ACTA general manager) interview, 1994.

12. Myra L. Frank & Associates et al., *Alameda Corridor Draft Environmental Impact Report*, August 1992, p. 1-3.

13. Ibid., pp. 1-4, 1-5.

14. Transportation Marketing Services, *Consolidated Rail Corridor Strategic Plan*, November 1988.

15. Dean Murphy, "Long Beach, Los Angeles Agree to Form Authority to Oversee Alameda Corridor," *Los Angeles Times*, July 23, 1989, pt. 9, p. 1; ACTA, "Written Testimony Prepared for House Subcommittee on Surface Transportation" March 15, 1994, p. 4; Janet Rea-Dupree, "Port-to-L.A. Rail Plans Approved," *Los Angeles Times*, January 24, 1993, p. J4; "An Alameda Corridor Reality Check with L.A. Harbor's Jon Thomas," *Metro Investment Report* IV:10 (March 1997), pp. 1, 16–18.

16. ACTA, "Written Testimony Prepared for the House Subcommittee on Surface Transportation," p. 6; Dan Weikel, "Alameda Corridor Project to Stop Releasing Ground Water," *Los Angeles Times*, December 11, 1999, p. B3; Joshua Lowe, "Decision on Corridor Put Off," *Long Beach Press-Telegram*, December 10, 1999, p. A13; "Alameda Corridor Project Updated: Jim Hankla's Candid Assessment," *Metro Investment Report* VII:9 (February 2000), pp. 8–9, 15.

17. Jerry B. Epstein, "A Robbery from Downtown to the Sea," *Los Angeles Times*, April 28, 1993, p. B7; Nora Zamichow, "Talks End on Rails to Link Ports, L.A.," *Los Angeles Times*, September 2, 1993, p. B1. A key negotiating uncertainty involved what the railroad owned in fee simple versus surface easements.

18. "Good Deal Would Benefit Everybody: Unclogging the Famed Alameda Corridor," *Los Angeles Times*, September 11, 1993, p. B7; Greg Krikorian, "Rail Projects Take Twists and Turns," *Los Angeles Times*, October 8, 1993, p. B3; Greg Krikorian, "Ports Agree to Buy Rights of Way for Alameda Corridor," *Los Angeles Times*, December 10, 1993, p. B3.

19. Bill Boyarsky, "Union Pacific's Stance Could Derail Corridor," *Los Angeles Times*, February 6, 1994, p. B1; "Officials, Union Pacific OK Pact on Alameda Corridor," *Los Angeles Times*, August 6, 1994, p. B2.

20. "Alameda Corridor Project Director Expands on the Challenge and Potential," *Metro Investment Report* II:6 (November 1994), pp. 9, 12.

21. ACTA, "Alameda Corridor Application for Federal Funds," 1993, pp. 2–4, 6, 8; ACTA, *The Alameda Corridor: Linking the United States to the World* (Huntington Park, Calif.: ACTA, September 1995), p. 5; LACMTA, "Executive Summary: The Transportation Plan for Los Angeles County," March 1995, p. 5; Hicks interview; and Steve Gleason (former manager of transportation planning, Port of Long Beach) interview, 1994.

22. "Alameda Corridor: On Track? Or Sidetracked by Funding Gap?" *Metro Investment Report* II:10 (March 1995), p. 11.

23. California Transportation Commission [CTC], *1993 Annual Report to California Legislature* (Sacramento, Calif.: CTC, December 1993), vol. 1, p. iv; Steve Dillenbeck, Port of Long Beach Executive Director, "Remarks," in *Hearings of the Assembly Task Force on the Alameda Corridor Project*, May 19, 1995; CTC, *1994 Annual Report to California Legislature* (Sacramento, Calif.: CTC, December 1994), vol. 1, p. i. See also William Fulton and Morris Newman, "State Transportation Fund Is Stalled," *San Diego Union-Tribune*, August 16, 1994, p. B7.

24. Mary Berglund (then-chairperson, CTC) interview, 1995.

25. "Prop. 185: Too Ambitious, Too Costly," *Los Angeles Times*, October 17, 1994, p. B8; James O. Goldsborough, "Peace Makes War on the State's Problems," *San Diego Union-Tribune*, August 4, 1994, p. B9.

26. ACTA, *The National Economic Significance of the Alameda Corridor* (Huntington Park, Calif.: ACTA, February 1994), pp. 4–5. For a methodological critique of the project's economic-impact analysis, see Erie, *International Trade and Job Creation in Southern California*, pp. 37–41. For an elaboration of the federal-funding strategy, see "Alameda Corridor: On Track?" p. 11.

27. Quoted in "Alameda Corridor: On Track?" p. 10.

28. Assemblywoman Martha Escutia, "Remarks," in *Hearings of the Assembly Task Force on the Alameda Corridor Project*, May 19, 1995; "Alameda Corridor Project Director Expands," pp. 12, 16; Glenn F. Bunting, "Officials Lobby for Port-to-L.A. Transit Corridor," *Los Angeles Times*, March 16, 1994, p. B3.

29. "Alameda Corridor Project Director Expands," p. 9; ACTA, "Port Access Demonstration Projects and the Use of Proposition 116 Funds," August 1, 1994.

30. Strategic Transportation Policy Group [STPG], "Update on Federal and State Advocacy Program," July 12, 1995, pp. 1–4; J. Michael Kennedy, "U.S. Funds for Alameda Corridor in Jeopardy," *Los Angeles Times*, March 31, 1995, pp. B1, B4; J. Michael Kennedy, "Congress Restores Alameda Corridor Funds," *Los Angeles Times*, April 6, 1995, p. B3.

31. STPG, "Update," p. 2; STPG, "Legislative Activities in Congress Relating to the Alameda Corridor Project," September 11, 1995, pp. 1–2.

32. STPG, "Update," p. 2; "Alameda Corridor Project Director Expands," p. 9; Jean Merl and James Bornemeier, "Clinton to Seek Loan for L.A. Rail Corridor," *Los Angeles Times*, March 19, 1996, pp. A1, A12; James Flanigan, "Diverse Interests on Track in Corridor," *Los Angeles Times*, March 20, 1996, pp. D1, D10; Jeff Leeds and James Bornemeier, "Alameda Corridor Gets Key Vote," *Los Angeles Times*, June 7, 1996, pp. B1, B6; Hicks interview. The idea for a federal loan (rather than a grant) reportedly first came from a mid-level staff person in Mayor Riordan's office.

33. Carmen Perez, President, Board of Harbor Commissioners, Port of Long Beach, and Fred Hemple, California Division Administrator, Federal Highway Administration, "Remarks," in *Hearings of the Assembly Task Force on the Alameda*

Corridor Project, May 19, 1995; Josh Meyer and Richard Simon, "Divided MTA Board Decides to Shift $50 Million to County," *Los Angeles Times*, September 8, 1995, pp. B1, B3; Jeffrey L. Rabin and Max Vanzi, "Legislature Rejects Aid Bills; County Crisis Worsens," *Los Angeles Times*, September 17, 1995, pp. A1, A21; "Sup'r Yvonne Burke's Perspective On: LACMTA, Budget, Alameda Corridor," *Metro Investment Report* IV:6 (November 1996), pp. 1, 15–17; U.S. General Accounting Office [GAO], *Surface Infrastructure: Costs, Financing and Schedules for Large-Dollar Transportation Projects* (Washington, D.C.: GAO, February 12, 1998), pp. 73–86; Dan Weikel, "Federal Study Faults Alameda Corridor Plan," *Los Angeles Times*, March 3, 1998, pp. A1, A15.

34. ACTA, *Alameda Corridor: A Project of National Significance* (Carson, Calif.: ACTA, October 2000), p. 4; "An Alameda Corridor Update: Project Moves into Construction Phase," *Metro Investment Report* VI:11 (April 1999), pp. 1, 12–13.

35. Ezunial Burts interview, 1994.

36. Reginald Tabor interview, 1994.

37. Ibid., and Johnson interview.

38. Hicks interview; ACTA Governing Board minutes (Huntington Park, Calif.), January 1993–December 1994.

39. Hicks interview; Planning Center, *Southeast Los Angeles County Sub-region Regional Comprehensive Plan Program: Subregional Strategy* (Los Angeles: Planning Center, January 1994).

40. Escutia, "Remarks"; Geraldine Knatz interview, 1994; and Hicks interview.

41. Kofi Sefa-Boakye, "A Test for Environmental Justice," *Los Angeles Times*, August 21, 1995, p. B9; David L. Hauser, "Alameda Rail Corridor Impact," *Los Angeles Times*, August 27, 1995, p. B8.

42. "Port Withdraws from Alameda Corridor Project," *Los Angeles Times*, August 13, 1994, p. B2; "Alameda Corridor Project Director Expands," pp. 16–17; Tabor interview; Johnson interview; and Burke Roche (then-member, ACTA Governing Board, and senior deputy to Los Angeles County Supervisor Yvonne Braithwaite Burke) interview, 1994.

43. Roche interview.

44. Bud Lembke, "Steering New L.A. to Harbor Rail Line Along Alameda St. Is a Lot Like Herding Cats," *California Corridors* 1:4 (April 28, 1995), pp. 1, 5; Knatz interview.

45. Johnson interview and Roche interview.

46. Hicks interview.

47. Tom Jackson (then-member of ACTA Governing Board and councilperson for the City of Huntington Park) interview, 1994; Michael Mitoma (then-member of ACTA Governing Board and mayor of the City of Carson) interview, 1994; Bill Boyarsky, "A Student of Back-Room Deals Hits Pay Dirt in Carson," *Los Angeles Times*, April 17, 1994, p. B1.

48. Stephen Gregory, "Business Roadblock?" *Los Angeles Times*, February 21,

1998, pp. D1, D3; Marla Dickerson, Lee Romney, and Vicki Torres, "Despite Wilson Order, Goals for Diversity Thrive Elsewhere," *Los Angeles Times*, March 13, 1998, pp. A1, A19; Dan Weikel, "Alameda Corridor Cities Demand Jobs for Residents," *Los Angeles Times*, March 8, 1998, p. B3.

49. "An Almost Secret Project That's Vital to L.A.'s Future," *Los Angeles Times*, September 6, 1997, p. B6; Richard Hollingsworth, Gateway Cities Partnership, "How Interdependent Are California's Urban & Rural Regions?" *Metro Investment Report* VIII:10 (October 2000), pp. 5, 16–17.

50. ACECA, *ACE: Gateway to America* (Irwindale, Calif.: ACECA, n.d.); ACECA et al., *Alameda Corridor–East Trade Corridor Plan*, p. 52; ACECA, *Alameda Corridor–East Project Funding Summary* (Irwindale, Calif.: ACECA, 2000); San Gabriel Valley Council of Governments, "San Gabriel Valley Grade Crossing Improvement Program: Summary of Key Findings," February 20, 1997; statement of the Honorable David Dreier, San Gabriel Valley Council of Governments, press conference, Pomona, California, February 28, 1997; Art Wong, "Add 60 Miles to Port-Rail Plan?" *Long Beach Press-Telegram*, September 27, 1997.

51. ACECA et al., *Alameda Corridor–East Trade Corridor Plan*, pp. 52–54.

52. Quoted in "Orange County Gateway's Rail Corridor Project Would Extend Alameda's Economic Benefits South," *Metro Investment Report* VIII:11 (December 2000), p. 14.

53. Ibid., pp. 4, 14, 15; BST Associates and L.A. County Economic Development Corporation, *OnTrac Trade Impact Study* (Placentia, Calif.: OnTrac JPA, 2002); Orange County Gateway, *Orange County Gateway Cost Benefit Analysis* (Placentia, Calif.: OnTrac JPA, September 1999); OnTrac, *Orange County Gateway: A Completely Grade-Separated Rail Corridor* (Placentia, Calif.: OnTrac JPA, 2000).

54. SCAG, *The Southwest Passage: A Strategic Proposal* (Los Angeles: SCAG, March 1997); SCAG, *Establish the Southwest Compact Region* (Los Angeles: SCAG, August 2000).

55. ACECA et al., *Alameda Corridor–East Trade Corridor Plan*, p. 56.

56. "Get It Done: An Eastern Rail Link Could Become a Reality," *San Diego Union-Tribune*, November 20, 1997; Dean Calbreath, "Hope for Rail Link to Plaster City Sidetracked," *San Diego Union-Tribune*, November 27, 1997, p. C2; San Diego Dialogue, *Improving Trade Infrastructure for a More Competitive Binational Region* (San Diego: San Diego Dialogue, June 1998), pp. 13–14. Regarding the project's economic feasibility, see SANDAG, *An Updated Market Study for the San Diego and Arizona Eastern (SD&AE) Railway* (San Diego: SANDAG, June 1999).

57. Meyer, Mohaddes Associates et al., *Port of Long Beach/Los Angeles Transportation Study: Executive Summary* (Anaheim, Calif.: Meyer Mohaddes Associates, June 2001).

58. U.S. Bureau of Transportation Statistics, *1996 National Transportation Statistics* (Washington, D.C.: U.S. Department of Transportation, 1996); SCAG,

CommunityLink 21 (Los Angeles: SCAG, 1998), p. 3/5; SCAG, *Interregional Goods Movement Study* (Los Angeles: SCAG, 1997).

59. SCAG, *CommunityLink 21*, Technical Appendix Part 1, pp. 181–89; SANDAG, *1994 Regional Transportation Plan* (San Diego: SANDAG, February 1994).

60. U.S. Commission to Promote Investment in America's Infrastructure, *Financing the Future* (Washington, D.C.: U.S. Department of Transportation, 1993); and Commission on Transportation Investment, *Final Report* (Sacramento, Calif.: Caltrans, January 1996). Also see CTC, *1997 Annual Report to California Legislature* (Sacramento, Calif.: CTC, December 10, 1997), vol. 1, pp. I-49 to I-56.

61. George Gray, *Impacts of the North American Free Trade Agreement in the Border Areas of the U.S. with Emphasis on the California Border with Mexico* (San Jose, Calif.: Mineta Transportation Institute, 1999), pp. 9–11; and Caltrans, *California Transportation Plan* (Sacramento, Calif.: Caltrans, December 1993), pp. 28–29.

62. SCAG, *CommunityLink 21*, pp. I-23, I-24, I-26.

63. Caltrans District 11, *California Border Briefing*; SANDAG, *2020 Regional Transportation Plan* (San Diego: SANDAG, April 2000), pp. 211–19.

64. Barton-Aschman & Associates, *The U.S.-Mexico Binational Transportation Planning and Programming Study, Task Reports 4 and 14* (Washington, D.C.: Federal Highway Administration, 1997), pp. 23–25, 38–40; SANDAG, *1994 Regional Transportation Plan*, p. 208.

65. Ken Sulzer (former executive director, SANDAG) interview, 2001; SANDAG, *1994 Regional Transportation Plan*, pp. 50–51, 55–61, 209.

66. SANDAG, *State Route 905: Freeway Needed to Otay Mesa Border Crossing* (San Diego: SANDAG, February 2001).

67. SANDAG, *State Route 125 South Tollway: New North-South Highway for International Border* (San Diego: SANDAG, January 2001).

68. SANDAG, *Rural Highway 94 Corridor Study* (San Diego: SANDAG, June 1999); SANDAG, *Feasibility of Opening an International Border Crossing at Jacumba-Jacumbé* (San Diego: SANDAG, June 2000).

69. San Diego Dialogue, *Planning for Prosperity in the San Diego/Baja California Region* (San Diego: San Diego Dialogue, 1993), pp. 30–31; Chris Kraul, "From Border City to Boom Town (No, Not Tijuana)," *Los Angeles Times*, October 5, 1997, p. D1; Rick Wartzman, "For New Port of Entry, Opening Is the Easy Part," *Wall Street Journal*, November 13, 1996, p. CA2; "Neglected Arteries," *San Diego Union-Tribune*, October 12, 1997, p. G2; Caltrans, *SR 7 Project Study Report* (Sacramento: Caltrans, 1997), pp. 1–4.

70. SANDAG, *Border Area Transportation: The Local, State, National and International Connection* (San Diego: SANDAG, November 1996), pp. 16–17; SANDAG, *Binational Coordination in the Southern California–Northern Baja California Region* (San Diego: SANDAG, March 2002); Steven P. Erie, *Toward a*

Trade Infrastructure Strategy for the San Diego/Tijuana Region (San Diego: San Diego Dialogue, 1999), pp. 19–24.

Chapter Seven

1. Los Angeles Department of Airports [LADOA], "LAX Unveils Its 21st Century Expansion Plan Options," *Metro Investment Report* IV:8 (January 1997), p. 11.

2. "By Default, L.A. Councilwoman Galanter Takes the LAX 'High Ground,'" *Metro Investment Report* VI:1 (June 1998), p. 17.

3. "Dan Garcia on What Candidates for Mayor of L.A. Should Be Discussing," *Metro Investment Report* VII:11 (April 2000), pp. 11, 12, emphasis in original.

4. Southern California Association of Governments [SCAG], *Regional Mobility Element: The Long Range Transportation Plan for the SCAG Region*, vol. 2 (Los Angeles: SCAG, June 1994), pp. 8-1 to 8-13; SCAG, *2001 Regional Transportation Plan* (Los Angeles: SCAG, April 2001), pp. 98–99.

5. SCAG, Economic Analysis Division, "RTP Input for JIT Manufacturing and the Region as a Trade Center" (draft memo), November 13, 1996, p. 4; Hamilton, Rabinovitz & Alschuler [HR&A], *Direct Economic Benefits of Expansion at LAX: Phase II-98 Cargo and Passenger Activity Growth to the Year 2015* (Los Angeles: HR&A, 1996); Steven P. Erie, John D. Kasarda, Andrew M. McKenzie, and Michael A. Molloy, *A New Orange County Airport at El Toro: Catalyst for High-Wage, High-Tech Development* (Irvine, Calif.: Orange County Business Council, 1999).

6. Jack Driscoll, "Airports Grapple with Growth and Environmental Demands," *Metro Investment Report* II:4 (September 1994), p. 10.

7. Jack Driscoll, "Will Master Plan Process Tame LAX's Unconstrained Demand?" *Planning Report* 9:7 (March 1996), p. 13; "Dan Garcia: Region's Needs Are Driving Airport Planning," *Metro Investment Report* V:11 (April 1998), pp. 1, 14, 15; Jack Driscoll, personal communication with author, 2001.

8. LADOA, "LAX Master Plan Aviation Activity Forecasts," January 1996; "Master Plan Facts," at www.laxmasterplan.org; HR&A, "Economic Benefits of Expansion at LAX: Phase II-98 Output and Job Benefits in the Year 2015," 1996; Dan Garcia, "LAX Master Planner Deposed," *Metro Investment Report* II:1 (June 1994), p. 4; Steven P. Erie, *International Trade and Job Creation in Southern California: Facilitating Los Angeles/Long Beach Port, Rail, and Airport Development* (Berkeley: California Policy Seminar, 1996), pp. 57–65.

9. "Limits to LAX Expansion: At What Price to the Region?" *Metro Investment Report* IV:4 (September 1996), p. 8; "LAX Master Plan: Finding a Balance Between Regional Economic Growth & Negative Local Impacts," *Metro Investment Report* IV:5 (October 1996), pp. 4, 5, 16, 17; Patrick McGreevy, "Will Bay Be Filled for LAX?" *Daily Breeze*, January 8, 1996, p. B1; Jim Radcliffe, "LAX Scraps Bay Runway from Its Plans," *Outlook*, September 12, 1996, p. B1.

10. Dan Garcia (then-L.A. airports commissioner) interview, 1995; Dan Garcia and Steven P. Erie, "Does Region's Future Depend upon a 6th Runway?" *Los Angeles Times*, December 15, 1996, p. M6.

11. Los Angeles World Airports [LAWA], "The LAX Master Plan: Executive Briefing," February 1998; Jack Graham, "Goods Movement at Los Angeles International Airport," Statement before the State Assembly Committee on Transportation, Los Angeles, California, December 12, 1997; Jack Driscoll, "Master Planning LAX—Phase III: Mitigating Impacts of Airport Growth," *Metro Investment Report* V:2 (July 1997), pp. 1, 10, 11, 17; "L.A. Airport Commissioner Ed Manning: Reconciling Economic Growth & Environmentalism," *Metro Investment Report* V:9 (February 1998), pp. 4, 12, 13.

12. Jim Newton, "Riordan Offers Smaller Airport Expansion Plan," *Los Angeles Times*, June 15, 1999, pp. B1, B2; "Is Mayor Riordan Now In Charge of LAX? Dan Garcia's Airport Board Resignation Letter," *Metro Investment Report* V:12 (May 1998), pp. 4, 5; "L.A. Airports Lose Their Leader: An Exit Interview with Jack Driscoll," *Metro Investment Report* VII:1 (June 1999), pp. 1, 16–18.

13. Carlyle Hall, "LAX Capitulates on Additional Runway—Is the Draft Master Plan Now a Placebo?" *Metro Investment Report* VIII:9 (February 2001), pp. 1, 14, 15, 19; Douglas P. Shuit, "Panel Rejects Full LAX Expansion," *Los Angeles Times*, March 2, 2001, pp. B1, B7.

14. LADOA, *Los Angeles International Airport Privatization Study* (Los Angeles: LADOA, May 1992); Ruth Galanter, "Airport Revenue and Mitigation Reform Package," March 1992.

15. Steven P. Erie, "Balancing a Budget at the Expense of L.A.'s Future," *Los Angeles Times*, May 23, 1993, pp. M1, M2; Robert W. Poole, Jr., "Who's Right on How Much LAX Is Worth?" *Los Angeles Times*, May 21, 1993, p. B7; Martin Tolchin, "'Airport for Lease': Los Angeles Mayor Finds Foes to Idea," *New York Times*, August 26, 1993, pp. A1, A7 (quote); Jill Leovy, "Lockheed Looks to Expand Its Airport Business," *Los Angeles Times*, May 31, 1994, pp. D1, D6.

16. Marc Lacey, "Panel Votes to Triple LAX Landing Fees," *Los Angeles Times*, June 29, 1993, pp. B1, B4; John Schwada, "Riordan Appoints Attorney to Handle LAX Revenue Issue," *Los Angeles Times*, July 17, 1993, pp. B1, B3; Ted Stein, "LA Airport President Ted Stein: A Candid Assessment of Future Plans," *Metro Investment Report* III:3/4 (August/September 1995), pp. 1, 12–15.

17. Steven P. Erie, "Riordan Beats the Airlines at City's Long-Term Expense," *Los Angeles Times*, December 5, 1993, pp. M1, M6; James Rainey, "40 Airlines Sue to Cancel Landing Fee Hike at LAX," *Los Angeles Times*, July 31, 1993, pp. B1, B2; Kenneth Reich, "City Gears Up to Fight Airlines over LAX," *Los Angeles Times*, August 2, 1993, p. B1; James Rainey, "Airlines Lose Round in LAX Fees Dispute," *Los Angeles Times*, October 26, 1993, pp. B1, B8; James Rainey, "Landing Fee Hike Threatens to Close LAX," *Los Angeles Times*, November 24, 1993, pp. A1, A3; David G. Savage, "Court Backs Airports on Fee Hikes," *Los Angeles Times*, January 25, 1994, pp. A1, A22; James F. Peltz, "City Hikes Landing

Fees at LAX by Another 32%; Airlines Protest," *Los Angeles Times*, June 22, 1995, pp. D1, D10; Jodi Wilgoren, "Most of Airport Landing Fee Increase Upheld," *Los Angeles Times*, December 23, 1995, pp. B1, B3.

18. James Bornemeier and James Rainey, "Congress Stalls Riordan's Plan for LAX Funds," *Los Angeles Times*, October 20, 1993, pp. A1, A15; James Rainey, "New Contract May Spice Up LAX Food," *Los Angeles Times*, December 3, 1994, pp. B1, B3; Harrison Shepard, "LAX Rejects Millions," *Los Angeles Daily News*, March 10, 2000, pp. 1, 17; Jeffrey L. Rabin, "L.A. Gave Up $117 Million in U.S. Funds for LAX," *Los Angeles Times*, December 1, 2001, pp. A1, A30.

19. "Deputy Mayor Keeley: The Business of L.A.'s Proprietary Departments," *Metro Investment Report* I:4 (September 1993), pp. 1, 8, 11–13; Michael Keeley, "LA Mayor's Office 'Benchmarking' City's Proprietary Departments," *Metro Investment Report* II:9 (February 1995), pp. 1, 11–13, 15; James Rainey, "Council OKs Law to Boost LAX Income," *Los Angeles Times*, August 7, 1993, pp. B1, B8; Richard Simon, "$54 Million Goes to City, Not Airport, U.S. Decides," *Los Angeles Times*, March 2, 1995, pp. B1, B3; John Schwada, "Airport Owes L.A. Millions, Audit Finds," *Los Angeles Times*, April 5, 1995, pp. B1, B5; L.A. City Controller's Office, "Analysis of Unreimbursed Costs Incurred by the General Fund of the City of Los Angeles on Behalf of the Department of Airports," March 1996; Jodi Wilgoren, "City Raises Debt Claim for LAX to $350 Million," *Los Angeles Times*, April 2, 1996, p. B3; Jean Merl, "City Reliance on Profitable Departments Threatened," *Los Angeles Times*, March 25, 1996, pp. B1, B3.

20. David Willman, "City Hired Lobbyist Despite Fraud Probe," *Los Angeles Times*, September 14, 1995, pp. B1, B3; David Willman, "Critics Question Hiring of Lobbyist," *Los Angeles Times*, September 15, 1995, pp. B1, B6; Federal Aviation Administration, "Policy and Procedures Concerning the Use of Airport Revenue," *Federal Register* 61:38 (February 26, 1996), pp. 7134–44; U.S. Senators John McCain and Wendell H. Ford to Mayor Richard Riordan, April 22, 1996; U.S. Representative Frank R. Wolf to Mayor Richard Riordan, May 13, 1996; Mayor Richard Riordan to U.S. Representative Frank R. Wolf, May 16, 1996; "Mayor Riordan vs. Congressman Wolf: Transferring Revenues from LAX to City's Gen. Fund," *Metro Investment Report* IV:1 (June 1996), pp. 19, 20; Jodi Wilgoren and James Bornemeier, "U.S. Officials Vow to Bar Use of LAX Funds," *Los Angeles Times,* May 2, 1996, p. B1; Air Transport Association [ATA], "LAX Is Focus as DOT Issues Airport Revenue Diversion Policy," *ATA News*, February 27, 1996. See also Jeffrey L. Rabin, "Mayor Orders Repayment of Diverted Funds," *Los Angeles Times*, March 28, 1997, pp. B1, B6.

21. Moody's Investors Service, *Moody's Municipal Credit Reports: Los Angeles Department of Airports, California—Los Angeles International Airport* (n.p.: Moody's Investors Service, April 1995), p. 7; Stein, "LA Airport President," pp. 1, 12; Geoff Maleman, "Airline Coalition Steps Up Campaign to Stop Airport Revenue Diversion," *LAX Reader*, May 1996, pp. 1–3; Erie, "Riordan Beats the Airlines at City's Long-Term Expense," pp. M1, M6; Steven P. Erie, "A Budget That

Pays Today's Bills with L.A.'s Future Growth," *Los Angeles Times*, May 19, 1996, p. M6; Marc Lacey, "American Grounds Its Renovation of LAX Terminal," *Los Angeles Times*, August 27, 1993, pp. B1, B8; Deborah Belgum, "LAX to Lower Landing Fees but Raise Levy on Passengers," *Los Angeles Times*, August 20, 1997, p. B3; Dan Garcia interview, 1995; John Ek (then-state government affairs director, ATA) interview, 1995; and Edward Merlis (then-senior vice president, federal affairs and airports, ATA) interview, 1995.

22. Driscoll, personal communication with author.

23. "Master Plan Facts," p. 6; Driscoll personal communication with author.

24. Steven P. Erie, Thomas P. Kim, and Gregory Freeman, *The LAX Master Plan: Facing the Challenges of Community, Environmental and Regional Airport Planning* (Los Angeles: Southern California Studies Center, University of Southern California, 1999), p. 9.

25. Ibid., pp. 11–13.

26. Ibid., p. 12; Robert Pinzler (former Redondo Beach city councilman) interview, 1998.

27. Jim Newton, "LAX Expansion Publicists Are Catching Flak," *Los Angeles Times*, April 19, 1998, pp. A1, A38; Dan Garcia, letter to author, February 2000; Shirley Leung, "Why Group Boosting LAX Went Nowhere," *Wall Street Journal*, March 31, 1999, pp. CA1, CA4.

28. Garcia letter to author.

29. Erie, Kim, and Freeman, *LAX Master Plan*, p. 22.

30. Ibid., pp. 21–24.

31. Garcia letter to author.

32. Ruth Galanter to Jack Graham, July 31, 1997; Ruth Galanter to Councilmember John Ferraro, October 30, 1997; Deborah Belgum and Jean Merl, "Hoping to Clip the Wings of LAX," *Los Angeles Times*, July 7, 1997, pp. B1, B3.

33. "By Default," pp. 1, 14–17; Sharon Bernstein, "Supervisors Seek a Voice in LAX Plans," *Los Angeles Times*, August 4, 1998, p. B1; "Regional Airport Authority Reactivated: LA Supervisors Reject LAX Master Plan," *Metro Investment Report* IX:1 (July 2001), pp. 1, 12, 13.

34. Erie, Kim, and Freeman, *LAX Master Plan*, pp. 38–39.

35. Belgum and Merl, "Hoping to Clip the Wings of LAX"; Mike Gordon, "Re: The Need for a Regional Airport Plan for Southern California," September 18, 1998; Jim Newton, "Broad Coalition to Fight Mayor's Vision for LAX," *Los Angeles Times*, March 30, 1999, pp. B1, B8; Mike Gordon, "Put Airports Where They're Most Needed," *Los Angeles Times*, May 17, 1999, p. B5; Jean Merl, "The Mayor Who Rallied LAX Foes," *Los Angeles Times*, February 6, 2001, pp. A1, A15; Robert L. Jackson, "12 House Members Oppose Massive Expansion of LAX," *Los Angeles Times*, May 4, 2001, p. B3.

36. Anonymous communication with author.

37. Beth Shuster, "Expanded Service Seen for Palmdale Airport," *Los Angeles*

Times, October 2, 1999, p. B7 (Galanter quote); Ian Gregor, "Deal May Ease Load for LAX," *Daily Breeze*, October 2, 1999, pp. A1, A7; Erie, Kim, and Freeman, *LAX Master Plan*, p. 13.

38. Erie, Kim, and Freeman, *LAX Master Plan*, p. 26.

39. Ibid., p. 27.

40. Information from www.lawa.org.

41. Douglas P. Shuit, "L.A., Inglewood Agree on Airport Noise, Traffic Issues," *Los Angeles Times*, February 7, 2001, p. B3; Erie, Kim, and Freeman, *LAX Master Plan*, pp. 27–28.

42. Marla Cone, "Jet Lag in Pollution Control," *Los Angeles Times*, March 18, 1997, p. B2; Michael Armstrong, SCAG Senior Aviation Planner, "Memorandum re ICAO Aircraft Emission Standards," July 28, 1999.

43. Erie, Kim, and Freeman, *LAX Master Plan*, pp. 29–30, 33.

44. Ibid., pp. 29–30.

45. Ibid., pp. 30–31.

46. Roy Hefner (member, LAX Area Advisory Committee) interview, 1998.

47. Erie, Kim, and Freeman, *LAX Master Plan*, pp. 28–32.

48. Dennis Zane/Urban Dimensions, "News Release: El Segundo Lawsuit Challenges LAX Expansion," November 22, 1999; LAWA, "News Release: Threatened El Segundo Lawsuit Is an Attempt to Control and Block LAX Master Plan Process," November 22, 1999; Jim Newton and Jean Merl, "El Segundo Sues L.A. over Airport Work," *Los Angeles Times*, November 25, 1999, pp. B1, B10; Douglas P. Shuit, "El Segundo Drops Suit over LAX Expansion," *Los Angeles Times*, February 17, 2001, p. B7.

49. Erie, Kim, and Freeman, *LAX Master Plan*, p. 23.

50. Shirley Leung, "LAX Must Answer Questions About Minority Communities," *Wall Street Journal*, November 15, 2000, pp. CA1, CA3; Manuel Pastor Jr. and Jim Sadd, *Environmental Justice and the Expansion of Los Angeles International Airport: A Brief Comment* (Los Angeles: Occidental College Environmental Studies Program, November 2000); Manuel Pastor Jr. and Jim Sadd, "Put LAX Expansion in a Holding Pattern Pending Further Research," *Los Angeles Times*, November 15, 2000, p. B9; Douglas P. Shuit, "Concerns Raised over Protecting Poor Communities," *Los Angeles Times*, April 28, 2001, p. B4; Jennifer Oldham, "LAX Study Called 'Fatally Flawed,'" *Los Angeles Times*, June 6, 2001, p. B4.

51. Erie, Kim, and Freeman, *LAX Master Plan*, p. 20.

52. SCAG, *Southern California Military Air Base Study* (Los Angeles: SCAG, August 1994); William Fulton and Paul Shigley, "Dug In for Battle: El Toro's Land Use Epic," *California Journal*, June 2001, p. 36. A fifth military air base, Point Mugu Naval Air Station, also was slated for conversion to a joint-use facility. However, its mission changed, and it was never closed.

53. Mary Ann Milbourn, "Another El Toro Airport Option," *Orange County Register*, July 1, 1996, pp. 1, 4.

54. Lorenza Munoz, "Airport Plan a Tough Sell in S. County," *Los Angeles Times*, April 23, 1998, pp. B1, B6; Jean O. Pasco, "Fight over El Toro Takes Toll on Taxpayers," *Los Angeles Times*, May 14, 2001, p. B4; Fulton and Shigley, "Dug In for Battle," pp. 34–35. The opposing sides spent tax dollars in different ways. Most of the county's share ($45 million) was spent on required CEQA documents. South county's share ($45 million) went largely for public advertising, lawsuits, and lobbying.

55. David Parrish, "North, South on Collusion Course on El Toro," *Orange County Register*, January 26, 1998, pp. 1, 3; "Riordan Backs Airport at El Toro Base," *Los Angeles Times*, December 8, 1998; Jean O. Pasco, "El Toro Controversy Invades L.A. County," *Los Angeles Times*, April 9, 2001, pp. B1, B4; Dana Rohrabacher, "Foes of an Airport at El Toro Have Their NIMBY Blinders On," *Los Angeles Times*, June 4, 2001, p. B11.

56. James Flanigan, "A Bullish Vote for the Future: El Toro Airport—Conversion Plan Is Key for Orange County," *Los Angeles Times*, November 16, 1994, pp. D1, D3; Shelby Grad and Jeff Gottlieb, "Where Will Orange County Land in 2020?" *Los Angeles Times*, May 26, 1998, pp. A1, A20, A21; Steven P. Erie, John D. Kasarda, and Andrew M. McKenzie, *A New Orange County Airport at El Toro: An Economic Benefits Study* (Irvine, Calif.: Orange County Business Council, 1998), pp. 1–5; Erie, Kasarda, McKenzie, and Molloy, *A New Orange County Airport at El Toro: Catalyst for High-Wage, High-Tech Economic Development*, p. 1–4; Thomas Edwards, "Pro-Airport: The County Reuse Plan Meets Our Economic, Aviation and Other Needs," *Orange County Register*, December 14, 1997, pp. 1, 4.

57. See sources in note 56.

58. Larry Agran, "Anti-Airport: The Best Non-aviation Uses Are Incompatible with a Commercial Airport," *Orange County Register*, December 14, 1997, pp. 1, 4; Clarence J. Turner, "How to Build an Airport That Will Fly," *Los Angeles Times*, May 10, 1998, p. B7.

59. James S. Granelli, "The Leader of the Pack in El Toro Dogfight," *Los Angeles Times*, May 10, 1998.

60. Mark Baldassare, *When Government Fails: The Orange County Bankruptcy* (Berkeley: University of California Press, 1998). When filing for bankruptcy, the supervisors also considered selling John Wayne Airport to raise needed money. Mark Platte, Matt Lait, and Chris Woodyard, "Officials Consider Selling Airport in Orange County," *Los Angeles Times*, December 28, 1994, pp. A1, A12.

61. "El Toro Report Card: A Failure of Process," *Los Angeles Times*, February 13, 2000; Lorenza Munoz, "Board Oks Mid-Size Airport at El Toro," *Los Angeles Times*, April 22, 1998, A1, A22.

62. Jean O. Pasco and Jodi Wilgoren, "There's More Than One Way to Scuttle an Airport," *Los Angeles Times*, May 27, 1998, pp. A1, A14; Peter Brennan, "Obscure Panel Now Focus of El Toro Annexation Battle," *Orange County Business Journal*, December 15–21, 1997, pp. 1, 28.

63. Pasco and Wilgoren, "There's More Than One Way to Scuttle an Airport";

Shelby Grad and Lorenza Munoz, "El Toro Debate Promises to Shake Up '98," *Los Angeles Times*, December 29, 1997, pp. A1, A18.

64. Jean O. Pasco, "Issues Litter the Runway to an El Toro Airport," *Los Angeles Times*, October 29, 2001, p. B3.

65. LAWA, "LAX Master Plan: Report to the City Council," June 16, 1998.

66. Shelby Grad and Lorenza Munoz, "Southland Airport Planners Face Frustrating Paradox," *Los Angeles Times*, December 29, 1997, pp. A3, A8, A24, A25.

67. Mara A. Marks and Fernando J. Guerra, "Opinions of Southern California's Local Elected Officials Regarding Air Transportation Infrastructure: A Report to Los Angeles World Airports" (report, Center for the Study of Los Angeles, Loyola Marymount University, Los Angeles), June 2001; Mara A. Marks, "Getting It Together? Local Elected Officials' Opinions Regarding Regionalism," *California Politics & Policy* 6:1 (2002).

Chapter Eight

1. Edward W. Soja, *Thirdspace: Journeys to L.A. and Other Real and Imagined Places* (Cambridge, Mass.: Blackwell, 1996), p. 238.

2. Abraham F. Lowenthal, L. Thomas Best Jr., and Michael Browrigg, "International Linkages," in Michael J. Dear, ed., *Atlas of Southern California*, vol. 1 (Los Angeles: Southern California Studies Center [SC2], University of Southern California, 1996), p. 27.

3. Los Angeles County Economic Development Corporation [LAEDC], *International Trade Trends & Impacts: The Los Angeles Region 2001 Results and 2002 Outlook* (Los Angeles: LAEDC, June 2002), pp. 1, 3.

4. U.S. Bureau of the Census, *Merchandise Trade for 2001: Selected Highlights*, FT 920 Series (Washington, D.C., 2002). Although in 2001 L.A. remained the nation's trade leader as measured by district of unlading, L.A.'s 8 percent slump in port-of-entry trade cost it its number one ranking relative to the New York region, which fell only 5 percent.

5. Roger M. Showley, "San Diego Plays Its Part in the Land That Baum Created," *San Diego Union-Tribune*, June 4, 2000, p. E1. See Mike Davis, *Ecology of Fear: Los Angeles and the Imagination of Disaster* (New York: Metropolitan Books, 1998), pp. 155–58, for a provocative view of the history of twisters in Los Angeles. The Soja quote is from Michael J. Dear and Steven Flusty, "The Iron Lotus: Los Angeles and Postmodern Urbanism," in David Wilson, ed., *Globalization and the Changing U.S. City* (Thousand Oaks, Calif.: Sage, 1997), p. 153.

6. Edward W. Soja, "Los Angeles, 1965–1992: From Crisis-Generated Restructuring to Restructuring-Generated Crisis," in Allen J. Scott and Edward W. Soja, eds., *The City: Los Angeles and Urban Theory at the End of the Twentieth Century* (Berkeley: University of California Press, 1996). Of course, some social critics discerned in Southern California trends of broader importance. Theodore Adorno and Max Horkeimer, Frankfurt school intellectuals in exile in the United

States during World War Two, saw Los Angeles's "culture industry" as symptomatic of the waxing "absolute power of capitalism." Mike Davis, *City of Quartz: Excavating the Future in Los Angeles* (London: Verso, 1990), pp. 48–49.

7. For examples of the L.A.-as-harbinger approach, see Michael J. Dear et al., eds., *Rethinking Los Angeles* (Thousand Oaks, Calif.: Sage, 1996); Allen J. Scott and Edward W. Soja, eds., *The City: Los Angeles and Urban Theory at the End of the Twentieth Century* (Berkeley: University of California Press, 1996); Michael J. Dear, ed., *From Chicago to L.A.: Making Sense of Urban Theory* (Thousand Oaks, Calif.: Sage, 2002). Also, D. W. Miller, "The New Urban Studies: Los Angeles Scholars Use Their Region and Their Ideas to End the Dominance of the 'Chicago School,'" *Chronicle of Higher Education*, August 18, 2001, pp. A5–A15; David Rusk, *Cities Without Suburbs*, 2d ed. (Washington, D.C.: Woodrow Wilson Center Press, 1995); Joel Garreau, *Edge City: Life on the New Frontier* (New York: Anchor Books, 1991), pp. 3, 283; Raphael J. Sonenshein, *Politics in Black and White: Race and Power in Los Angeles* (Princeton, N.J.: Princeton University Press, 1993); Mark Baldassare, ed., *The Los Angeles Riots: Lessons for the Urban Future* (Boulder, Colo.: Westview Press, 1994).

8. Marco Cenzatti, *Los Angeles and the L.A. School: Postmodernism and Urban Studies* (Los Angeles: Los Angeles Forum for Architecture and Urban Design, 1993). The best introduction to the L.A. School is Scott and Soja, *The City*. Also see Janet L. Abu-Lughod, *New York, Chicago, Los Angeles: America's Global Cities* (Minneapolis: University of Minnesota Press, 1999).

9. Edward W. Soja, *Postmodern Geographies: The Reassertion of Space in Critical Social Theory* (London: Verso, 1989), p. 193.

10. Allen J. Scott, *Metropolis: From Division of Labor to Urban Form* (Berkeley: University of California Press, 1988); Allen J. Scott, *Technopolis: The High-Technology Industry and Regional Development in Southern California* (Berkeley: University of California Press, 1993).

11. Steven Flusty and Michael J. Dear, "Invitation to a Postmodern Urbanism," in Robert A. Beauregard and Sophie Body-Gendrot, eds., *The Urban Moment: Cosmopolitan Essays on the Late-20th-Century* (Thousand Oaks, Calif.: Sage, 1999), pp. 26–27; Soja, "Los Angeles, 1965–1992," pp. 433–38; Edward W. Soja, *Postmetropolis: Critical Studies in Cities and Regions* (Oxford: Blackwell, 2000), pp. 233–63. Soja's thesis has been popularized by Garreau, *Edge City*. Garreau calls Los Angeles the "great-granddaddy" of edge cities (p. 3).

12. Soja, "Los Angeles, 1965–1992," pp. 438–42; Soja, *Postmetropolis*, pp. 156–88; Ash Amin, ed., *Post-Fordism* (Cambridge, Mass.: Blackwell, 1994).

13. Soja, "Los Angeles, 1965–1992," pp. 442–44; Soja, *Postmetropolis*, pp. 189–232; Christopher Jencks, *Heteropolis: Los Angles, the Riots, and the Strange Beauty of Hetero-Architecture* (London: Academy Editions, 1993). Compare David Rieff, *Los Angeles: Capital of the Third World* (New York: Simon & Schuster, 1991) and Xandra Kayden with Jennifer Resnick, "The Impact of Globalization on Los Angeles" (draft, Pacific Council on International Policy [PCIP], Los Angeles), 2001.

14. Soja, "Los Angeles, 1965–1992," pp. 445–48; Soja, *Postmetropolis*, pp. 264–97; Lawrence D. Bobo et al., *Prismatic Los Angeles: Inequality in Los Angeles* (New York: Russell Sage Foundation, 2000).

15. Soja, *Thirdspace*, pp. 193–94; Soja, "Los Angeles, 1965–1992," pp. 448–50; Soja, *Postmetropolis*, pp. 298–322; Davis, *City of Quartz*, pp. 221–64.

16. Soja, "Los Angeles, 1965–1992," pp. 345–57; Soja, *Postmetropolis*, pp. 323–48; Harvey Molotch, "L.A. as Design Product: How Art Works in a Regional Economy," in Allen J. Scott and Edward W. Soja, eds., *The City: Los Angeles and Urban Theory at the End of the Twentieth Century* (Berkeley: University of California Press, 1996), pp. 225–75.

17. Joel Kotkin, "The New Technopolis," *Los Angeles Times*, June 25, 2001, p. M1; David Friedman, "Taking on the Armani Radicals," *Los Angeles Downtown News*, October 26, 1998, p. 1.

18. Joel Kotkin, *The New Geography: How the Digital Revolution Is Reshaping the American Landscape* (New York: Random House, 2000), p. 18.

19. Ibid., pp. 80–109; Joel Kotkin and Yoriko Kishimoto, *The Third Century: America's Resurgence in the Asian Era* (New York: Crown, 1988), pp. 100, 125; Joel Kotkin, *Tribes: How Race, Religion and Identity Determine Success in the New Global Economy* (New York: Random House, 1993), pp. 165–68; Joel Kotkin, "California Becoming a Favorite Chinese Investment," *Los Angeles Times*, June 29, 1997, p. M1.

20. Kotkin, *New Geography*, pp. 18, 22, 80–82. Revealingly, the book had as its tentative title "Repealing Geography."

21. Joel Kotkin, *Southern California in the Information Age* (Los Angeles: Pepperdine University Institute for Public Policy and La Jolla Institute, June 1997), pp. 1–4; Kotkin, *New Geography*, pp. 14–16, 88, 101–5.

22. Kotkin, *New Geography*, pp. 1, 8. On the continuing importance of the geographical comparative advantage of Los Angeles in relation to both Asia and Mexico, see Stuart A. Gabriel, "Rethinking the Los Angeles Economy: Cyclical Fluctuations and Structural Evolution," in Michael J. Dear et al., eds., *Rethinking Los Angeles* (Thousand Oaks, Calif.: Sage, 1996), pp. 27–28.

23. David Friedman, "The New Economy," *Los Angeles Times*, February 6, 2000, p. M1; David Friedman, "The Politics of Growth," *Los Angeles Times*, September 17, 2000, p. M1; David Friedman, "Bubble Economy II: Coming Soon," *Los Angeles Times*, May 13, 2001, p. M1; Kotkin, *New Geography*, pp. 6–11, 38–44, 107–9.

24. Soja, *Thirdspace*, pp. 19–20, 61–65, 298.

25. Scott and Soja, *The City*, pp. 5, 18; Soja, *Postmetropolis*, p. 128.

26. Scott and Soja, *The City*, p. 436; Soja, *Thirdspace*, pp. 299–300; Soja, *Postmetropolis*, 226.

27. Davis, *City of Quartz*. For Soja's and Davis's ambivalent assessment of each other's work, compare Soja, *Thirdspace*, pp. 199–201, with Davis, *City of Quartz*, pp. 84, 86.

28. Davis, *City of Quartz*, pp. 128–38, 410–11.

29. On the polemical fisticuffs between the L.A. Schoolers and the New Boosters, see Nora Zamichow, "Apocalyptic Look at L.A. Sparks Literary Fistfight," *Los Angeles Times*, January 6, 1999, p. A1; Soja, *Postmetropolis*, pp. 245–46; Friedman, "Taking on the Armani Radicals," p. 1; Robert A. Jones, "The Truth Squad of History," *Los Angeles Times*, January 10, 1999, p. B1.

30. Joel Kotkin, *Back to the Renaissance? A New Perspective on America's Cities* (Los Angeles: Pepperdine University Institute for Public Policy, September 1997), p. 7.

31. Kotkin, "The New Technopolis," p. M1. One of the few discussions in Kotkin's books of the L.A.-area ports, LAX, and regional-trade infrastructure is found in Kotkin and Kishimoto, *Third Century*, p. 201. In newspaper op/ed articles, Kotkin occasionally endorses major port, rail, and airport projects but concentrates on attacking their environmental opponents. See, for example, Joel Kotkin, "Democratize the Economic Recovery," *Los Angeles Times*, April 13, 1997, p. M1; and Joel Kotkin, "City Planning: Reducing 'Big L.A.' to Size," *Los Angeles Times*, September 20, 1998, p. M1.

32. See Susan E. Clarke and Gary L. Gaile, "Local Politics in a Global Era: Think Locally, Act Globally," in David Wilson, ed., "Globalization and the Changing U.S. City," *Annals of the American Academy of Political and Social Science 551* (May 1997), pp. 28–43; and Janet E. Kodras, "Restructuring the State: Devolution, Privatization, and the Geographic Redistribution of Power and Capacity in Governance," in Kodras Staeheli and Colin Flint, eds., *State Devolution in America: Implications for a Diverse Society* (Thousand Oaks, Calif.: Sage, 1997), pp. 79–96.

33. Manuel Pastor Jr., *Widening the Winner's Circle from Global Trade in Southern California* (Los Angeles: PCIP, June 2001); Helzi Noponen, Ann R. Markusen, and Karl Driessen, *Trade and American Cities: Who Has the Comparative Advantage?* Working Paper 96 (New Brunswick, N.J.: Center for Urban Policy Research, Rutgers University, 1996); Cynthia A. Kroll et al., *Foreign Trade and California's Economic Growth* (Berkeley: California Policy Seminar, 1998).

34. Kroll et al., *Foreign Trade and California's Economic Growth*, p. ix.

35. LAEDC, *International Trade Trends & Impacts: The Los Angeles Region* (Los Angeles: LAEDC, May 2001), p. 17; Abraham F. Lowenthal et al., *Strengthening Southern California's International Connections: Trade and Investment Aspects* (Los Angeles: SC2, University of Southern California, 1996), pp. 1, 8.

36. Lisa M. Grobar, "Export-Linked Employment in Southern California," *Contemporary Economic Policy* 17:1 (January 1999), pp. 97–108; and LAEDC, *International Trade—Major Growth Industry for Southern California* (Los Angeles: LAEDC, 2001), p. 1.

37. Gordon Smith, "A Measure of Success: Ontario Warehouses Thrive Thanks to Strategic Location," *San Diego Union-Tribune*, October 11, 2001, pp. C1, C2.

38. Lowenthal et al., *Strengthening Southern California's International Connections: Trade and Investment Aspects*, p. 16; Jack Kyser (chief economist, LAEDC) interview, 2001; Port of Los Angeles, *Economic Benefits Generated by*

the Port of Los Angeles (Los Angeles: Port of Los Angeles, n.d.). Also see Grobar, "Export-Linked Employment in Southern California"; Ken Ackbarali and Jack Kyser, "International Trade in Southern California: Measuring Its Size and Growth" (draft, PCIP, Los Angeles), 1998; LAEDC, *International Trade Trends & Impacts: The Los Angeles Region 1998 Results and 1999 Outlook* (Los Angeles: LAEDC, April 1999).

39. Earl H. Fry, *The North American West in a Global Economy* (Los Angeles: PCIP, April 2000), pp. 11–12; Abraham F. Lowenthal et al., *Strengthening Southern California's International Connections: Boosting International Investment* (Los Angeles: SC2, University of Southern California, 1996), p. 17; California Trade and Commerce Agency, Office of Foreign Investment, *Foreign Direct Investment in California: Recent Activity* (Sacramento, Calif.: California Trade and Commerce Agency, January 2001), p. 1; Jack Kyser, quoted in Kayden, "Impact of Globalization on Los Angeles," p. 13.

40. Robert E. Scott, "NAFTA's Impacts on the States," *Online Supplement to the EPI Briefing Paper NAFTA at Seven* (Washington, D.C.: Economic Policy Institute, April 2001); Raul Hinojosa-Ojeda, Curt Downs, and Robert McCleery, *North American Integration Three Years After NAFTA* (Tucson, Ariz.: National Law Center for Inter-American Free Trade, 1997), pp. 4–6; Zeth Ajemian et al., "Application for Eligibility Certification for North American Development Bank Financing: Los Angeles County," June 4, 1996.

41. Hinojosa-Ojeda, Downs, and McCleery, *North American Integration Three Years After NAFTA*, pp. 4–6; Don Lee, "Taiwan, Mexico Help Fuel State Exports," *Los Angeles Times*, February 21, 1998, p. D1; Don Lee, "California Posts Gains Despite Asia," *Los Angeles Times*, June 12, 1998, pp. D1, D12; Paul Harrington and Neeta Fogg, "Growth and Change in the California and Long Beach/Los Angeles Labor Markets" (paper prepared for the U.S. Conference of Mayors), May 2001.

42. Pastor, *Widening the Winner's Circle.* Unfortunately, the analysis confounds places of employment and residence. Export and wage data are for industries. Racial and income data are for community residents. Yet people frequently do not work in the communities in which they live. Thus, Inglewood residents are deemed trade winners because of local industries' high relative exports and wages even though many city residents commute to jobs in areas classified as trade neutrals or strugglers. A more comprehensive analysis would explain the locational and hiring decisions of businesses with different export and wage profiles.

43. William Cline, *Trade and Income* (Washington, D.C.: Institute for International Economics, 1997); Pastor, *Widening the Winner's Circle*, pp. 5, 11, 12; LAEDC, *Manufacturing in the Los Angeles Five-County Area* (Los Angeles: LAEDC, July 2002), p. 10.

44. Information in this paragraph is from Stephen Cohen, "L.A. Is the Hole in the Bucket," *Los Angeles Times*, March 7, 1993, p. M1.

45. LAEDC, *International Trade Trends & Impacts* (2002), Table 19, p. 43.

46. Temple, Barker & Sloane, Inc., *The Economic Impact of the Ports of Los Angeles and Long Beach* (Lexington, Mass.: Temple, Barker & Sloane, Inc., October 1989); Gordon Palmer interview, 2001; Larry Cottrill (manager of master planning, Port of Long Beach) interview, 2001; Hamilton, Rabinovitz & Alschuler [HR&A], "Technical Memo #3: Existing Economic Conditions and Impact Relationships for LAX and Other Airports in the Southern California Region" (Los Angeles World Airports, Los Angeles), May 25, 1996; HR&A, "Table 1: Direct Economic Benefits of Expansion of LAX: Phase II-98 Cargo and Passenger Activity Growth to the Year 2015" (Los Angeles World Airports, Los Angeles), 1996. For an analysis of port, rail, and airport economic-impact studies, see Steven P. Erie, *International Trade and Job Creation in Southern California: Facilitating Los Angeles/Long Beach Port, Rail, and Airport Development* (Berkeley: California Policy Seminar, 1996), pp. 19–22, 38–41, 66–67.

47. Alameda Corridor Transportation Authority, *The National Economic Significance of the Alameda Corridor* (Huntington Park, Calif.: Alameda Corridor Transportation Authority, February 1994), pp. 4–5; Erie, *International Trade and Job Creation in Southern California*, pp. 40–41.

48. Regarding the forecasting procedure, see Erie, *International Trade and Job Creation in Southern California*, pp. 66–67. For 1994–2020, using the Southern California Association of Governments [SCAG] estimates, the region's trade megaprojects could generate between 21 percent (with substitution) and 29 percent (without substitution) of the projected employment increase in the region's core economic base. These forecasts were supplied by SCAG Chief Economist Bruce DeVine. Steven P. Erie, "Why Southern California May Be Unprepared for Its Destiny," *Los Angeles Times*, January 28, 1996, p. M6.

49. Steven P. Erie, John D. Kasarda, Andrew M. McKenzie, and Michael A. Molloy, *A New Orange County Airport at El Toro: Catalyst for High-Wage, High-Tech Economic Development* (Irvine, Calif.: Orange County Business Council, 1999), pp. 4-1 to 4-7; SCAG Aviation Staff, "Potential Impacts of Deleting El Toro from the Regional Transportation Plan" (memo), April 29, 2002, pp. 1–3; HR&A, "Table 2: Economic Benefits of Expansion of LAX: Phase II-98 Output and Job Benefits in the Year 2015" (Los Angeles), 1996. The LAX constrained estimate is extrapolated from SCAG's El Toro no-build analysis. For other costs associated with not building an El Toro airport, see Steven P. Erie, John D. Kasarda, and Andrew M. McKenzie, *A New Orange County Airport at El Toro: An Economic Benefits Study* (Irvine, Calif.: Orange County Business Council, 1998), p. 1-5.

50. Barbara Whitaker, "Deal Clears Way for Los Angeles Port Project," *New York Times*, March 7, 2003, p. A16; Deborah Schoch, "L.A. Port Air Cleanup Plan May Be a Model," *Los Angeles Times*, April 1, 2003, pp. B1, B10.

51. Gary Polakovic, "Finally Tackling L.A.'s Worst Air Polluter," *Los Angeles Times*, February 10, 2002, pp. B1, B8; Marla Cone, "Jet Lag in Pollution Control," *Los Angeles Times*, March 18, 1997, p. B2.

52. SCAG, *Discussion Paper on the Short-Term Economic Impacts and Poten-*

tial Long-Term Implications for Regional Aviation Following the September 11 Events (Los Angeles: SCAG, November 2001), p. 21; Steve Hymon, "LAX Heads State List of Attack Targets," *Los Angeles Times*, February 22, 2003.

53. Steven P. Erie, "At Competitive Disadvantage: San Diego's Infrastructure," *Metro Investment Report*, II:11 (April 1995), pp. 1, 12, 13; Jack Kyser, *The Linkages Between San Diego/Tijuana and Its Neighbors to the North* (San Diego: San Diego Dialogue, June 2000).

54. Steven P. Erie, *Toward a Trade Infrastructure Strategy for the San Diego/ Tijuana Region* (San Diego: San Diego Dialogue, February 1999), p. 18; Port of San Diego/San Diego Association of Governments [SANDAG], *Air Transportation and the Future of the San Diego Region* (San Diego: Port of San Diego/SANDAG, Fall 2000), p. 3.

55. Erie, *Toward a Trade Infrastructure Strategy for the San Diego/Tijuana Region*, p. 8.

56. Stephen E. Flynn, "Transportation Security: Agenda for the Twenty-First Century," *TR News*, November-December 2000, p. 3; "The Road Ahead: Assessing the Impact of September 11," *Journal of Commerce*, 2:38 (September 24–30, 2001); Stephen E. Flynn, "Beyond Border Control," *Foreign Affairs* 79:6 (November-December 2000), p. 57.

57. U.S. GAO, *Financial Management: Assessment of the Airline Industry's Estimated Losses Arising from the Events of September 11* (Washington, D.C.: GAO, October 5, 2001); Ricardo Alonso-Zaldivar, "Airport Security Stakes Rising," *Los Angeles Times*, July 7, 2002, pp. A1, A22; Toby Eckert, "Agency Wobbling on Takeoff," *San Diego Union-Tribune*, July 8, 2002, pp. A1, A5.

58. Greg Johnson, "Revenue Losses Hit Airport Operators," *Los Angeles Times*, September 26, 2001, p. C1; Ricardo Alonso-Zaldivar, "New Federal Security Mandates Mean Financial Crunch for Major Airports," *Los Angeles Times*, April 13, 2002, p. A19; Kelly Thornton, "Terrorism Insurance Difficult to Get, Costly," *San Diego Union-Tribune*, July 1, 2002, pp. A1, A13.

59. Mike Armstrong, SCAG Senior Aviation Planner, "Impact of Recent Events on Aviation Forecasts and Allocations" (memo), September 17, 2001 (quote); Lee Romney, "Impact of Attacks Felt Around LAX," *Los Angeles Times*, September 22, 2001, pp. C1–C2; Jennifer Oldham, "New Approach at LAX," *Los Angeles Times*, October 10, 2001, p. C1.

60. William Armbruster, "Air-Cargo Shippers Feel Effects," *Journal of Commerce*, September 24, 2001, pp. 22–24 (quote); William Armbruster, "FAA Tightens Security Rules," *Journal of Commerce*, October 10, 2001, p. 1; Dave Lenckus and Carolyn Aldred, "Policy Cancellations May Ground Aircraft," *Business Insurance*, September 24, 2001, p. 1; Greg Schneider, "Terror Risk Cited for Cargo Carried on Passenger Jets," *Washington Post*, June 10, 2001, pp. A1, A10.

61. James S. Granelli and E. Scott Reckard, "Air-Shipment Firms Incur Steep Losses," *Los Angeles Times*, September 28, 2001, pp. C1, C6; May Wong, "Global Commerce Faces Slower Pace," *San Diego Union-Tribune*, October 7, 2001, p. H2.

62. Flynn, "Beyond Border Control," p. 58; Flynn, "Transportation Security," pp. 4–5; Dennis L. Bryant, "Emphasis on Seaport Security Should Be Expected," *Journal of Commerce*, September 24, 2001, p. 10; Louis Sahagun, "Shipping Containers at Security Fore," *Los Angeles Times*, April 20, 2002, p. A14.

63. Bill Mongelluzzo, "Back-ups at West Coast Ports," *Journal of Commerce*, September 13, 2001, p. 1; Louis Sahagun, "Officials Call for Tighter Security at Harbors," *Los Angeles Times*, October 2, 2001, p. B10; Ricardo Alonso-Zaldivar, "Coast Guard Lists Toward Security Duty," *Los Angeles Times*, August 24, 2002, p. A8; Bill Mongelluzzo, "Cargo Surge Congesting L.A.," *Journal of Commerce*, July 1, 2002, p. 1.

64. Senator Bob Graham, "Maritime Security," *Washington Post*, January 9, 2002, p. A18; Richard Simon, "House Backs Port Security Bill in Fight on Terrorism," *Los Angeles Times*, June 5, 2002, p. A13; Toby Eckert, "Foreign Ports Join Terror Fight," *San Diego Union-Tribune*, August 24, 2002, pp. A1, A17.

65. Claudia H. Deutsch, "More Security, and More Strain, in Supply Chain," *New York Times*, October 9, 2001, p. C1; Bernard Simon, "Shake-up in the Shipping Industry," *New York Times*, October 10, 2001, pp. W1, W7; Daniel Machalaba and Rick Brooks, "After Terror Attacks, Shipping Goods Takes Longer and Costs More," *Wall Street Journal*, September 27, 2001, pp. A1, A8.

66. Daniel Machalaba, "State of the Union: America the Vulnerable?" *Wall Street Journal*, September 28, 2001, p. B4; Flynn, "Transportation Security," pp. 5–6; Flynn, "Beyond Border Control," pp. 58–62.

67. Flynn, "Beyond Border Control," p. 58; Courtney Tower, "Not Just-in-Time," *Journal of Commerce*, September 24, 2001, p. 28; Jeff Ashcroft, "Logistics Impact of the Attack on America," *Logistics/Supply Chain*, September 19, 2001.

68. Ken Ellingwood, "Gridlock Grips the Border," *Los Angeles Times*, October 6, 2001, pp. A1, A19; Chris Kraul, "After Attacks, Traffic of All Kinds Slows at U.S.–Mexico Border," *Los Angeles Times*, October 3, 2001, p. A19; Bob Filner, "The High Cost of Security," *San Diego Union-Tribune*, October 25, 2001, p. B13.

69. Richard J. Riordan and Amy B. Zegart, "City Hall Goes to War," *New York Times*, July 5, 2002, p. A21; Matea Gold, Patrick McGreevy, and Jennifer Oldham, "Rising Security Costs Worry L.A. Mayor," *Los Angeles Times*, March 25, 2003, p. B5.

70. Patrick McGreevy, "Harbor Cityhood Found Infeasible," *Los Angeles Times*, April 26, 2001, pp. B1, B9; Louis Sahagun, "A Power Shift to Port Side," *Los Angeles Times*, June 19, 2001, pp. B1, B10.

71. Matea Gold, "Hahn Seeks to Strengthen Councils," *Los Angeles Times*, August 4, 2001, p. B3; Office of the Mayor (Los Angeles), "Mayor Hahn Empowers Neighborhood Councils with Executive Directive Requiring General Managers to Meet Quarterly with Neighborhood Councils," July 24, 2002; Louis Sahagun, "L.A. Mayor Seeks Background Checks, More Patrols at Ports," *Los Angeles Times*, December 10, 2001, pp. B1, B9.

72. Matea Gold, "Low-Key Mayor Taking on Much Higher Profile in L.A.,"

Los Angeles Times, October 15, 2001, p. B4; Jennifer Oldham, "LAX Plan to Shift Focus to Security Issues," *Los Angeles Times*, September 26, 2001, pp. B1, B7; Steven P. Erie, "Hahn's $8 Billion LAX Plan More Political Finesse Than Regional Solution," *Metro Investment Report*, IX:12 (June 2002), pp. 1, 12, 13; Howard Fine, "$9.6 Billion Hahn Plan Too Large, Some Say," *Los Angeles Business Journal*, July 15–21, 2002, pp. 1, 12.

73. Jennifer Oldham, "Hahn Seeks to Shift Flights to Ontario Airport," *Los Angeles Times*, August 28, 2001, p. B3; Patrick McGreevy, "Hahn Sees Role for Palmdale Airport," *Los Angeles Times*, February 12, 2002, p. B6; Jennifer Oldham, "Hahn Plan Shifts LAX Burden to Other Cities," *Los Angeles Times*, July 3, 2002, pp. A1, A20.

74. James Sterngold, "Growing Pains for Los Angeles' Airport," *New York Times*, January 14, 2002, p. A10; Jean O. Pasco, "El Toro Airport Advocates Lost to a United Suburbia," *Los Angeles Times*, April 28, 2002, pp. B1, B10; "Airport Lesson: El Toro Battle Should Refocus San Diegans," *San Diego Union-Tribune*, March 12, 2002, p. B8; SCAG, *Discussion Paper on the Short-Term Economic Impacts and Potential Long-Term Implications for Regional Aviation Following the September 11 Events*.

75. James Flanigan, "New Power for New Mayor in a Globalized Economy," *Los Angeles Times*, June 4, 2001, pp. C1, C6; Matea Gold, "Hahn's Trade Trip to Mexico Comes to Close," *Los Angeles Times*, November 7, 2001, p. B6; Beth Shuster, "Hahn Makes Contracts and Contacts in Asia," *Los Angeles Times*, November 30, 2002, p. B6.

76. Information supplied by the Office of International Trade, Office of Mayor James K. Hahn, City of Los Angeles, 2002.

77. James Flanigan, "Interdependence Day," *Los Angeles Times*, July 2, 1997, pp. D1, D2; City of Los Angeles, Office of the Mayor, Executive Directive No. 2000–11: Mayor's Office of Protocol (July 1, 2000). Although he hosted an international-trade forum to show how small, minority-owned businesses could take advantage of new global opportunities, Riordan scuttled Bradley's trade office. Belatedly, he designated the Mayor's Office of Protocol to administer the city's sister-cities program and to coordinate international trade missions, cultural exchanges, and visits by foreign dignitaries.

78. In the area of trade development, Bradley created a mayoral trade office to oversee an active sister-cities program and to expand trade missions and meetings with foreign dignitaries. Bradley also followed Long Beach's lead and created foreign trade zones for the Port of Los Angeles, LAX, and other locales.

79. Quoted in LAEDC, *International Trade Trends & Impacts* (2001), p. 1.

80. See, for example, Manuel Pastor Jr., "Strategies to Expand L.A.'s International Role," *Los Angeles Times*, January 25, 1998, p. D2.

81. Areas may enjoy comparative trade advantages because of preexisting ties such as common language, nationality, or former colonial status. James Rauch argues that (at least for differentiated products) high search costs lead to trading net-

works (rather than markets) based on preexisting relations. Thus, regions such as Los Angeles, with large immigrant populations, may have a trade advantage with the immigrants' countries of origin. James E. Rauch, "Networks Versus Markets in International Trade," *Journal of International Economics* 48 (1999), pp. 7–35.

82. La Jolla Institute et al., *Business Leadership in the New Economy: Southern California at a Crossroad* (Claremont, Calif.: La Jolla Institute, July 1998), pp. 1–2.

83. California Technology, Trade and Commerce Agency, *Southern California World Trade Guide, 2001–2002* (Sacramento: California Technology, Trade and Commerce Agency, 2001), pp. 26–32; Trade Development Alliance of Greater Seattle, Washington Council on International Trade, and Washington State Department of Commerce, Trade and Economic Development [CTED], *Tools of the Trade: A Directory of International Trade Organizations in Washington State* (Olympia, Wash.: CTED, Winter 1999). The scarcity of governmental export financing for the region's small- and medium-sized firms also looms as a local trade impediment. See Abraham F. Lowenthal, *Strengthening Southern California's International Connections: Regional-International Development Priorities* (Los Angeles: SC2, University of Southern California, 1996), p. 14.

84. See LAEDC, *Annual Report 1999–2000* (Los Angeles: LAEDC, 2000); "EZ Burts: New President, New Agenda for L.A. Area Chamber of Commerce," *Metro Investment Report* V:2 (July 1997), pp. 1, 9, 14.

85. "LA's Economic Action Summit Nov. 1st: Prioritizing the Region's Needs Post-9/11," *Metro Investment Report*, IX:4 (October 2001), pp. 1, 12, 13; Kroll et al., *Foreign Trade and California's Economic Growth*, pp. x, xi.

86. Nancy Cleland, "Making Waves on the Waterfront," *Los Angeles Times*, June 30, 2002, pp. C1, C4. Also see James A. Regalado, "Organized Labor and Los Angeles City Politics: An Assessment in the Bradley Years, 1973–1989," *Urban Affairs Quarterly* 27:1 (September 1991), pp. 87–108.

87. Jean O. Pasco, "SCAG Bill Could Cause Loss of Transit Funds," *Los Angeles Times*, August 30, 2002, p. B3.

88. Joel Kotkin, "L.A. May Avoid Recession's Worst," *Los Angeles Times*, November 11, 2001, p. M3.

89. For 2020 regional trade forecasts, see LAEDC, *The 60 Mile Circle: Reconnecting Our Neighborhoods to the Region* (Los Angeles: LAEDC, 2002); State of California, *Global Gateways Development Program* (Sacramento, January 2002).

90. James Flanigan, "Port Issues Go Far Beyond Labor Dispute," *Los Angeles Times*, June 30, 2002, pp. C1, C4; Deborah Schoch, "Designs Offered to Keep Freight Moving," *Los Angeles Times*, March 21, 2003, pp. B1, B8; Deborah Schoch, "Some Say Go Slow on Plans for Long Beach Freeway," *Los Angeles Times*, March 27, 2003, p. B6.

91. James Flanigan, "Going Places: Inland Empire Keeps Adding Jobs with Transportation and High Tech," *Los Angeles Times*, March 13, 1996, pp. D1, D6; SCAG, *The New Economy and Jobs/Housing Balance in Southern California* (Los Angeles: SCAG, April 2001).

Index